Anthropological Research in North East India:

Retrospect and Prospect

Anthropological Research in North East India:

Retrospect and Prospect

Editors:

Jibon Kumar, Sarit K. Chaudhuri & Huidrom Suraj Singh

GYAN

Indira Gandhi Rashtriya Manav Sangrahalaya
(National Museum of Mankind Bhopal)

Published, 2020

Published by

Gyan Publishing House
5, Ansari Road
Daryaganj, New Delhi-110002
Phone: 9811692060
E-mail: books@gyanbooks.com

and

Indira Gandhi Rashtriya Manav Sangrahalaya
Shamla Hills, Bhopal
Phones: 0755-2661290, 2661319
Fax: 91-755-2661458

Printed at: G. Print Process, Delhi.

Cataloging in Publication Data--DK
Courtesy: D.K. Agencies (P) Ltd. <docinfo@dkagencies.com>

Anthropological research in North East India : retrospect & prospect / editors, Jibon Kumar, Sarit K. Chaudhuri & Huidrom Suraj Singh.
pages cm
Contributed articles.
ISBN 9788121218146 (HB)

1. Anthropometry--India, Northeastern. 2. Tribes--Health and hygiene--India. 3. Tribes--India--Social conditions. I. Kumar, Jibon, editor. II. Chaudhuri, S. K. (Sarit Kumar), editor. III. Indirā Gāndhī Rāshṭrīya Mānava Saṅgrahālaya, publisher.

LCC GN635.I4A58 2019 | DDC 305.8009541 23

Contents

Section - II
Ethno-Medicine

Section - III
Socio-Cultural

Section - IV
Ethno-Archaeology

List of Contributors

Abhijit Guha, Professor, Department of Anthropology, Vidyasagar University, Midnapore (*email: abhijitguhavuanthro@rediffmail.com*)

Ak. Bojen Meetei, Associate Professor, P.G. Department of Anthropology, D.M. College of Science, Imphal (*email: bojenmeeteiak@gmail.com*)

Anindita Sinha, Assistant Professor, Tripura Government Law College, Agartala, Tripura (*email: a.asinha@yahoo.co.in*)

Arundhati Devi Maibam, Associate Professor, P.G. Dept. of Anthropology, D.M. College of Science, Imphal (*email: arundhati.maibam@yahoo.com*)

Arup Bera, Professor, Department of Anthropology, Mahishadal Girl's College, Purba Medinipur, West Bengal (*email: arup.ndg@gmail.com*)

B.T. Langstieh, Associate Professor, Department of Anthropology, North-Eastern Hill University, Shillong (*email: langstieh.banrida@gmail.com*)

C.S.B. Marak, Research Scholar, Department of Anthropology, North-Eastern Hill University, Shillong (*email: chinmarak@gmail.com*)

Chaithu Sonia Aimol, M.Sc., P.G. Department of Anthropology, D.M. College of Science, Imphal (*email: soni_sairol_7@live.com*)

Chungkham Supriya Devi, Research Scholar, Department of Anthropology, University of Delhi, Delhi (*email: supschungkham@gmail.com*)

Duka Devi Chhetri, Research Scholar, Department of Anthropology, Sikkim University, Sikkim (*email: chhetriduka@yahoo.in*)

Esther Lalremkim, Post Doctoral Fellow, Department of Anthropology, Manipur University, Canchipur (*email:remkim@gmail.com*)

Grace Mary Vaiphei, Research Scholar, P.G. Dept. of Anthropology, D.M. College of Science, Imphal (*email: vaipheigrace@gmail.com*)

H. Sorojini Devi, Associate Professor, P.G. Department of Anthropology, D.M. College of Science, Imphal (*email: sorojinihijam@yahoo.in*)

Henry Konjenbam, Research Scholar, Department of Anthropology, Manipur University, Manipur (*email: henrykonjengbam745@gmail.com*)

Hoineilam Kipgen, Research Scholar, Department of Anthropology, North-Eastern Hill University, Shillong (*email: hoineilamkips@gmail.com*)

Jangkhomang, Research Scholar, Department of Anthropology, North-Eastern Hill University, Shillong (*email:mhaokip37@gmail.com*)

Kamlengthang Khongsai, MSc Student, P.G. Department of Anthropology, D.M. College of Science, Imphal (*email:lenpukhongsai99@gmail.com*)

Konsam Renu Devi, Assistant Professor, Department of Anthropology, W.M.G. College, Thoubal, Manipur (*email: renu_konsam2006@yahoo.co.in*)

Ketousienuo Kuotsu, Research Scholar, Department of Anthropology, North-Eastern Hill University, Shillong (*email:ketousienuo@gmail.com*)

Kh. Manglembi Devi, Associate Professor, P.G. Department of Anthropology, D.M. College of Science, Imphal (*email:manglembi10@gmail.com*)

Kh. Narendra Singh, Associate Professor, Department of Anthropology, Assam University, Diphu Campus, Diphu (*email: kh.singh@rediffmail.com*)

Ksh. BeliyaLuxmi Devi, Research Scholar, Department of Anthropology, Manipur University, Manipur (*email: beliya.kshetri@yahoo.in*)

Leivon Khamnu Kom, Research Scholar, Department of Anthropology, North-Eastern Hill University, Shillong (*email: khamnuleivon@gmail.com*)

Lorho Mary Maheo, Associate Professor, P.G. Department of Anthropology, D.M. College of Science, Imphal (*email:marylorho@gmail.com*)

Maibam Monoranjan Singh, Assistant Professor, P.G. Department of Anthropology, D.M. College of Science, Imphal (*email:monomaibam@yahoo.com*)

Mariam Jamatia, Research Scholar, Department of Anthropology, North-Eastern Hill University, Shillong (*email:mariamj1589@gmail.com*)

Menaka Devi, M.Sc. Student, P.G. Department of Anthropology, D.M. College of Science, Imphal (*email:menakanong@gmail.com*)

Monsumi Barooah, Research Scholar, Amity Institute of Anthropology, Amity University, Noida, U.P. (*email: monsumib9@gmail.com*)

Naorem Naokhomba Singh, Research Scholar, Department of Anthropology, North-Eastern Hill University, Shillong (*email:naokhombanaorem@gmail.com*)

Ngathem Pungfa Singh, Associate Professor, P.G. Department of Anthropology, D.M. College of Science, Imphal (*email:pungfa@gmail.com*)

N. Sanatombi Devi, Research Scholar, P.G. Department of Anthropology, D.M. College of Science, Imphal (*email: nsanatombi87@gmail.com*)

P. Binodini Devi, Associate Professor, P.G. Department of Anthropology, D.M. College of Science, Imphal (*email:binodini96@gmail.com*)

P. Dhaneshwari Devi, Associate Professor, Department of Anthropology, Kha Manipur College (*email: dr.okramdhaneshwari@gmail.com*)

Pourinliu Kamei, MSc Student, P.G. Department of Anthropology, D.M. College of Science, Imphal.

R. Khongsdier, Professor, Department of Anthropology, North-Eastern Hill University, Shillong (*email:rkhongsdier@hotmail.com*)

Ramananda Ningthoujam, Research Scholar, Department of Physical Education and Sports Science (*email: ramanand.ningthoujam5@gmail.com*)

Ratna Tayeng, Doctoral Scholar, Department of Anthropology, Rajiv Gandhi University, Itanagar (*email:ratnatayeng991@gmail.com*)

Romeo Bungdon, General Secretary, All Manipur Tribal Union, Manipur (*email:romeopakan@gmail.com*)

Rongnyoo Lepcha, Research Scholar, Department of Anthropology, Sikkim University, Sikkim (*email:lepcharongnyoo@gmail.com*)

Rv. Khanchuila, Post Doctoral Fellow, Department of Anthropology, Manipur University, Canchipur (*email: khanchuila11@gmail.com*)

Sangay Diki Bhutia, Research Scholar, Department of Anthropology, Sikkim University, Sikkim (*email:bhutiasangaydiki92@gmail.com*)

Shangpam Kashung, Post Doctoral Fellow, Department of Anthropology, Gauhati University, Guwahati (*email:shangpamkashung9@gmail.com*)

Singtitla Vashum, Research Scholar, Department of Anthropology, Manipur University, Canchipur (*email: vs.singtit@gmail.com*)

Soibam Jibonkumar Singh, Professor, Department of Anthropology, Manipur University, Canchipur (*email: drjibonkumar@yahoo.com*)

Sudipta Ghosh, Assistant Professor, Department of Anthropology, North-Eastern Hill University, Shillong (*email: sudipta@nehu.ac.in*)

S. Sumanta Singh, Assistant Professor, P.G. Department of Anthropology, D.M. College of Science, Imphal (*email:ssumantasingh@gmail.com*)

T. Inaobi Singh, Associate Professor, Department of Physical Education and Sports Science, Manipur University, Canchipur (*email:drinaobisinght@gmail.com*)

T. Lyngdoh, Department of Anthropology, North-Eastern Hill University, Shillong.

Tenzing Zangmu Lepcha, Research Scholar, Department of Anthropology, Sikkim University, Sikkim (*email: tenzingzangmu@gmail.com*)

Thiyam Rabikanta Singh, Associate Professor, P.G. Department of Anthropology, D.M. College of Science, Imphal (*email:trabikanta123@gmail.com*)

Thoudam Bedita Devi, Tutor cum Research Scholar, Department of Anatomy Sikkim Manipal Institute of Medical Sciences, Sikkim (*email: thnoubi@gmail.com*)

Vihousienuo Neli, Research Scholar, Department of Anthropology, North-Eastern Hill University, Shillong (*email:atsivilhou@gmail.com*)

Y. Roshni Devi, M.Sc., P.G. Department of Anthropology, D.M. College of Science, Imphal (*email:roshniynam94@gmail.com*)

Yogesh Sharma, Research Scholar, Department of Anthropology, Sikkim University, Sikkim (*email: jshon58@gmail.com*)

Zimic Urapum, Research Scholar, P.G. Department of Anthropology, D.M. College of Science, Imphal (*email:zimicurapam@gmail.com*)

Introduction

North East India (NEI) is considered as one of the most culturally and ecologically diverse regions of the world. It is the eastern most region of India inhabited by different ethnic groups. It comprises of seven sister states (Arunachal Pradesh, Assam, Manipur, Meghalaya, Mizoram, Nagaland and Tripura) and the state Sikkim is also included very recently to this North Eastern Region (NER). It is the homeland of a large number of ethnic groups who came from different directions by various routes of migration at different historical times. These ethnic groups belong to different racial elements and have diverse socio-cultural traditions. The major racial element that lives in this region includes Mongoloids and Australoids. The tribal populations of NEI belong to three major linguistic families such as Austro-Asiatic, Siamese-Chinese and Tibeto-Burman. The Tibeto-Burman linguistic group numerically predominates in the NE region.

North East India, occupying an area of 2,61,2185 sq.km constitute about 7.9 percent of the total area of the country. NER is surrounded by international boundaries with China, Tibet, and Bhutan on the north; Myanmar on the east and Bangladesh on the south. NE states are connected with the mainland India only through West Bengal with a long narrow passage on the West. The total population of NEI according to 2011 census is 4,57,72,188 individuals which constitutes nearly 4 percent of the total population of India as a whole. The overall density of population is 170 person/Km^2. The region has been the home to as many as 345 different diverse ethnic communities which are more than one third of the total number of tribes in India having different socio-cultural and ethno-linguistic characters. It includes 172 Scheduled Tribes, 31 Scheduled Castes, 34 other Backward Communities and 108 general communities. Distribution of tribal population in NER varies significantly from one state to others. The highest tribal population is observed in Mizoram which constitute 94.4 percent of the total state's population. In Meghalaya and Nagaland, the percentage of tribal population is quite high reaching more than 86 percent of the total state's population. The least frequency of tribal population is observed in Assam (12.4 percent).

Most of the communities have their own socio-cultural characteristics which make them unique in their own ways. They have rich cultural tradition which is more or less embedded in their habitat. From the earlier times, it has been the interest of the anthropological researchers from different parts of the globe to understand the society and culture of this region against the backdrop of nomothetic and ideographic researches. Of late, these small communities have undergone a sea-change in respect of their ways of life, both tangible and intangible, owing to the deep impact of exogenous and endogenous multidimensional factors adding a new dimension to the already existed man environment relationship of these societies. At present, various smaller communities of this region are also facing the dilemma of ethnic identity. This in turn gives birth to the competing problems of both inter- and - intra community conflicts as well as movements, focussing around the ethnic interest and also against the authority. On the top of this, lack of skills and infrastructure development, unemployment, particularly among the educated youth also breed various social problems. Social scientist, especially social anthropologist, are keen in understanding such problems and seeking for remedial strategies from earlier times. Under such socio-cultural circumstances, North East India remained, still remains and will remain the fertile field for social researches.

Apart from the social perspectives of the people, the region is also archeologically rich. It is often considered the meeting point of the two great cultural traditions: Sub Indian archaic and East Asian cultural traditions. Archaeological remains of the early human civilization somehow suggest the possibility of culture contact between the people of these two parts of the continent and further throw light on the consequent diffusion of the cultures leading to the formation of a unique syncretised culture on the region. Not only do these artefacts illustrate the type of settlement, social organization of these early human civilizations, they also suggest human survival in this region in the early course of human migration and settlement. In biological sense, it may also be interpreted that the adaptive response of humans towards the harsh environment might have resulted in physical and physiological variation of those archaic humans.

The peopling of India is a matter of investigation but the peopling of the north eastern region is still more complicated. The possibility of out of India migration to East Asia through North East India has been inferred highlighting the region as a corridor of human migration to East Asia, Attempts to validate this inferences have also been made through genetic and non-genetic studies. At the same time, variation of these peoples in term of their morphological characteristics from those of other Indian populations makes it more doubtful. Genetically, it is claimed that the people of this region has more resemblance or affinity with those of East Asia. Genetic structure of each population becomes more rigid because of endogamous nature of these groups of people. More or less, the selection pressure on these populations also varies depending on the ecological niche or environmental habitation. The region is also prone to various infections and epidemics which pose a threat to the health of the people. At the Same time changing lifestyle and physical activities also enhance the health problems resulting in the rise of various complex disorders. Such a condition attracts the academic attention of various researchers, academicians, health scientists including anthropologist who are very much concerned for the health promotion and management in this region.

An exhaustive and comprehensive study of the various ethnic communities of this region on a holistic approach i.e from prehistoric, social, cultural, economic, political and biological aspects can only be accomplished through in depth anthropological research. In this regards, the anthropological knowledge of North East India has enlarged to a great extent by the establishment of the Regional Centre of the Anthropological Survey of India at Shillong in 1953. However, the academic department of anthropology was first started at Cotton College in 1947, followed by Gauhati University in 1948. After the establishment of Regional Centre of Anthropological Survey many universities have opened anthropology department in NEI. Dibrugarh University started anthropology department in the year 1966, North Eastern Hill University in 1981, Manipur University in 1984, Rajiv Gandhi University in 2001 initially as Department of Tribal Studies. Later in the year 2012, it got bifurcated as a separate Department of Anthropology), Assam University in 2010, Sikkim University in 2013 and recently Nagaland University in the year 2013. After the establishment of anthropological departments in North East India, various anthropological research works has been carried out from different perspectives. Anthropologists started targeting on different issues related with different communities of North East India. The future prospect of anthropological research in the region is of paramount importance and need of the hour too. In fact, the region can be considered a hotspot of Anthropologist for understanding human issues and diversity. Considering this diversity and rich human environment relationship reflected in different cultural traditions and morphological characteristics, there are prospects for academic deliberation from different perspectives.

In this edited book, a total of forty four research articles were contributed by different scholars on various issues highlighting the current trends of Anthropological Research particularly in North East India. The present edited book is grouped into four sections viz Biological Anthropology, Ethno-Medicine, Socio-Cultural and Ethno-Archaeology based on the theme of the contributed articles.

The first section of this edited book **Biological Anthropology** includes a total of sixteen research papers on Anthropometric and Physiological profile of various ethnic groups, Reproductive and child health, Nutritional status, Diseases and its risk factors, and Trends of Physical Education Program in School. Authors' tries to highlights the present issues and problems faced by the mother, children, adolescent and current trends of anthropological research in different ethnic groups inhabiting in North East India.

Ak. Bojen Meetei and S. Jibonkumar Singh explored to determine **body composition and anthropometric profile of Indian Elite Wushu (Sanshou and Taolu) players** of Indian National Team, Manipur participating 9th World Wushu Championships, 2007 at Beijing. Authors suggest that Indian male elite Sanshou players have low body fat within desirable range, high fat free mass, total body water and grip strength as compared to Taolu players. Male Sanshou players were significantly heavier and taller than the Taolu players. Similarly, women Sanshou players are also found to have significantly higher body fat, free fat mass, heavier body weight and higher body height than the Taolu players. The study conclude that low fat percent, high grip strength, high fat free mass, low percent fat and low BMI may consider important parameters for successful competitive performance in both Sanshou and Taolu players.

Ghosh S. Lyngdoh and Marak CSB studies **anthropometric characteristic of the adults' males of War-Jaintia population of Nongtalang village, Jaintia Hills district Meghalaya**. The study reveals that adult War Jaintia males found to smoke daily and chew tobacco regularly. However, the rates of alcohol consumptions show very less frequency. Anthropometric findings revealed that War-Jaintia males are generally short in stature with medium shoulder, narrow pelvis and they have medium and long face. The paper concludes that War-Jaintia males do not show significance difference with other populations of North-east India.

The paper entitled **Anthropometric, Blood Pressure and Haemoglobin Aspects of Chothes of Chandel District, Manipur** by Chaithu Sonia Aimol and H. Sorojini Devi reported significant differences between male and female with respect to BMI, WHR, blood pressure and haemoglobin levels among the Chothe tribe of three villages of Chandel district, Manipur. Males are taller in height, heavier in weight and higher in systolic and diastolic blood pressure as well as less anaemic while compared with females. On the other hand, the paper reveals higher incidence of high risk WHR among Chothe women than male.

Henry Konjengbam made an attempt to understand the **correlation between stature and foot dimension among the Kom of Thayong village, Senapati District, Manipur**. Author suggests that knowing the index values, stature of an individual of a particular community can be safely estimated from the foot size and vice versa. Study reveals that foot length provides the best estimate of stature in both males and females as it indicate the highest correlation value and regression equation provides greater reliability than multiplication factor. According to the author, there is need to conduct more studies among people of different region and ethnicity so that stature estimation becomes more reliable and identity of an individual is easily established. Such studies will also help in medico-legal cases in establishing identity of an individual in mass disasters, accidents, bomb explosion etc as opined by the author.

Konsam Renu Devi examines the fertility of women in her paper title **A study on fertility of the women of Ithing village, Manipur**. The study reveals high Crude Birth Rate of 25.55 during the year 2010. The mean age at menarche and that of menopause of the women were found to be 14.22 years and 44.95 years respectively, that is, the reproductive span of the Ithing women is 30.73 years. The mean age at marriage is observed to be above the national average. Age Specific Fertility Rate and the Total Fertility rate are 144.28 and 4.11 respectively. Author reports high fertility rate among the studied population suggesting low socio-economic status leading to early marriage is one of the possible reasons for high fertility rate among the Ithing women.

Hoineilam Kipgen and B.T. Langstieh's paper **Cultural behaviour in relation to maternal child health among the Thadou-Kuki of Senapati District, Manipur** focuses on the importance of education and its vital roles played in woman's life which reflects on not only herself but also on her offsprings, family and society at large. According to the authors, education on planned parenthood or guides to parental education, maternal and child health services through outreach programmes on awareness, prevention and cautionary measures on health issues have always been taken on a positive outcome even in the remotest local village administration.

A cross sectional **study on height, weight, and haemoglobin status of Chothe children of Manipur** aged between 6 to 12+ years belonged to three villages of Purum Tampak, Purum Lainingkhun and Purum Khullen of Chandel district, Manipur was conducted by H. Sorojini Devi and Y. Roshini Devi focussing on nutritional health status. Body height, weight and haemoglobin level of each child were measured using standard norms. Study reports that prevalence of anaemia was more common among the Chothe boys than girls. Regarding nutritional status, the studied children are reported to be shorter and lighter than the Indian children at all ages reported by ICMR.

Ramananda Ningthoujam and T. Inaobi Singh's paper titled **Present trends of physical education program in school** highlights the new model of physical education program and its importance in schools. The new model aims at overall development including socio-ecological factors and optimal health benefits of the students. Authors opined that the new model is intended to provide expanded opportunities for physical activity beyond regularly scheduled Physical Education time. Moreover, authors also give more importance to development of healthy life style. Several new activities were proposed to introduce in the new model of physical education program which includes home play activities, dance, games and sports, other movement activities, parents participation activities, community based physical activity program, weekly assessment of children (FITNESSGRAM), diet and nutrition physical activity program, and physical activity literacy program.

Thoudam Bedita Devi carried out research work on Meitei male Population of Manipur focusing on **morphological study of head dimensions of Meiteis: A secular trend**. Author hypothesised that the population might have experienced a secular trend in Head Length, Head Breadth and Cephalic Index from earlier generation to the present generation. According to the findings of the study, author suggest that even though the size of the head increases, head shape remains more or less unchanged because of the fact that head shape or form depends more on pre-established constitutional hereditary factors and less on environmental factors as compared to head size for which environmental factors has a great influence on genetic factor.

Water-borne diseases such as cold fever, scabies, diarrhoea, worm infestation, typhoid and jaundice were commonly observed in Karang Island, an area of land completely surrounded by Loktak lake. The paper also reveals that unavailability of potable water, poor sanitation and hygiene, low socio-economic conditions, and cultural practices associated with consumption of drinking water were the main determinants of water borne diseases. The results of the study indicate need for intervention strategies to control water borne morbidities among the inhabitants of Karang Island, Manipur. It is the outcome of **study on water borne morbidities of Karang Islet, Manipur** conducted by Ksh. BeliyaLuxmi Devi.

Duka Devi Chhetri explores demographic study to describe the **Differential fertility and mortality among the Khasi women of Siden village, Meghalaya**. The study highlights the fertility and mortality rates in relation with certain socio-economic conditions. The number of live birth was observed to be higher than the mean number of surviving children among women who have completed family size. Family income was found to play an important role in determining the fertility and mortality rate. Findings of the study also indicate that education level of the mothers doesn't influence on the fertility and mortality rate in the present studied Khasi female population.

Socio-economic factors influences on nutritional status among the Khasi women of Meghalaya by Yogesh Sharma discuss possible risk factors that influence nutritional status. The present study was undertaken among Khasi females of Saiden village, Ri-Bhoi district, Meghalaya to find the nutritional status in relation with socioeconomic conditions, lifestyles and food habits. According to the author, prevalence of overweight/obesity among Khasi females of Saiden village is influenced by certain socioeconomic factors like family income, occupation and inactive physical activities. Food habits especially the consumption of non-vegetable foods was also found to play an important role in determining the nutritional status in the present research.

Singtitla Vashum and Soibam Jibonkumar Singh's paper title **Strategies for Contraception, Bodily Effects, and Speculations related to Contraceptive Methods: A case study of the Tangkhuls** explores the use of different contraceptive methods as a means of family planning among Tangkhuls of Manipur. The study indicates that people used contraception for various reasons such as spacing, pregnancy complication, mother's health risk, and for family planning. Most of the women used it between the interval of three and more children. Their findings clearly indicate that people use contraception after they got their desired number of children. Authors also reported negative side effects of the use of contraception faced by the people and it is the main reason for not using contraception by some sections of the studied population.

The paper titled **Ageing change in body composition among the Tangkhul males of Manipur** by H. Sorojini Devi and Zimic Urapum discusses change in body composition due to ageing. They have reported that with the increase of age there is decline in stature, body weight, waist and hip girth as well as various skinfold such as sub-scapular, supra-illiac, abdominal, medial calf, bicep and tricep as ageing reduces metabolic rate with functional decline of all organs which contribute to reduction in resting metabolic rate (RMR) leading to change in body composition. Development of body composition components such as fat percent , body fat and lean body mass also varied with age. Authors have opined that changes in body composition with ageing are also influenced by many factors such as nutrition, life style, occupation and income.

Leivon Khamnu Kom and Prof. R. Khongsdier examine the **Opportunity for natural selection in relation to age at marriage and household income among Kom population of Churachandpur District in Manipur**. According to Crow's as well as the modified method by Johnston and Kensinger, results of the study shows negative association with age at marriage of the mothers and household income and contribute more towards differential fertility rather than differential mortality. The total index (I) shows higher contribution towards the fertility component among the study Kom population which supports the contention that due to better public health care and other modern facilities which gives a positive outcome on the lower contribution of mortality for the evolutionary mechanism through natural selection. Authors conclude that fertility is seen to be more important as compared to mortality in the manifestation of natural selection in the study population.

Lorho Mary Maheo, Pourinliu Kamei and Menaka Devi's paper titled **Reproductive and child health: a comparative study between the Koms of Khoirentak and the Chothes of Purum Tampak village, Manipur** deals with women reproductive health along with infant and child care practices prevailing in the focused areas. An attempt has also been made to compare two ethnic groups viz Koms of Khoirentak, Churachandpur District and Chothes of Purum Tampak, Chandel District inhabiting in different socio-environmental conditions. Most of the women are aware of birth control measures and they gave less importance to traditional health care system particularly in reproductive health. Similar reproductive and child health conditions were observed in both Kom and Chothe community despite having different ethnic background as well as living in different socio-environmental conditions. However, the present study indicates urgent need to intensified promotional activities of mother and child health (antenatal care, safe delivery, immunization, small family and adequate child spacing) for overall betterment of the community's health.

The second section **Ethno-Medicine** consists of six research papers on traditional health care practices adopted by different ethnic groups of North East India. Some of the papers try to highlight the significance of ethno-medicinal practices in present days which are being influenced by advance western medical sciences. Moreover, impacts of Christianity on the traditional healing practices are also discussed in this section.

Kh. Narendra Singh explained the significance and **role of traditional medicine in primary healthcare practices among the Karbis of Assam, India**. Karbi Anglong is one of the rich repositories of medicinal plants in the northeast India. Traditional medical system still plays an important role in health care behaviour among the Karbis. Causes of an illness and healing system are found to be associated with the magico-religious beliefs. Along with herbal treatment, magico-religious practices are still occupying a significant position in their indigenous methods of treatment. In-depth study using anthropological methods and approaches are very much essential to understand the indigenous health seeking behaviour from emic perspective.

A case study on **Ethnomedical practices by Lepchas of Tingshim village, Sikkim** was studied by Tenzing Zangmu Lepcha. It focuses on common health problems, health care practices, magico religious practices and modern health care practices among the villagers. Different varieties of plants are used for medicinal purpose as well as animal products are also sometimes used for healing different diseases. Food poisoning is something that a person gives to some other by mixing it in their food as believed by the people. ICDS centre of Tingshim village provides medical and nutritional facilities to children. It also provides nutritional powder to pregnant women that continue till their baby reaches the age of three. Moreover, money has been sanctioned for the distribution of dry fruits to adolescent girls of the village but has not started yet. Author suggests that the development in term of health is of good quality in the Tingshim village.

Naorem Naokhomba Singh's paper titled **Ethnomedicine and its significance in Meitei society** deals with traditional medical system practices by the Meitei. Study highlights the important roles of Maibas (male practitioners) and Maibis (female practitioners) in traditional health care system. Most of the illness and diseases are treated with indigenous medicinal plants and organic matters with praying deity in traditional health care system. The local and traditional healers are still practicing in treating certain medical conditions which is not able to replace by modern physicians with the advance tools and techniques. In some conditions magico-religious methods such as incantation of spells, oracles, performing healing rituals, prayer, offering of food items, fruits, vegetables and flowers to the spirits are use to dealt the health problems associated with possession of evil spirits and deities. Author suggests the necessities to promote and preserved traditional healing practices for the future generations as well as it will also help in conserving the indigenous medicinal plants.

Indigenous health care practices of Vaiphei community of Kangvai in Churachandpur district, Manipur was studied by Grace Mary Vaiphei and Arundhati Devi Maibam. According to the Vaiphei community, illness is cause by evil spirits. Evil spirits are believed to dwell in many strange places causing mental and physical illness. Nine folk classes of illness are identified among the studied population. They are skin diseases, pain and ache, fever, cuts, wounds and bites, gynaecological problems, supernatural diseases, associated diseases, fatal diseases and seasonal diseases. Both medicinal plants and animal parts are used for medicine. Findings of the study highlights that modern medicine has become a better option with its easy availability and affordability. The rich indigenous knowledge on health care practices among the Vaiphei is gradually replace by modern medicine. Authors express the need to conserve the indigenous health care knowledge for common ailments having comparatively less side effects.

Ketousienuo Kuotsu explores the **Impact of Christianity on the traditional healing practices among the Angami Naga, Nagaland**. Before the adoption of Christianity, Angami have rich traditional health care practices. Regular appeasement to the deity was made in the form of offerings by laying an egg, pieces of meat, rice – beer and morsel of food in the field, outside the village, jungle and in the village gate to obviate the wrath of malevolent spirits. All the unnatural deaths, diseases, famines, plagues, natural calamities and misfortunes were believed to be the wrath of evil spirits. However, the traditional form of healing illness and the role of shamans began to decline and got replaced by dispensaries and health centres after the advent of Christianity. Church has become an integral part in the life of the Angamis. The study concludes that introduction of Christianity in the Angami region played a commendable role in the life of the tribal population.

The traditional healers of Khurkhul use a holistic approach in dealing with health and illness by providing treatment for physical, psychological, spiritual and other social symptoms. The people of Khurkhul have their own concepts of the causes and curing of diseases. As such, disease is viewed as a supernatural phenomenon governed by a hierarchy of vital powers beginning with the most powerful deity followed by lesser spiritual entities, ancestral spirits, living persons, animals, plants and other objects as reported by the author Ngathem Pungfa Singh in his paper title **Traditional Healers of Khurkhul**.

In third section **Socio-Cultural** studies include nineteen research papers on different dimensions such as Man and Environment, Social change, Impact of modernity, Christianity and Hinduism, Governance, Socio-Political Organization, Life in inter-state borderlands, and inter tribal marriages. The present section also highlights studies focusing particularly on women like Domestic violence against women, women role and status in the society, Gender inequality, and socio-cultural risk factors for diseases among women.

Arup Bera examines critically a research project which was undertaken by the Anthropological Survey of India under its Eleventh Five Year Plan Project – Man and Environment on his paper entitles **A Critical Review of the Man in Biosphere: Khangchendzonga Biosphere Reserve (KBR) Project of Anthropological Survey of India**. The review report mentioned that, "Biosphere Reserves are *special entities* for both the people and the nature and are living examples of how human beings and nature can co-exist while respecting each other's needs". The region is special in nature and not natural. Author explores the dialectic of life of the people living in the KBR region and documented how the life of the people was portrayed.

The paper title **Peril in the Harbor: Domestic violence and women's autonomy in north-east India** by Anindita Sinha states that various forms of violence have a strong cultural component associated with gender norms prevailing in the society. Study reveals that among the states of NER, all forms of violence against women (VAW), especially sexual violence, are relatively lower in the tribal dominated states, viz. Meghalaya, Mizoram, Nagaland and Sikkim. It is alarming to note that all forms of VAW are abysmally high in Tripura and in fact, Tripura and Assam evince rates of domestic violence as well as physical and sexual violence much higher than the all-India average levels. Overall, Meghalaya seems to be safest place for women as far as intimate partner violence (IPV) is concerned and in fact, sexual violence is almost absent in the state. According to the author, policy interventions at the community level and sustained rises in women's autonomy and education seem indispensable for reducing domestic violence in NER.

Notable contributions of Tarak Chandra Das, one of the founders of professional and academic Anthropology in India, in the field of ethnographic study is briefly discussed by Abhijit Guha in his review paper titled **Chirus, Purums, and how social changes in North East India provided new windows for T.C. Das**. Das earned his international fame through his research on the Purums of Manipur. Author also highlights one of the important research works on ecological analysis of the Chiru society, North East India having contemporary relevance which had largely gone unnoticed. North East India provided TC Das with a new window to turn Anthropology towards application and nation building and he was really running ahead of his time.

Chungkham Supriya Devi's paper titled **Emoinu Model in Contemporary Meitei Society** discusses the impact of modernization on Goddess Emoinu's codes of conduct on Meitei women and in Meitei society. Modernization has brought various changes in traditional way of living of the Meitei society. It opens the entrance of women in education and in economic activities. Both working and non-working women helps in the economy of the family. Men are kept much higher in status than women; despite it women ideas are considered and have an important role in decision making. Author highlights that modern Meitei women are less aware of the prescribe behavior of the Goddess Emoinu.

The paper title **Gender Inequalities as key driver of the HIV/AIDS epidemic among the tribes of Jaintia Hills, Meghalaya** by Monsumi Barooah highlight the effects of HIV/AIDS in the society/ the impediments faced by women in the HIV/AIDS epidemic due to gender inequalities. According to the author, both male and female should recognize that men's efforts will bear most fruit in a climate of encouragement and understanding. Women need to be encouraged to continue to empower and protect themselves, as well as to speak and live their truths as autonomous sexual beings. They deserve help and support in standing up to male domination where that is the case. At the same time it must be remembered that women are powerful and not helpless victims of male oppression. Author suggests that they are proactive participants and full partners in the fight to halt the HIV/AIDS epidemic.

Rv. Khanchuila examine gender socialization at different stages of childhood and to evaluate how gender values of the society is reproduced through socialization process in her paper title **Gender socialization of children among the Tangkhuls of Manipur**. Gender streamlining among the Tangkhuls starts right from the time the child is conceived. The values of femininity depict patience, caring attitude, understanding nature, and a homemaker which is manifested in the way they assign duties, the nature of their games, etc. The values of masculinity portray men with a daring character, protector, etc. The values of patriliny and patriarchy interfere in all the process of socialization. Moreover, author also narrated the value of patriarchy in the way elders soothe the girl child protectively which indicates men as the protector of their women.

Shangpam Kashung made an attempt to understand how much the status of women has been improved under the influence of modernity and Christianity in his paper titled **Influence of Modernity and Christianity on the status of Tangkhul Women**. People aware of the importance of women's education and it increased the status of women. They got employed and they no longer depend only on agriculture for economy. Tangkhul women have equal political rights and freedom as male guaranteed under the Indian Constitution after the introduction of modern political system. But the question of gender equality remains as no picture of women inheriting immovable properties after improving in many aspects. Author opined that despite gender inequality, the influence of Christianity and modernity proved beneficial in many ways.

Jangkhomang's paper title **Modernisation and Change: Transition of youth organisation among the Kukis** highlight the importance of dormitories and change in the youth organisational structural set up if any with the coming of modernisation, with special reference to the Kukis. In present days many changes had been observed in the age old traditional institutions of the Kukis. The institution of *Lawm* and *Sawm* which had been the centre of village social life have now been replaced by modern youth organization like the youth clubs at the village level and students organizations at the students level. According to the author, the youth club of present day may be described as representing both the tradition institution of *Lawm* and *Sawm*, as it fulfilled certain criteria of both, while keeping in mind that the education work being carried out by modern educational institutions. One of the main objectives of these organizations is to preserve and protect the traditional culture and customs as concluded by the author.

The role of women in traditional institution among the Jamatia of Tripura was studied by Mariam Jamatia. Women in the *Jamatia* community were confined to the four walls of the house. They treated as non-permanent member of the society and they were left to the background. Women had no share or role in the political and administrative set-up of the society. With the arrival of the adult franchise they were given a platform where they were able to raise their voice and participate in decision making. The present paper tries to give a glimpse of the role of women played in the traditional institution and its changes due to influence of modern developments.

Rituals of Harvest: A Study on Paddy Harvest Rituals and Change among the Angami Nagas of Kigwema Village, Nagaland authored by Vilhousienuo Neli deals with the harvesting of paddy, the rituals conducted, and how it has undergone changes over the years. The cultivation of rice is the major occupation of the people of Kigwema village. A change in the traditional practices in the case of performing pre and post harvest of paddy is seen with the coming of Christianity. Although, the harvesting and threshing of paddy is the same, in the present scenario with better connectivity and transportation, the workload of bringing in paddy home from the field has been affected. Social change in a society is inevitable and continuous. Modern amenities, development in various sectors and spread of Christianity in Kigwema has resulted in certain changes and modification in relation to the harvesting of paddy and connected rituals were witnessed.

Romeo Bungdon narrates an outlines on the PAKANs who have been living with much unsung recognition on his paper title **Pakan: A Historical**

Nomenclature of Ethnic Affinity. The PAKAN tribe is one of the ancient brave warriors originated from Yunnan province of China who are then scattered in countries like Myanmar, Borneo Island (Malaysia), Chittagong (Bangladesh), NE of India and other Southeast Asian countries. Author attracts new challenges of anthropological deeper research on such thousands of years lapsed study fields. According to him, it is never too late yet and it is believed that anyone who is striving and has such solace of thirst on new discoveries shall venture wisdom to re-integrate the fragments of such consunguity for paving higher achievement of natural historical facts in the North East region of India.

Esther Lalremkim and Soibam Jibonkumar Singh's paper title **Socio-Economic and Cultural changes among Hmar from pre-Christian period to present: A Comparative study** explores the past and present socio-cultural aspects and also gives detail information on the transformation that has taken place in Hmar society and the ways Hmar society has retained their customs and traditions. Various traditional customs and practices are given up in the name of Christianity while in certain spheres of activities and ways of life it shows impressive results. The Hmar society is no longer static; it has change and is changing. If this continued, the rich traditional cultures and indigenous systems may be lost. Some indigenous customs and practices are too fast disappearing from the society without any replacement set in. Author recommends that cultures and traditions, dresses, folklore and songs, fashion, indeed the totality of Hmar life style should be regularly and with passionate practiced, properly recorded and preserved and proudly and widely promoted.

The paper title **Socio-political and Cultural Existence of Monsang Naga Tribes: Retrospective Outlook** by P. Dhaneshwari Devi attempts to understand Monsang Naga Tribes through social anthropological aspects. The present study focuses on socio-political structure that includes family; clan; marriage; divorce; mating pattern; inheritance property; political organisation; social structure; occupation, festivals and death. The Monsang tribal communities are segregated in two major clans namely Simputi and Rinheti. Each clan is divided in some other sub groups. The coming of Christianity sometime in the 1920s and conversion to the new religion brought-forth many changes in the socio-economic and material culture of the Monsang Nagas. Indeed, the study is deeply concerns on the retrospective outlook.

Status of Khasi women were described in Rongnyoo Lepcha's paper title **Status of women among the Khasi's of Saiden village, Meghalaya**. According to the study the Khasi society known to be matrilineal and the women do exercise certain privileges still the main authority behind the mask of matrilinity is always a male. They only have privileges in certain spheres like inheritance of property and the decision making sphere also seem to be more or less equal with the men. But in the political and religious sector the women of the village have very less participation as well as low status. Women though have a very high status culturally in the Matrilineal Khasi society they are still trying to gain a lot more socially. Women are regarded to be *kabalang Shi-bor* (having one power) in local term *kakyntheikabalangShibor* meaning women having only one power; this is how a Khasi woman is perceived by the society.

Ratna Tayeng focused on understanding **Life in the Inter-State borderlands of Assam and Arunachal Pradesh**. Author demonstrates how the Assam- Arunachal Pradesh border comes into being and how borderlanders and their respective government's construct, negotiate and experience this reality and how people, who live along and are divided by state borders, have adjusted to the borderland situation and what strategies they have adopted in their socio-cultural life. The people living in this regions have been living along the boundary engage in individual occasion, influences cultures, exchange among people. The administrative boundary of the state does not stand in the way of the rational choice of markets for economic transaction. Foothill regions of Assam-Arunachal Border, traditionally which was supposed to be the place of economic exchange between the hills people and the plains, turned into a violence ground with the emerging ideas of 'territoriality'. Author narrates the situation of this long foothills bordering Assam and Arunachal Pradesh became more complex when Assam's demand for inclusion of reserved forest and contiguous areas inhabited by Assamese emerged out.

Sangay Diki Bhutia explains the village governance in a matrilineal society of Meghalaya in her paper title **Village governance in a matrilineal society of Meghalaya: a case study of Saiden village**. Author argues about the gendered relational aspects within the political process and practice. Most of the village decisions are taken by the village headman and all the household decisions are by the male subject in contrast to the popular conception that the women of K*hasi, Garo* and *Jaintia* communities enjoy more or less egalitarian social status. Meghalaya being a matrilineal society, women are considered to be valued both in socio economic religious and legal status. However, the representation of women in political process and at the state legislative is comparatively almost nil in many parts of the state. Patriarchal structures are very strong particularly in the political sphere. The present study indicates the age old practice of village headman and the social exclusion of women in the local governance. Author tries to give some suggestions in her paper for the women political empowerment process within the given structural components of these communities.

Arundhati Devi Maibam identified cultural factors that make women vulnerable to cervical cancer in her paper title **Cervical cancer and cultural vulnerabilities of Meitei women**. Socio-cultural practices such as early marriage, multiple pregnancies and unhygienic sanitary practices were identified as factors that increased the vulnerability of women to cervical cancer. 62.96 percent of the women married at ≤ 18 years and 75.92 percent had ≥3 pregnancies. 90.74 percent had the habit of using traditional reusable cloth as sanitary napkin. Bathing in unenclosed space accounted for 66.66 percent of the total study sample. The study showed various cultural vulnerabilities that expose women to cervical cancer. Author suggests that cultural practices such as early marriage, multiple pregnancies, sexual silence, childbearing decision and personal hygiene are habits which can be changed to prevent cervical cancer. Primary and secondary prevention mechanisms such as awareness creation, vaccination and screening targeting particularly the women at high risk should be widely initiated and strengthened.

Maibam Monoranjan Singh and Arundhati Devi Maibam's paper title **Inter-tribal marriage among the Thangal tribe of Manipur - continuity and change** discuss the status and extent of intertribal marriage among the Thangal, its impact on language and to identify the reasons for change in the age-old practice. Despite a growing trend of intramarriage among the Thangal, inter-tribal marriage is still practised. The traditional practice of exogamy and recruitment of wife from other groups has not only led to a high degree of miscegenation but also to a high degree of mixture in language. A shift from the native Thangal to a new *lingua franca* called *Lamjan* in some Thangal villages is a distinct sign of language shift. Authors express the need of timely intervention to check the gradual shift with well formulated policies. Unless a resolution to learn and promote Thangal language is adopted, chances of complete loss of the heritage within a few decades cannot be ruled out.

The impacts of Hinduism on the Meitei society by S. Sumanta Singh and Thiyam Rabikanta Singh attempt to study the impact of Hinduism on the Meiteis who have been settling mainly in Manipur, India. The Hinduisation process almost engulfed the indigenous social values of the people to be assimilated into a totally Hindu society. The effects and influences of Brahmanical religious propagation and popularization paved the way of classifying the social stratification of people with the immigrant Brahmins taking the topmost rung of the social ladder in the Meitei society. The new religious order in the local Meitei society was also vividly seen in many aspects and respects of the Meitei social and cultural heritages, festivals, rites, rituals, dramatic ballets, devotional choirs, folk and modernized songs, etc. Author highlights the progress of revivalism of the Meitei cultic and ethnical cultural revivalists is still running though certain elements in a fusion manner of the two religious faiths are observed. Sanamahi, the household deity was worshipped and the belief system around Sanamahi was used for the revivalist movements.

Section four **Ethno-Archaeology** of the present edited book contain three research papers on subsistence pattern towards understanding ethnographic postulates, Monuments – changes and its continuity, and survival of gathering economy.

The paper title **subsistence pattern of the Poumais, towards understanding of the application of Ethnographic postulates of the study of Ethno archaeology** by N. Sanatombi Devi and Kh. Manglembi Devi devoted to the study of archaeological ethnography of the Poumais on the one hand and probable theoretical application of the ethnographic postulates derived from the study of the Poumai subsistence pattern to the understanding of the prehistoric culture of Manipur on the other. The Oinam people are still practicing gathering, hunting, fishing, agriculture and weaving as a part of their way of life and that the prehistoric man also led a life of gathering and hunting. Weaving as revealed by the ethnography of the Oinam people is in the domain of household chores and consequently it is the monopoly of that Women folk.

Kh. Manglembi Devi and Kamlenthang Khongsai reported **Changes and continuity of monuments among the Chothes of Purum Tampak village, Manipur** in connection with the different stages of their life cycle with a view to elucidating the changing scenario in the life ways of the people under study. The idea of keeping monuments or memorials either for the self-glorification or for the welfare of the people is still alive in the mind of the Chothes. The Pre-Christian monuments are found associated with symbolic expressions connected with activities of the deceased. However, all these are, at present, replaced by Christian symbol, i.e. Cross mark. Study concludes that the activities of a person or persons which were once transmitted from generation to generation through the symbolic inscriptions made on the monuments are now replaced by monuments inscribed with historical facts.

Survival of gathering economy with reference to the Liangmai tribe by P. Binodini Devi sheds light on the nature of procurement as well as distribution and consumption, which can give some clue to the reconstruction of past human economy. The Liangmai tribe still preserve their aged-old gathering traditions. They use to collect various plant foods as vegetables, spices, and fruits, in addition to the hunted meats of animals and birds. They also catch fishes and insects from the nearby water logging areas to meet their food supplement. Till date they are practicing their simple technology for their food production and consumption. Author suggested that types of food items, nature of procurement, and consumption that are practising by this tribe, which can give some clue to the reconstruction of past human lifestyle and economy.

The present book identifies different anthropological issues, social and nutritional problems, uses and beliefs of traditional health practices followed by different ethnic groups, mother and child health condition and practices, social changes, domestic violence, political and governance, religion, ethno-archaeology, economy, monuments and so forth. Under such dynamic socio-cultural circumstances and ethnic diversities, North East India remained, still remains and will remain the fertile field for anthropological researchers.

SECTION - I

BIOLOGICAL ANTHROPOLOGY

1

Body Composition and Anthropometric Profile of Indian Elite Wushu Players

Ak. Bojen Meetei & S. Jibonkumar Singh

Introduction

Wushu encompasses all types of Martial Arts. It is a very dynamic combative sport originated from China. At present, there are hundreds of different Wushu styles. Despite this great diversity, an Olympic Wushu style was recently created to standardize the rules, techniques, and competition patterns for inclusion one of the Olympic events. World wushu games were also held in Beijing Olympic of 2008. Artioli, et al., (2008) reported that Olympic Wushu seems to be highly anaerobic-dependent combat sport. Low body fat, high flexibility, leg anaerobic power, isometric strength, and moderately high arm anaerobic power seem to be important for successful competitive performance. Competitive Wushu is composed of two disciplines of Taolu and Sanshou (Sanda). Taolu includes the official and standard forms, rotating movement with short and log weapons. Movements are evaluated with respect to accuracy, power and speed. In Sanshou, fights are differently classified with respect to the weight of men and women. Wushu competitions are held in three 2 minute rounds by considering 1 minute for rest between the two rounds.

In the modern world, there are trends towards more systematic training and selection influencing the anthropometric profile of players who compete at the highest level (Stolen et al., 2005). Body composition, anthropometric dimension and morphological characteristics play a vital role in determining the success of an athlete (Keogh, 1999; Rico-Sanz, 1998 and Wilmore & Costil,1999). Anthropological studies have also been carried out in other sports, including gymnastics, volleyball, basket ball, rock climbing, swimming, freestyle wrestling, and ten pin bowling to mention a few (Callan et al., 2000; Cleassens et al., 1999; Khosla, 1984; Tan et al., 2000; Toriola et al., 1987; Watts et al, 1993; Yamamura, 1999). These studies have found that, in each sport, elite athletes fit a certain physical or anthropometric profile. One study concluded that the lack of 'proper physique' could hinder successful sports performance at the Olympic Level (Toriola et al., 1987).

Russian elite male wushu taolu athletes had a sum of six skin folds of 30.81 mm, while their recreational Sanshou colleagues recorded a value of 42.19 mm (Pieter & Gagonin, 1994). Zhuo et al., 1984 reported that male Taiji quan athletes had 13.9 percent of relative body fat. Although body fat will depend on weight division, combative sports where fast movements are required may most likely call for a low fat mass to enhance the weight –to-strength ratio. Nevertheless, even if fast and slow techniques are part of one's sport, such as in pencak silat and taiji quan a more desirable amount of fat would still be preferable. Too much fat will most likely deter the athlete from achieving peak performance in her or his chosen sport (Sinning, 1985).

Roy, et al, (2006) highlighted that male wushu players of Manipur have less amount of fat percent (17.32 ± 2.29) compared to female wushu players (22.77 ± 2.77) and is statistically significant ($p < 0.01$). Several literatures on combat sports reveals that athletes who grapple with opponents (i.e., wrestlers and judokas) have markedly low body fat, high anaerobic and aerobic power and explosive strength (Franchini et al., 2007; Sharrati, et al., 1986; Thomas et al., 1989) whereas athletes who engage in strike opponents(i.e., karate and taekwondo players) have markedly high aerobic capacity, flexibility (Heller,1998; Toskovic et al., 2004). Olympic wushu contest combine both grappling and striking techniques, but there is no enough scientific literatures regarding the body composition and anthropometric attributes of wushu athletes. Determining the body composition and anthropometric profile of elite wushu players is needed for predicting the most potential factors which enhance the performance level. Thus, the purpose of the present study was undertaken to determine body composition and anthropometric profile of Indian Elite Wushu players and to predict the most potential factors influencing higher performance in the success of wushu (Taolu and Sanshou) competitions.

Materials and Methods

Subjects were the probable men and women wushu athletes of Indian National Team. Twenty two men and fourteen women Indian elite wushu athletes took part in the study during the preparatory Intensive Coaching camp held from 25th September to 25th October, 2007 at Imphal, Manipur for participating 9th World Wushu Championships, 2007 at Beijing. Body composition analyzer, anthropometer and hand grip dynamanometer were used for collecting data of the study. For statistical analysis, descriptive statistics, t-test and linear regression were computed with the help of SPSS Version 15.0.

Results

Table 1.1 shows descriptive statistics and t-test of Indian Male Sanshou and Taolu players. By analysing the data it reveals that significant differences are observed in all the parameters except age. Male sanshou players are found to have higher average age as compared to taolu players. Sanshou players are significantly taller in body height and heavier in body weight as compared to taolu players. The mean body weight of sanshou players (24.28 ± 3.30 kg) is significantly heavier than the taolu players (21.86 ± 1.98 kg). However, the average weight of sanshou is found to have within the normal range of BMI. Taolu players are significantly weaker in grip strength in right hand (41.38 ± 4.95 kg vs. 51.23 ± 7.60 kg.) and in left hand (39.94 ± 4.91 kg vs. 51. 92 ± 9.27 kg.) as compared to sanshou players.

Table 1.1: Descriptive Statistics and t-test between Indian Elite Male Sanshou and Taolu players

Variables	*Male Sanshou Players (n=13)*		*Male Taolu Players (n=9)*		*t- value*	*p-value*
	Mean	*SD*	*Mean*	*SD*		
Age (yrs)	25.38	4.56	23.77	2.22	1.097	0.287
Body weight (kg)	73.41	14.51	59.34	5.85	3.114	0.006*
Body height (cm)	173.30	6.57	163.81	4.56	4.000	0.001*
Percent Fat (%)	10.67	4.75	7.20	2.59	2.201	0.040*
BMI (kg/m²)	24.28	3.30	21.86	1.98	2.135	0.045*
Total Body Fat (kg)	8.46	5.26	4.27	1.78	2.654	0.018*
Total Body water (kg)	47.64	7.24	39.81	3.34	3.408	0.003*
Fat Free Mass (kg)	65.08	9.93	54.40	4.55	3.395	0.003*
Hand Grip Right (kg)	51.23	7.60	41.38	4.95	3.403	0.002*
Hand Grip Left (kg)	51.92	9.27	39.94	4.91	3.928	0.001*

*P <0.05

By looking at table 1.2 female sanshou players are found to have higher in average age than the taolu players. Statistically significant differences are observed in body weight, body height, BMI, fat free mass, right hand grip. As expected, women sanshou players have significantly higher in body height, fat free mass and right hand gript strength. Sanshou players are significantly heavier than the taolu players (62.77± 9.25 kg vs.50.11± 2.83 kg).

No significant differences are observed in age, percent fat, total body fat, total body water, and left hand grip strength.

In table 1.3 reveals the linear regression between hand grip strength (right) and anthropometric variables and body composition among the Indian male elite wushu players. It was undertaken with hand grip strength as dependent variables. Results shows that grip strength had influenced positive impact on body composition and anthropometric parameters. The amount of variation explained by right hand grip strength ranged from 21 percent (age) to 67 percent (body height). It indicates that body height can influenced

67 percent of variation to accelerate right hand grip strength and it is followed by total body water (66 percent) and fat free mass (66 percent).

Table 1.2: Descriptive Statistics and t-test between Indian Female Elite Sanshou and Taolu Players

Variables	Female Sanshou Players (n=6)		Female Taolu Players (n=8)		t- value	p-value
	Mean	SD	Mean	SD		
Age (yrs)	22.50	1.760	21.87	3.52	0.435	0.672
Body weight (kg)	62.77	9.15	50.11	2.83	3.272	0.018*
Body height (cm)	161.12	4.69	154.77	3.66	2.740	0.022*
Percent Fat (%)	22.42	7.11	16.80	2.23	1.870	0.113
BMI (kg/m²)	24.10	2.90	20.91	1.05	2.566	0.043*
Total Body Fat (kg)	14.53	6.27	8.45	1.41	2.334	0.063
Total Body water (kg)	35.32	3.20	31.93	4.63	1.618	0.132
Fat Free Mass (kg)	48.23	4.39	41.66	2.11	3.380	0.012*
Hand Grip Right kg)	35.00	4.19	27.87	3.82	3.265	0.008*
Hand Grip Left (kg)	30.50	4.94	25.53	1.89	2.342	0.057

*P<0.05

Table 1.3: Linear Regression between Hand Grip Strength (Right) and Anthropometric Variables and Body Composition among the Indian Male Elite Wushu Players

Variables	B	SeB	Beta	Adj R^2	t	P
Age (yrs)	1.084	0.417	0.503	0.215	2.602	0.017*
Body weight (kg)	0.490	0.079	0.811	0.640	6.193	0.000**
Body height (cm)	0.911	0.138	0.828	0.670	6.612	0.000**
Percent Fat (%)	1.254	0.319	0.660	0.407	3.926	0.001*
BMI (kg/m²)	1.869	0.435	0.693	0.454	4.299	0.000**
Total Body Fat (kg)	1.226	0.284	0.694	0.456	4.313	0.000**
Total Body water (kg)	0.954	0.147	0.823	0.662	6.484	0.000**
Fat Free Mass (kg)	0.697	0.108	0.823	0.661	6.471	0.000**

*P<0.05; **p<0.001

Table 1.4 reveals the linear regression between right hand grip strength and anthropometric variables and body composition among the Indian female elite wushu players. Right hand grip strength was taken as dependent variable while body composition and anthropometric parameters as independents variables. Results shows that grip strength had a positive impact on body composition and anthropometric parameters. The amount of variations as explained by the right hand grip strength was observed with different impact ranged from 1 percent (body mass index) to 40 percent (body height). It indicates that body height can influenced highest percentage (40 percent) of impact on right hand grip strength and it is followed by fat free mass (35 percent).

Table 1.5 shows the comparison between the present data of Indian Male elite wushu players and other available secondary data. The Brazilian wushu team were found to have average older age (26.6 yrs), heavier body weight

(76.96 kg), taller in body height (178.66 cm) and higher total body fat (9.5 kg) as compared to Indian male wushu players. Interestingly we found that elite Manipuri wushu players are younger in age (21.3 yrs), lighter in body weight (57.7 kg) and shorter in body height (165.84 cm) than the Brazilian and Indian male wushu players.

Table 1.4: Linear Regression between Hand Grip Strength (right) and Anthropometric Variables and Body Composition among the Indian Female Elite Wushu Players

Variables	*B*	*SeB*	*Beta*	*Adj R^2*	*T*	*P*
Age (yrs)	-0.240	0.537	0.128	0.066	-0.447	0.663
Body weight (kg)	0.284	0.152	0.469	0.155	1.840	0.091
Body height (cm)	0.691	0.221	0.669	0.402	3.121	0.009*
Percent Fat (%)	0.162	0.275	0.106	0.071	0.370	0.718
BMI (kg/m²)	0.539	0.578	0.260	0.010	0.931	0.370
Total Body Fat (kg)	0.254	0.291	0.244	0.019	0.872	0.400
Total Body water (kg)	0.609	0.308	0.496	0.183	1.976	0.072
Fat Free Mass (kg)	0.728	0.257	0.634	0.352	2.838	0.015*

*$P<0.05$

Table 1.5: Comparison between the present data Wushu Players and Other Available Secondary Data

Men's Team/ players of Two Countries and State	*Age (yrs)*	*BW (kg)*	*BH (cm)*	*BMI (kg/m²)*	*TBF (kg)*	*FFM (kg)*
Brazilian National Wushu Team (Artioli et al.,2008	26.6	76.96	178.66	24.12	9.5	-
Manipuri Elite Wushu players (Meetei,2003)	21.3	57.27	165.84	20.85	7.38	50.19
Indian Men Wushu Team,2007 (present study)	25.38	73.41	173.30	24.28	8.46	65.08

BW=Body Weight, BH=Body Height, BMI=Body Mass Index, TBF=Total Body Fat, FFM=Fat Free Mass

Discussion

Body composition is one of the important factors contributing to sports performance. Assessment of body composition is an important component of the ongoing monitoring of athletes interested to improve their performance level. The present study shows that Indian elite wushu team have low body fat, percent fat, high fat free mass and hand grip strength. Compared with other combat athletes that are grappling and striking based, wushu fighters have similar fat content, but less fat than non competitive martial arts practitioners. Olympic wushu players can be characterised by a mixture of grappling, throwing and striking techniques seems to be required the same capacities as other combat sports. (Douris et al., 2004).

Several related literature reveals that sportsmen who are involved with their competitors (Judo and wrestling) obviously have a high anaerobic capacity and power while in such sports, there are low body fat and high aerobic capacity (Artioli et al., 2009; Callister et al., 1991; Franchini et al., 2011). However, in wushu, there is a combination of taking and striking which require the aforementioned physical preparation in a combinational form to be succeeded; with respect to the lack of the literature about physiological traits of Wushu, knowing these traits can lead to the success of sport teams (Artioli et al., 2009). As Kazemi (2010) reported, martial arts require muscle power with the maximum power and endurance since the muscular structure of lower limb plays an important role due to implementing fast and powerful movements performed over combat and replace the weight of body. Of course, agility, harmony and balance complete the mentioned abilities.

Although ranges of percent BF for sports participants are related to successful performance within a sport, athletic performance cannot be accurately predicted solely on the basis of body composition. All the components of physique - body size, structure, and composition are significant determinants of competitive success. Toriola et al (1987) reported that lack of proper physique could hinder successful sports performance at the Olympic level. Earlier studies have looked at anthropometric variables in terms of potential indicator of athletic performance. The findings of present study are supported by the earlier studies in various anthropometric characters. In fact, sanshou players were found heavier in body weight and higher in body height than the taolu players in both sexes. The results indicate that specific physique is required for a specific sporting event. Sinning (1985) reported that taller individuals, who have longer levers (limbs) and a higher centre of gravity, have the advantage in jumping and throwing events, whereas shorter individuals have the advantage when the body must be rotated around an axis, such as in diving and gymnastic events. Indian male and female elite taolu players were found shorter in body height, higher fat free mass and lighter body weight than sanshou players. It facilitated translocation of body weight in different angles, jumping and faster rotation of body with short and long weapons.

Evidence from sports participants in various age groups has demonstrated an inverse relationship between fat mass and performance of physical activities requiring translocation of the body weight either vertically, such as in jumping, or horizontally, as in running (Boileau & Lohman, 1977; Malina, 1992; Pate et al., 1989). Excess fatness is detrimental to these types of activities because it adds mass to the body without additional capacity to produce force. Because acceleration is proportional to force but inversely proportional to mass, excess fat at a given level of force application will result in slower changes in velocity and direction (Boileau and Lohman, 1977; Harman and Frykman, 1992). Excess fatness also increases the metabolic cost of physical activities that require movement of the total body mass (Buskirk and Taylor, 1957). Thus, in most performances involving movement of the body mass, a relatively low percent BF should be advantageous both mechanically and metabolically (Boileau and Lohman, 1977). Franchini et al., (2007) also reported that percent fat is negatively correlated with performance in activities and body mass locomotion.

For males, concerns about attaining low fat mass are especially prevalent if they compete in sports such as wrestling, boxing, and martial arts that require participants to reach a certified body weight classification. Similar trend of attaining low body fat mass and percent fat are observed among the Indian elite sanshou players. They have low body fat (8.46 kg) and percent fat (10.67 percent). This potential advantage of a low percent BF for successful performance in these sports is evident. However, there are negative implications for health and performance when weight reduction is carried to extremes. The levels of percent BF considered being minimal levels compatible with good health are 5 percent for males and 12 percent for females (Lohman, 1992). Optimal health body fat in adults' non- athletes is 12-18 percent (10-25 percent) for men and 16-25 percent (18-30 percent) for women (Wilmore et al., 1986).

The body fat percent for elite athletes varies largely by sports. Swimmers especially female swimmers, have percent body fat higher than long distance runners. As we know the game style of sanshou and taolu is totally different and accordingly anthropometric characters and body composition are also different. Indian sanshou players have higher fat mass, percent fat and lean body mass as compared to taolu payers. In indicates that the game of sanshou, as punching, striking and grappling features, are associated with a desirable fat mass,(8.46 kg) percent fat (10.67 percent), higher grip strength(51.92 kg) and higher fat free mass (65.08 kg). In contrast, Indian male taulu players have less fat mass (4.27kg), percent fat (7.20 percent) and optimal level of fat free mass (54.40 kg).

As sanshou players is a weight classified sports and composite game of judo, taekwondo, boxing and wrestling , it has been suggested that the functional variables viz. less body fat, higher fat free mass, medium body height and weight are associated with better performance. Kubo et al (2006) reported that high level judo players should have low body fat. It has been suggested that high percent body fat may be a discriminator for success. Callister et al (1991) found that more successful male players (those with more international success or competition points) maintained lower body fat percentages.

Conclusion

The findings of the present study suggest that Indian male elite sanshou players have low body fat within desirable range, high fat free mass, total body water and grip strength as compared to taolu players. Male sanshou players were significantly heavier and taller than the taolu players. Similarly, women sanshou players are also found to have significantly higher body fat, free fat mass, heavier body weight and higher body height than the taolu players. It is concluded that low fat percent, high grip strength, high fat free mass, low percent fat and low BMI may consider important parameters for successful competitive performance in both Sanshou and Taolu players.

The results of this research can be used in team selection as well as in the intensive national training and coaching camp. Thus, coaches should focus on the development of these characteristics/components in the lower-level players to attain a better performance. Another aspect that coaches need to consider is the measurement of hand grip strength which can accelerate punching, throwing and grappling power.

Acknowledgements

We are greatly thankful to the Indian elite wushu players and coaches who took part in this study. We also thank department of anthropology, Manipur University for providing body composition analyser and anthropometric instruments.

References

Artioli,G.G., Gualano, B., Franchini, E., Batista, RN., Polacow, V.O., & Lancha Jr A.H. (2009). Physiological, performance, and nutritional profile of the Brazilian Olympic Wushu (kung-fu) team. *The Journal of Strength & Conditioning Research 23,* (1), 20-25.

Boileau, R.A. & T.G. Lohman (1977). The measurement of human physique and its effect on physical performance. *Orthopedic Clin.N. Am. 8*(3), 563-581.

Buskirk, E., and H. L. Taylor (1957). Maximal oxygen intake and its relation to body composition with special reference to chronic physical activity and obesity. *J. Appl. Physio. 11*(1), 72-78

Callan, S.D., Brunner, D.M., Devolve, K.L., Mulligan, S.E., Hesson, J., Wilber, R.L.& Kennedy, J.T. (2000). Physiological profiles of elite freestyle wrestlers. *Journal of Strength and Conditioning Research 14*(2), 162-169.

Callister, R., Callister R.J., Staron, R.S., Fleck, S.J., Tesch. P. & Dudley, G.A. (1991). Physiological characteristics of elite Judo athletes. *Int J Sports Med, 12*(2), 196–203

Claessens, A.L., Lefevre, J., Beunen, G. & Malina, R.M. (1999). The contribution of anthropometric characteristics to performance scores in elite female gymnasts. *Journal of Sports Medicine and Physical Fitness, 39*(4), 355-360.

Douris,P, Chinan,A, Gomez, M.Aw,A, Steffens,D, and Weiss, .(2004). Fitness level of of middle aged martial art practitioners. *Br J Sports Med.,38* (2),143-147

Franchini, E., Matsushigue, K.A.,Vecchio, F.B., Artioli, G.G.(2011). Physiological profiles of elite judo athletes. *Sports Med. 41*(2),147–166.

Franchini, E., Nunes, A.V, Moraes, J.M., & Del Vecchio, F.B. (2007). Physical fitness and anthropometric profile of the Brazilian male Judo team. *J.Physiol Anthropol 26*(2), 59-67.

Harman, E.A.,& P.N. Frykman (1992). The relationship of body size and composition to the performance of physically demanding military tasks. In: B.M. Marriott and J. Grumstrup-Scott (eds.). *Body composition and physical prtformance: Application for the Military Services Washington D.C.*: National Academy Press, pp. 105-118

Heller, J., Peric,T., Dlouha, R, Kohlikova, E, Melichna, J, & Novakova, H.(1998) Physiological profiles of male and female taekwondo (ITF) black belt. *J. Sports Sci, 16*(3), 243-249

Kazemi, M., Perri, G., Soave, D. (2010). A profile of 2008 Olympic taekwondo competitors. *The Journal of the Canadian Chiropractic Association, 54*(4), 243-249

Franchini, E., Del Vecchio F.B., Matsushigue, K.A., Artioli, G.G. (2011).Physiological profiles of elite judo athletes. *Sports Med.*,41(2), 147-66.

Keogh, J. (1999). The use of physical fitness scores and anthropometric data to predict selection in elite under-18 Australian rules football team. *J Sci Med Sport, 2*(2), 125–133.

Khosla, T. (1984) Physique of female swimmers and divers from the 1976 Montreal Olympics. Journal of American Medical Association 252(4), 536-537.

Kubo, J., Chishaki, T., Nakamura, N., Muramatsu, T., Yamamoto, Y., Ito, M., Saitou, H. & Kukidome T. (2006). Differences in fat-free mass and muscle thicknesses at various sites according to performance level among judo athletes. *J Strength Cond Res, 20*(3): 654–657.

Lohman,T.G. (1992). Basic Concepts in Body Composition Assessment (pp. 1-6); Body Density, Body water, and Bone Minerals: Controversies and Limitations of the Two-Component System (pp.7-4); Prediction Equations and Skin folds, Bioelectric Impedance, and Body Mass Index (pp.37-56); and Estimating minimal weight and percent fat in athletes (pp.109-118). In: *Advances in Body Composition Assessment.* Champaign, Illinois: Human Kinetics Books.

Malina, R.M. (1992). Physique and body composition: Effect on performance and effects on training, semistarvation, and overtraining. In: K.D. Brownell,J. Rodin, and J.H.Wilmore (eds.) Eating, body weight, and performance in Atheletes. Philadelphia Lea & Febiger,pp. 94-114.

Meetei, AK.B. (2013). Kinanthropometric variables and physical fitness ability of male elite and non-elite players of Manipur, Unpublished Ph. D. Thesis, Manipur University, Canchipur.

Pate, R.R., Slentz, C.A. & Kattz, D.P. (1989). Relationship between skin fold thickness and performance of health related fitness test items. *Res. Quart. Exerc. Sports 60*(2), 183-189.

Pieter,W.& Gagonin, S.(1994). Body composition of elite and recreational Russian athletes. International Conference on Current Research Into Sport Sciences, St. Petersburg Research Institute of Physical Culture, St. Petersburg, Russia, July 28-30

Rico-Sanz, J. (1998). Body composition and nutritional assessments in soccer. *Int J Sport Nutrition, 8*(2), 113-123.

Roy, S..L., Singh, J. A.k., Meetei, K..K., and Singh, T.L. (2006). Body Composition of SAI Scheme Trainee of Manipur in Weight Category Sports. *Journal of Sports and Sports Sciences, 29* (1), 27-36

Sharrati, M.T., Taylor, A.W.& Song, T.M.(1986). A physiological profile of elite Canadian freestyle wrestlers. *Can J Appl Sport Sci 11*(2), 100-105.

Sinning W.E. (1985). Body composition and athletic performance. In. Clarke D.H., Eckert H.M., (editors), *Limits of human performance*. The academy papers #18 Eds: Champaign, IL: Human Kinetics Publishers, pp. 45-56.

Stolen, T., Chamari, K., Castagna, C., & Wisløff, U. (2005). Physiology of Soccer: An Update. Sports Medicine, 35(6), 501- 536.

Tan, B., Aziz, A.R. and Chuan, T.K. (2000). Correlations between physiological parameters and performance in elite ten-pin bowlers. *Journal of Science and Medicine in Sport, 3*(2), 176-185

Thomas,S.G., Cox,M.H., Legal,Y.M, Verde,T.J.& Smith,H.K.(1989). Physiological profiles of the Canadian National Judo Team. *Can J Sport Sci, 14*(3), 142-147

Toriola, A.L., Adeniran, S.A. & Ogunremi, P.T. (1987). Body composition and anthropometric characteristics of elite male basketball and volleyball players. *Journal of Sports Med phys fitness, 27*(2), 235-238

Toskovic, N.N., Blessing, D, & Williford, H.N. (2004). Physiological profile of recreational male and female novice and experienced Taekwondo practioners. *J. Sports Med Phys Fitness, 44*(2): 164-172

Watts, P.B., Martin, D.T. & Durtschi, S. (1993). Anthropometric profiles of elite male and female competitive sport rock climbers. *Journal of Sports Sciences 11*(2), 113-117.

Wilmore, J.H., Buskirk, E. R., DiGirolama, M., & Lohman, T.G. (1986). Body composition: A round table. The Physician and sports medicine, 14(3), 144-162.

Wilmore, J. H., & Costill, D. L. (1999). *Physiology of Sports and Exercise.* Champaign: Human Kinetics, 9. 490–507

Yamamura, C. (1999). Physiological characteristics of well-trained synchronized swimmers in relation to performance scores. *Internal Journal of Sports Medicine 20*(4), 246-251

Zhuo, D., Shephard, R., Plyley, M., & Davis, G. (1984). Cardio-respiratory and metabolic responses during tai chi chuan exercise. *Canadian Journal of Applied Sport Science, 9*(1), 7-10.

2

Morphological characteristics of adult War-Jaintia Males from Jaintia Hills District, Meghalaya

Sudipta Ghosh, T. Lyngdoh and C S B. Marak

Physical anthropology has been defined as the study of man's biological behaviour in time and space. Physical anthropologists have been mainly concerned with the study of human origins and human evolution as well as varieties of mankind in different parts of the world. One of the main objectives of Physical anthropology is to understand the process of human evolution and variation. Evolution is considered as the development of dissimilarities in morphological and genetic characteristics between the ancestral and descendent population (Dobzhansky, 1951). The advancement of the science of genetic now-a-days has conceived human evolution as the change in gene frequencies of population from generation to generation. The study of human growth and development in various human populations is also the new dimension of Physical anthropology. According to Richard and Kavanagh (1945), growth is a fundamental attribute of all organisms that manifests itself by change in size of an individual or in the number of organisms that manifests itself by change in size of an individual or in the number of organisms in unit environment. Mitchell (1962), defines it as the summation of those coordinated biological and chemical processes that are initiated with the fertilization of the ovum and terminated with the attainment of the body size and conformation of the physiological capabilities characteristic of the species and the hereditary background of the individual. Meridith (1957), conveys somewhat similar ideas when he writes physical growth includes a gamut of changes sometimes sub group under such captions as morphological differentiation, dimensional growth, propotional development and structural maturation. Anthropologists have helped in designing the spaceship for the convenience of the astronauts. They have made valuable contribution in designing of aircrafts, uniforms, and other specialized equipments for defence personnel, Butner-Janusch (1966) has rightly stated that evolution is also necessarily viewed as changes in the morphology of the organism through time. The comparative morphological similarities and differences among individual and population can be studied with the help of anthropometry. The anthropometry invented by J.S Elshwz, a German Physician in 17th century refers to measurement of human body and its various portions. It encompasses a wide variety of measurement procedures for determining endless number of body dimensions

Anthropometry as defined by Juan Comas is "Systematics techniques for measuring and taking observations on man his skeleton, the skull, the limbs, trunks, etc. as well as the organs by the most reliable means and scientific methods. It enables us to find the quantitative expression of the form of body, various traits of which undergo changes in varying degrees from birth to death in health and disease. Further, populations living in different climatic conditions have different ethnic origin and their off-springs often present interesting differences in body form and proportion. It is also an important indicator to evaluate the physical status of individuals and populations which in turn highlights the nutritional status of the populations and the history of their economic development. According to Tanner (1994), 'The variation between the heights of the individuals within a sub population is indeed largely dependent on differences in their genetic endowment; but the variation between the means of groups of individuals (at least within an ethnically homogenous population) reflects the cumulative nutritional hygienic disease and stress experience of each of the group.

The present study aims to study the anthropometric characteristics of War Jaintia males with special reference to body shape, size, head and face indices. An attempt was also made to compare War Jaintia males with other North-east population with respect to their anthropometric measurements.

Materials and Methods

Data for the present study had been conducted among the War Jaintias of Nongtalang village, West Jaintia hills district, Amlarem Block, Meghalaya. The following measurements are considered for the present study such as Height vertex, sitting height vertex: (v-sitting plane), body weight, Biacromial Breadth (a-a), Bicristal Breadth (ic-ic), maximum head length. Maximum head breadth, nasal length, nasal breadth, Bizygomatic Breadth, Bigonial Breadth (go-go), Total facial height (n-gn), Minimun Frontal breadth, Morphological superior Facial height (n-pr). Instrument use: Anthropometer, spreading calliper, sliding calliper, weighing machine. Martin's classification of stature is employed in the present study.

Classification of stature (Martin classification)

Categories	*Ranges (cm)*
Very short	130-149.9
Short	150-159.9
Below medium	160-163.9
Medium	164.166.9
Above medium	167.169.9
Tall	170-179.9

Body mass index (BMI) is the ratio obtained by dividing the body weight by stature.

Body Mass Index= Body Weight/Stature^2 (m)

After calculating body mass index, it was categorised according to the classification of WHO Asian cut off.

Classification of Body Mass Index (WHO, Asian cut off)

Categories	*Ranges*
Under Weight	-18.5
Normal Weight	18.5-22.9
Over Weight	23+

Classification of sitting height index (Guiffrida-Ruggeri)

Categories	*Ranges*
Brachycormic	-50.9
Metriocormic	51.0-52.9
Macrocormic	53+

Classification of Relative biacromial breadth index (Burgsch)

Categories	*Ranges*
Narrow shoulder	-22.0
Medium Shoulder	22.1-23.0
Broad Shoulder	23.1+

Classification of Relative bicristale breadth index (Burgsch)

Categories	*Ranges*
Narrow pelvis	-22.0
Medium pelvis	22.1-23.0
Broad pelvis	23.1+

Classification of cephalic index (Martin and Saller)

Categories	*Ranges*
Hyperdolichocephalic	-70.9
Dolichocephalic	71.0-75.9
Mesocephalic	76.0-80.9
Brachycephalic	81.0-85.4
Hyperbrachycephalic	85.5+

Classification of nasal index (Martin and Saller)

Categories	*Ranges*
Hyperdolichocephalic	54.9
Dolichocephalic	55.0-69.9
Mesocephalic	70.0-84.9
Brachycephalic	85.0-99.9
Hyperbrachycephalic	100+

Classification of Morphological total facial index (Martin and Saller)

Categories	*Ranges*
Hyperdolichocephalic	-78.9
Dolichocephalic	79.0-83.9
Mesocephalic	84.0-87.9
Brachycephalic	88.0-92.9
Hyperbrachycephalic	93+

Classification of Morphological total facial index (Martin and Saller)

Categories	*Ranges*
Hypereuryene	-42.9
Euryene	43.0-47.9
Mesene	48.0-52.9
Leptene	53.0-56.9
Hyperleptene	57+

Classification of Jugo-Mandibular index (Lundborg-Linders and Saller)

Categories	*Ranges*
Very narrow	<69.9
Narrow	70.0-74.9
Medium	75.0-79.9
Broad	80.0-84.9
Very Broad	85.0+

Classification of Jugo-Frontal Index (Lundborg-Linders and Saller)

Categories	*Ranges*
Very narrow	<69.9
Narrow	70.0-74.9
Medium	75.0-79.9
Broad	80.0-84.9
Very Broad	85.0+

Results and Discussion

The adult Jaintia males have high percentage of smokers with respect to the non-smokers. Out of 200 samples, 152 males are smokers (76 percent) and 48 males are non-smokers. It can also be inferred from the present study that there is huge differences in smoking status such as 82.89 percent of the smokers are engaged in daily smoking, 5.26 percent of them are frequent smokers, and 11.84 percent are occasional smokers. Habit of drinking and its frequency is also shown in the same table; where it was found that 143 (71.5 percent) and 57 (28.5 percent) are non-drinkers and drinkers respectively. Out of 57 drinkers, frequency of its habit was also observed, where 43.86 percent of the drinkers are engaged in daily, 17.54 percent of them are frequent drinkers and 38.60 percent are occasional drinkers. Chewing of tobacco and

Table 2.1: Smoking, alcohol consumption and tobacco chewing habit among adult Jaintia males

Categories	*Frequency*	*Percentage*
	Smoking Habit	
Non Smokers	48	24
Smokers	152	76
	Smoking frequency among smokers	
Daily	126	82.89
Frequently	8	5.26
Occasionally	18	11.84
	Alcohol consumption	
Non drinker	143	71.5
Drinkers	57	28.5
	Frequency of alcohol consumption	
Daily	25	43.86
Frequently	10	17.54
Occasionally	22	38.60
	Tobacco chewing	
Non chewers	92	46
Chewers	108	54
	Frequency of tobacco chewing	
Daily	83	76.85
Frequently	5	4.63
Occasionally	20	18.52

its frequency is also shown in the same table where 108(54 percent) are chewers and 92 (46 percent) are non-chewers and out of total chewers 83(76.85 percent), 5(4.63 percent) and 20(18.52 percent) are daily, frequently and occasional chewers respectively.

Self-reported morbidity patterns of adults have been collected for the past 12 months and during the present study as shown in the table 2.2. Morbidity pattern of the Jaintia males is found that cold and cough are the most prevalent illness pattern; whereas, only a few cases of diarrhoea/ dysentery, malaria, asthma and gastritis are recorded among the Jaintias of present study. In the past 12 months 85.71 percent were suffering from cold and cough, 11.90 percent from diarrhoea/dysentery and 2.38 percent from malaria. The present study also infers that cold and cough account 53.33 percent , asthma 6.67 percent and gastritis 40.00 percent .

The different anthropometric measurements of the war Jaintia adult males of Nongtalang village of Jaintia village are shown in Table 2.3. The table shows that height varies from 141 to 176 cm and the mean is found to be 157.16± 6.20. It is found that the sitting height vertex varies from 61.50 to 95.00 and the mean is found to be 82.55±4.03. The body mass or weight varies from 37.00cm to 86.00 cm and the mean is found to be 52.07±8.61.

Table 2.2 Self-reported morbidity patterns in adults of War Jaintia males

	Category	*Frequency*	*Percentage*
Past 12 months	Cold and cough	36	85.71
	Diarrhoea/Dysentry	5	11.90
	Malaria	1	2.38
Present study	Cold and cough	8	53.33
	Respiratory disorder	1	6.67
	Others	6	40.00

The biacromial breadth varies from 25.00cm to 52.00cm and the mean is found to be 35.74±2.63. The bicristal breadth varies from 18.00cm to 33.20 cm and the mean is found to be 26.67 cm±2.06. The maximum head length is recorded from 20.00 to 15.00 and the mean is found to be 17.90±0.74. The maximum head breadth of the of the adult males varies from 12.30cm to 17.00cm and the mean is found to be 15.18±0.64. Two measurements were taken on nose i.e. nasal length and nasal breadth. It is observed that the nasal length and nasal breadth varies from 3.60cm to 4.82cm and 2.80cm and 4.50cm respectively. The mean nasal length is 5.00 ± 2.52 whereas the mean nasal breadth is 3.59± 0.34. The bizygomatic breadth varies from 9.50 (cm) to 13.60 (cm) and thfrome mean is found to be 11.45 ±0.79 (cm). The bigonial breadth ranges between 8.00 to 14.00 with the mean is found to be 11.09±0.66. The morphological total facial height varies from 8.90cm 12.50cm and the mean is found to be 11.09±0.66. The minimum frontal breadth varies 10.5cm to 14.5cm and the mean is found to be 12.22cm±0.82.

The morphological superior facial height varies from 4.00cm to 8.50cm and the mean is 6.41±0.60. In body measurements, maximum variation is observed in body weight (8.61 cm), as evident from standard deviation. This further suggest that sort mass related measurements vary more than linear measurements in any population. In head and face measurement, the greatest variation is observed in nasal height/length (2.52) in the present population.

Classification of stature among the War Jaintia males such as short, below medium, very short, medium above and tall are shown in Table 4. From the above table it is found that 54 percent fall under short category, followed by below medium 21.50 percent , very short 11 percent and medium 7 percent . Negligible percentage of medium (4 percent) and tall stature (2.5 percent) was observed among the Jaintia males.

Table 2.3: Distribution of anthropometric measurements in adult War Jaintia

Name of the measurements	*Average*	*Maximum*	*Minimum*	*Standard Deviation*	*Standard Error mean*
Body Measurements					
Height vertex	157.16	176.00	141.00	6.20	0.44
Sitting height	82.55	95.00	61.50	4.03	0.29
Body weight	52.07	86.00	37.00	8.61	0.61
Biacromial breadth	35.74	52.00	25.00	2.63	0.19
Bicristal	26.67	33.20	18.00	2.06	0.15
Head and Face measurements					
Maximum head length	17.90	20.00	15.00	0.74	0.05
Maximum head breadth	15.18	17.00	12.30	0.64	0.05
Nasal length	5.00	4.82	3.60	2.52	0.18
Nasal breadth	3.59	4.50	2.80	0.34	0.02
Bizygomatic breadth	11.45	13.60	9.50	0.79	0.06
Bigonial Breadth	10.69	14.00	8.00	0.86	0.06
Total facial height	11.09	12.50	8.90	0.66	0.05
Minimum frontal breadth	12.22	14.50	10.50	0.82	0.06
Morphological superior facial height	6.41	8.50	4.00	0.60	0.44

Table 2.4: Classification of stature among the War Jaintia adult males

Sl. No	*Categories*	*Frequency*	*Percentage*
1	Very short	22	11
2	Short	108	54
3	Below medium	43	21.50
4	Medium	14	7
5	Above medium	8	4
6	Tall	5	2.50

Table 2.5: Body mass index among adult Jaintia males

Sl. No	*Categories*	*Frequency*	*Percentage*
1	Underweight	30	15
2	Normal weight	155	77.50
3	Over weight	15	7.50

Classification of body mass index between underweight, normal weight and overweight are shown the table 2.5. From the above table it is revealed that majority falls under the Normal weight category 77.5 percent , followed by underweight 15 percent and overweight 7.50 percent .

Table 2.6: Relative sitting height index/ cormic index among Jaintia males

Sl. No	*Categories*	*Frequency*	*Percentage*
1	Brachycormic	42	21
2	Metriocormic	72	36
3	Macrocormic	86	43

The table 2.6 shows that 43 percent fall under macrocormic followed by metriocormic (36 percent) and brachycormic (21 percent).

Table 2.7: Relative biacromial breadth index among Jaintia males

Sl. No	*Categories*	*Frequency*	*Percentage*
1	Narrow shoulder	53	26.50
2	Medium shoulder	74	37
3	Broad shoulder	73	36.50

Classification of relative sitting height or cormic index among Jaintia males are shown in the table 2.7. The table reveals that 37 percent of the population fall under medium shoulder category, followed by broad shoulder (36.50 percent) and narrow shoulder (26.50 percent).

Table 2.8: Relative bicristale breadth index among Jaintia adult males

Sl. No	Categories	Frequency	Percentage
1	Narrow pelvis	200	100
2	Medium pelvis	0	0
3	Broad pelvis	0	0

In classification of relative biacromial breadth index, it is observed that 100 percent population falls under narrow pelvis.

Table 2.9: Cephalic index among War Jaintia males

Sl. No	*Categories*	*Frequency*	*Percentage*
1	Hyperdolichocephalic	1	0.50
2	Dolichocephalic	3	1.50
3	Mesocephalic	28	14
4	Brachycephalic	74	37
5	Hyperbrachycephalic	94	47

Classification of Cephalic index between Hyperdolichocephalic, Dolichocephalic, Mesocephalic, Brachycephalic and Hyperbrachycephalic among Jaintia males are shown in table 2.9. It shows that 47 percent fall under Hyperbrachycephalic, followed by brachycephalic 37 percent , mesocephalic 14 percent , dolichocephalic 1.5 percent , and hyperdolichocephalic 0.5 percent. Negligible percentages are either dolichocephalic 1.50 percent or heperdolichocephalic 0.50 percent .

Table 2.10: Nasal Index among War Jaintia adult males

Sl. No	*Categories*	*Frequency*	*Percentage*
1	Hyperleptorrhine	0	0
2	Leptorrhine	53	26.50
3	Messorhine	125	62.50
4	Platyrrhine	20	11
5	Hyperlatyrrhine	0	0

The above table 2.10 reveals that 62 percent fall under Messorrhine category, followed by leptorrhine 26.50 percent and platyrrhine 11 percent . Negligible percentage of Jaintia males are either hyperleptorrhine or hyperplatyrrhine.

Table 2.11 shows that 69 percent fall under the category of hyperleptoprosopic, which is followed by leptorosopic 19.50 percent , mesoprosopic 5.50 percent , euryprosopic 3.50 and hypereuryprosopic 2.50 percent .

Table 2.11: Morphological total facial index among War Jaintia adult males

Sl. No	*Categories*	*Frequency*	*Percentage*
1	Hypereuryprosopic	5	2.50
2	Euryprosopic	7	3.50
3	Mesoprosopic	11	5.50
4	Leptorospic	39	19.50
5	Hyperleptoprosopic	138	69

Table 2.12 reveals that 40.50 percent fall under hyperleptene category, which is followed by leptene 31.50 percent , mesene 21 percent , euryne 5 percent and hypereuryene 2 percent . Negligible percentage of Jaintia males are either euryne 5 percent or hypereuryne 2 percent .

Table 2.12: Morphological upper facial index among War Jaintia adult males

Sl. No	*Categories*	*Frequency*	*Percentage*
1	Hyperleptorrhine	0	0
2	Leptorrhine	53	26.50
3	Messorhine	125	62.50
4	Platyrrhine	20	11
5	Hyperlatyrrhine	0	0

Table 2.13: Jugo-mandibular index among War Jaintia adult males

Sl. No	*Categories*	*Frequency*	*Percentage*
1	Very narrow	0	0
2	Narrow	0	0
3	Medium	6	3
4	Broad	21	10.50
5	Very broad	173	86.50

The table 2.13 shows that 86.50 percent fall under the category, very broad, followed by broad, 10.50 percent and medium 3 percent . Negligible percentage of Jaintia males is either narrow or very narrow. 100 percent of the population fall under very broad category of Jungo frontal index (Table 2.14).

Table 2.14: Jugo frontal index among War Jaintia adult males

Sl. No	*Categories*	*Frequency*	*Percentage*
1	Very narrow	0	0
2	Narrow	0	0
3	Medium	0	0
4	Broad	0	0
5	Very broad	200	100

The above table shows that stature of Khasi males (159.60 cm) are found to be tallest and War Jaintia are the shortest (157.16 cm). The mean stature of Pnar and Khasi shows significant difference with the present study. In respect to sitting height vertex, the highest value is found among the War Jaintia (82.55 cm) and the lowest is among the Pnar (81.63 cm). The mean shows a significant difference for Khasi but not for Pnar when compared with the War jaintias. With respect to head length, the highest value is found among the Pnar (18.45 cm) whereas the War Jaintia's has the lowest value (17.9 cm). The mean differs significantly with Khasi whereas Pnar are non-significant when compared with the War Jaintias.

In respect to the head breadth, the present study on War Jaintia adult males (15.18 cm) is found to be highest and the Khasi has the lowest value (14.17 cm). The mean shows that in head breadth Khasi and Pnar differs non-significantly. In respect to nasal length, the War Jaintia is found to be highest (5.00 cm) and the Pnar has the lowest value (4.93 cm). Both Khasi and Pnar differ non-significantly with respect to the mean of nasal length. In respect to

Table 2.15: Comparison between War Jaintia and other North-east populations

Population	*N*	*Statistic*	*Stature (cm)*	*Sitting Height (cm)*	*Head Length (cm)*	*Head Breadth (cm)*	*Nasal Length (cm)*	*Nasal Breadth (cm)*	*Morphological upper facial height (cm)*	*Total Facial height(cm)*	*Weight (kg)*	*Source*
War Jaintia	00		157.16	82.55	17.9	15.18	5	3.59	6.41	11.09	52.07	Present study
		S.D	6.2	4.03	0.74	0.64	2.52	0.34	0.6	0.66	8.61	
Pnar	65		159.07	81.63	18.45	15.08	4.93	3.66	6.69	11.63	-	Vanlalremuatal Lushai, 2010
		S.D	1.06	0.59	0.18	0.12	0.07	0.04	0.07	0.10	-	
		t-value	4.15	0.39	0.19	0.05	0.22	0.03	0.92	0.28	-	
Khasi	1		159.60	81.72	18.12	14.17	4.97	3.82	6.71	11.23	52.53	Ketouneinuokuotsu, 2003
		S.D	0.93	0.55	0.10	0.09	0.05	0.04	0.06	0.08	0.87	
		t-value	5.42	2.83	4.4	0.54	0.01	8.57	0.22	0.09	0.05	

nasal breadth, the highest is found among the Khasi (3.82 cm) and the War Jaintia has the lowest value (3.59 cm). There is a significant difference in the mean nasal breadth among Khasi whereas it is not significant for Pnar when compared with the War Jaintias. In respect to morphological upper upper facial height the Khasi has the highest value (6.71 cm) and the lowest is among the War Jaintia (6.41 cm). The mean shows that Pnar and Khasi differ non-significantly with the present study. In respect to morphological total facial height, the Pnars has the highest value (11.63 cm) and the lowest is among the War Jaintia (11.09 cm). The mean shows that Pnar and Khasi differ non-significantly with the present study. In respect of weight, Khasi has the highest value (52.53 kg) and the adult male of War Jaintia has the lowest value (52.07 kg). The mean shows that Khasi differs non-significantly with the present study.

The present study is an investigation of anthropometric characteristic of the adults males of War-Jaintia population of Nongtalang village, Jaintia Hills district Meghalaya. A total of 200 adult males were measured between the age group of 18 to 65 years. Each subject was measured for 14 different anthropometric characteristics. The result of the present investigation reveals that adult War Jaintia males showed high percentage of smokers and tobacco chewers and they are found to smoke daily. However, alcohol consumptions showed lower percentage as compared to the alcohol consumers. Anthropometric findings revealed that War-Jaintia males are generally short in stature with medium shoulder and narrow pelvis. Nasal anthropometry showed that they have medium and long face. However, in respect to the nutritional status majority of War-Jaintia males showed normal weight. The t-test result showed that, War-Jaintia males does not show significance difference with other populations of North-east India.

References

Buettner-Janusch. 1966. *Origins of Man.* London: Wiley

Buxton, L.H.D. 1925. The People of Asia. London.

Dobzhansky, Th. 1951. Genetics and the origin of species *(New York: Columbia University Press)*

Meredith, H.V. 1957. A descriptive concept of physical development. In D.B. Harris, The concept of development. Minneapolis. *Psychological Bulletin*, 1955, 52, 194-216.

Mitchell, H .S. 1962. Nutrition in relation to stature. *J Am Diet Assoc*. 40:521–4.

Richards, O.W & A.J Kavanagh. 1945. The analysis of growing form, in Le Gros Clark, W.E and Medawar, P.B., eds., on growth and form presented to D. Arcy ThompsonWentworth Thomps Oxford. *Clarendon press, Oxford*, p. 188-230.

Tanner, J. M. 1994. Introduction: Growth in height as a mirror of the standard of living. In J. Komlos (Ed.), Stature, living standards, and economic development: Essays in anthropometric history (pp. 1– 6). Chicago: *University of Chicago Press.*

3

Anthropometric, Blood Pressure and Haemoglobin Aspects of Chothes of Chandel District, Manipur

Chaithu Sonia Aimol[*] *and H. Sorojini Devi*[*]

Introduction

Anthropometric parameters such as height, weight, body girths, skinfold thicknesses and indices play important role in predicting the various health risks. Waist circumference (WC) is an indicator of deep adipose tissue and it is related to fat mass. It is a convenient and simple measurement which correlates closely with WHR. It is a convenient and simple measurement which correlates closely WHR and is an approximate index of intra-abdominal fat mass and total body fat (Lean et al., 1996). Changes in WC reflect changes in risk factors. Moreover, sex differences in central body fat distribution exist among different populations (Bhadra et al., 2002). Obesity has become an important public health problem in many countries since it is linked with many diseases. Deposition of excessive adipose tissue mass in the trunk region is linked with an increased risk for hypertension (Harris et al. 2000), type-II diabetes mellitus (Seki et al. 2002). Obese individuals with excess fat in the abdominal region are at particular risk of the adverse health consequences. The WHO (1998) recognized obesity as a major public health epidemic disease, in developed as well as in developing countries. Jean Vague (1956) classified two types of obesity i.e. android/ visceral or upper body obesity which is the accumulation of adipose tissue within the abdomen, particularly, in the waist region and gynoid or lower body obesity. However, the incidence of obesity was found to be higher among women than men (Pi –Sunyer, 1994).

Many studies have shown that in many countries there is alarming rise obesity among males and females. Not only among the adult individuals, has the prevalence of obesity to the younger generations too. Khongsdier (2001) has pointed that the increase in rural-urban migration along with change in dietary and physical activity patterns is likely to condition many individuals to obesity and its associated diseases such as diabetes, hypertension, etc. The global trend of obesity has reached in every corner of the world. Chingmila (2013) and Monika (2014) also found approximately 50 percent of males and females suffering from obesity among the Rongmei and Kom tribes of Manipur. Generally, obese people have high blood pressure.

Haemoglobin is an important respiratory pigment of blood and performs an important function of oxygen carrier and it also takes part in carbon dioxide transport. Haemoglobin is produced in red bone marrow and normal synthesis of haemoglobin requires an adequate supply of iron. Haemoglobin constitutes 90-95 percent of the red blood corpuscle. Anaemia is defined as a haemoglobin level of less than <12 g/dL in females and <13 g/dl in males. It is an indication of either dietary deficiency or an underlying pathologic process or disease (Looker, 1997). The normal value of haemoglobin ranges from 13-17.0 g/dL in male and 12-16 g/dl in female. However, chronic diseases (liver disease, gastrointestinal problem, renal disease, colon disease), bone marrow disorder, thallasemia, sickle cell anaemia are all responsible for the prevalence of anaemia commonly among elderly patients. Clinical examinations such as mean corpuscular volume, red cell distribution, serum iron, total iron binding capacity, serum ferritin and reticulocyte count (Bernard and Karnard, 2004). Iron deficiency in the diet is the most common cause of nutritional anaemia in the world and is more common in the rural children from poor socio -economic status (Ghai et al., 2008*)*. After 50 years of age, prevalence of anaemia increases with advancing age and exceeds 20 percent among those 85 years and older. Verma et al., (2012) found among adult men with a total of 53.2 percent , in which 34.3 percent for mild, 17.7 percent for moderate and 1.2 percent for severe; and in case of women a total of 70.1 percent was reported, out of which 48.7 percent for mild, 19.9 percent for moderate and 1.5 percent for severe. Majority of them belonged to a lower socio-economic and lower socio-demographical status. Studies on the aspects of hypertension and anaemia among the north east population are very rare. Therefore, the present study has been taken up among the Chothe adult men and women of three villages namely, Purum Tampak, Purum Lainingkhun and Purum Khullen of Chandel district, Manipur to study anthropometric, blood pressure and haemoglobin status of Chothe adult individuals.

Material and Methods

A total of 186 (95 =males and 91= females) cross sectional data of Chothe males and females ranging in age 18-80 years were chosen for the present study. All individuals belonged to Chothe tribe of three villages of Purum Tampak, Purum Lainingkhun and Purum Khullen of Chandel district of Manipur. Anthropometric measurements viz., height, weight, triceps skinfold, subscapular skinfold, supra iliac skinfold, abdominal skinfold, hip girth and waist girth were measured following the norms of Weiner and Lourie (1969). Blood pressure of each subject was examined according to Chatterjee, (1992) and classified according to DHHS, JNC, (2003). Waist hip ratio (WHR) of each subject was computed and classified as per DGSP, (2007). Haemoglobin estimation was done of each child using the Sahli's method (Georgieva, 1989).

Statistical analysis

Statistical constants such as mean, standard deviation (SD) and t test were computed using SPSS version 16 and one way analysis of variance by using Excel software.

Results

Mean values of anthropometric parameters, blood pressure and Hb of men and women are given in table 3.1. It is observed that as a general trend males are taller in height (157.55cm), heavier in weight (56.87 kg), higher in systolic BP (134.87 mmHg), diastolic BP (88.38 mmHg) and Hb (13.94 G/dl) as compared with females. However, in all skinfold measurements of triceps (17.68 mm), subscapular (21.72 mm), supra iliac (14.88 mm) and abdominal (21.78), girth measurements of hip girth (90.68 cm) and waist girth (87. 76 cm) and also waist hip ratio (0.94) females show larger means than male counterparts. Statistically, significant variations are observed except in abdominal skinfold, hip girth and waist girth in between the two sexes in the comparison of anthropometric, blood pressure and haemoglobin (Hb) level (Table 3.1).

Table 3.1: Statistical constants of anthropometric, blood pressure and haemoglobin level of men and women

		Male (n=90)			*Female (n=91)*			
	Variables	*Mean*	*SE*	*SD*	*Mean*	*SE*	*SD*	*t value*
1.	Height	157.57	0.49	4.82	148.14	0.57	5.50	12.57*
2.	Weight	56.76	0.90	8.78	52.73	1.06	10.07	2.82*
3.	Triceps skf.	10.74	0.42	4.15	17.65	0.56	5.43	9.87*
4.	Subscapular skf.	15.98	0.73	7.08	21.72	0.76	7.27	5.47*
5.	Supra-iliac skf.	11.15	0.84	4.71	14.88	0.59	5.60	3.62*
6.	Abdominal skf.	21.02	0.90	8.77	21.78	0.75	7.14	0.65
7.	Hip girth	90.13	0.66	6.48	90.68	0.79	7.54	0.53
8.	Waist girth	85.73	1.06	10.34	87.76	1.26	12.07	1.24
9.	Waist hip ratio	0.93	0.08	0.75	0.94	0.09	0.90	2.63*
10.	Systolic BP	134.78	1.87	18.24	112.95	1.85	17.71	8.30*
11.	Diastolic BP	88.38	1.01	9.86	83.28	1.17	11.19	3.29*
10.	Hb.	13.94	0.17	1.66	12.89	0.13	1.23	4.77*

Note: df= 184, t=1.98, height and girths in cm, weight in kg, skinfold in mm, and Hb in g/dl, skf=skinfold

Table 3.2 highlights the various mean values of anthropometric, systolic, diastolic and Hb of various age groups of males. Age group wise distribution of means indicates that the highest in stature (158.33 cm) triceps skinfold (12.05 mm) with highest Hb level (15.13g/dl) are found at 18-29 years. Thereafter, the age group of 40-49 years show significant changes in body weight with highest mean (60.33 kg) , sub scapular skinfold (17.21 mm), abdominal skinfold (22.60 mm) and hip girth (93.75 cm) have been observed. During 70-79 years, there are marked changes in supra iliac skinfold (12.47 mm), waist girth (93.50 cm) with corresponding waist hip ratio of 0.95. Most advanced age group of 70-80 years has the highest of systolic pressure (157.78 mmHg) and diastolic pressure (95.85 mmHg) among males. Analysis of variance indicates significant differences in waist girth (F- ratio=3.18), waist hip ratio (F-ratio=4.195), systolic pressure (F- ratio=5.009), diastolic (F-ratio=2.552) and Hb (F-ratio= 3.307) at 5 percent level among the various age groups of males.

Table 3.2: Mean values of anthropometric, blood pressure and haemoglobin of males of various age groups

SL no	*Variables*	*18-29 yrs*	*30-39 yrs*	*40-49 Yrs*	*50-59 Yrs*	*60-69 yrs*	*70-80 yrs*	*F ratio*
1.	Height	158.33	158.14	158.06	158.05	157.83	155.07	0.763
2.	Weight	58.15	58.12	60.33	57.54	53.22	53.20	1.000
3.	Triceps skf.	12.05	11.88	10.31	9.51	9.76	10.97	0.977
4.	Sub-scapular skf.	15.69	16.65	17.21	15.68	15.43	15.33	0.480
5	Supra-iliac skf.	10.01	11.78	10.70	12.40	9.56	12.47	0.691
6.	Abdominal skf.	18.44	22.19	22.60	21.91	20.15	20.82	0.418
7.	Hip girth	89.77	89.96	93.75	90.75	86.31	90.27	1.384
8.	Waist girth	78.65	82.96	93.23	82.66	83.33	93.50	3.184*
9.	Waist hip ratio	0.88	0.92	0.89	0.92	0.95	1.06	4.195*
10.	Systolic BP	123.26	128.06	129.17	135.40	140.0	152.78	5.099*
11.	Diastolic Bp	83.88	86.78	87.0	86.0	90.71	95.85	2.552*
12.	Hb.	15.13	14.45	13.53	13.93	13.77	12.88	3.307*

Note: $F_{0.05}$ (5, 90)=2.33, skf=skinfold

Table 3.3 highlights the various mean values of anthropometric measurements, blood pressure and hemoglobin of various age groups of females. Distribution of mean values indicates that females belonging to the age group 18-29 years have the highest mean values of height (149.97 cm) with HB (13.30 g/dl). Other highest in body weight (59.25 kg), triceps skinfold (20.11 mm), subscapular skinfold (26.49 mm) and hip girth (94.59 cm) are observed among the women aged 30-39 years. Women aged 60-69 years have the largest in supra iliac skinfold (17.20 mm), abdominal skinfold (26.0 mm), waist girth (89.89 cm), waist hip ratio (0.98) and diastolic pressure (90.0 mmHg). Old Old women aged 70-80 years show the highest in only systolic pressure (145.56 mmHg). Analysis of variance indicates significant differences in all parameters except in triceps skinfold, systolic BP and Hb in the comparison of males of different age groups.

Table 3.3: Mean values of anthropometric, blood pressure and haemoglobin of females

Sl. No.	*Variables*	*18-29 yrs*	*30-39 yrs*	*40-49 yrs*	*50-59 yrs*	*60-69 yrs*	*70-80 yrs*	*F ratio*
1.	Height	149.97	149.82	149.41	149.80	148.73	141.08	5.759*
2.	Weight	49.89	59.25	52.62	52.60	53.11	48.88	7.178*
3.	Triceps skf.	18.65	20.11	18.27	18.25	16.32	14.35	1.837
4.	Subscapular skf.	22.63	26.49	22.37	22.35	21.84	14.58	3.598*
5.	Supra-iliac skf.	15.24	16.97	14.78	14.74	17.20	10.44	5.601*
6.	Abdominal skf.	24.06	23.68	22.33	22.30	26.00	12.42	3.873*
7.	Hip girth	90.18	94.59	92.39	92.39	93.00	81.44	4.991*
8.	Waist girth	76.14	89.55	81.60	81.80	89.89	83.61	5.783*
9.	Waist-hip ratio	0.84	0.96	0.94	0.94	0.98	0.97	4.723*
10.	Systolic BP	118.42	126.15	122.75	128.93	146.11	145.56	1.841
11.	Diastolic BP	77.36	81.65	82.00	84.28	90.0	84.44	6.838*
10.	Hb.	13.30	12.75	13.00	13.00	12.73	12.53	0.672

Note: $F_{0.05}$ (5,86)=2.33

Table 3.4 represents frequency distribution of WHR cut off values of Chothe men and women. It is apparent that 37.89 percent of the total males are overweight and another 17.89 percent are in the obese I, having a total of 55.78 percent . In case of women, 26.37 percent is in the overweight and a very high percentage (61.54 percent) is in the obesity criteria. Thus a total of 87.91 percent have suffered from overweight and obesity. Although, men outnumber females in overweight, women are extremely higher in obesity than men.

Table 3.4: Various grades of waist-hip ratio of men and women

		Males (n=95)					*Females (n=91)*	
SL.No.	Classification	Ranges	F	p.c	Classification	Ranges	f	p.c
1.	Normal	<0.90	42	44.21	Normal	<0.80	11	12.09
2.	Overweight	0.90-0.99	36	37.89	Overweight	0.80-0.84	24	26.37
3.	Obesity	>1.00	17	17.89	Obesity	>0.85	56	61.54
		Total	95	99.99			91	100

Table 3.5 focuses various grades of systolic and diastolic of Chothe adult individuals. Frequency distribution pattern indicates that the number of males suffering from hypertension I and II are 27.37 percent and 11.57 percent respectively. Thus a total of 38.94 percent males are suffering from hypertension stage I and II. Another 45.26 percent males constitute prehypertension group. Among the females, 16.48 percent and 7.7 percent , have been suffering from hypertension stage I and II having a total of 24. 18 percent . A high percentage of 50.27 percent of the total females are in the prehypertension grade.

Table 3.6 highlights the prevalence of anaemia among the adult Chothe males and females. While observing the prevalence of anaemia among these people, it is observed from the table that majority of 65 males (68.42 percent) and 66 females (72.53 percent) have normal haemoglobin values greater than >13 and > 12 g/dl. Number of cases / individuals who suffer from mild is 29 (30.53 percent) males and 25 (27.47 percent) females; while for moderate case is represented by only 1 (1.05 percent) male. No woman has been found to suffer from moderate and none of them are suffered from severe anaemia.

Table 3.5: Various grades of Systolic and diastolic pressure of men and women

				Males (n=77)		*Females(n=91)*	
SL. No	*Classification*	*Ranges SBPmm Hg*	*Ranges DBP mm Hg*	*f*	*p.c*	*F*	*p.c*
1.	Normal	90-119	60-79	15	15.79	23	25.27
2.	Prehypertension	120-139	80-89	43	45.26	46	50.27
3.	Stage 1 hypertension	140-159	90-99	26	27.37	15	16.48
4.	Stage II hypertension	=160	=100	11	11.57	07	7.70
			Total	95	99.99	91	100

Table 3.6: Various grades of haemoglobin levels of men and women

			Males(n=77)			*Females (n=91)*	
SL. No	*Classifcation*	*Ranges (g/dl)*	*f*	*p.c*	*Ranges (g/dl)*	*F*	*p.c*
1.	Severe	<8	-	-	<7	-	-
2.	Moderate	8.1-10	01	1.05	7.1-9	-	-
3.	Mild	10.1-13	29	30.53	9.1-12	25	27.47
4.	Normal	>13	65	68.42	>12	66	72.53
		Total	95	100		91	100

Discussion

Result of anthropometric parameters indicates that males are taller in height (157.55cm), heavier in weight (56.87 kg), higher in systolic (134.87 mmHg), diastolic (88.38 mmHg) and Hb (13.94 g/dl) as compared with females. However, in all skinfold measurements of triceps (17.68 mm), subscapular (21.72 mm), supra iliac (14.88 mm) and abdominal (21.78), girth measurements of hip girth (90.68 cm) and waist girth (87. 76 cm) and also waist hip ratio (0.94) females show larger means than male counterparts. Taller in height and heavier in weight among males are due to bigger anatomy of males than women. On the other, genetically, women have larger adipose tissue as compared with males, therefore larger mean values in skinfold and girth measurements and are found amongst them (table 1).

Age group wise distribution of mean values of males indicates that maximum stature (158.33 cm) and triceps skinfold (12.05 mm) with highest Hb level (15.13g/dl) are found among the young men aged 18-29 years. Due to secular trend, younger age group males are taller than elder ones. Thereafter, the age group of 40-49 years show significant changes in body weight (60.33 kg) sub scapular skinfold (17.21 mm), abdominal skinfold (22.60 mm) and hip girth (93.75 cm). Old aged males of 60-79 years also show highest in supra iliac skinfold (12.47 mm), waist girth (93.50 cm) with corresponding waist hip ratio of 0.95. Oldest men of 70-80 years, the highest of systolic pressure (157.78 mmHg) and diastolic pressure (95.85 mmHg) are found.

Distribution of mean values of females shows that the highest mean values of height (149.97 cm) with Hb (13.30 g/dl) are found among the young women of 18-29 years. Women aged between 30-39 years also have the other highest means in body weight (59.25 kg), triceps skinfold (20.11 mm), subscapular skinfold (26.49 mm) and hip girth (94.59 cm). 60-69 years aged women also have the highest in supra-iliac skinfold (17.20mm), abdominal skinfold (26.0 mm), waist girth (89.89 cm), waist hip ratio (0.98) and diastolic pressure (90.0 mmHg). Women whose ages are 70-80 years show the highest mean in only systolic pressure (145.56 Mm hg). Body fat and blood pressure increase with increasing age of the individuals (table 2 &3).

WHR cut off values of Chothe men and women shows that in men, 37.89 percent of the total males are overweight and 17.89 percent are in the obese I whereas 26.37 percent of the total women are overweight and a very high percentage (61.54 percent) represents obesity among women. Thus a total of 55.78 percent and 87.91 percent are for both sexes suffering from overweight and obesity. Although, men outnumber females in overweight, number of women is extremely higher in the obesity criteria than men, which is in conformity with the study of Pi-sunyer (1994). During the course of ageing, more fat is accumulated among women than men (Marion, 1977).

Various grades of systolic and diastolic pressures of Chothe adult individuals indicates that males and females suffering from hypertension I and II are 27.37 percent and 11.57 percent respectively with a total of 38.94 percent . Among females, it is found that 16.48 percent and 7.7 percent forming a total of 24.18 percent are in the hypertension stage I and II. High numbers of men (45.26 percent) and women (50.27 percent) have prehypertension in the present study. Persons with prehypertension are likely to have greater risk of developing hypertension (Greenland et al., 2004). Therefore, many Chothe individuals may have high risk of developing hypertension unless they do not control their blood pressure.

Anaemia grades of men and women indicates that number of cases who suffered from mild is 30.53 percent for males and 27.47 percent for females, but moderate case is represented by only 1 male. None of them have suffered from moderate and severe anaemia. Majority of males (68.42 percent) and (72.53 percent) have normal haemoglobin values greater than >13 and > 12 g/dl.

Conclusion

The present study has led to the conclusion that although more females are in the obesity criteria than males the later are more in number suffering from hypertension as well as anaemia as compared with females. In both cases nearly 50 percent of both sexes also suffer from prehypertension condition. Although certain genes that are responsible for obesity that are recognized, it is needless to say that no single gene interacts in vacuum. High consumption of saturated fat and large consumption of carbohydrates may also lead to overweight and obesity among the people. In the present study, obesity and anaemia occur at the same time and the reason behind this is that the causes are different in the two forms. The food responsible for obesity is not responsible for normal or higher haemoglobin level. Iron containing foods such as green leafy vegetable might be lacking in the diet of the Chothes, therefore, some section of them suffered from mild form of anemia, and the main cause of anemia is due to dietary iron deficiencies (Gai et al., 2008). It will be extremely helpful having a proper knowledge of and understanding of the causes and controlling factors of these problems for having a positive health for all.

References

Bernard, M. and M.D. Karnath. 2004. Anaemia in the adult. *Review of Clinical Signs.*

Bhadra, M., Mukhopadhyay, A. and Bose, K. 2002. Adiposity,central body fat distribution and blood pressure among young Bengalee adults of Kolkata, India; Sexual dimorphism. *J. Physiol. Anthropol.*, 21: 273- 276.

Chatterjee CC. 1992. Human Physiology. Medical Allied Agency, Culcatta,

Chingmila Shimrah, 2013. *Correlation between anthropometric variables and BMI among Rongmei males and Females.* Msc Dissertation, Manipur University.

Department of health and human services, Joint national committee, US. 2003.

DGSP (Dt. Gesellschaft five sport medi in & prevention C.V):S1-leitlinie Vorsorgeuntersuchungim sport. 2007.

Gai, O. P., P. Gupta, and V.K. Paul. 2008. Essentials *of Pedtatrics.* Dr. Ghai , Delhi.

Georgieva, S.A.1989 . *Essentials of Physiology*, Mir Publishers, Moscow *J. Obs.*9,147-153.

Harris MM, Stevens J, Thomas N, Schreiner P, Folsom AR. 2000. Associations of fat distribution andobesity with hypertension in a bi-ethnic population: The ARIC study. Atherosclerosis Risk inCommunities Study. *Obes Res*, 8: 516–524.

Jean Vague MD. 1956. The Degree of Masculine Deferentiation of Obesities (A Factor Determining Predisposition to Diabetes, Athrosclerosis, Gout, and Uric Acid Calculous Disease. Am. J. Clin. Nutr. 4(1), 20-34.

Khongsdier, R. 2001. Body mass index of adult males in 12 populations of Northeast India. *Ann. Hum. Biol.* 28, 374 – 383.

Lean, M. E. J., Han, T. S. and Deurenberg, P. 1996. Predicting body composition by densitometry from simple anthropometric measurements. *Am. J. Clin. Nutr*. 63 : 4-14 (1996).

Looker, A. M.D Carroll .1997. *Prevalence of iron deficiency in the United States.* JAMA 277: 973-976.

Marion JL. 1977. Biology of Ageing. Blackie and London.

Monika, M. 2014. *Health Status of Males and Females of Kom Tribe of Manipur. Msc dissertation,* Manipur University.

Pi - Sunyer F X. 1994. Obesity. In: Modern Nutrition in Health and Disease. Shils M E, Olson J A and Shike M (Eds.), Lea and Febiger, London, 984-1006.

Seki A, Takigawa T, Ito T, Fukuoka E, Takahashi K, Kira S. 2002. Obesity and the risk of diabetes mellitus in middle-aged Japanese men. *Acta Med*

Okayama, 56: 255–260.

Verma Pratima, Singh Shraddha ,GhildiyalArchna, Kumar Ashutosh, Krishna Ahilesh. 2012. Prevalence of anaemia in adults with respect to socio-demographic status blood groups and religion in north indian population**.** *Int J. Biol Med Res. 3(4): 2422-2428.*

Weiner, J.S. and Lourie, J.A., 1969. *Human biology- A guide to field methods, International biological programme,* Handbook no.9, Blackwell scientific publications.

WHO. 1968. *The first ten years of The World Health Organisation*, Geneva.

4

A study of correlation between stature and foot dimension among the Kom of Thayong village, Senapati District, Manipur

Henry Konjengbam

Introduction

Identification of an individual is the backbone of forensic investigations. Estimation of stature forms a basic domain of the investigation process in unknown and co-mingled human remains in mass causalities and natural disasters. In situations like mass destruction even experienced forensic experts feel difficulties in the identification of the bodies. Anthropometry traditionally has a prime role to play in the identification of human materials in the field of forensic anthropology. The estimation of stature from extremities forms an integral part in the process of identification of deceased individuals and it has been observed that dimensions from the lower extremity of the body have greater association with body height than those from the upper extremity. Estimation of stature from the foot dimensions has considerable forensic value in developing descriptions of suspects from evidences at the scene of the crime and in corroborating height estimates from witnesses. A number of studies have tried to document the relationship between stature, foot length (FL) and foot breadth (FB) among different human populations utilizing linear and multiple regression statistical equations. Stature reconstruction is important as it provides a forensic anthropological estimate of the height of a person in the living state – playing a vital role in identification of individual. Height estimation by measurement of various long bones has been attempted by several workers with variable degree of success. Each worker has derived his own formula for calculating the stature from long bones. The present study attempts to depict the occurrence of foot types, basing on relative length of first and second toes, incidence of homotypes and heterotypes of the individuals among the males and females of Kom tribe of Thayong village, it also covers report on measurements of stature, foot length, foot breadth and body weight. Another important aspect of the study is the examination of co-relation between stature and body weight, stature and two foot dimensions, viz. length and breadth, foot length and foot breadth. It aims at probing if there is constant ratio of stature and foot size at different height so that stature of individuals of a particular community can safely be estimated from the foot size and vice versa.

Materials and Methods

The sample consists of 96 males and 109 female individuals ranging in age from 18 – 45 years. They have been chosen randomly from Thayong Kom Village, Senapati district, Manipur. Apparently healthy and un – defective individuals (any disease, deformity, injury, fracture, amputation or record of any surgical procedures) were selected for the study. Several Anthropometric measurements were taken using Anthropometer and sliding caliper along with contour tracing of left foot only. The height of the individual was measured between the vertex and floor, with the person standing erect, in anatomical position and the head in the Frankfurt plane, using a standing height measurement instrument. Foot length was measured as the distance from the most prominent part of the heel backward to the most distal part of the longest toe (1st or 2nd). The left foot is considered as recommended by International Agreement at Geneva 1912 (Comas, 1972). The measurements and contour tracing of foot were performed on plane surface in the absence of any sort of foot wear by following the conventional technique (Singh and Bhasin, 1968). Foot dimensions, length and breadth, were measured from the drawings. Foot types are determined basing on the relative length of first and second toes. When the big toe is longer than the second one, it is assigned to as 'T' (tibiale) type, when the second toe is longer than the first toes, it is assigned to as ; 'F' (fibula) types, when the big toe and second toe are equal in length the type of the foot is called 'O' type (Minami and Korin, 1952). When the length of the 1st toe and 2nd toe is equal in both feet, it is classified as homotype foot and when the length of the 1st toe and 2nd toe in both feet is not equal, it is classified as heterotype foot (Minami and Korin, 1952). Measurement and land marks taken are; height vertex or stature, foot length, foot breadth, foot contour and body weight or weight. Karl Pearson's co-efficient of correlation 'r' is calculated for the examination of correlations between stature and foot length, stature and foot breadth and foot length and breadth, etc.

Results

From the study it is observed that 'O' type of foot is found to be the most frequent one, followed successively by 'T' type and lastly by 'F' type in both males and females. Therefore, the foot type of the Kom of Thayong village shows a trend of O>T>F (Table 4.1).

Table No. 4.1: Frequencies of Incidence of T, F, And O Types of Foot.

		Foot Type			
		T (N, %)	*F (N, %)*	*O (N, %)*	*Total*
Male	f	59 (30.73)	55 (28.65)	78 (40.62)	192 (100)
Female	f	79 (36.24)	49 (22.48)	90 (41.28)	218 (100)
Total	f	138 (33.66)	104 (25.36)	168 (40.98)	410 (100)

Table no. 4.2 displays the sex-wise occurrence of homotype and heterotype of foot. It is seen that homotype occurs more frequently than the heterotype in both the sexes. Among males, 'OO' homotype is more prevalent with 33.33 percent than the 'TT' and 'FF' homotypes with 28.13 percent and 22.92 percent respectively. In the case of female, 'OO' and 'TT' homotypes is equally distributed with 34.86 percent each but greater than the FF homotype with 22.92 percent .

Table No. 4.2: Frequency Distribution of Homotypes and Heterotypes of Foot

	Homotypes (N, %)			*Heterotypes (N, %)*						*Total*
	TT	*FF*	*OO*	*TF*	*FT*	*OT*	*TO*	*OF*	*FO*	
Male	27(28.13)	22(22.92)	32(33.33)	0	1(1.04)	0	4(4.17)	8(8.33)	2(2.08)	96(100)
Female	38(34.86)	19(17.43)	38(34.86)	0	0	1(0.92)	2(1.83)	4(3.67)	7(6.42)	109(100)
Total	65(31.71)	41(20.00)	70(34.15)	0	1(0.48)	1(0.48)	6(2.93)	12(5.85)	9(4.39)	205(100)

The values of coefficient of correlation 'r' are given in Table 4.3. Significant statistical positive correlations between all the measurements, stature and foot length, stature and foot breadth, foot length and breadth, are seen in both male and female. It is thus evident that as the stature increases both the length and breadth of foot also increase. Consequently the latter two measurements are also closely related. The value of 'r' for the stature and foot length shown by female and male is 0.595 to 0.683 respectively while the value of 'r' for stature and foot breadth shown by female and male is 0.259 to 0.508 respectively. The value of 'r' for the foot length and foot shown by female and male is 0.356 to 0.488 respectively. The relationship between the stature and foot length is, however, closer than that of the stature and foot breadth as is evident from the values of 'r'.

The linear regression equations for estimation of stature from two foot dimensions, i.e. foot length and foot breadth from Kom males and females are shown in Figure I, II, III and IV. These linear regression equations are formulated based on the correlation values as given above. It has also been suggested that for estimation of stature, regression equation provides greater reliability than multiplication factor (Bhavna and Nath 2007; Jibonkumar and Lilinchandra 2006).

Table No. 4.3. The values of 'r' (coefficient of correlation) of stature –foot length, stature –foot breadth, foot length and breadth among male.

Coefficient of correlation	*Correlation r value*	
	Male	*Female*
Stature-Foot Length	0.683*	0.595*
Stature-Foot Breadth	0.508*	0.259*
Foot length- Foot Breadth	0.488*	0.356*
* Correlation is significant at the 0.05 level		

This simple regression equation can be safely used to estimate height of individuals of Kom community. The stature was estimated for each individual from the linear regression equations and compared with the observed stature, and found that the difference between the estimated stature from the observed stature ranges from ~5 cm to ~8 cm. The estimation of stature from foot length, using linear regression equations is found to be most reliable as compared to foot breadth.

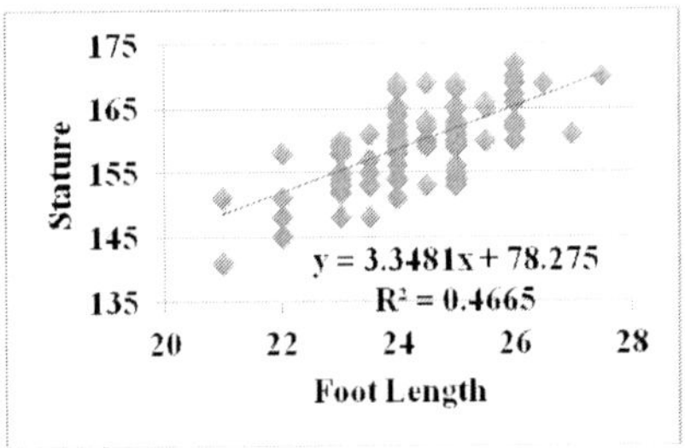

Figure 4.1: Regression Equation of Stature and Foot length of male

Discussion

The estimation of stature can play a role in determining gender, identity, and, many more things that are helpful to identify human remains. This study has a positive strength, firstly, this study is the first of its kind among the Kom community, and secondly, all the measurements were conducted by a single person, which provided uniformity in data gathering. In this study, it is observed that 'O' type of foot is found to be the most frequent one, followed successively by 'T' type and lastly by 'F' type in both males and females as compared to other studies. Therefore, the foot type of the Kom of Thayong village shows a trend of O>T>F where as other previous study show a trend

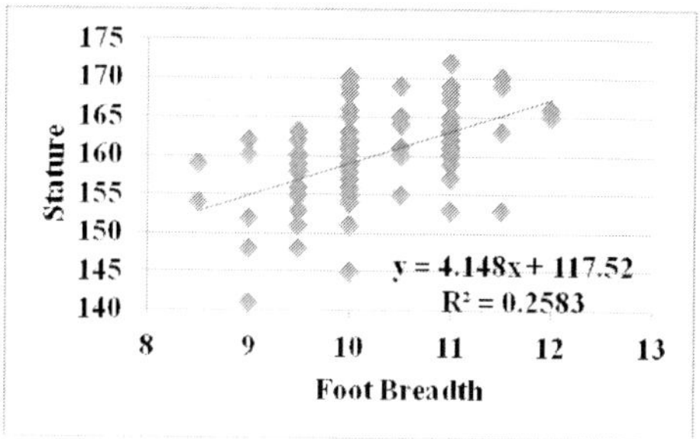

Figure 4.II: Regression Equation of Stature and Foot breadth of male

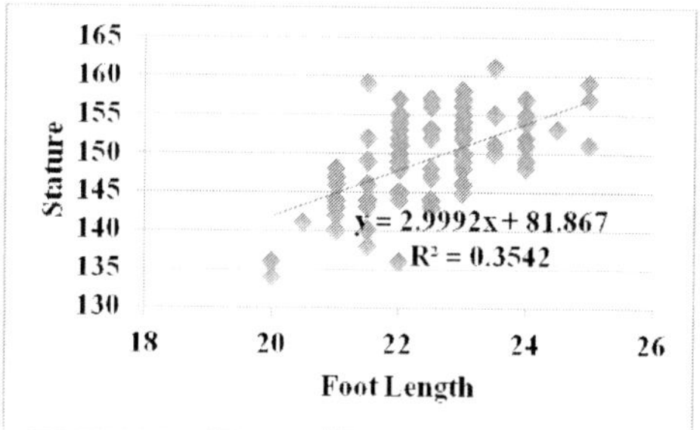

Figure 4.III: Regression Equation of Stature and Foot length of female

of T>O>F. This may be due to population variation or small sample size. Homotype foot is more frequent than heterotype foot. Among the homotypes, 'OO' homotype is more prevalent than the 'TT' and 'FF' homotypes in the case of male while in the case of female, 'OO' and 'TT' homotypes seems to equally distributed but greater than the 'FF' homotype. The value of Karl Pearson's correlation coefficient "r" for examination of co-relationship between all the measurements; stature and foot length, stature and foot breadth, foot length and foot breadth in both male and female shows significant statistical positive correlation. The linear regression equation derived from foot length for estimation of stature showed a greater statistically significant relationship in both the genders. Patel et al., (2007) carried out a study in Gujarat region and it is found that the correlation co-efficient between height and foot length as +0.65 in males and +0.80 in females which was most significant and also derived regression equation to calculate the height from foot length in both males and females.

Qamra et al., (1980) suggested that a true relationship existed only between foot length and stature, and the relationship in other combination of variables

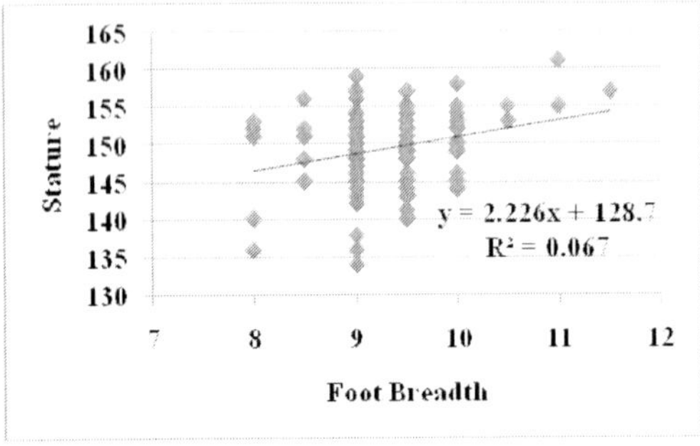

Figure 4.IV: Regression Equation of Stature and Foot breadth of female

was affected to a great extent by foot length alone. They found a good correlation of height with foot length (male: r = 0.69 and female: r = 0.70) and foot breadth (male: r = 0.42 and female: r = 0.47). Giles and Vallaneligham (1991) also suggested that foot length display a biological correlation with height and height of an individual can be safely estimated from foot length. Singh and Phookan (1993) also suggested that foot length is a better indicator of stature than foot breadth while studying the male population of Assam. Sonali and Ashish (2012) reported that all the parameters correlate significantly with stature but foot length in both the sexes depicts higher correlation coefficient with stature ('r' = 0.850) than that any of the parameter and also suggested that multiple linear regression analysis is better over simple linear regression analysis for estimating accurate stature.

However, multiplication factors derived from studies conducted by various research workers such as Patel et al. 2016, Qamra et al, Giles and Vallaneligham, Singh and Phookan are not similar with our findings. The variation obtained in multiplication factors values of above measurements in different population is the direct outcome of the variation in the morphology of different population group. In this present study, the significant correlation of stature with foot length in males and females is 0.683 and 0.595 respectively. And the significant correlation of stature with foot breadth in males and females is 0.508 and 0.259 respectively. From the above correlation value, it is a well-known fact that the stature of an individual can be safely estimated from foot length than the foot breadth.

Conclusion

The present study suggest that knowing the index values, stature of an individual of a particular community can be safely estimated from the foot size and vice versa. Length of the foot shows closer relation with the stature than does by breadth of the foot. Foot length provides the best estimate of stature in both males and females as it indicate the highest correlation value and regression equation provides greater reliability than multiplication factor. It is evident that as the stature increases both the length and breadth of foot also increase. Increase in stature is followed by increase in both the length and breadth of foot in a more or less constant ratio. There are lot of variations in estimating stature from foot dimensions among people of different region, race. Therefore, there is need to conduct more studies among people of different region and ethnicity so that stature estimation becomes more reliable and identity of an individual is easily established. It will also help in medico-legal cases in establishing identity of an individual in mass disasters, accidents, bomb explosion etc. As the sample is somewhat small, it may have some limitations but this study will pave the way for future research in this field.

References

Bhavna and Surinder Nath (2007). Estimation of stature on the basis of measurements of the lower limb. © *Kamla – Raj 2007, Anthropologist*, 3: 219-222.

Comas J. (1972). *Manual of Physical Anthropology*. Springfield. C.C. Thomas.

Giles E. and Vallandigham P.H. (1991). Height estimation from foot and shoeprint length. *J Forensic Sci,* 36(4): 1134-1151.

Jibonkumar and Lilinchandra (2006). Estimation of Stature Using Different Facial Measurements Among the Kabui Naga of Imphal Valley, Manipur. © *Kamla-Raj 2006 Anthropologist*, 8(1): 1-3.

Minami and Korin (1952). The digital formula in Japanese fetus, II – Study on the relative length between the 1st and 2nd toe. *Okajimas Folia Anatomica Japonica*, 24:295-305.

Patel S. M., Shah, G.V., and Patel S.V. (2007). Estimation of height from measurements of foot length in Gujarat region. *J. Anta. Soc. India*, 56(1):25-27.

Qamra SR, Jit I, Deodhar SD (1980). A model of reconstruction of height from foot measurement in an adult population of Northwest India. *Indian J Med. Res.* 71:77-83.

Sarkar S.S. (1958). Morphological characters of human foot. *Proc. Nat. Ins. Sc.* 24: 209-228.

Singh I.P. and M.K Bhasin (1968). *Anthropometry*. Kamla – Raj Enterprises, Delhi, India.

Singh T.S. and Phookan M.N. (1993). Stature and foot size in four Tai communities of Assam, India. *Anthropol Anz,* 51(4):349- 355.

Sonali Khanapurkar and Ashish Radke (2012). Estimation of stature from the measurement of foot length, hand length and head length in Maharashtra region. *Indian journal of basic and applied medical research*, 1(2): 77-85.

5

A Study on Fertility of the Women of Ithing Village, Manipur

Konsam Renu Devi

Introduction

Fertility indicates the reproductive performance i.e., child bearing of a woman. The child bearing is, basically a biological function, but is influenced by socio-economic factors as well as social customs, values and norms related to various aspects of child bearing. It is a positive force through which the population expands counteracting the force of attrition caused by mortality (Bhende and Kanitkar, 2004). Human fertility is very important to keep the family going on. The growth of world population entirely depends on human fertility. There is no period of human history in the past when a deliberate attempt was made to check human fertility. But in the present times, human fertility has become a major problem because of the trend of population growth that threats the development of a society. In the present paper an attempt has been made to report on the fertility performance of the women of Ithing Village, Manipur. Ithing Village selected for the present study is a typical island village surrounded by the Loktak Lake which is the largest fresh water lake in Manipur. It lies within the jurisdiction of Bishnupur District. The distance of the village is about 50 kms away from Imphal town. The total population of the village during the period of study, i.e., during March to September 2010 is found to be 1173, comprising 606 males and 567 females distributing in 5 lineal groups. The family is patrilineal and patrilocal. Newly married sons establish a new family of their own at the earliest as it is found difficult to support a family mainly by fishing.

Materials and Methods

The present study was carried out during March to September, 2010. The data were collected from the whole village. There were 205 households during the time of investigation. The relevant information was collected through interview method. Altogether 201 ever-married women were interviewed with the help of specially designed questionnaire schedule. Husbands and also other members of the family were also interviewed whenever necessary. For collection of data on age at menarche, age at marriage, age at first delivery, and age at menopause, retrospective method was followed. Standard statistical techniques were used to evaluate the data.

Observation and Discussion

Table 5.1 shows the distribution of the 201 women in five yearly age groups. The maximum number of women falls between 27-32 years of age group followed by age group of 21-26 years and 33-38 years age group.

Table 5.1: Distribution of women according to present age

Age group(years)	*Number of women*	*Percentage*
15-20	13	6.48
21-26	42	20.90
27-32	60	29.85
33-38	42	20.90
39-44	34	16.92
45-49	10	4.98
Total	201	100.03

Table 5.2 shows the distribution of age at menarche among the Ithing women. Highest percentage of the women (25.37 percent) attained their age at first menstruation at the age group of 15 years followed by the age group of 13 and 14 years respectively (21.64 percent and 15.67 percent). The mean menarcheal age of the Ithing women is found to be slightly higher (14.22 ± 0.07) than the Meiteis of Imphal valley, i.e., 13.56 ±0.18 years (Devi, 2010).

Table 5.2: Distribution of age at menarche among the Ithing women

Age (years)	*No. of women*	*Percentage*
10	2	1.49
11	5	3.73
12	13	9.70
13	29	21.64
14	21	15.67
15	34	25.37
16	17	12.69
17	7	5.22
18	5	3.73
19	1	0.75
Total	134	99.99

Mean ± S.E. 14.22 ± 0.07, S.D. 0.85

Distribution of women by age at marriage is shown in table 5.3. Age at marriage is one the important determinants of fertility. It is the beginning of the reproductive span of a woman's life .The low age at marriage of the female increases fertility and mortality by providing longer duration and higher incidence of maternal and infant mortality (Bhattacharya, Singh and Singh, 1994). Highest number of the Ithing women (55.56 percent) married at the age group between 15-19 years followed by age group between 20-24 (23.38 percent) years .Women between 30 - 34 years represent the lowest frequency (3.48 percent). The mean age at marriage of the Ithing women is 19.16 ± 0.32 years.

Table 5.3: Distribution of Ever-married women by their Age at Marriage

Age (Years)	*No. of Women*	*Percentage*
10-14	17	8.46
15-19	112	55.72
20-24	47	23.38
25-29	18	8.96
30-34	7	3.48
Total	201	100.00

Mean± S.E. 19.16 ± 0.32, S.D. 4.52

Age at first childbirth

Distribution of ever married women according to their age at first childbirth is presented table 5.4. It is observed that majority of the women (51.24 percent) had their first child birth during the age group of 20-24 years followed by the age group of 15-19 years (34.83 percent) . The mean age at first child birth is 20.86 ± 0.14years.

Table 5.4: Distribution of Ever-married women by their Age at First Childbirth

Age (years)	*No. of Women*	*Percentage*
Below 15	2	0.99
15-19	70	34.83
20-24	103	51.24
25-29	24	11.94
30-34	2	0.99
Total	201	99.99

Mean ± S.E. 20.86 ± 0.14, S.D. 2.84

Age Specific Marital Fertility Rate

Age Specific Marital Fertility Rate of Ithing women is presented table 4.5. From this table it is observed that fertility did not continue up to the end of the reproductive period, i.e., upto 49 years of age but it is observed only upto 39 years of age. When the ASMFR for the different age cohorts are compared, it is observed that the peak of reproduction in the present population is reached in the age cohort of 20-24 years of age (230.79). The second highest peak is 222.22, age cohort being 15-19 years. The total Age Specific Marital Fertility Rate population is to be 144.28. The Total Fertility Rate, that is, the average number of children that would be born alive to a woman during her lifetime, who would be subjected to age specific fertility rates of a given year of Ithing women is found to be 4.11.

Table 5.5: Age Specific Marital Fertility Rate

Age Cohort	*No. of Live Births*	*No. of Women*	*ASMFR*
15-19	2	9	222.22
20-24	9	39	230.79
25-29	12	63	190.48
30-34	4	41	97.56
35-39	2	24	80.00
40-44	-	25	-
45-49	-	-	-
Total	29	201	144.28

Age at menopause

The distribution of women by their age at menopause is shown in table 5.6. The phenomenon of menopause is not sharply terminated at any particular point of time (Talukdar, 1977). Compared to age at menarche, age at menopause shows a high range of variation in a number of populations (Treolar, 1974). In the present study, out of 201 ever married women, 76 have attained menopause. Highest number of women, i.e., 27.63 percent attained their menopause in between 46-47 years. The mean age at menopause among them is 44 .95 ± 0.23 years. This value is lower than the Meiteis of the Imphal valley which is 48.5 years (Devi, 2010).

Table 5.6: Distribution of age at menopause among the women of Ithing Viiiage

Age (years)	*No. of Women*	*Percentage*
34-35	3	3.95
36-37	2	2.63
38-39	4	5.26
40-41	4	5.26
42-43	9	11.84
44-45	15	19.74
46-47	21	27.63
48-49	11	14.37
50-51	4	5.26
52-53	3	3.95
Total	76	99.99

Mean ±S.E. 44.95 ± 0.23, S.D.2.17

Table 5.7: Distribution of the different Rates and Ratio of Fertility

Name of the population	*CWR*	*CBR*	*TFR*
Ithing (2010)	388.70	25.55	4.11

Distribution of the different rates and ratios of fertility is presented in table 5.7. CWR of the present population is 388.70, CBR is 25.55 and TFR is 4.11. The CBR of the present study is found to be higher than the population of Manipur which is 15.8 and The Total Fertility Rate of Ithing women (4.11) is also higher than that of Manipur (2.4) according to 2011 Census. Thus the present study reveals a high fertility rate.

Conclusion

The present study shows 30.73 years of reproductive life span among the Ithing women. Their mean age at menarche is 14.22 years and mean age at menopause is 44.95 years. The mean age at marriage is 19.16 years and the mean age at first child birth is 20.86 years .The Total Fertility Rate is 4.11. Thus the present study exhibits high fertility rate .Low socio-economic status leading to early marriage is the main reason for high fertility rate among the Ithing women.

References

Bhattacharya, B., K.K. Singh, U Singh 1994 Proximate Determinants of Fertility in eastern UttarPradesh. *Human Ecology*: *The International Journal of Population Biology and Genetics.*

Bhende, A. and T. Kanitkar 2004 *Principles Of Population Studies*. Mumbai: Himalaya Publishing House.

Devi, P. 2010 *Vehicular Pollution in Imphal.* Unpublished Doctoral Thesis, Manipur.

Talukdar, S.1977. On Age At Menopause in India. *Man in India* .57(4): 345-449.

Treolar, A.E. 1974. Menarche, Menopause and Intervening Fecundity. *Human Biology*. 44 (6): 89-107.

http://www.wikipedia *free encyclopaedia*

6

Cultural Behaviour in relation to Maternal Child Health among the Thadou-Kuki of Senapati District, Manipur

Hoineilam Kipgen and B.T. Langstieh

Introduction

Globally maternal health advancement and healthcare improvements have been key topical issues to address preventable maternal and child deaths overall staging for a conscious effort to address and adopt 'safe motherhood' programmes worldwide. The evidences of improvement have been supported by WHO (2012) reports that states that maternal mortality worldwide has dropped by 47 percent since 1990. At the national scenario, preventing deaths to mothers associated with pregnancy and childbirth has been one of the greatest challenges before our nation in this 21st century. Women are the prime caretakers of family and bearers of children and any repercussion on their health affects the family as a whole. Women in India face constraints not only in obtaining health services but also in expressing health needs (Modi, Moitra, Patel, Kapadia, & Kantharia, 2013).

According to the UNCF Report 2014, substantial global progress has been made in reducing child deaths. During the last 25 years, the number of under-five deaths worldwide has declined from 12.7 per million in 1990 to 6.3 million in 2013. While that translates into around 17,000 fewer children dying every day in 2013 than in 1990, it still implies the deaths of about 17,000 children under age five every day in 2013. About half of under-five deaths occur in only five countries namely India, Nigeria, Pakistan, Democratic Republic of the Congo and China. India at 21 percent and Nigeria at 13 percent together accounted for more than a third of all under-five deaths. As a nation,

India holds the highest recorded neonatal deaths at one million each year with 65.4 percent of all births occurring mostly at home and 75.3 percent of births in rural areas occur at home (IIPS, 2007). It may be noted that despite the great importance of the subject, no information is available regarding the details of the causes of deaths (IIPS, 2001 and Freeman *et.al.* 2005). The NFHS-4 (2015-16) reported that, in Manipur infant and under-five mortality rate in both rural and urban areas were 22 percent and 30 percent respectively.

Maternal and child health is strongly associated with beliefs and practices around pregnancy and childbirth which has implications for the health of the child and mother after the birth (Choudhury *et al.*, 2012).mIn Northeast India, except for the NFHS 1, 2 and 3 data which provide a broad macro-level estimation on maternal and child health parameters regionally represented by politically demarcated eight states; very few but limited studies are available from the region relating to the population-specific and/or ethnic group related to micro-level understanding on culture, language and communication, behaviour, beliefs and local health practices. Thus in the present study we would like to examine the cultural behaviour in relation to maternal child health as a case-study from among the Thadou-Kuki of Senapati district, Manipur.

Materials and Methods

The present study was conducted among 551 households of the Thadou-Kuki of Tuilang-hom Block in Senapati district, Manipur. The anthropological fieldwork was conducted on nine (9) villages namely, Chalwa, Gelnel, Tujang Vaichong, Kotlen, Songjang, Songpijang, Selsi, Govajang and Phoikon during the period of January 2013-February 2014.With the help of a structured schedule, data was collected and recorded by interviewing the 560 ever-married women aged 15-49 years.

Data on maternal care and child health

Data on maternal care which includes pregnancy and birth histories, details of antenatal care and delivery care received during their past pregnancies from married women was collected with the help of an interview schedule. These include information on the number of antenatal visits, stage of pregnancy at first abdominal check-up (first trimester, second trimester and third trimester), place of delivery, persons conducting delivery and reasons for no antenatal check-up, etc. In addition, the respondents were asked whether they received tetanus toxoid injection and iron/folic acid tablets or syrup during their pregnancies.

Statistical analysis

Data entry and compilation of the demographic data was done on MS Excel data sheets and the collected data was analysed using SPSS.

Findings

The background characteristic of respondents in the present study is shown in Table 6.1. The total number of mothers was 560 with maximum representation of more than one hundred participants in the age groups of 25-39 year old. Ninety five percent of the respondents were married followed by separated and widow at 0.36 percent and 3.93 percent . Majority of the mothers belong to low income group 49.46 percent subsequently with the middle income and high income group at 26.79 percent and 23.75 percent respectively. With regards to education 31.79 percent mothers had no formal education, primary 24.64 percent , upper primary 19.64 and higher secondary above 8.04 percent. More than half of the mothers lived in nuclear type of family. The primary occupation of the mothers is cultivator followed by housewife, weaving, shopkeeper and Anganwadi/ASHA worker.

Table 6.1: Background characteristics of mothers (n=560)

Characteristics		*N*	*%*
Education	No schooling	178	31.79
	Primary	138	24.64
	Upper Primary	110	19.64
	Secondary	89	15.89
	Higher secondary and above	45	8.04
Marital Status	Married	536	95.71
	Separated	2	0.36
	Widow	22	3.93
Family	Nuclear	551	98.39
	Joint	9	1.61
Income	LIG	277	49.46
	MIG	150	26.79
	HIG	133	23.75

Antenatal care

The findings of the present study revealed that registration and ANC visits of the expectant mothers seems to be taken on a slightly serious note with a comparatively high number of 62 percent overall cases of registration. These were done at the government hospital (41 percent), Private Doctor's clinic (4 percent) and ASHA (17 percent). A sizeable number of mothers (38 percent) responded that they never got themselves registered at the time of pregnancy. One of the main reasons mentioned was basically due to ignorance and lack of knowledge from their part as reported in 30 percent of the mothers while a sizeable 5 percent do not feel the necessity of registration. From among those mothers who reside in remotely located villages lack of facility was the respond in 3 percent cases. Ante Natal Check-up (ANC) visits was reported by 55 percent of the mothers which means that the remaining 45 percent mothers never undertook this opportunity with reasons given that it was not necessary (26 percent), no time to go (9 percent), lack of knowledge (5 percent) and others (6 percent).

There is clear association between infant mortality rate and lack of poor quality antenatal care (Chandrasekhar, Rao, Nair, & Kutty, 1998). World Health Organisation has recommended a minimum of 4 antenatal care visits for low risk pregnancy in women (Mathai, 2005). Most women who did not receive health care during pregnancy said this was because they thought it was unnecessary (International Institute of Population Sciences & Macro International, 2000). It is currently estimated that 16 percent of the rural population lives more than 10 km from any medical facility (Bhalla, 1995).

Table 6.2: ANC utilisation by 294 mothers who had availed the MCH services

Ante Natal Check-Up	*No. of mothers (n=294)*	*(per cent)*
Period of ANC visits		
First trimester	152	51.7
Second trimester	111	37.6
Third trimester	31	10.5
Frequency of antenatal check-up		
1 time	68	23.1
2 times	77	26.2
3 times	93	31.6
4 times	37	12.6
More than 5 times	19	6.5
Place where antenatal care was received		
PHC	161	54.8
CHC	87	29.6
Private	46	15.6

Table 6.2 shows the characteristics of ANC visits by the 294 mothers who had availed the MCH services. It may be noted here that from the total number of 534 mothers taken for the present study, only 294 mothers (55 percent) have availed the ANC visits. The result depicted on the table 6.2 is inclusive of all mothers irrespective of the number of pregnancies per mother. Of mother's who attended ANC visits (51.7 percent) made their first ANC visits during the first trimester of pregnancy, 37.6 percent in second trimester and 10.5 percent in third trimester. The place where ANC visits was received were PHC (54.8 percent), CHC (29.6 percent) and private (15.6 percent). The table further shows that majority of mothers (50.7 percent) had ANC visits for three times or more during their pregnancy.

It may be observed from Table 6.3 that the basic maternal health examination such as abdominal check-up's, body weight and blood pressure measures were the most commonly reported in 82 percent and above cases while other tests such as blood test, ultra sound, urine test, etc. which incurred an extra expenditure were reported in few cases at 20 percent and below. The expected date of delivery and nutrition advice were also the most common pre-natal information given in 66.7 percent and 54 percent women. Contradicting to post natal care where advice were expected to be given on breastfeeding, keeping the baby warm, family planning and the need for institutional delivery, very few women reported receiving such advice.

Table 6.3: Maternal health examination and advice given to mothers (n=294) during antenatal check-up

Maternal health examination	*No. of mothers*	*Percentage*
Abdomen examined	289	98.3
Weight	262	89.1
BP	242	82.3
Delivery date told	196	66.7
Nutrition advice given	158	53.7
Blood test	61	20.7
Ultrasound done	58	19.7
Urine Test	43	14.6
Breast examined	14	4.8
Delivery advice given	25	8.5
Advice given on:		
Breastfeeding	56	10.0
Keeping the baby warm	31	5.5
Family planning	96	17.1
Need for Institutional Delivery	96	17.1

Overall it may be noted that among the 294 mothers who attended regular ANC visits only 25 percent reported unsatisfactory results that the medical check-up was hurriedly done; while a sizeable 28 percent and 47 percent reported that the medical attendants had satisfactory and somewhat enough time to perform their duty in the ANC. Interestingly 62.6 percent of the mothers reported that the motivation for the antenatal check-up was 'self-motivated' while 32 percent reported that they were motivated by a family member, 3.7 percent by the ASHA and 1.7 percent by others. Thus, it may be concluded that the 55 percent of the mothers in the present study does show that they are quite aware and does take a serious concern when it comes to taking care of themselves during their childbearing years. Included in this group are those mothers who have attained a slightly higher level of education influencing their decision making processes and initiatives.

The access and availability of those who receive the iron and folic acid tablets (IFA) where it is found that only about 30.7 percent received the IFA, 7.5 percent could afford to purchase and the remaining 61.8 percent of the mothers never availed the IFA tablets (Table 6.4). It was reported that IFA is taken more seriously towards the last trimester period of pregnancy only among the133 women which is 24.9 percent out of the 534 mothers. Very few mothers (n=204) responded to the question whether doses of iron was taken during last pregnancy of which 133 mothers replied in the positive and 58 mothers replied in the negative while 13 mothers responded that they could not take the iron tablets due to reasons of health complaints. With reference to the Tetanus Toxoid (TT) injection for immunisation of both mother and child, 87.5 percent responded 'Yes' and 12.5 percent did not take the injections. A considerable number of mothers withdraw themselves to getting only a one time or one shot injection (15.8 percent), twice and more than three times injection shots were also reported from 42 percent of the mothers. This decline in the number of mothers using the TT injection was primarily due to the unavailability of injections as a free supply in the health centre, the unaffordable and lack of knowledge about the benefits of these injections.

Table 6.4: Pre-natal services availed by mothers

	No. of mothers (n=534)	*Percentage*
IFA tablets/bottles		
Received	164	30.7
Purchase	40	7.5
No	330	61.8
Dosage of Iron during the last pregnancy (n=204)		
Taken	133	65.2
Can't take	13	6.4
No	58	28.4
TT injection (n=534)		
Yes	467	87.5
No	67	12.5
No. of times for TT injection (n=467)		
1	74	15.8
2	196	42.0
3^+	197	42.2

Post natal care

The childbirth and delivery among the Thadou-Kuki mothers in the present study in which it was found that 86.9 percent child delivery cases take place at home and only 13 percent are at hospital (CHC or PHC). Also the fact that 83.2 percent of all deliveries are assisted by the local *Dais* or midwives who in most cases are self-taught with no formal training except their hands-on experience in childbirth deliveries in the area (Table 6.5). As the location of the study area is in rural setting it was reported that the number of trained nurse is relatively lower and most of the assistance during childbirth had taken place with the help of the local midwife or dais. For those admitted to hospital childbirth delivery was attended by hospital staff (13 percent), trained nurse or auxiliary midwife (2.5 percent) and others (1.2 percent). It may be noted that 95.4 percent of the mothers had reported normal delivery while 46 percent caesarean. The check-up within 48 hours after delivery was reported only by those who had availed hospital delivery (12.7 percent) while the remaining 87.3 percent did not attend any check-up. One of the main reasons for non-check-up was that there was no doctor available in the village and for some women who had a natural normal home delivery the thought of a post natal check-up was considered not necessary even though lack of knowledge and far distance were also some concerns in some women.

Table 6.5: Childbirth and Delivery as reported from 519 mothers

	No. of mothers (n=519)	*Percentage*
Place of Child Delivery		
Home	451	86.9
Hospital	68	13.1
Assistance during child birth		
Hospital staff	68	13.1
Dais	432	83.2
Nurse	13	2.5
Others	6	1.2
Last delivery conducted		
Normal	495	95.4
Caesarean	24	46
Check-up within 48 hours after delivery		
Yes	66	12.7
No	453	87.3

Restriction during pre and post natal period

The findings revealed that women's diet were rigidly controlled during pregnancy. Women were advised not to eat crab, egg, monkey meat, turmeric, fermented things, larva or pupa of bees, mushroom, papaya and twin fruits. Most of the women mentioned that consuming all this would result to infant born with foamy spit or bubbly saliva, body covered with white substance, child tends to be hyperactive, gives bad odour during delivery, child shivers like the fluttering wings of the bees and likelihood of conceiving twins. They also reported that family members, mainly mother-in-law encouraged for traditional practices with regard to food restriction. Apart from all these restrictions, the Thadou-Kukis believed that if a pregnant woman eats the meat of a fawn or gallbladder of a porcupine (*sakuling*) it helps her in easy delivery. Also the activity of the expectant mother seems to be having higher responses among mothers who worked until the late stage of their pregnancy with 70.94 percent reported cases of enduring hard agricultural work and cultivation of crops as compared to those mothers with lesser sedentary activities.

Together with diet pregnant women were also prohibited from socialising at night and refrain from drinking spring water and water keep/left overnight in the field as she could invite spirits lurking to follow her and harm the baby.

Similarly, avoid turning their back towards the fire or hearth, cutting of hair, on doing so the womb cannot come out easily during childbirth. Similar to the findings of Krishnakumari (2012) among the Andro and Kwakeithel population of Manipur, the Thadou-Kukis too believed that a pregnant woman as well as the father of the child should not participate in funeral rites. At this stage, she and her husband cannot kill any living creature or certain mystically dangerous animal else his wife may miscarry or bear an abnormal or deformed child. Killing of snake is also restricted because on doing so; the tongue of the child will take after the fang of a snake.

Consumption of chicken boil soup after delivery is very common among the Thadou-Kuki. Most of the women mentioned that after giving birth intake of boil soup of cow shank and chicken, sugarcane, brown sugar, fish, milk, rice beer, ghee and boil vegetables gives them energy and initiate in production of breast milk. With regards to feeding practices 50.5 percent mother breastfeed within 24hours after delivery. About 41.1 percent of the mothers discarded the initial milk (colostrum) as it was considered impure and harmful for the child. And majority of the mothers breastfeed their child till 2 years of age.

The child mortality or recorded deaths among children below 14 years of age are shown in Table 6.6. Child mortality has further been classified into 4 subgroups namely, Neo-natal (0-7days), Infant (>1 years), Toddler (1-4 years) and Juvenile (5-14 years) deaths. Out of the total number of 1940 live-births, the recorded number of deaths in male children was 974 (50.21 percent) and 966 (49.79 percent) in female children respectively. The total number of child deaths is 221 at 11.04 percent which shows to be slightly higher among male children at 123 (6.34 percent) than 98 (5 percent) among female children. Child mortality is found to be highest among the Neo-natal (0-7days) period at 5.77 percent and lowest at the Juvenile (5-14 years) period at 0.93 percent . It further shows that child mortality decrease with increase in age group in the studied population.

The child mortality and related causes of child deaths among the present studied population of Thadou-Kuki are shown in Table 6.7. The table further shows the comparison between the total number of live-births that is an incident count occurring with particular recordings of death prevalence in those specific age groups namely – neonatal (less than 1 week after birth); less than 1 month after birth, below 1 year, 4 years and 14 years respectively. From further categorization of the causes into a medically reported symptom versus a non-medical cause is listed in table 6.9. It is found that non-medical causes were highly reported (67.27 percent) in Not known/Don't know cases mostly lined to a cultural belief in unnatural causes of death. Among the Thadou-Kuki and their cognate ethnic Chin-Kuki groups too, a belief in the existence of an evil or malevolent spirit is pervasive. The evil spirit is known as *'Kaose'* in local parlance (Haokip, 2011). Noticeably among the Thadou-

Table 6.6: Child mortality which includes Neo-natal 0-7days; Infant >1yrs; Toddler 1-4yrs and Juvenile 5-14yrs mortality

Total no. of mothers	*Total no. of live-births*			*Child Mortality Rate*												*Total child deaths*		
				0–7 days			*> 1 yr.*			*1 – 4 yrs.*			*5 - 14 yrs.*					
	M	*F*	*Total*	*M*	*F*	*Total*	*M*	*F*	*Total*	*M*	*F*	*Total*	*M*	*F*	*Total*	*M*	*F*	*Total*
560	974	966	1940	61	51	112	30	19	49	21	20	41	11	7	18	123	97	220
%	50.21	49.79	100	3.14	2.63	5.77	1.55	0.98	2.53	1.08	1.03	2.11	0.57	0.36	0.93	6.34	5.0	11.34

Table 6.7: Child mortality and related causes of child deaths among the present studied population of Thadou-Kuki

Age / Days	*No. of Children*	*M*	*F*	*Causes of Death*
0 – 7 days	112	61	51	Don't know/Not known, lack of care during delivery, *kaose*, Premature delivery, Gynae problem, hard work, etc.
8 – 28 days	3	1	2	Don't know, *kaose*
29 days - 1 year	46	29	17	Cold diarrhoea, Not known, , lack of care, *kaose*, abnormal, fever, etc
1 – 4 year	41	21	20	Cold diarrhoea, Not known, malaria, *kaose*, fever, jaundice, heartcase, etc.
5-14 year	18	11	7	Not known, Diarrhoea, Typhoid, Fever, Drown in water, Naga Kuki conflicts, Multiple tooth eruption, etc.
Total	220	123	97	

Kuki the belief in *'Kaose'* seems to be universally occurring especially in children below the age of 4 years. Medical causes relating to symptoms of diarrhoea, typhoid, malarial fever, jaundice, and other medically known causes was reported at 32.73 percent .

Table 6.8: Nature and causes of deaths reported in the present study

Age Group	*Medical*	*Non-Medical*	*Total*	*%*
0-7 days (N, %)	10 (8.85)	103 (91.15)	113	5.83
< 1 month (N, %)	...	3 (100)	3	1.36
< 1yr (N, %)	22 (48.89)	23 (51.11)	45	2.53
1-4yr (N, %)	29 (69.05)	13 (30.95)	42	2.11
5-14yr (N, %)	11 (64.71)	6 (35.29)	17	0.93
Total (N, %)	72 (32.73)	148 (67.27)	220	11.40

Nature and causes of deaths reported in the present study are shown in Table 6.8. Causes of death are categorized into two groups namely medical and non-medical. The Medical causes of death includes Pre-mature delivery, Gynae problems, Diarrhoea, Cough, Cold, Fever, Tuberculosis, Chest pain, Heart problems Jaundice, Malaria, Vomiting, Typhoid, Multiple tooth eruption, Liver problem, etc. On the other hand, Non-Medical causes of death are Not known (not aware), *Kaose*, lack of care, hard work, displacement during Naga-Kuki conflict, etc.

Thus, summarising the findings from the present study we may conclude that maternal child health services provided in this rural population from Manipur seems to indicate that perhaps poverty and lack of access to basic health needs may not always be the hindrance or causal factor for distress in health outcomes. During pregnancy more foods were restricted and considered taboo, than were promoted or allowed. Neonatal deaths was reportedly high (5.77 percent) followed by infant and child mortality. Regarding the details of the causes of deaths fieldwork information revealed that there were more cases of non-medical causes relating to superstitious beliefs and practices (*Kaose*) and lack of care.

Factors contributing to higher child mortality rate or child deaths could be due to fact that most child deliveries accounting 86.9 percent is at home and 13.1 percent in hospital. As the location of the study area is in rural setting it was reported that the number of trained nurse (2.5 percent) is relatively lower and most of the assistance during childbirth has taken place with the help of untrained dais (83.2 percent).

No doubt education has a vital role to play in a woman's life which is reflected in health outcomes on not only herself but on her offspring(s), family and society at large. Education on Planned Parenthood or guides to parental education, maternal and child health services through outreach programmes on awareness, prevention and cautionary measures on health issues have always been taken on a positive outcome even in the remotest local village administration. These should be encouraged in right earnest to help cater to the needs of those not receiving the formal school education in the villages. Education albeit formal or informal ways of learning plays an important role in dissemination of knowledge with a conscience for better discretionary 'decision making' processes for one self and the society in which we live.

References

Bhalla, A. S. (1995). *Uneven development in the third world: a study of China and India. Basingstoke,* UK: Macmillan.

Chandrasekhar, S., Rao, R. S., Nair, N. S., & Kutty, P. R. (1998). Socio-demographic determinants of antenatal care. *Tropical Doctors, 28(4),* 206-209.

Choudhury, N., Moran, A.C., Alam, M.A., Ahsan, K.Z. & Rashid, F.R. 2012. Beliefs and practices during pregnancy and childbirth in urban slums of Dhaka, Bangladesh. *BMC Public Health*, 12: 791.

International Institute of Population Sciences and Macro International. (2007). *National Family Health Survey,* (NFHS-3), 2005-2006, IIPS: Mumbai.

International Institute of Population Sciences and Macro International. (2015-2016). *National Family Health Survey,* (NFHS-4), 2015-2016, IIPS: Mumbai.

International Institute of Population Sciences and Macro International. (2000). *National Family Health Survey,* (NFHS-II), 1998-1999, IIPS: Mumbai.

Krishnakumari, P. (2012). *Perspective of the Reproductive Health in Manipur*. New Delhi: Akansha Publishing House.

Mathai, M. (2005). Patterns of routine antenatal care for low risk-pregnancy: RHL commentary. The *World Health Organisation Reproductive Health Library,* No.8. Oxford: update Software Ltd.

Modi, A., Moitra, M., Patel, B. H., Kapadia, P., & Kantharia, S. L. (2013). Women's Health: Profile and Practices of Anganwadi Workers. *Indian Journal of Maternal and Child Health, 15(2),* 1-11.

UNCF REPORT. (2014). *Levels and Trends in Child Mortality.* The UN Inter-agency Group for Child Mortality Estimation. Pp. 1-30.

World Health Organisation. (2012). *Merck for mothers*: WHO Issue New Maternal Mortality Data.

7

Study on Height, Weight and Haemoglobin Status of Chothe Children of Manipur

H. Sorojini Devi and Y. Roshni Devi

Introduction

The velocity or rate of growth naturally reflects the child's health status. Although, there are certain norms of the growth pattern of height and weight during the growing stages of children, both the parameters are greatly influenced by environmental and genetic factors. Significant changes in weight can be observed over periods of few days. In developing countries such as west and east Africa, north and south Asia and Indian subcontinents, the overall prevalence of stunting and underweight was found to be high in all the above mentioned countries ranging from 48-56 percent for stunting and 34-62 percent for underweight (Mittal, 2005). Boys in most countries are tended to be significantly more stunted and underweight than girls in all countries. The main nutritional problem facing by the school age children are low height low weight and anaemia, vitamin deficiency etc, which is revealed by many recent studies. As per report of the National Nutrition Monitoring Bureau and National Institute of Nutrition nearly 43.8 percent children suffered from moderate degree of protein energy malnutrition, 8.7 percent suffer from extreme forms of malnutrition and only 9.9 percent of the children are normal. In India, malnutrition is the direct cause of death of 500,000 children every year (Parvathi, 2001).

It is also reported that pre-school and school children suffer from anaemia. Nutritional anaemia was defined in 1968 by WHO in the technical report as "a condition in which the haemoglobin content of the blood is lower than the normal as a result of a deficiency of one or more essential nutrients, regardless of the cause of such deficiency." Iron deficiency in infants and adolescents causes mental retardation and damages the immune system, predisposing children to a wide range of disorder (WHO, 2001). Haemoglobin is an important respiratory pigment of blood and performs an important function of oxygen carrier and it also takes part in carbon dioxide transport. Haemoglobin is produced in the red bone marrow and normal synthesis of haemoglobin requires an adequate supply of iron. It is able to function only when it is contained in erythrocytes (red blood corpuscles). Iron deficiency in the diet is the most common cause of nutritional anaemia in the world and is more common in the rural children from poor socio - economic status (Ghai et al., 2008*)*.

Various scientists (Medhi et al., 2006; Singh et al., 2007; Saheb and Prasad, 2009; Devi and Singh, 2009; Kaveri and Ruth, 2011 and Sinha et al., 2012) have taken up many research works on the aspect of nutritional status and prevalence of anaemia of school children of various communities. Therefore, the present study is expected to throw light on the study of height, weight and haemoglobin status of Chothe children aged between 6+ to 12+ years of three villages of Purum Tampak, Purum Lainingkhun and Purum Khullen of Chandel district, Manipur.

Material and Methods

A cross sectional data of 180 (95 =boys and 85= girls) Chothe children aged between 6+-12+ years were randomly chosen for the present study. All children belonged to three villages of Purum Tampak, Purum Lainingkhun and Purum Khullen of Chandel district, Manipur. The age of each child was recorded from the date of birth. Anthropometric measurements of height and weight were measured from each child following the norms of Weiner and Lourie (1969). Height and weight of the children have been compared with the standard data of ICMR. Haemoglobin estimation was done of each child using the Sahli's method (Georgieva, 1989) and classified according to Sinha et al., (2012).

Statistical analysis

Statistical constants such as mean, standard deviation (SD) and t test were computed using SPSS version 16 and one way analysis of variance by using Excel software.

Results

Table 7.1 focuses the statistical constants of mean, standard error of mean (SE), standard deviation (SD), and t values of height of boys and girls. It is observed from the table that at 6_+ years and 9+ years boys are slightly taller with 111.21 cm and 126.93 cm than girls counterpart of the same age groups. Thereafter, on reaching 10+ years, girls catch up in height till 12+ years with mean values 131.83 cm, 136.65cm and 139.69 cm respectively as such become taller than boys whose mean statures are 128.87cm, 132.62 cm and 138.25 cm. Statistically, sex variations have not been shown at all age groups in height.

Table 7.1: Statistical constants of mean, standard deviation and t value height of boys and girls

		Boys(n=95)				*Girls(n=85)*			
Age (yrs)	*N*	*Mean*	*SE*	*SD*	*N*	*Mean*	*SE*	*SD*	*t value*
6+	14	111.21	0.66	2.30	11	110.36	1.04	3.47	0.69
7+	15	116.64	1.22	4.06	12	114.65	1.09	3.80	1.21
8+	12	121.05	1.04	3.60	12	121.00	0.99	3.46	0.03
9+	13	126.93	0.91	3.00	13	125.66	1.40	5.08	0.76
10+	14	128.87	1.28	3.84	11	131.83	1.56	5.18	1.46
11+	13	132.62	1.21	4.20	11	136.65	2.32	7.69	1.54
12+	15	138.25	1.54	6.54	15	139.69	0.99	3.86	-0.79
Total	95				85				

Table 7.2 highlights mean and t values of weight of boys and girls. It is apparent from the table that as in the case of height, boys dominates over girls in weight at 7+ and 9+ years with mean weight 20.23 kg and 26 kg than girls counterpart whose means weight are 16.90 kg and 22.66 kg of the respective age groups. Hence, girls overtake boys counterpart at 8+ years, 10+ years, 11+ years and 12+ years. It may be said that adolescent growth spurt occurs earlier among girls than boys as a general trend. Therefore, girls are heavier than boys during adolescent stage. As such, girls show better nutritional status as compared to boys. No significant difference is found in the comparison of weight of boys and girls (Table 7.2).

Table 7.2: Statistical constants of mean, standard deviation and t value weight of boys and girls

		Boys(n=96)				*Girls(n=95)*			
Age (yrs)	*N*	*Mean*	*SE*	*SD*	*N*	*Mean*	*SE*	*SD*	*t value*
6+	14	16.00	0.60	2.06	11	16.90	0.67	1.57	1.00
7+	15	20.21	0.52	1.75	12	18.71	0.74	2.58	1.69
8+	12	21.50	0.74	2.57	12	22.66	0.91	2.83	0.97
9+	13	26.00	0.53	1.78	13	25.07	0.45	1.38	1.35
10+	14	26.23	0.51	4.55	11	27.98	1.42	4.72	0.79
11+	13	30.00	1.55	5.39	11	30.63	0.82	2.73	0.36
12+	15	32.50	1.10	4.70	15	33.81	1.22	4.73	0.82
Total	95				85				

Table 7.3 highlights comparison of mean height and weight of the present children with those of ICMR data. It is apparent that mean height of present study boys ranges from a minimum of 111.21 cm to 138.25 cm at the age group 6+-12+ years, while in case of ICMR data the mean height ranges from 118.9 cm to 148.90 cm. In case of girls also, a large differences can be observed in the comparison of stature. At 6+ years, the ICMR data shows that the mean

height is 117.73 cm, while it is only 110.36 cm. A value of 10 cm difference is seen at 12+ years in the comparison of girls. In case of weight also, the present study boys have a mean weight of only 16.0 kg at 6+ years as compared with 22.14 kg of ICMR (1994). Such low weight for age cannot be compensated at all ages. The same trend occurs in case of girls whose mean weight ranges from 16.92 kg – 33.81 kg as compared with ICMR data (21.56 kg – 42.97 kg). Therefore, the present study height and weight of Chothe boys and girls are shorter and lighter as compared to the standard data of affluent Indian children of ICMR, at all ages.

Table 7.3: Comparison of mean height and weight of children with those of ICMR data

	Boys Height		*Girls Height*		*Boys Weight*		*Girls Weight*	
Age (yrs)	*ICMR*	*Present Study*	*ICMR*	*Present Study*	*ICMR*	*Present*	*ICMR*	*Present study*
6+	118.90	111.21	117.73	110.36	22.14	16.00	21.56	16.90
7+	123.32	116.64	122.65	114.65	24.46	20.21	24.45	18.71
8+	127.86	121.05	127.22	121.00	26.42	21.50	25.97	22.66
9+	133.63	126.93	133.08	125.66	30.00	26.00	29.82	25.07
10+	138.45	128.87	138.90	131.83	32.29	26.33	33.58	27.98
11+	143.35	132.62	145.00	136.65	35.26	30.00	37.17	30.63
12+	148.90	138.25	150.98	139.69	38.78	32.50	42.97	33.81

Comparison of height of present study boys with other data of height of Kom and Scheduled caste boys has revealed that the present study boys are intermediate in mean height in maximum number age groups between the Kom and the Scheduled caste boys, while the Kom boys are the tallest of all except in age group 6+ years (108.89 cm). On the other side, the Scheduled caste boys stand as the shortest in stature except comparatively high in two age groups of 6+ years and 12 + years with 110.75 cm and 140.04 cm respectively (Table 7.4). Analysis of variance show significant variation in height among the three groups boys in 7+, 9+ 11+ and 12+ years (F-ratio=3.45, 3.99,4.29 and 4.28, P<0.05).

Table 7.5 highlights comparison of height of present study girls with other data shows that the Chothe girls are the shortest in mean height among the three groups, while Kom girls are the tallest in maximum number of age groups except the 6+ years and 8 + years , which have the 2nd highest mean values with 110.25cm and 121.35cm respectively. Among the three groups, the Scheduled caste girls have represented the intermediate group in between the Chothe and Kom girls. However, no significant differences have been shown in the comparison of height among the girls (all P>0.05), statistically.

Table 7.4: Comparison of Height of Present Study Boys with Others Data

	Chothe boys (n=95)			*Scheduled caste boys (n= 271)*			*Kom boys (n=84)*			
Age (yrs)	*N*	*Mean*	*SD*	*N*	*Mean*	*SD*	*N*	*Mean*	*SD*	*F-ratio*
6+	14	111.21	2.30	37	110.75	3.96	17	108.89	3.83	1.878
7+	15	116.64	4.06	37	115.44	3.56	11	117.70	1.53	3.45*
8+	12	121.05	3.60	37	120.43	3.40	10	121.24	2.14	0.239
9+	13	126.93	3.00	39	123.37	4.53	11	125.41	1.44	3.99*
10+	14	128.87	3.84	44	128.54	3.75	11	129.18	3.05	0.147
11+	13	132.62	4.20	37	132.38	4.67	14	136.14	2.32	4.29*
12+	15	138.25	6.54	40	140.04	3.78	10	142.91	4.26	4.28*
Total	95			271			84			

Table 7.5: Comparison of Height of Present Study Girls with Others Data

	Chothe girls (n=96)			*Scheduled caste girls (n= 269)*			*Kom girls (n=85)*			
Age (yrs)	*N*	*Mean*	*SD*	*N*	*Mean*	*SD*	*N*	*Mean*	*SD*	*F-ratio*
6+	11	110.36	3.47	39	109.15	3.03	17	110.25	4.81	0.036
7+	12	114.65	3.80	34	116.58	3.34	11	117.44	2.16	2.099
8+	12	121.00	3.46	49	121.66	2.64	12	121.35	3.26	0.219
9+	13	125.66	5.08	37	126.13	3.04	13	127.30	1.57	0.861
10+	11	131.83	5.18	41	130.45	3.92	10	131.91	4.82	0.758
11+	11	136.65	7.69	31	137.31	4.80	12	138.88	2.96	0.577
12+	15	139.69	3.86	38	141.36	5.84	10	143.46	2.53	1.650
Total	85			265			85			

Table 7.6 shows that the Chothe boys have the highest mean body weight in 9+ years (26.0 kg) and 11+ years (30.0 kg) with second highest in 10 + years (26.23 kg) and 12 + years (32.50 kg), and the lowest in 3 remaining age groups. The Kom boys also reveals the highest in 7+ years (21.45 kg), 8+ years (22.6 kg) and 12+ years(34.20 kg) and 2nd highest in the remaining age groups, except 10+ years, which has the third highest (25.09 kg) among the comparison of mean weights. On the other hand, Scheduled caste boys have the lowest mean body weight in 3 age groups with highest means in 6+ years and 10+ years with 18.95 kg and 26.55 kg respectively and 2nd highest in 7+ years 8+ years. Statistically, significant variation is indicated in only 9+ years (F ratio=6.04, $P<0.05$) among the boys in the comparison of weight.

Table 7.7 focuses comparison of weight of present study girls with others data. It is observed that majority of the age group Chothe girls have represented the lowest means in weight as many as in 6+ years, 7+ years, 11+years and 12+ years, but 9+ years and 10+ years have shown the highest mean values having with 25.09 kg and 27.98 kg respectively among the comparing groups, while 8+ years has the second highest of all. Interestingly, the Kom girls have the highest and 2nd highest among the age groups, while the scheduled caste girls have the highest and 2nd highest in 2 each age groups and the lowest in the remaining 3 age groups. Significant difference is observed in only 8+ years (F- ratio=4.56, P<0.05) among the girls of three populations.

Table 7.6: Comparison of Weight of Present Study Boys with Others Data

	Chothe boys (n=96)			*Scheduled caste boys (n= 271)*			*Kom boys (n=84)*			
Age (yrs)	*N*	*Mean*	*SD*	*N*	*Mean*	*SD*	*N*	*Mean*	*SD*	*F- ratio*
6+	14	16.00	2.06	37	18.95	1.75	17	18.23	2.65	0.419
7+	15	20.21	1.75	37	20.22	1.69	11	21.45	1.12	2.627
8+	12	21.50	2.57	37	22.08	1.91	10	22.60	1.64	0.821
9+	13	26.00	1.78	39	23.46	2.16	11	24.09	1.81	6.04*
10+	14	26.23	4.55	44	26.55	2.97	11	25.09	3.02	0.895
11+	13	30.00	5.39	37	28.24	3.24	14	29.35	3.77	1.124
12+	15	32.50	4.70	40	32.08	2.95	10	34.2	3.99	0.897
Total	95			271			84			

Note: df(2,67) =3.14, df(2,62) =3.14, df(2,56) =3.16,df (2,62) =3.14,df(2,68) =3.10, df (2,63) =3.14, df (2,64)=3.14

Table 7.7: Comparison of Weight of Present Study Girls with Others Data

	Chothe girls (n=95)			*Scheduled caste girls (n= 269)*			*Kom girls (n=85)*			
Age (yrs)	*N*	*Mean*	*SD*	*N*	*Mean*	*SD*	*N*	*Mean*	*SD*	*F- ratio*
6+	11	16.90	1.57	39	18.17	1.51	17	18.0	1.83	2.66
7+	12	18.71	2.58	34	20.35	1.84	11	20.09	1.58	3.12
8+	12	22.66	2.83	49	22.10	2.10	12	24.42	2.81	4.56*
9+	13	25.07	1.38	37	23.95	2.47	13	25.0	2.67	2.33
10+	11	27.98	4.72	41	26.49	3.14	10	27.80	3.88	0.768
11+	11	30.63	2.73	31	31.94	4.08	12	34.08	3.47	2.57
12+	15	33.81	4.73	38	35.29	5.98	10	38.30	5.90	1.88
Total	95			265			85			

Note: df (2,65) =3.14, df (2,65) =3.14, df (2,72) =3.13, df (2,62)=3.14, df (2.53) =3.15, df (2,62) =3.14

Table 7.8 indicates the prevalence of anaemia among Chothe school age (6_+-12_+ years) boys and girls. The percentage of anaemic boys falling in various grade are 6.32 percent , (severe) 10.53 percent (moderate) and 17.89 percent (mild). Thus, the total percentage of anaemia is 34.74 percent . Among girls, the prevalence is 28.23 percent in which 4.70 is in the severe form, 9.41 percent for moderate and 14.12 percent for mild form of anaemia. Prevalence of anaemia observed among Chothe boys and girls are 34.74 percent 28.23 percent respectively. Majority of boys and girls (65.26 percent and 71.76) are having normal haemoglobin level greater than 11.9 g/dl.

Table 7.8: Haemoglobin status of Chothe boys and girls

		Boys(n=95)		Girls(n=85)	
Haemoglobin level (g/dl)	Classification	F	p.c	p.c	p.c
<10	Severe	06	6.32	04	4.70
10.0-10.9	Moderate	10	10.53	08	9.41
11.0-11.9	Mild	17	17.89	12	14.12
>11.9	Normal	62	65.26	61	71.76
Total		95	100.0	85	99.99

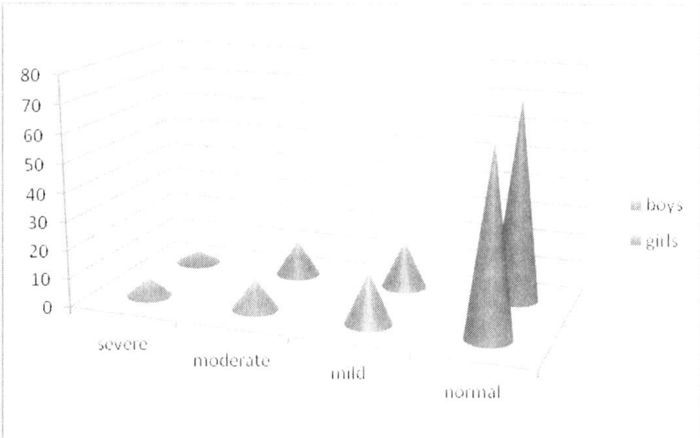

Fig. 7.1: Grades of haemoglobin levels of boys and girls

Discussion

From the above result and observation, it is revealed that in the height of the children, girls are taller in height and heavier in weight as compared with boys after attaining 10+ years onwards suggesting that adolescent growth spurt is found earlier among the girls than boys. Such a trend was also observed among the scheduled caste and Kom tribal boys and girls of Manipur (Devi, 2013, 2016).

In the comparison of height of boys of three groups, the Chothe boys are intermediate between Kom and Scheduled caste boys, while the Kom boys are the tallest of all. Analysis of variance show significant variation in height among the three groups boys in 7+, 9+ 11+ and 12+ years. Again among the girls also, Kom girls are found to be the tallest in majority of age groups, while the Chothe girls are the shortest of all and the Schedule caste are the intermediate group. However, no significant differences have been shown in the comparison of height among the girls (all P>0.05), statistically.

In the comparison of body weight, the Kom boys stand in having highest and second highest in maximum number of age groups, while the Chothe and Kom boys share the same number of age groups in having the highest, second highest and the third highest in weight mean values. So it may be said that the Kom boys show better height than the others. However, significant variation is not revealed except in 9+ years among the boys in the comparison of weight. In case of girls the highest and second highest weight means are observed among the Kom girls as compared with the Chothe and Scheduled caste girls. The Chothe girls represent the highest number of age groups having lowest mean values of body weight. Therefore, they are the shortest of all, although some age group reveals highest and second highest means. Significant difference is observed in only 8+ years. The Chothe and Kom population have more or less same fecilities in terms of market and assess to food as compared with those of Scheduled caste population, but variations in height and weight are exhibited amongst them. Environmental and genetic factors might play in producing such variations.

Further, anaemia is prevalent among the boys, in which 6.32 percent is in the severe form, 10.53 percent and 17.89 percent are in the moderate and mild form. Thus, the total percentage of anaemia is 34.74 percent . As of girls, 4.70 percent represents severe, 9.41 percent and 14.12 percent are in the moderate and mild grade respectively, forming a total of 28.23 percent which is lower than the scheduled caste boys and girls with 64.20 percent and 55.02 percent respectively (Devi, 2013). Among the Kom boys and girls, the overall prevalence of anaemia was 64.28 percent for boys and 63.52 percent for girls (Devi, 2013). Among the tribal school children of Rajasthan, Vyas and Choudhry (2005) revealed that 93.7 percent children suffer from anaemia with highest in moderate form (60.2 percent) and followed by severe grade (32.9 percent) anaemia, which was contrastingly higher than the present study boys and girls.

Conclusion

Finally, it has led to the conclusion that observed accelerated growth during the adolescent stage of girls with taller stature than boys after reaching 10+ years onwards is a general trend. Height and weight growth pattern of the present study children as compared with other Kom and Scheduled caste children of the same age groups have revealed that the Chothe boys were intermediate in statue group in between the two, but girls were the shortest and lightest of all in maximum number of age groups under study. Anaemia of boys (34.74 percent) and girls (28.23 percent), although were not so high as compared with those of scheduled caste boys and girls with 64.20 percent and 55.02 percent respectively (Devi, 2013). Among the Kom boys and girls, the overall prevalence of anaemia was 64.28 percent for boys and 63.52 percent for girls (Devi, 2013). Among the tribal school children of Rajasthan (Vyas and

Choudhry, 2005) revealed that 93.7 percent children suffer from anaemia with highest in moderate form (60.2 percent) and followed by severe grade (32.9 percent) anaemia which was contrastingly higher than the present study boys and girls.

References

Devi, Vedamani and K. Saratchandra Singh. 2009. Nutritional status of the children of Tarao tribe of Manipur. *Ind. J. Phys. Anthrop. & Hum Genet.* 25: (1-2): 199-204.

Devi Hijam Sorojini. 2013. Nutritional status of the Scheduled caste children of Manipur. *Frontier Anthropology. Vol 2: 87-97.*

Devi, H. Sorojini. 2013. Prevalence of anaemia among the Scheduled caste school children of Manipur *J. of International Review of Social Sciences and Humanities,* 6(1):8-12.

Devi Hijam Sorojini and M. Shymchand Meitei. 2016. Assessment of Low Height, Low Weight and Haemoglobin Status among the Kom School Children in Three Villages of Churachandpur District, Manipur. *In Health and iIllness.(eds)* M.C. Arunkumar, Tonjam Joshila Chanu and Pebam Krishnakumari. Akansha Publishing House, New Delhi.

Gai, O. P., P. Gupta, and V.K. Paul, 2008.Essentials *of Pedtatrics.* Dr. Ghai , Delhi.

Georgieva , S. A. 1989 . *Essentials of physiology*, Mir Publishers, Moscow.

I.C.M.R. 1994. *Nutrient requirements and recommended dietary allowances for Indians.* New Delhi.

Kavery, R. And S. J. K. Ruth, 2011. Nutritional status of HIV positive children.Ind. J. Nutr. Dietet.48:98-104.

Medhi, G.K., A. Barua and J. Mahanta, 2006. Growth and nutritional status of school age children (6-14years) of tea garden worker of Assam. *J. Hum. Ecol.*,19 (2):83-85.

Mittal, S. 2005. *Health and Nutrition for School Age Child* . Isha Books , Delhi.

Parvathi, S. 2001.Malnutrition in Indian Children, Soc. wel. 48(6): 28-34.

Saheb, S.Y and M. RajendraPrasad 2009. Physical growth and nutritional status of the Lambadi children of Andhra Pradesh.*J. Hum. Ecol.*, 11(3): 195-206.

Sinha, A.K., Sanjay Yadav, Md. Nazrul Islam, BirendraYadab and BijayAryal. 2012. Assessment of anaemia based on hb levels in children of 2 to 12 years age group in Biratnagar, Nepal. *Int. J. Pharmaceutical & Biol. Archives*. 3(30): 552-554.

Vyas, S. and Choudhry, M., 2005. Prevalence of anaemia in Tribal school children. *J . Hum . Ecol* . 17(4): 289-291.

Weiner, J.S. and J.A. Lourie, 1969.*Human biology- A guide to field methods, International biological programme, Handbook* no. 9, Blackwell scientific publications.

WHO. 1968. *The first ten years of The World Health Organisation*, Geneva.

WHO. 2001. *Iron deficiency anaemia, assessment prevention and control. A Guide for Programme Managers.* Geneva.

8

Present Trends of Physical Education Program in School

Ramananda Ningthoujam and T. Inaobi Singh

Physical education (PE) program has been creating, implementing, and evaluating in promoting lifelong wellness among the school children. Students learn how to make healthy food choices, reduce time playing video games and watching television. Previously, the PE program has been removed from the school curriculum as schools everywhere strive to improve the academic performance of their students, many have cut physical education and recess periods to leave more time for sedentary classroom instruction. Over the years, researchers and educators have revised their PE curricula and training programs to meet the six NASPE (National Association of Sport and Physical Education) guidelines.

The school PE programmes are designed to increase daily levels of physical activity for all school-age children and youths. Fundamental Movement Skill Manipulative—Sending (roll, bowl, slide, strike, underhand throw/toss) and non-locomotor movement viz. bend, curl, hold, lift, lower, pull, push, stand, stretch, reach, swing, twist, turn are taught in the PE class. PE programme is designed to teach children and adolescents the skills necessary to be active outside of physical education class, on the weekends, during vacations, and ultimately the rest of their lives. It also focus upon teaching students tactical understanding before dealing with the performance of skill, as such it offers a tactical approach to games teaching emphasizing game performance over skill performance (Griffin, Mitchell & Oslin, 1997; Werner, 1989).

Recent trends in PE program

One of the drawbacks in Education system as far as physical Education is concerned is that the academic scenario has progressively improved. Physical Education has not really change the methodology for the last 30/40 years. The traditional conventional method where in many children are playing a sports sharing one ball with huge group in which every child does not get a chance to play. However, researchers and educators have revised their PE curricula and training programs to meet the six NASPE (National Association of Sport and Physical Education) guidelines: (i) demonstrates competency in motor skills and movement patterns needed to perform a variety of physical activities, (ii) demonstrates understanding of movement concepts, principles, strategies, and tactics as they apply to the learning and performance of physical activities, (iii) participates regularly in physical activity, (iv) achieves and maintains a health-enhancing level of physical fitness, (v) exhibits responsible personal and social behavior that respects self and others in physical activity settings, and (vi) values physical activity for health, enjoyment, challenge, self-expression, and/or social interaction.

In India, many sports organisation (LEAPSTART, EDUSPORTS, KOOH SPORTS, SPORTS MENTOR, PEFI, YAS, SAI, PE colleges, etc) are taking initiatives which runs physical Education program in School and colleges with the objective of developing physical education program. They main objective is provide sports education in children from the grass root level. Sports education includes basics movement's skills, locomotion, basic skills of the games, rules and regulations of the games, nutritional knowledge, team cohesion, etc. Besides, new teaching strategies (ASAP principles for warm-up, 80/20 rules, use of music, limited space activities, home plays, etc) are used during the PE class which are fun activities compared with the traditional style of teaching. Many researches expressed that one of the drawback of PE program is that it is not having fun and it is like a military training. They use age appropriate equipment, conduct regular assessment of the child, and prepare reports for their parents, and early talent identification of the child. The equipment used by them is modified according to their anatomical structure. For early childhood, fluff ball, ribbons, balloon, bean bags is used in catching and throwing lessons. The foam balls were used to teach kicking and trapping in small children. Fun activities like parachute which teach them team work, and develop their upper body strength are taught during PE classes.

SPARK (Sports, Play, and Active Recreation for Kids) is another pioneer organisation that has been contributing in the systemic reform of physical education (PE) since 1989. In addition to the six guidelines of NASPE, SPARK supports Healthy People Goals (HPG) 2010: a) PE classes make every effort to engage students in moderate to vigorous physical activity (MVPA) at least 50 percent of class time without sacrificing academic achievement or student enjoyment of PE, b) SPARK focus on positive health outcomes of students. These include physical fitness and sports skills, c) SPARK programs include strategies that promote behaviour and environmental change techniques, and d) SPARK also follows ASAP (As Soon As Possible) activity to avoid the lengthy instruction in Physical education class.

Health optimizing physical education (HOPE) through physical education

The National Association for Sport and Physical Education (NASPE) is now endorsing the concept of Comprehensive School Physical Activity Programs (CSPAP) that are designed to increase daily levels of physical activity for all school-age children and youths. It involves all the socio- ecological factors that affect the child so as to achieve the optimal health benefits. They are Individual, Interpersonal, Organizational, Community and Public Policy (Figure 1).

A CSPAP is intended to provide expanded opportunities for physical activity beyond regularly scheduled Physical Education time - including before, during and after school, as well as opportunities outside of school (e.g., at home and in the community) (APPENDIX-I). School physical education (PE) will flourish only when its programs are perceived as being of public importance. Currently many children enjoy it and parents often say it is important, but PE is far from prospering (McKenzie & Lounsbery, 2009). A new CSPAP curriculum model called Health Optimizing Physical Education (HOPE) that can be used to help Primary to High School (P-12) students to acquire knowledge and skills for lifelong participation in physical activity that contributes to optimal health benefits. HOPE aim at developing the public health goal for students to accrue adequate amounts of current physical activity and be prepared for an active lifestyle in adulthood.

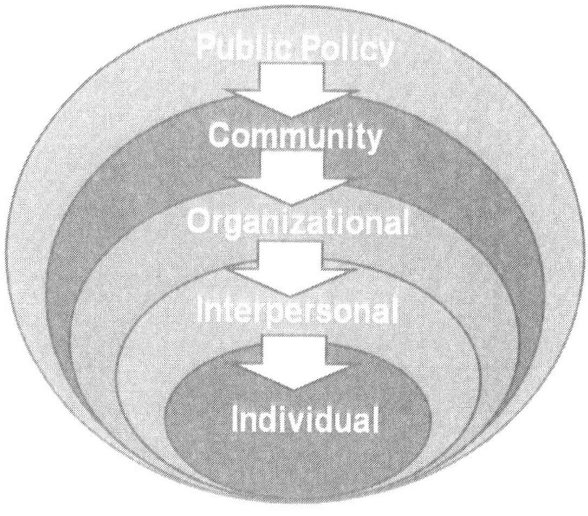

Figure 8.1: Socio-Ecological Factors (Metzler et al., 2013)

Teaching games for understanding in Physical Education

Teaching Games for understanding (TGFU) are designed to elicit the players'/students tactical awareness and skill development from situated learning experience enabled by the teacher/coach/Physical Educationist. The model of TGFU is discussed below: (a) Game Participation: The learning in Physical education starts with games participation in a modified game or real games. At this stage the formative assessment takes place, (b) Game Appreciation: Through game play students are given the chance to enjoy and experience of learning, (c) Tactical Awareness: Through game play students are encourage to identify attacking and defending strategies and implements successful tactical action, (d) Making appropriate decision: In dynamic situation students make real time decisions. These could be with or without the ball, (e) the skill execution: Do the students have the ability to convert their decisions into actions? Can they execute the correct skill to enable their team to succeed? (f) Performance: Students take part in full or modified game applying all new knowledge and skills. This is the time for summative assessments (Figure 8.2).

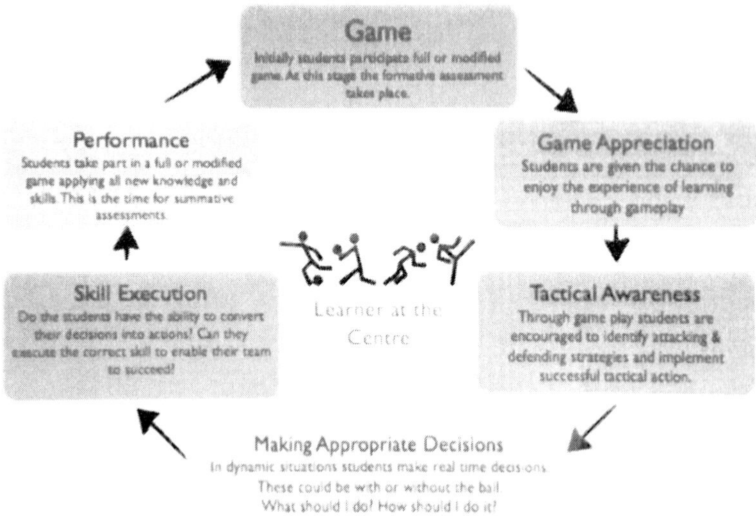

Figure 8.2: TGFU Model (Naomi Hart, 2010)

Technical and Tactical Skills in PE class

Participating in a physical education programme not only increases health and fitness of the students but also learn a variety of technical and tactical skills. The learning model of a child is shown in Figure 8.3.

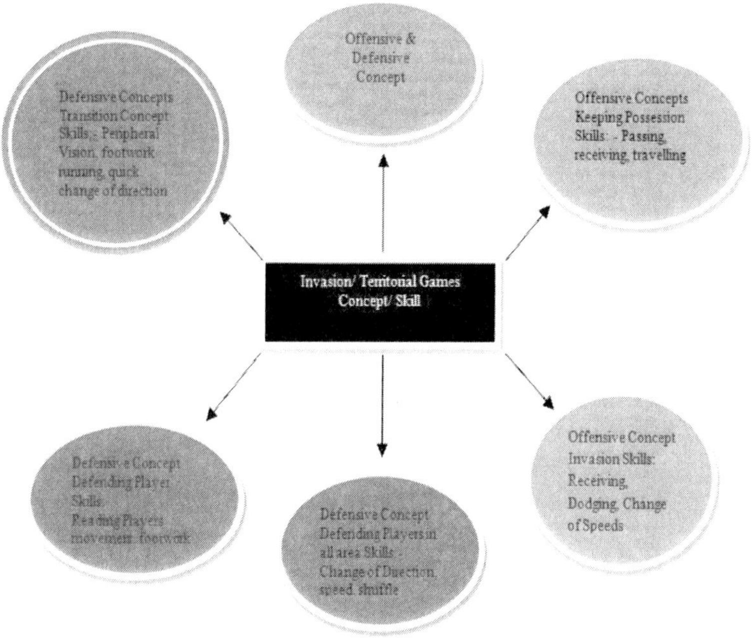

Figure 8.3: Technical and Tactical Skill in PE Class

(Adapted with permission from Linda Griffin, Joy Butler 2005)

Conclusion

New model for PE program aims at developing not only students, but it involves all the socio- ecological factors that affect the child so as to achieve the optimal health benefits viz. Individual, Interpersonal, Organizational, Community and Public Policy. The new models are research based program for lifelong participation in physical activity by the students to make them healthy and well-being. A new model is intended to provide expanded opportunities for physical activity beyond regularly scheduled Physical Education time - including before, during and after school, as well as opportunities outside of school (e.g., at home and in the community).. Before, during and after school program are developed to teach them healthy life style. Home play activities, dance, games and sports, other movement activities, parents participation activities, community based physical activity program, weekly assessment of children (FITNESSGRAM), diet and nutrition physical activity program, physical activity literacy program, etc are introduced recently in PE programs.

References

Charles E. Basch (2010)"Healthier Students Are Better Learners: A Missing Link in School Reforms to Close the Achievement Gap". EQUITY MATTERS: Research Review No. 6.http://www.sparkpe.org/physical-education-resources/academics-physical-activity/#sthash.gsHpeiFD.dpuf

How Does Physical Activity Affect Academic Performance? http://www.sparkpe.org/blog/how-physical-activity-affects-academic-performance/# sthash. Sa 8 W1Nwp.dpuf

Linda Griffin, Joy Butler (2005) Teaching Games for Understanding. Saskatchewan Physical Education Association.

Metzler et al (2013), Health Optimizing Physical Education (HOPE): A New Curriculum Model, Journal of Physical Education, Recreation & Dance, Volume 84, Issue 4, 2013 pages 41-47, DOI:10.1080/07303084.2013.773826

Mike Metzler, Thomas McKenzie, Rebecca Ellis, Hans van der Mars and Shannon Williams (2013).Health Optimizing Physical Education (HOPE): A New Curriculum Model. Handout for AAHPERD.

Naomi Hart (2010), Teaching Games for Understanding, naomihartl.weebly.com/blog/archives.

Physical Education, Physical Activity and Academic Performance, Summer (2009), A national program of the Robert Wood Johnson Foundation, with direction and technical assistance provided by San Diego State University. active living research.org.

Sallis, J. F., & McKenzie, T. L. (1991). Physical education's role in public health. Research Quarterly for Exercise and Sport, 62,124–137.

Stewart G. Trost and Hans van der Mars (2009), Why We Should Not Cut P.E.Health and Learning Pages 60-65 Volume 67 | Number 4.

"The Association Between School-Based Physical Activity, Including Physical Education, and Academic Performance" Report by the Centers for Disease Control and Prevention.

http://www.sparkpe.org/physical-education-resources/academics-physical-activity/# sthash. IRWpxZbj.dpuf.

http://activelivingresearch.org/files/ALR_Brief_ActiveEducation_Summer2009.pdf.

http://www.sparkpe.org/physical-education-resources/academics-physical-activity/#sthash. iz3305Xg.dpuf .

APPENDIX-I: HOPE Program Strands

Learners acquire knowledge and skills for lifelong participation in physical activity for optimal health benefits

Strand	*Learning Outcome/s*	*Learners*	*Examples of Units, Learning Activities, Events*	*SEM Band (See Fig. 1)*	*Comments*
Before/During/After school extended PA programming	Promote high rates of MVPA and health-related knowledge to supplement the scheduled PE program	P-12 students	-SPARK-After School -Intramurals -Before school Walking Club -"Drop in time" in gym	Individual	Instruction can be provided by the Physical Education teachers, other subject teachers, parent volunteers.
Sport, games, dance, and other movement forms	To learn sport, games dance and other movement forms as a source of lifelong participation in PA.	P-12 students	-Skill themes -Team sports -Individual sports -Games -Outdoor/Adventure -International dance -SPARK-PE	Individual	Sports, games, and dance should have high rates of MVPA and over 50% activity time in classes. This strand will look much like many current Physical Education instructional units.
Family/home education,	To teach parents, guardians, and other family members to promote PA, better diet, etc. at home.	Parents, guardians, and other family members and caregivers	-School/parent organization programs -How to read FITNESSGRAM® reports -Healthy cooking courses -Behavior change strategies -School newsletters	Individual Interpersonal Organizational Policy	Opportunities should be sought to provide parents/guardians with knowledge and other resources they can use to promote regular physical activity and other health-enhancing behaviors for their children at home. Teachers are not expected to be the main source of expertise—their role is to find ways to lead parents/guardians and children to these resources.
Community-based PA programming	To promote PA opportunities for children in community settings	P-12 students	-Youth sports -Recreation programs -VERB Scorecard	Individual Community	The teacher's role is to locate community-based opportunities for PA and to provide linkages to them
Health-related fitness	To promote weekly MVPA according to national standards To promote individual achievement to "Healthy Fitness Zone" (e.g. on FITNESSGRAM)	P-12 students	-High MVPA units -Making personal physical activity plans -Strategies for physical activity at home -Knowledge of Health Related Fitness	Individual	The primary purpose is to increase knowledge and MVPA that can improve health related fitness and enjoyment of physical activity. Improved performance on fitness tests should be viewed as the secondary outcome in this strand.

(Contd ...)

Diet and nutrition for physical activity	To learn and demonstrate knowledge of diet and nutrition that enhances PA	P-12 students, Parents/guardians, School food staff, School admin.	-Units on diet and nutrition for PA -Seminars for parents -Analysis of school vending machine program -Consultations with school food staff	Individual Interpersonal Organizational Community Policy	Other than the content units for P-12 students, teachers will need the support and assistance of community nutrition experts
Physical Activity Literacy - Consumerism - Technology - Advocacy	To acquire knowledge and appreciation that can increase and enhance participation and enjoyment of PA	P-12 students, Parents/guardians, Other teachers, School food staff, School admin., Community Organizations	-PA health fair at school -Guest speakers from the PA business community -Guest speakers from community advocacy organizations -Seminar on finding web resources for PA -Seminar on buying PA equipment and clothing	Individual Interpersonal Organizational Community	In addition to the content units for P-12 students, teachers will need the support and assistance of many school and community experts.
Integration of HOPE across all school subjects (including recess)	To increase (non-PE) teachers', school administrators' and school staff's knowledge of and support for children's PA and improved dietary habits	P-12 students, PE teachers, Other teachers, School administrators	-Integrated content units with other subjects -Classroom Activity Breaks (e.g., *Take10!*) -Seminar on promoting high PA and positive socialization in recess	Individual Interpersonal Organizational	HOPE teachers must recognize common learning outcomes across subjects and to inform other teachers of those shared outcomes in order to establish a need for integrated units and instruction.

Source: Metzler et al., 2013 reproduce with permission from Aahperd Handout

Note: PA; physical activity, MVPA; moderate to vigorous physical activity

9

Morphological Study of Head Dimensions of Meiteis: A Secular Trend

Thoudam Bedita Devi

Study of morphological and anatomical features of man, a concern of the anthropologist and anatomist have played a major role in understanding the morphological and anatomical variation from evolutionary and racial point of view of human mankind both at individual as well as population level. As far as biological understanding of personal, ethnic and racial identity is concerned, cephalo-cranial part is the most important dissected component of human body. It is true that cephalo-facial anthropology is an important tool for determining the morphological and anatomical features of the head and face which can steer the anthropological, anatomical and forensic investigations (Cvetkovic et al., 2014).At the same time cephalo-facial dimensions and indices are the simplest and most efficient tool for studying racial differences (Chaturvedy and Harneja, 1963), population variations and sexual dimorphism (Ilayperuma, 2011,) identification of race, ethnicity, gender, age etc. (Del Sol, 2005). Cephalo-facial dimensions experience change during growth and development period and reach its peak growth between 16-20 years of life (Kondu et al., 1999; Knutson et al. 2001)and finally attains maturity there after.The interaction of both genetic and environmental factors determines the phenotypic expression of inter and intra population variations in cephalo-facial dimensions (Kasai et al., 1993; Mehta and Gupta, 2008; Cvetkovic et al., 2014), though hereditary factor mainly affects the head shape while environmental factors have lesser influence (Golalipour, 2006; Sanna et al., 2015).Changes in the head dimensions can be more influenced by climate, nutrition, sleeping pattern in infancy, migration, and socio economic status (Hoppa and Garlie, 1998; Bharati et al., 2001; Weninger, 1979; Kouchi, 2000). Again variation in head and face depend on many factors such as ethnicity, genetic influence, traditions, nutrition, certain pathological conditions, environment and climate (Rexhepi and Meka 2008). Cephalic index which explains the relationship of maximum head breadth and maximum head length simply describes the head shape of an individual and also at the population level. Cephalic Index is very frequently used cephalo-facial parameter for studying secular trend (Larsen, 1997; Kouchi, 2000). Cephalic Index can be used for identifying sexual differences (Williams et al. 1995) and also for racial variations (Shah and Jadav, 2004).In one of the study among Japanese immigrants in Hawai, it was observed that they had increased head breadth and decreased head length and as a result higher cephalic index than their parents (Heravi and Zieaee, 2002). Findings of Koh et al. (2001) says that from the beginning of 20th century brachycephalization has been taking place. Similarly head shape can also change from one generation to the next (Eroje et al. 2010). However, change in head form and shape subsequent generation of a population takes place over a long period of time (Nakashima, 1986).

Though quite a number of scholars have worked on secular trend in cephalo-facial measurements on different population groups of the world, report from Indian population is comparatively very few. Such a scanty nature of data on Indian population more particularly among the populations of North East India calls for undertaking a pioneering research on the Meitei male Population of Manipur steered by the hypothesis that the population might have experienced a secular trend in Head Length, Head Breadth and Cephalic Index from earlier generation to the present generation.

Material and Methods

For the purpose of present study, data were collected from randomly selected unrelated 100 Meitei male adults of Bishnupur district, Manipur. Meiteis are the most populous community inhabiting in the valley districts of Manipur. The age of the subjects ranges between 20 to 60 years. Only two head measurements viz. Maximum Head Length (*glabella to opisthocranion*) and Maximum Head Breadth (*euryon to euryon*) were measured with the help of blunted knob Martins spreading calliper following the techniques laid down by Weiner and Lourie (1969). Relevant index i.e. Cephalic Index was calculated using the formula $\frac{\text{Maximum Head Breadth}}{\text{Maximum Head Length}} \times 100$ and classified based on the conventional categories of Saller. Appropriate statistical treatment was given for a systematic and scientific presentation of the data.

Results and Discussion

It has been observed that Maximum Head Length and Maximum Head Breadth (Table 9.1) of the Meitei population have experienced a secular change towards increasing size from the last generation to the present generation. On comparing Maximum Head Length of the present Meitei population with that of Singh (1992), it is observed that the present generation have longer head length than the earlier generation. As revealed by the findings, the Meiteis of last generation (Singh, 1992) generally have short (31 percent), medium (43 percent) and long head (20 percent) in contrast to short (6 percent), medium (41 percent) and long head (43 percent) of the present generation (present study).With this variation in frequency percent distribution, the two generations show significant difference in Maximum Head Length when examined statistically ($^{L\ 2}$ = 34.27, d.f.= 3). As stated above Meiteis of present generation have longer head (=18.65±0.06 cm) than previous generation (= 18.05±0.06 cm) which display a statistically significant difference (t = 7.06, table 9.3).

Table 9.1: Distribution of Maximum Head Length and Maximum Head Breadth of Meitei Males of Manipur (following Conventional categories of Lebzelter and Saller)

Parameter	*Conventional category*	*Range (in mm)*	*Singh (n=100, 1992)*	*Present study (n=100, 2016)*	*Chi Square Value*
Maximum Head Length (in mm)	Very short	≤ - 169	4	0	χ^2 = 34.27*
	Short	170 - 177	31	6	
	Medium	178 - 185	43	41	
	Long	186 - 193	20	43	
	Very long	194 - ≤	2	10	
Maximum Head Breadth (in mm)	Very narrow	≤ - 139	--	2	χ^2 = 12.32*
	Narrow	140 - 147	35	12	
	Medium	148 – 155	49	52	
	Broad	156 – 163	16	31	
	Very broad	164 - ≤	--	3	

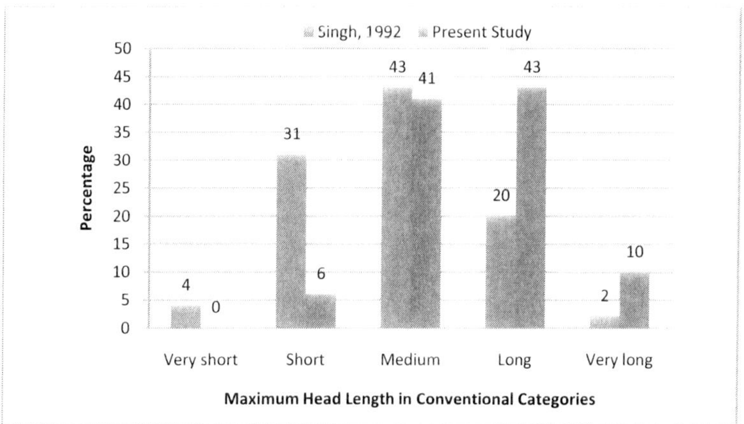

Figure 9.1: Frequency percent distribution of Maximum Head Length according to Conventional Categories

Similar pattern of increase in Maximum Head Length holds true for Maximum Head Breadth as well. It is clearly evident from table 9.3 that Meiteis of present generation have a broader head (= 15.32±0.06cm) than the previous generation (= 14.99±0.06 cm) which reveals a significant difference (t =3.88, table 9.3) thereby displaying a positive secular trend towards an overall increase in head breadth.

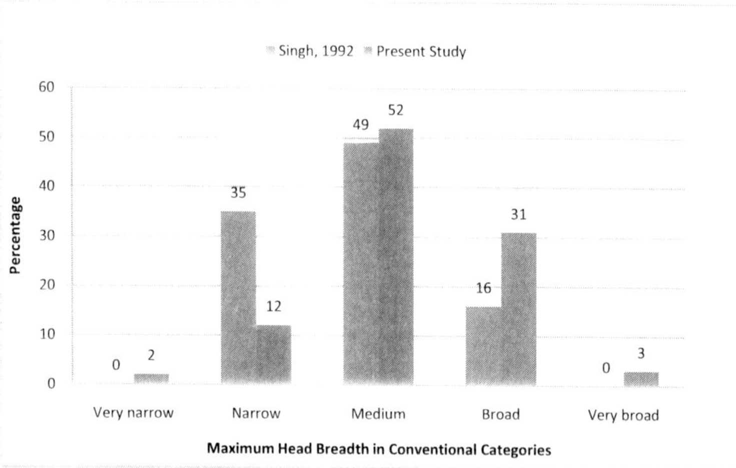

Figure 9.2: Frequency Percent Distribution of Maximum Head Breadth in Conventional Categories

Again considering the frequency percent distribution (table 9.1) based on different conventional categories, it is observed that as many as 35 percent of the population of earlier generation had narrow head as compared to only 12 percent of the present generation. Though medium size head occur highest in both the populations (49 percent for earlier generation and 52 percent for present generation), the frequency of broad head is found to occur almost double time higher in the present study (31 percent) as compared to earlier generation (16 percent). In short, more number of people (84 percent) of earlier generation had narrow to medium head, while more number of people (83 percent) of present generation have medium to broad head, thereby showing statistically significant difference ($x^2 = 12.32$, d.f.= 1) in the frequency percent distribution.

Table 9.2: Distribution of Cephalic Index of Meitei Males of Manipur (following Conventional categories of Saller)

Cephalic Index	*Range*	*Singh (n=100, 1992)*	*Present study (n=100, 2016)*
Dolichocephalic	71.0 – 75.9	3	3
Mesocephalic	76.0 – 80.9	29	39
Brachycephalic	81.0 – 85.4	41	38
Hyperbrachycephalic	85.5 – 90.9	24	30
Ultrabrachycephalic	91.0 - ≤	3	0

($x^2 = 1.83$; p-)

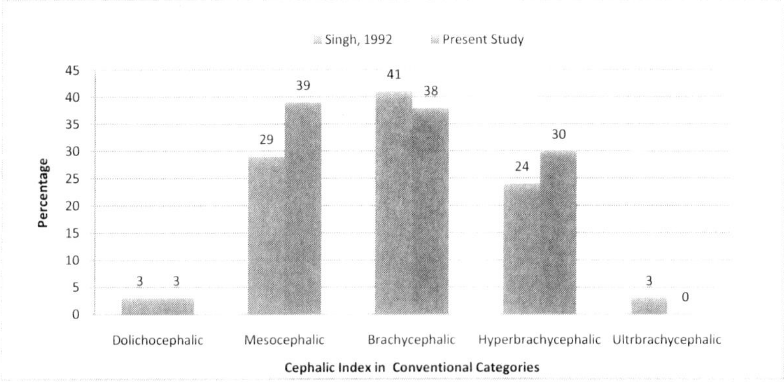

Figure 9.3: Frequency Percent Distribution of Cephalic Index in Conventional categories

Looking into the cephalic index, the Meitei population of present generation have lower mean value (82.23±0.41) than the previous generation (83.25±0.43) showing a negative secular trend, though no statistically significant difference (t=1.72, table 9.3) is observed. This decrease in the mean value of cephalic index in the present generation of Meitei population from the previous generation by 1.02 is mainly because of greater increase in head length (0.60 mm) as compared to head breadth (0.33mm). This finding is in agreement with those reported by Sanna et al.,(2015) among the Sardinian, but contrasting to that of Korean adults among whom there is greater increase in Head Breadth as compared to Head Length (Koh et al. 2001) and among Japanese children (Kouchi, 2000). The reason for decreasing cephalic index may possibly be because of better nutrition, improved socio-economic conditions, nutrition, better health care and changing living conditions of the present Meitei population, as similarly described by Cvetkovic (2014) who worked among the Serbian school children. Therefore as a result of decreasing cephalic index, the population is gradually experiencing debrachycephalization. Similar findings were also reported among the Sardinian Children (Sanna and Soro, 2000; Sanna and Palmas, 2003); among the Hungarian (Gyenis, 1994; Magyar et al. 2006); among the Zena children (Zellner et al., 1998); among the Croatian (Buretic et al., 2007) among Russian children (Gordina et al., 2011) and among Ogbia tribe of Bayesla State (Eroje et al. 2010). However, the mean values of cephalic index of both the Meitei populations indicate that their head shape fall under the brachycephalic category (table 9.2). Again, the frequency percent distribution of different head form reveals no statistical significant difference between the populations as evidenced from chi square value (χ^2 = 1.83, table 9.2).

In short, the population is experiencing a secular trend towards increasing head length and head breadth but decreasing cephalic index because of greater increase in head length than head breadth. Even though the size of the head i.e. head length and head breadth increases, head shape remains more or less unchanged in both the populations because of the fact that head shape or form depends more on pre-established constitutional hereditary factors and less on environmental factors as compared to head size for which environmental factors has a great influence on genetic factor.

Table 9.3: Mean and Standard Deviation of Head Length, Head Breadth and Cephalic Index of Meitei Males of Manipur

Source	*Maximum Head Length*		*Maximum Head Breadth*		*Cephalic Index*	
	Mean	*SD*	*Mean*	*SD*	*Mean*	*SD*
Singh (n=100, 1992)	18.05±0.06	0.63±0.04	14.99±0.06	0.50±0.04	83.25±0.43	4.31±0.31
Present study (n=100, 2016)	18.65±0.06	0.58±0.04	15.32±0.06	0.61±0.04	82.23±0.41	4.07±0.06
t value	7.06*		3.88*		1.72	

References

Bharati S., Som S., Bharati P. and Bhasulu T. S. Climate and Head form in India. *Am J. Human Biol.* 13:626-634. (2001).

Buretic-Tomljanovic A., Giacometti J., Ostojic S., and Kapovic M. Sex specific differences in cephalo-facial traits in Croatia: The impact of environment in small geographic area. *Ann. Hum. Biol.*, 34: 296-314.(2007).

Chaturvedi R. P. and Harneja N. K.A cephalometric study of Human Skulls. *J. Anat. Soc. India.* 12: 93-96. (1963).

Cvetkovic M., Stevo N. and Milos N. 20. Secular change in cephalic index- a study of Serbian School Children, *GENETIKA.* 46(2): 561-568.(2014).

Del Sol M. 2005. Indice cephalico en un grupo de individuosmapuches de la IX Region de Chile. *Int. J. Morphol.*, 23(3) 241-246. Cited inAlves H. A,., Santos M. I. M. P., Melo F. C. I. and Wellington R. Comparative study of cephalic Index of the population from regions of the North and South of Brazil. *Int. J. Morphol.*, 29(4): 1370-1374.(2011).

Eroje, M. A., Fawehimmi, H. R. Jaja B. N. and Yasker, I. Cephalic Index of Ogbia Tribe of Bayesla State. *Int. J. Morphol.* 28(2): 389-392.(2001).

Godina E. Z. Secular Secular Trend in some Russian populations. *Anthropol. Anz.*, 68: 367-377.(2011).

Golalipour, M. J. The effect of ethnic factor on cephalic index in 17-20 years old females of North of Iran. *Int. J. Morphol.* 24(3): 319-322.(2006).

Gyenis G.Rapid change in head and facial measurements in university students in Hungary. *Anthropol. Anz.*, 52: 149-158.(1994).

Heravi, F. And Zieaee, H. 2002. Assessing the importance of cephalic and facial indices in a group of 12 years old boys in Mashhad. *Beheshti Univ. Dent. J.*, 20 : 119-124

Hoppa R.D., Garlie T. N.Secular change in the growth of Toronto children during the last century. *Ann. Hum. Biol.* 25: 553-561(1998).

Ilayperuma I. Evaluation of cephalic Indices: A clue for racial and Sexual diversity.*Int. J. Morphol.* 29(1): 112-117(2011).

Kasai K. L. C., Richard T. and Brown T.Comparative study of craniofacial morphology in Japanese and Australian aboriginal population. *Hum. Biol.,* 65: 821-834.(1993).

Knutson B., Momenan R., Rawlings R. R., Fong G.W. and Hommer D.Negative association of neuroticism with brain volume ratio in healthy humans. *Biol. Psychiatry*, 50: 685-690 (2001).

Kondu S., Wakatsuki E. and Sibagaki H. A. Somatometric study of head and face in Japanese adolescents. *Okajimas Folia Anat. Jpn.*, 76: 179-185.(1999).

Kouchi M.Brachycephalization in Japan has ceased. *Am. J. Phy. Anthropol.* 112: 339-347.(2000).

Larsen, C. S.*Bioarchaeology.* Cambridge University Press (1997).

Magyar L., Bellovits O. and Bujdoso G.Changes in anthropological data of Hungarian child and adult population during the last thirty years based on family study conducted by the Department of Forensic Medecine at Budapest. *Anthropol. Anz.*, 64: 227-241.(2006).

Mehta O. P. and Gupta D. S. A study of cephalometric appraisal of the inheritance of craniofacial patterns in Gurkhas. *J. Indian Soc. Pedod. Prevent Dent.* 121:124.(2008).

Nakashima, T. 1986. Brachycephalization in the head form of school girls in North Kyushu. *J. UOEH*, 8:411-4. Cited in Ilayperuma I. Evaluation of cephalic Indices: A clue for racial and Sexual diversity. *Int. J. Morphol.* 29(1): 112-117.(2011).

Rexhepi. A. and Meka, V.Cephalofacial Morphological characterics of Albanian Kosova population. *Int. J. Morphol.* 26(4): 935-940.(2008).

Sanna E.and Palmas I. Change in Body and Head Dimensions in urban Sadinian children (3-5years) from 1986-2001.*Ann. Hum. Biol.,* 12: 782-791.(2008).

Sanna E., Nicola M., Patrizia M. and Maria E. D. Body and Head dimensions in Sardinia (Italy) support different intensities of relative secular trends. *J. Anthrop Sc.* 93:157-162(2015).

Sanna E. and Soro M. R. Anthropometric changes in urban Sardinian children 7-10 years between 1975-1976 and 1996.*Ann. Hum. Biol.,*12: 782-791.(2000).

Shah, G.V. and Jadav , H.R.The Study of Cephalic Index in Students of Gujarat. *J. Anat. Soc. India.* 53(1): 26-26 (2004).

Singh, S.J.Anthropological Variations on the Meitei of Manipur and Assam. Unpub. Ph.D. Thesis. Manipur University.(1992).

Weiner, J.S. and J.A. Lourie. *Human Biology:A Guide to Field Methods.* IBP Handbook No.9,Blackwell Scientific Publications, Oxford. (1969).

Weninger M. As to the influence of climate on head form. *Anthropol. Anz.* 37: 18-26.(1979)

Williams, P. L., Bannister, L. H., Dyson, M., Collin, P., Dussek, J. E. and Ferguson J. W. M. *Grays Anatomy Skeletal System.* 38th Edn. Churchill Livingstone, Edinburg, London, pp;609-612.(1995).

Zellner K., Jaeger U. And Kromeyer-Hausechild K. The phenomenon of debrachycephalization in Jena School Children. *Anthropol. Anz.*, 56: 301-321.(1998).

10

A study on Water borne Morbidities of Karang Islet, Manipur

Ksh. BeliyaLuxmi Devi

Introduction

Human body is constituted of 66 percent water. Water is a lifesaver, but it can also be a major threat to human life: when it is contaminated and resulting to water borne diseases. Water-borne diseases are usually those diseases caused when a person drinks, bathes in, washes with or prepares food with water that has been contaminated by bacteria, viruses or parasites, usually from human or animal waste (www.worldvision.ca). Man's health may be affected by the ingestion of contaminated water either directly or through food; and by the use of contaminated water for purpose of personal hygiene and recreation, (Park, 1995). Diseases such as cholera, diarrhoea, dysentery, hepatitis A, typhoid, scabies, worm infestation, malaria and jaundice are some of the diseases caused by contaminated water and poor sanitation. Literature reveals that every 90 seconds a child dies from a water-related disease. Water-related diseases affect more than 1.5 billion people every year. Water, sanitation and hygiene related disease kills nearly 1 million people each year. 160 million children suffer from stunting and chronic malnutrition linked to water and sanitation. Diarrhoea is the 3rd leading cause of child death, a majority of which are water-related. In low and middle-income countries, 1/3 of all healthcare facilities lack a safe water source according to World Health Organization and UNICEF Joint Monitoring Programme (JMP). (2015). Again in low- and middle-income countries, 38 percent of health care facilities lack any water source, 19 percent do not have improved sanitation and 35 percent lack water and soap for hand washing. Half of the world's hospital beds are filled with people suffering from a water-related disease. Globally, at least 1.8 billion people use a drinking-water source contaminated with faeces (https://thewaterproject.org). Absent, inadequate, or inappropriately managed water and sanitation services expose individuals to preventable health risks (https://thewaterproject.org).

The internal environment of man himself and the external environment surrounding him determine the health status of an individual, a community and a nation. Lack of safe drinking water is the prime reason of much of the ill health in the underdeveloped world. Water-borne diseases are a leading cause of morbidity and mortality and are still a major public health problem in India (WHO-1994).

With all these in background, and steered by the hypothesis that there will be high prevalence of water borne morbidities among the people of Karang islet of Manipur, an attempt has been made to explore the water –borne morbidities prevalent in this Village and its contributing factors in the present study . Karang, is an islet village of Loktak lake in Bishnupur district of Manipur about 55 km on the south west of Imphal, the capital of Manipur. The village is surrounded by water on all sides and canoe and motor boat are the only means of transport (plate 10.1). Though the work of Tombi (1992) and Saratchandra (1997) have worked on the floating hut dwellers of Loktak Lake none have as yet attempted to touch the people of Karang Village with special reference water borne morbidities. The village is inhabited by 1394 individuals according to the head count by the village authority. The main occupation of the people of the village is fishing and in general their socioeconomic conditions are low. The village has 234 households and all families have toilet constructed within their homestead under Nirmal Bharat Abhiya from 1999 to 2012 called the Total Sanitation Campaign, or TSC. India is a land of villages and about 80 percent of its population lives in villages. The problem of sanitation therefore is one of" Rural sanitation". Surveys have shown that 90 percent of the population "go to the open fields" for defecation. This habit of indiscriminate fouling of the surrounding with human excreta is generations-old and rooted firmly in the cultural behaviour of the Indian village people. The problem in rural sanitation is how to overcome the resistance of the village people, and induce them to use sanitary latrines (Park-1995).

Even though all the families have toilets constructed within their home-stead, many people defecates in water while boating out for fishing during early in the morning. Some families have constructed pig sty and coops (plate 10.3) mainly near the shore, so faecal matters are seen floating in water. The same water is used for cooking, drinking, bathing, washing clothes and cleaning utensils. Water level of Loktak Lake increases during rainy season and houses near the water are often inundated during rainy seasons. The water purity also changes seasonally, during the month of December to July they get pure water and during the month of August to November water usually got rotten and contaminated due to abundantly available of unwanted thick marshy land with grasses floating in the water as well as garbage thrown into the lake by dwellers in the floating huts (plate 10.2). During this season people mostly suffer from water-borne morbidities like cold fever, scabies, diarrhoea etc. The colour and odour of the lake water is reported to change due to rotten grasses and water hyacinth. It was observed that air temperature ranged between 11-33°C, water temperature between 16-32°C, pH ranged between 6.05-9.10, dissolved oxygen between 4.05-14.18 mg/l, biochemical oxygen demand between 1.51-10.65 mg/l, free CO2 between 0-35 mg/l, total dissolved solids between 50-150 ppm, phenolphthalein alkalinity between 0-20 mg/l, total alkalinity between 35-90 mg/l, conductivity between 90-220 μS/cm and transparency between 29-162cm (Jogesh and Dey, 2014). The pattern of arrangement of different houses on the slope ridge of the village is a noteworthy feature.

Plate 10.1. Canoe the means of transport

Plate 10.2. Floating hut of Loktak Lake

The houses are arranged very densely one above another in tiers. The construction of latrines amongst these congested houses is limited by the geographical topography of the village site. If one constructs one kutcha / pit latrines in his own homestead, problems of bad odour as well as sometimes running down of over flowed faecal matters towards the low lying houses especially during the rainy season take place. Thus, in order to avoid such awkward situations, the villagers are compelled to answer the call of the nature in the nearby lake – an age-old ongoing trend handed down for many years. The same situation is faced by the people in case of drainage system also.

Material and Methods

For the purpose of present study (Survey period July to October 2016), out of the 234 households 168 were selected for a survey using simple random sampling technique. This constitutes 71.8 percent of the total number of households, in the village. The total population of selected household is 979 (M=536, F=443) individuals thus having a sex ratio of 826 females per 1000 males. Structured interview schedule and personal observation methods was employed as survey tool for collection of data pertaining to hygienic practices related to use of drinking water and morbidity pattern among the surveyed population.

The parameters considered for the present includes information such as

1. Distribution of waterborne morbidities based on age, sex and literacy
2. Sanitation and hygienic pattern of use of water- water storage methods, water filtering technique, washing of hands before meal and defecation, treatment of drinking water, removal of water from the storage utensils, cleaning of utensils, and main source of water pollutants.

Results and Discussion

It is evident from table 10.1 that types of water-borne morbidities in the surveyed population are cold fever, skin infestation, diarrhoea, worm infestation, jaundice and typhoid fever. It is observed that out of the total 171 individuals suffering from water borne morbidities cold fever account for highest prevalence (35.67 percent) with a highest incidence rate of 62.37. Skin infestation accounts for 26.90 percent , with an incidence rate of 46.99, diarrhoea for 18.13 percent (incidence rate-31.66). In India Diarrhoea is a major public health problem like in other developing countries. An estimated 1.8 billion episodes of Diarrhoea occur each year and 3 million children under the age of 5 years die of diarrhoea (WHO, 1999). Jaundice, worm infestation and typhoid fever also occur in the incidence rate of 16.34, 10.21 and 7.14 respectively (table 10.1, fig. 10.1)

Plate 10.3. Contaminated water by animal and human activities

Table 10.1: Frequency percent distribution of Water-borne Morbidities of Karang Village

Type of Morbidity	*F*	*PC*	*Incidence Rate*
Cold fever	61	35.67	62.37
Skin infestation	46	26.90	46.99
Diarrhoea	31	18.13	31.66
Worm infestation	10	5.84	10.21
Jaundice	16	9.36	16.34
Typhoid fever	7	4.09	7.14
Total	171	100	

Table 10.2 reveals that water borne morbidities are found to be prevalent more among males than females as per the present findings. But when compared statistically for different types of morbidities in both the sexes, no significant difference is observed as shown by $\chi^2 = 4.7$, d.f=7, $p<0.05$. This may be because biologically, immunity of males is comparatively lower than females. At the same time another probable reason is that males by occupation (fishing) are more frequently exposed to outdoor activities in the lake water meant for catching fish., As per the record of Primary Health centre, it was recorded that Cough has the highest frequency of 24 both male and female infected from waterborne morbidities and the lowest frequency of infection found to be on skin infestation. The present findings however, differs from the records of the last three months collected from Primary health centre (table 10.3).The reason of this difference between actually occurred incidence and reported cases is because of the fact that males usually do not report their cases in the primary health centre. Another reason for not approaching to health centre is that

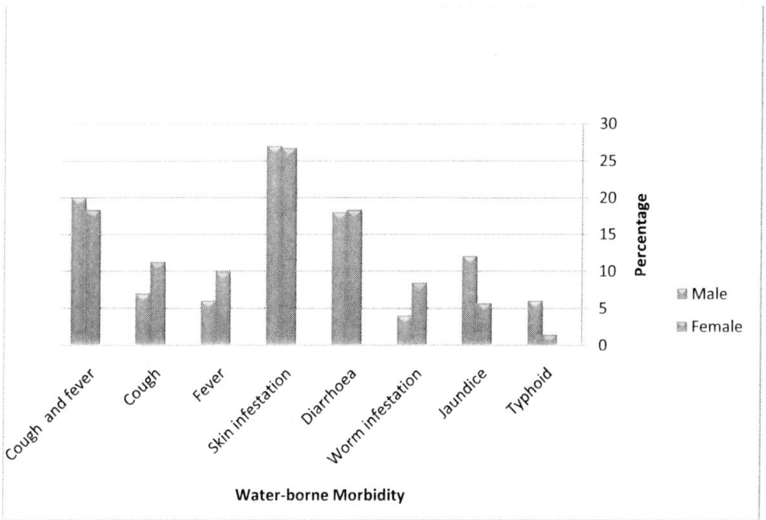

Fig 10.1. Sex wise distribution of Water -borne Morbidity

they considered waterborne morbidities as part of their life cycle they faced every now and then and take it easy.

Table 10.2: Sex-wise distribution of Water borne Morbidities in the Surveyed Population

Water-borne Morbidity	*Male*		*Female*		*Total*	
	f	*PC*	*f*	*PC*	*f*	*PC*
Cough and fever	20	20	13	18.3	33	19.30
Cough	7	7	8	11.27	15	8.77
Fever	6	6	7	9.86	13	7.60
Skin infestation	27	27	19	26.76	46	26.90
Diarrhoea	18	18	13	18.31	31	18.13
Worm infestation	4	4	6	8.45	10	5.85
Jaundice	12	12	4	5.63	16	9.36
Typhoid	6	6	1	1.41	7	4.09
Total	100	100	71	100	171	100

Table 10.3: Health Report for last 3 months from Primary Health Centre

Waterborne morbidities	*July*		*August*		*September*		*Total*
	Male	*Female*	*Male*	*Female*	*Male*	*Female*	
Cough	4	5	6	3	5	1	24
Fever	1	3	1	3	-	2	10
Diarrhoea	4	-	-	-	-	1	5
Skin infestation	-	3	-	1	-	-	4
Total	9	11	7	7	5	4	43

It is also evident from table 10.4 that incidence of water-borne morbidity decreases gradually with increasing age up to 60 years of age, beyond which it again increases. The incidence of water borne disease is seen to occur highest among the children of the age group ≥5 years (63.93 percent) followed by 5-10 years of age (27.94 percent) and 10-20 years (20 percent) and least for the age group 20-60 years (10.89 percent). After 60 years it further increased to 14 percent from water-borne morbidities. On the whole nearly one fourth of the infected population belongs to children below 5 years. Around 15 percent of all water borne morbidities prevalent in the village affect the elderly (>60 years) group. It is also reported from many studies that with unsafe water, there is serious concern for children, especially those under the age of three. They tend to spend more time playing in areas with high risk of contamination. Their small body size makes them more susceptible to diarrhoea-related dehydration (which can be deadly). Since many kids in the developing world suffer from malnutrition, their immune systems are weaker and less able to fight off infections (www.worldvision.ca). Nearly 1 out of every 5 deaths under the age of 5 worldwide is due to a water-related disease. (https://thewaterproject.org).

Table 10.4: Age-wise Distribution of Water borne Morbidities

Age Group	*Population*	*Frequency infected*	*per cent of infected per cent to the total population Age wise population*
≥5	61	39	22.81 63.93
5-10	68	19	11.11 27.94
10-20	190	38	22.22 20.00
20-60	560	61	35.67 10.89
60≤	100	14	8.19 14.00
Total	979	171	100

Fig 10.2 reveals that highest episode of water borne illness (32 percent) occurred among the illiterate group of the surveyed population and least (10 percent) people with educational standard of graduation and above. Thus, the illiterate sections of the population are more vulnerable to water-borne diseases than the educated section of the surveyed population. From the socio-demographic profile of the population it is seen that literacy rate of the studied population is 61.97 percent which is lower than the literacy rate of Manipur 68.90 percent (Bose, 2001). The incidence of Water-borne morbidities decreases with the increase of educational standard. This is because of the fact that with attainment of higher education they become more aware of waterborne morbidities and thus take care of preventive measures.

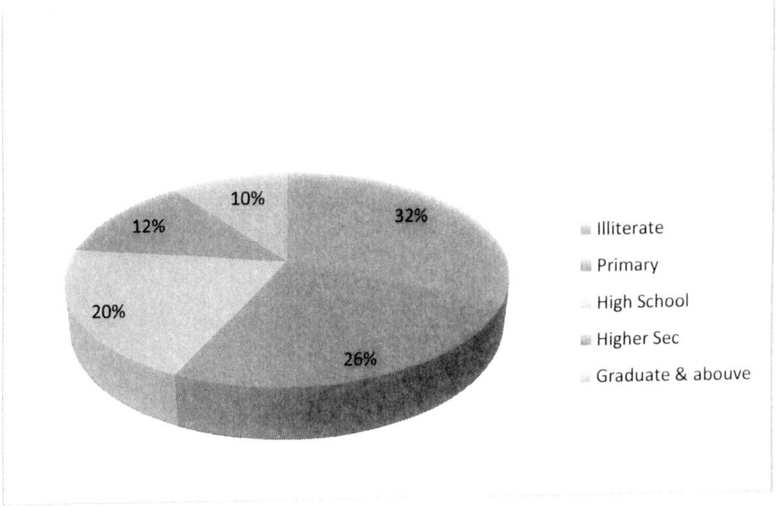

Fig. 10.2 Prevalence of Water borne Morbidity and Literacy

The diseases associated with contaminated water remain amongst the most serious public health problems for much of the world's population

(Wynngarden, 1992). There are neither tube wells nor hand pumps in village. The main source of water therefore is met from the lake. Out of the 168 household surveyed 100 percent of the household depend on the lake as sole source of water for drinking as well as other uses. As far as sanitary and personal hygiene is concerned, as many as 59.52 percent of them wash their hand with plain water after defecation as compared to only 40.48 who used detergent. Similarly 79.17 percent wash their hands before having food as compared to only 20.83 who used soap. The practice of washing utensils (plate 10.4) with ash (18.45 percent) and plain water (1,19 percent) are also seen though most of them (80.36) used detergents. As many as only 4.17 percent of the household cleaned the vessels daily in which they stored drinking water, 62.5 percent cleaned in weekly basis and 33.33 percent reported cleaning the vessel twice a week (table 10.5).

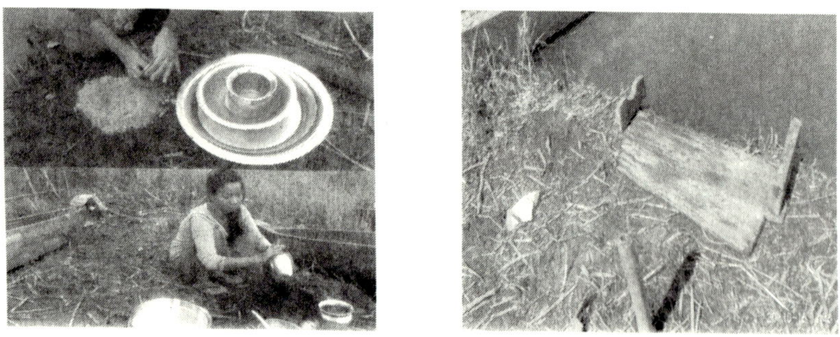

Plate 10.4. Ash being used for cleaning and plain water for washing utensils

Table 10.5: Frequency percentage distribution of Different ways of Cleaning and Washing

Cleanliness and washing	*Ways of Washing and Cleaning*	*Frequency*	*%*
Hand after defection	Plain water	100	59.52
	Detergent	68	40.48
Hand before food	Plain water	133	79.17
	Soap and water	35	20.83
Cleaning of utensils	Detergent	135	80.36
	Plain water	2	1.19
	Ash	31	18.45
Cleaning of Water container	Once a week	105	62.5
	Twice a week	56	33.33
	Daily	7	4.17

All the 168 households surveyed in the population store water for drinking and 100 percent of them used covered vessels for storing drinking water. It is observed that 91.67 percent of the families used plastic drum (plate 10.5) for storage of water while only 2.38 percent used stainless steel vessel. As many as 51.78 percent of the household used cup or vessel without handle to take out drinking water from stored vessel where in they dipped their fingers in water while taking out the water and 47.62 used cup with handle and only 1 family found to use taps on vessel where drinking water is being stored (table 10.6). Types of treatment method used by the villagers for household used are boiling, conventional method of filtration using cloth (plate 10.7) and modern water filter and alum treatment. Even though the water is being filters impurities are found settling at the bottom of the container (plate 10.6). The availability of safe and adequate drinking water and sanitary measures has a direct bearing on the working conditions and health of the people and their capacity for optimum production. The report reveals that out of 168 households only 27.97 percent used boiled water for drinking and 72.02 percent does not boil water for drinking. While access to safe drinking water and sanitation have been proven to be essential to good health, and while the availability of water is a requisite for socio-economic development, there also exists a cause and effect relationship between water, health and development (Shukla, 1988).

Plate 10.5. Plastic drum for water storage

Plate 10.6. Impurities settled at the bottom

Plate 10.7. Filtering water with cloth

Plate 10.8 Earthen pot for water storage

Table 10.6: Frequency and percentage distribution of Storage and Treatment of Water

Storage and Treatment of water	*Modes of treatment*	*Frequency*	*%*
Storage of drinking water	Aluminium Pot	10	5.95
	Plastic drum	154	91.67
	Steel pot	4	2.38
Type of vessel used for taking out water	With handle	80	47.62
	Without handle	87	51.78
	With tap	1	0.59
Treatment of drinking water	Boiled	47	27.97
	Raw/Unboiled	121	72.02
Types of filtering	Modern filter	66	39.29
	Cloth	102	60.71

It is also evident from table 10.6 that 60.71 percent use cloths for filtering water (plate 10.7) and only 39.29 percent found to be used modern filter. Illness can be prevented by ensuring that drinking water remains clean from the point of collection to the point of consumption. This is possible by storing drinking water in clean, covered vessels and by using a ladle for taking out the water (UNICEF, WHO and UNESCO-1997).

Conclusion

The study indicates that low literacy rate; low socio-economic status; unavailability of potable water; ignorance, poor hygienic practices and cultural practices associated with consumption of drinking water etc. were found to be the determinants of high incidence of morbid condition in the village.

The study indicates that some strategies are needed to ensure safe drinking water to the community. The study shows that lack of awareness is a major problem among the community. One of the solutions can be creating awareness amongst the people in the surveyed population. To implement this suggestion and bring it to reality there is a need to formulate scientifically designed intervention strategies to create awareness amongst the people. Provision of safe drinking water is of utmost priority that goes hand in hand with education of the people. There has to be system for pumping the water from lake to the convenient site on the island and proper treatment of the water and its distribution. Perhaps, it is imperative that the community learns to take up the responsibility of ensuring that the drinking water remains safe and this would be one step towards the community taking their health in their own hands.

References

Bose Ashish,:*Population of India, 2001Census Results and Methodology*, B. R. Publishing Co., Delhi (2001)

Govt. of India,:*National Child Survival and Safe Motherhood Programme*, Govt of India (1994).

Jogesh Laishram and Mithra Dey,:*Water Quality Status of Loktak Lake, Manipur, Northeast India and Need for Conservation Measures: A Study on Five Selected Villages* (2014)

Park,K,:*Preventive and Social Medicine* Banarsidas Bhanot Publisher, Jabalpur (1995)

Saratchandra, K. : *Ecology of the Loktak Lake of Manipur and its Floating Hut Dwellers* (1997).

Shukla S. R.:*National water supply and sanitation progm., National health Program* (series8), National institute of health and Family welfare (1988).

Tombi Singh,H.: *Impact of Loktak Hydel Project on the Environment of Manipur. Technical Report (1991-92),* DSTE,Govt.of Manipur (1992).

UNICEF,WHO and UNESCO,: *Facts for life-A communication Challenge*. UNICEF India country office (1997).

WHO,:*Reading on Diarrhoea:Student Manual*, WHO,Geneva (1994)

World Health Organization and UNICEF Joint Monitoring Programme (JMP). (2015) Progress on Drinking Water and Sanitation, 2015 Update and MDG Assessment.

www.worldvision.ca/ourwork/Our-Stories/Pages/Factsheet-Cholera-and-Waterborne-Disease.aspx (retrieved on27th Sept 2016, 10.30 pm)

www.thewaterproject.org/water-scarcity/water_stats (retrieved on 28th Sept 2016, 9.45 p.m.)

Wynngarden: *Cecil text book of Medicine* vol.1 Pub.by W.B Saunerscompany, Philadelphia (1992).

11

Differential Fertility and Mortality among the Khasi Women of Siden Village, Meghalaya

Duka Devi Chhetri

Demography is the scientific study of human populations, primarily with respect to their size, structure, and current and future development. It also deals with the study of population quality. Absolute number of persons (or the size of the population), age, sex, demographic events like births, deaths, marriages, divorce, migration, etc. are important demographic factors. In demographic trend, fertility and morality are important features for calculating population movement. Fertility is known to vary rather widely among the adults of every population. Such fertility variation between different groups is called differential fertility. Mortality variation between different groups is called differential mortality. The numbers of births and deaths that take place are themselves influenced by the size and age distribution of the population. The difference between the number of births and deaths, natural change, is a key determinant of population size and growth. If there are more births than deaths, a population will experience natural increase. Conversely, if more deaths occur than births, a population will experience natural decrease (Reddy and Sudha, 2010). Biological as well as socio-cultural factor are responsible for differential fertility and mortality among the human population (Reedy and Sudha, 2010). Further, it is also highly affected by different cultural practices, socioeconomic and environmental factors, as seen in many different cultures and societies.

The demographic transition theory (DTT) was arguably the founding paradigm of international demography. The demographic transition theory suggested that the fertility transition would result from structural changes linked to a general modernization process that included economic development, industrialization, and urbanization (Heuveline, 2003). Apart from death rate and birth rate, migration is also an important factor for the change in demographic structure of a population. During the time of hunter and gatherer, human population is very small and it remained integrated well within the boundaries of the ecosystem/landscape. With settlements appearing with the advent of agriculture about 10,000 years ago, the exploitative phase of the human population started growing rapidly.

The world experienced dramatic population growth during the twentieth century, with the number of inhabitants doubling from 3 to 6 billion between 1960 and 2000. India, too, saw a very rapid population growth during this period from 448 million to 1.04 billion and to 1.21 billion in 2010. The effects of past and projected future demographic change on economic growth in India are the main focus. Global population grew at roughly 2 percent per annum from 1960-2000, a level that is unsustainable in the long term, as it translates into population doubling every 35 years. India's population is currently growing at a rate of 1.4 percent per year, far surpassing China's rate of 0.7 percent. The differential between India and China will result in India surpassing China with respect to population size in less than 20 years (Bloom, 2011). While most of the developing countries perceive their fertility as too high, while many developed countries are concerned for too low fertility rates (Hartmann, 2010).

Fertility and mortality are fundamental determinants of population growth in order to understand the changes in human population structure. Studies all over the world have brought forth evidences in support of contention that the socioeconomic and socio-cultural milieus of a population have tremendous impact on the fertility and mortality component of that population (Kapoor et al. 2003). Biological as well as socio-cultural factor are responsible for differential fertility and mortality among the human population (Reedy and Sudha, 2010).

Economic and social changes such as industrialization, urbanization, and increase educational level accelerated a decline in mortality. Economic development triggered health improvements (e.g., sanitation, refrigeration of food) which first reduced infant mortality because infants are more responsive than adults to initial mortality declines. In 2011, the total number of children in the age-group 0-6 years is reported as 158.79 million which is down by 3.1 percent compared to the child population in 2001(163.84 million). Children of today are citizens of tomorrow, which is why, it is extremely important to ensure proper health care facilities as well as adequate nutritional intake for the Children. It is now globally acknowledged that investment in human resource development is a pre requisite for any nation (Kullar, 2013). The relationship between fertility and mortality rate shows a close association with the rise and decrease in the level of income. From the time of Malthus onward, economists, demographers and other social scientists have been debating whether and how high fertility and rapid population growth affect economic outcomes, and vice-versa.

Age at marriage is one of the factors that play a significant role in determination of fertility rate of the population (Somola et al. 2006) There are others factors which is responsible for the demographic differential among the population. Urbanization is believed to reduce fertility because children are less likely to contribute to house hold production and more difficult to supervise in an urban setting. Urbanization has a direct effect on mortality, especially on infant mortality, given the aggregate advantages of cities in terms of basic sanitation like clean water, sewerage and garbage collection, health services, etc. This helps to reduce foetal deaths through prenatal care, paediatric care and better coverage through vaccination campaigns (Patil et al. 2002). Moreover, urbanization is correlated with greater access to better sexual and reproductive health services that allow effective regulation of fertility.

The relationship between fertility and mortality rate shows a close association with the rise and decrease in the level of income. From the time of Malthus onward, economists, demographers and other social scientists have been debating whether and how high fertility and rapid population growth affect economic outcomes, and vice-versa. Economists and demographers in the most part agree that important ingredients of improved living standards, such as urbanization, industrialization and rising opportunities for non-agrarian employment, improved educational levels and better health, all lead to change parental perceptions of the costs and benefits of children, leading in turn to lower fertility (Karaman and Goldstein, 2010). In other words, there is no longer much debate about whether or not improved economic conditions, whether at the family level or the societal level, lead to lower fertility. There are, of course, important differences among countries, and even within countries, regarding the timing and the pace of these changes, but there is a causal relationship running from improved living standards to lower fertility (Karaman and Goldstein, 2010).

Mother education and socio-economic condition give a huge contribution to fertility and mortality rate of the children. So many factors are responsible behind it. Firstly, at the general level, it is useful to distinguish between the influences of the female education on desired family size, the relationship between planned numbers of births. Secondly, educated women are likely to be less dependent on their sons as sources of social status and old age security and this too may lead to the reduction in family size. Thirdly, in relationship between maternal education and children mortality, educated women are likely to be more knowledgeable about nutrition, hygienic and health of the children (Marthi et al. 1995).The relation between female educational levels with fertility has a crucial bearing change in the fertility and mortality rate. Indeed, female education plays a key role in the social development approach (Dreze, 2001). Previous studies have suggested that a large body of Indian and International evidences point to the role of rising female education in lowering fertility rate. A woman's level of education is essential to explain fertility movements. Higher educational attainment has been shown to be associated with more prenatal care. In total, higher female education is universally associated with lower and delayed fertility (Norville et al. 2003).

Considering the above available data and its significance, a demographic study was conducted among the Khasi Women of Siden village, Meghalaya. In the present study, an attempt was made to describe the differential fertility and mortality among the Khasi Women of Siden village.

Materials and Method

The present study was conducted in Saiden village, Re-Bhoi district of Meghalaya from 20th January to 8th February 2015. No statistical sampling technique was applied in the selection of individual and household for the present study. The entire demographic data were collected from 71 women through interview using structural schedules visiting house to house survey. Information on age, sex, marital status, occupation, place of birth, place of residence etc, was collected. The fertility and mortality schedules was completed by filing information on the numbers of conception, numbers of live births, birth orders, age, sex, marital status of each offspring, numbers of death children, cause of death, if any, reproductive wastage (abortion and still births)through in-depth interview with each of the married women. Special attention also made to collect data on socio-economic parameter like occupation, household income, household expenditure, educational attainment of household members especially married women, religious affiliation, age at marriage, awareness and adoption of the family planning method etc. Data pertaining to individual characteristics, fertility, mortality, household income, and educational status were collected from the studied population.

Individual Characteristics

It includes name of the informants, its relationship with the head of the household, tribes, religion, total numbers of family members, age, sex, marital status, place of birth and place of residence etc.

Fertility

Data on fertility includes the pregnancy history of each woman, present age of mothers, age at marriage, age at first child birth, total number of conception, total numbers of live births, birth order, sex and marital status of each offspring.

Mortality

Data on mortality includes number of dead children, sex, age at death, causes of death, number of reproductive wastage (still birth, spontaneous and induce abortion) etc. In the present study, we have divided morality into two groups, namely, infant mortality and juvenile mortality.

Household Income

Data on household income were collected directly from the head of the household or the women who interviewed. They were cross checked taking into considerations some aspects of socio-economic conditions like housing condition, type of occupation, land holding. Per capita income of household was classified into following three categories namely High income group (HIG) (>Rs.5674); Middle income group (MIG) (Rs.2500-5674) and Lower income group (LIG) (<Rs.2500).

Educational status

Data on educational attainment of individuals were classified into four categories, namely, secondary, higher secondary and graduate and above. The primary level of education includes those individuals who studied up to class V. In the secondary level of education, we included those individuals who attended standard VI to X. Higher secondary level of education included those who attended standard XI to XII. In the graduate and above level of education, we included those individuals who have completed graduation and those pursuing higher studies

Statistical analysis

All the parameters taken were analysed statistically to find out the mean and the standard error. In order to test the level of significance, *t*-test, Anova and chi-square test have been used. MS-Excel software was used for all statistical analyses of the present research.

Results

The mean and standard errors of the age at marriage and age at first child birth is mentioned in Table 11.1.It is found that the mean age at marriage was higher among males (28.15±0.79 years) than females (22.35±0.59 years). The differences were statistically significant (t=5.861; p<0.05). Similarly, the mean age at first child birth was also higher in males (29.56±0.78 years) than females (23.76 ±0.61 years).The t-test indicates that the difference between males and females with respect to age at first child was highly significant (t=5.84; p<0.05).

Table 11.1: Mean age at marriage and first child birth among males and females of the Saiden village

Sex	Numbers	Mean age of marriage ±SE	Mean age at first child birth ± SE
Male	71	28.15±0.79	29.56±0.78
Female	71	22.35±0.59	23.76±0.61

t=5.861; df=138; p<0.05 t= 5.845; df=138; p<0.05

Table 11.2 shows the completed family size among the Khasi females of the present study. For measuring complete family size, we have considered only those women who were 40 years and above. The mean of live birth children and surviving children to such mothers were 3.11± 0.19 and 2.44±0.20 respectively.

Table 11.2: Completed family size of the females of Saiden village

Number of women above 40 years	Number of live birth children	Number of surviving children	Mean live birth of children ±SE	Mean surviving children ±SE
32	119	89	3.11±0.19	2.44±0.20

Table 11.3: Number of live birth by age at marriage of the females of Saiden village

Age of marriage	No of mothers	No. of live births	Mean live birth ±SE
≤19	-	-	-
20-24	3	4	1.33± 1.27
>25	68	217	3.19± 0.14

$t=3.023$; $df=2$; $p>0.05$

The mean number of live births by age at marriage of females is given in Table 11.3. It was found that the mean number of live births was lower among females who married at the age between 20–24 years (1.33±1.27) than those who married above 25 years of age (3.19±0.14).

Table 11.4: Infant mortality, juvenile mortality and reproductive wastage

Parameters	*Frequency*
Numbers of mothers	71
Total no of pregnancies	258
No of live births	221
No of death before 1 year	5
No of deaths between1 to 14 years	2
Infant mortality rate %	2.26%
Juvenile mortality rate%	0.09%
Total no reproductive wastage	19
Reproductive wastage %	7.36%

The above table shows the frequency of infant mortality, juvenile mortality and reproductive wastage of the study population (Table 11.4). Out of 221 live births of the mother of all ages, five live births died before the age of 1 year and two live births died between 1 to14 years of age. The frequency of the infant and juvenile mortality rate was 2.26 percent and 0.09 percent respectively. It indicates that mortality rate especially infant mortality is little high than juvenile mortality in this population. The table further indicates that the rate of reproductive wastage out of total pregnancies was7.36 per cent.

Table 11.5: Age specific fertility rate among females of Saiden village

Age group of mothers	*Number of mothers*	*Numbers of live births*	*Age specific rate*
15-19	-	-	-
20-24	71	221	3.10
25-29	68	217	3.19
30-34	63	210	3.33
35-39	52	184	3.53
40-45	40	148	3.70
45+	26	103	3.96
Total fertility rate (TFR)			20.81

Table 11.6: Fertility rate by the income level of the family of Saiden village

Income	*No. of mothers*	*No. of live births*	*No. of surviving*	*Mean live birth± SE*	*Mean surviving ±SE*
Low	33	127	91	3.84±0.19	2.75± 0.21
Middle	20	62	55	3.10± 0.27	2.75± 0.27
High	18	32	28	1.78±0.37	1.55 ±0.35

(Live Birth: $F=6.067$; $p<0.05$; Surviving Birth: $F=2.073$; $p>0.05$)

The mean live birth 3.84±0.19 was found slightly higher in low income family followed by middle income family (3.1±0.27) and high income family (1.78±0.37). The differences in the mean live births in different income levels were statistic (Table 11.6).

Table 11.7: Infant mortality rate by income level of the family of the Saiden village

Income	*No of live birth*	*No of infant*	*Infant mortality*
Low income	127	3	2.36%
Middle income	62	2	3.23%
High income	32	---------	--------

$x^2=0.114$; df=1; $p>0.05$

Table 11.8: Infant mortality rate by educational level of mothers of the Saiden village

Education	*Number of live birth*	*Number of infants death*	*Infants morality %*
Primary	121	3	2.48%
Secondary	73	2	2.73%
Graduate+	27	---------	-----------

$X^2=0.011$; df=1; $p>0.05$

The frequency of infant mortality rate was slightly higher among the middle income family (3.23 percent) than low income group (2.36 percent).

low income group (2.36 percent) (Table 11.7). The infant mortality rate in relation to educational level of the mother of the present study is given in Table 11.8. The table shows that the infant mortality rate was more or less the same between the primary (2.48 percent) and secondary (2.73 percent) level of education of the mothers.

The mean age at marriage and mean age at first child birth in the present study is found to be significantly lower in females than males. The number of live birth is higher than the mean number of surviving children among women who have completed family size, i.e. mothers who married only once and live continuously in wedlock till attainment of the age 40 years. The present study shows that the mean numbers of live birth per mothers of all the age groups are found more or less the same. Similarly, the mean numbers of surviving children per mother of all the age groups are also found more the or less the same. The mean number of live birth is higher among women married at age of twenty five years and above. The infant mortality rate is higher than the juvenile mortality rate. The frequency of the reproductive wastage in the present study population is lower than that other study (Haloi, 2014). The fertility rate in the present population is moderately high. The probable reason could be due to the reproductive behaviour and reproductive decision, inadequate facilities of family planning in the village, lack of proper education about family planning method, etc. (Saikia,2005).

Demographic parameters such as fertility and mortality are reported to have associated with various biological and socio-economic factors. Socio-economic status of the family plays an important role in fertility and mortality rate of the population. The present study shows that fertility rate is higher among women belong to the low income family. It further indicates that the fertility rate tends to decrease with increasing the level of the income of the family. Similarly, the number of surviving children also decreases with increasing the level of income of the family. Several studies suggested that the economic conditions influence the fertility rate of an individual (Dey and Goswami, 2009).The economic conditions play a more important role on the determination of the fertility behaviour. The increasing participation of the females into the labour market, lead them to postpone childbearing, as they do not want to lose their gained power and skills by giving up their jobs to take care of their new born children. Women in the higher income group are more aware of all basic facilities like good education, health care, nutrition and so on. Further, the changing economic value and the rising cost of children in urban life and the desire of parents to promote better health and education for their children prompted fertility decline in developed countries, and this could be expected to soon reduce fertility in developing countries as well (Breierova and Duflo, 2002). Background characteristics of mothers, such as education also play an important role. In the present study we also observed that education of the mothers influence the fertility rate in the population. The present research indicated that the fertility rate tend to decreases with increasing the level of education of the mothers. A large body of Indian and International evidence points to the role of rising female education in lowering fertility rate. A better educated woman not withstanding her residence may experience different fertility to uneducated woman (Ushie et al. 2011). Educated women are aware and more knowledgeable about the desired family size, family planning, planned numbers of births etc. Educated and employed women are more likely to use contraception than those who have little education and who are not employed (Al-kandari, 2007). Further, educated women are likely to be less dependent on their sons as sources of social status and old age security and this too may lead to the reduction in family size.

Infant mortality is slightly higher in the middle income group than the lower income group. There is no case of infant mortality in the higher income group in the present research. The mortality rate shows more or less the same between the primary level of education and secondary level of education of the mothers. The present study further indicated that there is no case of infant mortality among the higher educated women. Educated women are likely to be more knowledgeable about nutrition, hygienic and health of the children (Marthi et al. 1995). The relation between female educations with fertility has a crucial bearing change in the fertility and mortality rate. Indeed, female education plays a key role in the social development approach (Dreze, 2001). However, education doesn't play an important role in infant mortality rate in the present research.

In conclusion, the present study among Khasi women of Saiden village highlights the fertility and mortality rates in relation with certain socio-economic conditions. The mean number of live birth and surviving children in all the age groups are found more or less the same. However, the number of live birth is higher than the mean number of surviving children among women who have completed family size. Family income plays an important role in determining the fertility and mortality rate. However, the education level of the mothers doesn't indicate much influenced on the fertility and mortality rate in the present studied Khasi female population.

References

Al kandari YY 2007. Fertility and its relationship with socio cultural factor in Kuwaiti society. *Eastern Mediterranean Health Journal*, 13(6):1364-1371.

Breierova L, Duflo E 2002. The impact of education on fertility and child mortality: Do father really matter less than mother? http://economics.mit.edu/files/738. (Accessed on 15 May 2015).

Census 2011. Meghalaya profile. http://www.census2011.co.in/census/state/meghalaya. html (Accessed on 15 May 2015).

Dey S, Goswami S 2009. Fertility pattern and its correlates in northeast India. *Journal of Human Ecology*, 26(2):145-152.

Dreze J 2001. Fertility, education development: evidence from India. *Population and Development Review*, 27(1):33-63.

Haloi A 2014. Fertility differentials of marriage and their reproductive wastage in a Muslim population of rural northeast India. *Human Biology Review*, 3(1):1-14.

Hartmann AM 2010. Fertility and economic growth. http://pure.au.dk/portal-asb-student/files/12445/Thesis_AM-Hartmann.pdf (Accessed on 20 May 2015)

Heuveline P 2003. Mortality and Fertility Interactions: New Insights from Recent Population Dynamics in Cambodia http://www.prgs.edu/content/dam/rand/www/external/labor/ seminars/adp/pdfs/adpheuveline.pdf (Accessed on 15 May 2015).

Kapoor AK, Kshatriya GK, Kopoor S 2003. Fertility and mortality differential among the population group of Himalayas. *Human Biology*, 75 (5):729-747.

Karaman DD, Goldstein JR 2010. The increasing importance of economic conditions on fertility. MPIDR working papers WP-2010-014, Max Plank, Institute for demographic research, Rostock, Germany.

Kullar DR 2012. India a comprehensive geography. New Delhi, Kalyani publishers.

Lapang EK 2010. Project work on the packages of the integrated child development scheme (ICDS) with special reference to Saiden Aganwandi centre-I-Ri-Bhoi district, Meghalaya (unpublished).

Marthi M, Guio AN, Dreze J 1995. Mortality, fertility and gender bias in India: A district level analysis. *Population and Development Review*, 21(4):745-782.

Norville C, Gomez R, Brown RL 2003. Some causes of fertility rates movements, IIPR Insurance and Pension Reports No.2003-02, Institute of Insurance and Pension Research, University of Waterloo.

Patil AV, Somasundaram KV, Goyal RC 2002. Current health scenario in rural India. *Australian Journal of Rural Health*, 10(2):129-135.

Reddy KSN, Sudha G 2010. Factors affecting fertility and mortality: A Case study among the Setti Balija community of Andhra Pradesh. *Anthropologist*, 12(4):271-275.

Saikia US 2005. High fertility in Khasi tribes of north east India-A repercussion of the fear of identity loss. http://iussp2005.princeton.edu/papers/51588 (Accessed on 12 May 2015)

Somola TD, Nabakumar W, Jibonkumar S 2006. Fertility study among the Ithing of Manipur, India. *The Internet Journal of Biological Anthropology*, 1(1).

Ushie MA, Ogaboh AAM, Olumodeji EO, Attah F 2011. Socio-cultural and economic determinants of fertility differentials in rural and urban Cross Rivers State, Nigeria. *Journal of Geography and Regional Planning*, 4(7):383–391.

WHO 2009. World Health Statistics. Geneva, World Health Organization.

12

Socio-Economic Factors Influences on Nutritional Status among the Khasi Women of Meghalaya

Yogesh Sharma

Nutritional anthropology is well established branch of anthropology which encompasses the disciplines of nutritional science and anthropology. This field is concerned with those anthropological phenomena which impinge upon the nutritional status of human beings. The scope of this discipline includes man's evolution, history and culture, and his adaptations to nutritional variables under various environmental conditions represent the focal materials in nutritional anthropology. Nutritional status of the people of a country is mainly influenced by the food they intake regularly. Taking improper amount of food results in malnutrition (that is overweight, obese or under weight) which ultimately affects physical well-being of people. Nutritional status of people is closely linked with dietary fat intake. It is considered as the intake of food in relation to the body dietary needs. Good nutrition with an adequate, well balanced diet combined with regular physical activity is a corner stone of good health. Poor nutrition can lead to reduced immunity, increased susceptibility to disease, impaired physical and mental development and reduced productivity (WHO, 2010). Intake of a diet sufficient to meet or exceed the needs of the individual will keep the composition and function of the individuals within the normal range. This equilibrium is disturbed by three processes, namely, decreased intake, increased requirements and altered utilization. When this disequilibrium occurs, then loss of body tissue ensues. The lacks of nutrients produce a series of metabolic change in relation to energy and protein metabolism within hours or day of reducing nutrients intake long before demonstrable anthropometric changes (Jeejeebhoy, 1987).

Rates of overweight continue to rise across all regions. The increasing problems of overweight and Obesity are occurring throughout the world effecting all ages. Health professionals around the world are concerned and trying to figure out why the problems of obesity are increasing (Stettler and Shelly, 2006). They argued that obesity contributes to a variety of ailments including heart disease, diabetes, sleep disorder, high blood pressure, breathing problems and even cancer (Stettler and Shelly, 2009). Overweight was once associated mainly with high income countries. But in 2011, 69 percent of the global burden of overweight children under five years old was in low and middle income countries.

Normal and healthy food are best for the human body. The main link between our eating habits and obesity is how much food we eat. Earlier, when people were farmers or hunter gatherers, they didn't have easy access to food and so people eat small portions and few meals a day. However, within creasing modernization, urbanization and rapid socioeconomic development, it becomes easier to get food, and people began eating more meals a day and bigger portions (UNICEF, 2013). Besides, we live very sedentary life styles. In other words, we don't get up and move enough. Technology and modern life have made things very easy for us. We have remote control for our televisions and our stereos, so we don't have to get up to change the channel. We can pop food into the microwave and go watch television while cooking dinner instead of standing in the kitchen for hours. We can drive or ride public transportation instead of walking to work, school or the shopping center. We sit in front of computer, televisions or video games all day. Such sorts of lifestyles led to the increasing problem of overweight and obesity and its consequences. Therefore, the present study has been undertaken among Khasi females of Saiden village, Meghalaya to find the nutritional status in relation with socioeconomic conditions, lifestyles and food habits.

Review of literature

Malnutrition is a major public health and economic problem of global significance. Prevalence rates of either obesity or underweight are increasing in all parts of the world, both in affluent western countries and in poor nations. Men, women and children in different age groups are affected with the problem of over nutrition and under nutrition. Indeed, overweight, obesity and health problems associated with them are now so common that they are replacing the more traditional public health concerns such as under nutrition and infectious disease as the most significant contributors to global ill health. In 1995, the excess adult mortality attributable to over nutrition was estimated to be about 1 million, double the 0.5 million attributable to under nutrition (Bjorntorp, 2001). The aetiology of malnutrition is multi-factorial. The rapid socioeconomic development, modernisation, increasing urbanisation, nutrition transition, motorised transportation and overall sedentary lifestyles are considered as important determinants of overweight and obesity worldwide.

Young women and mothers face many underlying challenges to meet their nutritional needs, which include poverty, lack of education on healthy diets, infant care, and access to diverse variety of affordable nutritious foods, health care, and sanitation. Gender inequality and restrictive cultural practices also results in unequal and/or insufficient access to adequate nutrition. Several studies indicated that women with a body mass index below normal show a progressive increase in mortality rates as well as increased risk of illness. Women of the reproductive age are amongst the most vulnerable to malnutrition (Grima and Genebo, 2002).

Women are generally vulnerable to under nutrition especially during pregnancy and lactation where the foods and nutrient requirements are more during that period. The demographic consequences of the lower status in women has expressed in various forms such as female infanticide, higher death rate for women compared to men, lower sex ratio, lower literacy rate in female, lower level of employment of women in the non-agricultural sector as compared to men. Most Indian mothers are nutritional anaemic and have short pregnancy interval which could have been easily prevented. Several studies underscore the relationship between maternal nutrition and incidence of low birth weight. Generally, at household level, cultural norms and practices and socio-economic factors determines the extent of nutritional status (Rao, 2010).

The high fertility of Indian women is one of the most detrimental socio-cultural influences on nutritional status. Because the metabolic stresses of pregnancy and lactation may not be adequately compensated by dietary intake before, during or even after these physiological processes. During pregnancy, women access to foods is even more restricted in the traditional Indian house-hold through taboos and ritual observances, which are widely documented in both rural and tribal populations. Maternal education had a significant influence on nutritional status. Several studies indicated that malnutrition is a serious health concerns that Indian women face. It threatens their survival as well as that of their children. The negative effects of malnutrition among women are compounded by heavy work demands, by poverty, by child bearing and rearing and by special nutritional needs of women, resulting in increased susceptibility to illness and consequently higher morbidity. A recent study indicated that the impact of nutritional status of mother is more pervasive than the impact of other factors on birth weight. The dietary intake of rural pregnant women was lower than the recommended level (Rao, 2010).

Study in Ethiopia shows the relationship between nutritional status of women and children with economic status, education level, occupation etc. (Garima and Genebo, 2002). Household economic status is one of the most important determinants of child and women nutritional status. The economic status of households is an indicator of access to adequate food supplies, use of health services, availability of improved water source and sanitation facilities, which are prime determinants of child and maternal nutritional status. A study of DHS survey conducted in developing countries shows that women from low economic status households were most affected by malnutrition (Grima and Genebo, 2002). Another study in the Southern Nations, Nationalities and People Region (SNNPR) of Ethiopia show that women from low economic households were most affected by malnutrition (Grima and Genebo, 2002). According to them, educational status of women is also one of the factors of malnutrition. Women who received even a minimum education are generally more aware than those who have no education of how to utilize available resources for the improvement of their own nutritional status and that of their own families. Education may enable women to make independent decisions, to be accepted by other household member and to have greater access to household resources that are important to nutritional status. This study shows that the higher level of education, lower proportion of undernourished women in Ethiopia (Grima and Genebo, 2002). Education is one of the most important resources that enable women to provide appropriate call for their children growth and development. Studies in the Philippines, Libya, Uganda and Ethiopia show a decreased incidence of malnutrition among young children with increase in the level of mother's education (Grima and Genebo, 2002).

In many cases, family dietary patterns can be partially attributed to genetic and hereditary factors. Dietary patterns become established in children from about age 1-2 onwards and to a great extent persist throughout life. The diets of younger children tend to be more similar to that of their parents than the diets of older children. It is thus important to try to ensure that children's diets are as varied as possible from an early age. A diet comprising many different nutrients as well as a many different flavours, textures, and colours will not only ensure adequate nutrition and development but will also encourage acquisition of the capacity to make appropriate choices between food items. Such "diet training" is particularly critical for children at the pre-school stage because this is the period during which the child learns to exercise control over his or her impulses and environment. Adolescence is a time when food habit are finalized, laying the foundation for adult nutritional status. Nutritional problems among American women are reflected in high rates of overweight and obesity as well as eating disorder which can lead to underweight. An adequate family diet is good for the child's health and provides a solid foundation for the future, when the child will gradually come to spend more time away from home, at school and elsewhere (Juan, 2006).

Materials and Methods

Period and duration of study

The present study was conducted in Saiden village, Re-Bhoi district of Meghalaya from 20th January to 8th February 2015. Saiden village lies between 26pNorth latitude and 89p East latitude half way between Guwahati and Shillong in the national highway number 40 (NH-40). Saiden derived its name from a water body Umpyrli running parallel to the Guwahati-Shillong national highway. According to the oral history, the name Saiden came from the words *Sai* and *den* which means a thread like rock. This rock is at *Thwei Saiden* near old Saiden (*Nongrim Saiden*), south of the present Saiden village. No statistical sampling technique was applied in the selection of individual and household for the present study. Data from 200 females were collected from the village by survey of house to house visit. A brief household census based on the data gathers during the study work is given in the table below:

Brief census of the village

Total house	*Pakka house*	*Kaccha house*	*Total population*	*No. of male*	*No. of female*	*Nuclear family*	*Joint family*	*Extended family*
201	191	10	1142	561	581	149	49	3
Religion								
Christian	Traditional		Other					
190	5		6					
Education								
Primary	Secondary	High secondary		Graduate		PG	MPhil	No data
254	405	170		127		30	5	150
Occupation								
Farmer	Private	Govt. Job	Student	House wife		Retired	Jobless	
153	152	140	501	130		25	40	

Anthropometric data

Cross-sectional data on 200 Khasi females aged between 6 and 75 years was collected for the present study. The data was collected through random sampling method following a survey of house to house visit. The subjects were divided as a children (6-13 years), adolescents (14-19years) and adults (20+ years). An anthropometric rod and a weighing scale to the nearest of 0.1 cm and 0.5 kg respectively was used to measure height and weight with subjects wearing light clothes following the standard technique of Lohman et al. (1998).

Data on socio-economic conditions

Data on household income were collected directly from the subjects or the head of the households. The incomes were cross-checked against certain aspects of socio-economic conditions like housing condition, types of occupation, land holding and monthly expenditure. The per capita monthly income of the households was classified as follows - High income group (HIG) (>Rs. 5000); Middle income group (MIG) (Rs. 2100-5000); Low income group (LIG) (<Rs. 21000). Data on educational attainment of individuals were classified into four categories, namely, primary, secondary, higher secondary and graduate and above. The primary level of education includes those

individuals who studied up to class V. In the secondary level of education, we included those individuals who attended standard VI to X. Higher secondary level of education included those who attended standard XI to XII. In the graduate and above level of education, we included those individuals who have completed graduation and those pursuing higher studies.

Data on occupation of each subject were classified into five categories such as government employee, private, student and housewife. Data on age and marital status were also collected for the present study.

Data on physical activity, television time and food habits

Information on physical activity/exercise, television watching and food habits were collected from each subject following a recalled method of one week periods. The data on television time were divided into three categories: less than or equal to two hours, between three to four hours and five hours and above. Data on moderate physical activity was classified into three groups, viz less than or equal to one hour, between two to three hours and four hours and above. Data on food habits, especially non-vegetables intake were divided into one-two times a week, three-four times a week and five times and above.

Statistical Analysis

The data were analyzed using MS-Excel software for the present research. The parameters taken were analyzed statistically to find out the mean, standard deviation for the anthropometric measurements. Prevalence of overweight/obesity has been evaluated using Asian cut-off points (WHO 2000). According to Asian cut-off points, BMI $\geq$27.5kg/m^2 has been considered as obese, BMI between 23.5-27.4 kg/m^2, considered as overweight, BMI between 18.5-23.4kg/m^2 indicates normal and BMI below 18.5kg/m^2 considered as underweight. Prevalence of overweight/obesity was calculated in relation to different socio-economic conditions, physical activity, television time and food habits. In order to test the level of significance, both t-test and chi square have been used in the present study. Women who are pregnant at the time of the survey or women who had given birth during the two months preceding the survey were excluded from the analysis.

Results

Table 12.1 shows basic data on mean height, weight and BMI with standard deviation of Khasi females of Saiden village. The table shows that mean height (150.68±4.45) was found higher among adults. The mean height (147.57±6.68) and mean height (129.28±12.36) were found among adolescents and children respectively. The differences were statistically significant ($F=130.24$; $p<0.05$). Similarly, the mean weight (49.29±8.13) was found higher among adult females. The mean weight (42.56±5.05) and mean weight (27.57±9.71) were found among adolescents and children respectively. The differences in the mean weight were significant at F=112.34; p<0.05. The same result was also found for BMI. The mean BMI values 21.71±3.49, 19.49±1.64 and 16.05±2.981.76 were found among adults, adolescents and children respectively. The distributions of mean BMI in different age groups were statistically significant (F=52.10; p<0.05).

Table 12.1: Basic data on mean height, weight and BMI among children, adolescents and adult females

Age group	*Number*	*Mean height(cm)± SD*	*Mean weight(kg)±SD*	*Mean BMI±SD*
6-13	43	129.28±12.36	27.57±9.71	16.05±2.98
14-19	44	147.57±6.68	42.56±5.05	19.49±1.64
20+	113	150.68±4.45	49.29±8.13	21.71±3.49
F (p-value)		F=130.24; p<0.05	F=112.34; p<0.05	F=52.10; p<0.05

The table 12.2 shows the nutritional status among children, adolescents and adult Khasi females of Saiden village. The table shows that the frequency of overweight/obese (30.09 percent) was higher among the adult females. This was followed by the frequency of overweight/obesity among children (2.32 percent). However, the frequency of underweight (90.69 percent) was higher among children. The frequency of underweight 29.54 percent and 15.04 percent was found among adolescents and adults respectively. The differences in the distributions of different BMI values in different age groups were statistically significant (x^2=96.47; df=4; p<0.05).

Table 12.2: Distribution of different BMI values among children, adolescents and adult females

Age group	*Number*	*Under weight*	*Normal*	*Over weight/ Obese*	χ^2 *(p-value)*
6-13	43	39(90.69%)	3(6.67%)	1(2.32%)	96.47 (p<0.05)
14-19	44	13(29.54%)	31(70.54%)	0(0.00%)	
20+	113	17(15.04%)	62(54.87%)	34(30.09%)	

The distribution of BMI values in relation to economic condition of the family in different age groups are given in table 12.3. The table indicated that the frequency of overweight/obesity (9.09 percent) among children was higher in higher income family. Again, the frequency of underweight 95.83 percent, 100 percent and 72.72 percent were found among children in lower income, middle income and higher income family respectively. Among adolescents, the prevalence of underweight was higher among middle income group (50.00 percent) followed by lower income group (33.33 percent). Among the adult females, the frequency of overweight/obesity (55.55 percent) was found higher in high income group. The frequency of overweight/obesity 23.07 percent and 21.27 percent was found among the middle income group and low income group respectively. The frequencies of underweight 20.51 percent,

12.76 percent and 11.11 percent were found in the middle income group, lower income group and higher income group respectively.

Overall distribution of BMI values in relation with income among Khasi females is given in table 12.4. The higher frequency of overweight/obesity (34.04 percent) was found among higher income group. This was followed by frequency of overweight/obesity among middle income group (16.36 percent) and lower income group (10.20 percent). The frequencies of underweight 38.22 percent, 36.36 percent and 23.40 percent were found among lower income group, middle income group and high income group respectively. The differences in the distribution of BMI values in relation with income were statistically significant (χ^2=12.85; df=4; p<0.05).

Table 12.3: Distribution of BMI values in relation with income group among children, adolescents and adult females

Age group	Income group	Number	Underweight [p.c/in bkt]	Normal [p.c/in bkt]	Overweight/ Obese [p.c/in bkt]
6-13	Lower income	24	23(95.83.)	1(4.16)	0(0.00)
	Middle income	8	8(100.00)	0(0.00)	0(0.00)
	High income	11	8(72.72)	1(18.18)	1(9.09)
14-19	Lower income	27	9(33.33)	18(66.66)	0(0.00)
	Middle income	8	4(50.00)	4(50.00)	0(0.00)
	High income	9	0(0.00)	9(100.00)	0(0.00)
20+	Lower income	47	6(12.76)	31(65.97)	10(21.27)
	Middle income	39	8(20.51)	22(56.41)	9(23.07)
	High income	27	3(11.11)	9(33.33)	15(55.55)

Table 12.4: Overall distribution of different BMI values in relation with income group among females

Income group	*Number*	*Underweight*	*Normal*	*Overweight/Obese*	*χ^2 (p-value)*
Lower income	98	38(38.22%)	50(51.02%)	10(10.20%)	
Middle income	55	20(36.36%)	26(42.27%)	9(16.36%)	12.85 (p <0.05)
High income	47	11(23.40%)	20(42.55%)	16(34.04%)	

Distributions of different BMI values in relation to educational levels in different age groups are given in table 12.5. Among children, the frequency of overweight/obesity (9.09 percent) was found higher among those who attained secondary education. The frequencies of underweight 63.63 percent and 100 percent were found in primary education and secondary education respectively. Among adolescents, the frequency of underweight 100 percent, 31.25 percent and 18.18 percent was found among the primary education, secondary education and higher secondary level of education respectively. In case of adults, the frequency of overweight/obesity (40.54 percent) was found higher among the secondary level of education. The frequencies of overweight/obesity 28.12 percent, 23.80 percent and 21.73 percent were found among adult females who attained graduate and above level of education, high secondary education and primary education respectively. The frequency of underweight was found higher among the primary level of education (21.73 percent). This was followed by secondary education (19.04 percent), higher secondary (13.51 percent) and graduate and above level of education (9.37 percent).

The overall distributions of overweight/obese and underweight in relation with educational levels among Khasi females of Saiden village are given in table 12.6. The table shows that the frequency of overweight/obesity (28.12 percent) was found higher among females who attained graduate and above level of education. Whereas, the frequency of overweight/obesity 8.92 percent, 20.00 percent and 15.62 percent was found among primary, secondary and higher secondary level of education. However, the frequency of underweight (67.85 percent) was found relatively higher among primary level of education than the graduate and above level of education (9.37 percent). The frequency of underweight 18.75 percent and 27.50 percent was found among higher secondary and higher secondary education respectively. The differences were statistically significant (└ ^{2}=43.09; df=4; p<0.05).

Table 12.5: Distribution of BMI values in relation with education levels among children, adolescents and adult females

Age group	*Education*	*Number*	*Underweight*	*Normal*	*Overweight/ Obese*
6-13	Primary	32	32(100p.c)	0(0.00p.c)	0(0.00p.c)
	Secondary	11	7(63.63p.c)	3(27.22p.c)	1(9.09p.c)
14-19	Primary	1	1(100p.c)	(0.00p.c)	0(0.00p.c)
	Secondary	32	10(31.25p.c)	22(68.75p.c)	0(0.00p.c)
	Higher Secondary	11	2(18.18p.c)	9(81.81p.c)	0(0.00p.c)
20+	Primary	23	5(21.73 p.c)	13(56.52p.c)	5(21.73p.c)
	Secondary	37	5(13.51 p.c)	17(45.94p.c)	15(40.54p.c)
	Higher Secondary	21	4(19.04p.c)	12(57.54p.c)	5(23.80p.c)
	Graduate+	32	3(9.37p.c)	20(62.5p.c)	9(28.12p.c)

The distribution of BMI values in relation to marital status among adult Khasi females of Saiden village are given in table 12.7. The table shows that the frequency of overweight/obese (39.02 percent) was higher among married females than the unmarried (7.14 percent). The frequency of underweight (17.85 percent) was higher among unmarried than married (4.63 percent). The differences in the distribution of different BMI values in relation with marital status among adult females were statistically significant (└ 2=9.99; df=4; p<0.05).

Table 12.6: Overall distribution of BMI values in relation with educational levels among females

Education	*Number*	*Under weight*	*Normal*	*Overweight/ Obese*	χ^2 *(p-value)*
Primary	56	38(67.85 p.c)	13(23.21p.c)	5(8.92 p.c)	43.09 (<0.05)
Secondary	80	22(27.50p.c)	42(52.50p.c)	16(20.00p.c)	
Higher Secondary	32	6(18.7 p.c)	21(65.62 p.c)	5(15.62 p.c)	
Graduate+	32	3(9.37 p.c)	20(62.50p.c)	9(28.12 p.c)	

Table 12.7: Distribution of BMI values in relation with marital status among adult females

Age group	*Number*		*Underweight*	*Normal*	*Overweight/ Obese*	χ^2 *(p-value)*
20+	Unmarried	28	5(17.85p.c)	21(75.00p.c)	2(7.14p.c)	9.99 (p<0.05)
	Married	82	12(4.63p.c)	38(46.34p.c)	32(39.02p.c)	
	Separated	3	0(0.00p.c)	3(100p.c)	0(0.00p.c)	

Table 12.8 shows the overall distribution of BMI values in relation with occupation among adult females. The frequency of overweight/obesity was found higher among the government employee (50.00 percent) followed by housewife (30.61 percent), private employee (12.50 percent) and students (2.83 percent). The frequency of underweight (49.54 percent) was observed higher among those who are still students as compare to government employee (8.82 percent) and house wife (24.50 percent).

Table 12.8: Overall distribution of BMI values in relation with occupation among adult females

Occupation	*Number*	*Underweight*	*Normal*	*Overweight/obese*	χ^2 *(p-value)*
Student	109	54(49.54p.c)	53(48.62p.c)	2(1.83p.c)	6.616 (p>0.05)
Govt. Employee	34	3(8.82p.c)	14(41.17p.c)	17(50.00p.c)	
House wife	49	12(24.48p.c)	22(44.89p.c)	15(30.61p.c)	
Private	8	0(0.00p.c)	7(87.5p.c)	1(12.50p.c)	

The frequency of overweight/obesity and underweight in relation with television watching is given in table 12.9. This table shows that the frequency of overweight/obesity 7.14 percent was found higher among children who spent between three to four hours on television watching. The frequency of underweight 89.65 percent and 92.86 percent was found among children who watched television below two hours and between three to four hours respectively. The underweight frequencies 26.82 percent and 66.67 percent were found among adolescents who watched television two hours and below and between three to four hours respectively. In case of adults, the frequency of overweight/obesity (30.64 percent) was reported higher among those who spent two hours and below on watching television. The frequency of underweight 15.04 percent was also reported among adults watching television two hours and below.

Overall distribution (table 12.10) shows that the frequency of overweight (18.57 percent) was higher among those who spent two hours and below on television watching than between three to four hours television watching (5.88 percent). The frequency of underweight among females who spent three to four hours on television watching was 88.24 percent whereas it was 29.50 percent among those who spent between two hours and below on watching television.

Table 12.9: Distribution of BMI values in relation with television watching among children, adolescents and adult females

Age group	*Television time per day*	*Number*	*Underweight*	*Normal*	*Overweight/ Obese*
6-13	≤2hrs.	29	26(89.65p.c)	3(10.34p.c)	0(0.00p.c)
	3-4hrs.	14	13(92.86p.c)	0(0.00p.c)	1(7.14p.c)
14-19	≤2hrs.	41	11(26.82p.c)	30(73.17p.c)	0(0.00p.c)
	3-4hrs.	3	2(66.67p.c)	1(33.33p.c)	0(0.00p.c)
20+	≤2hrs.	113	17(15.04p.c)	62(54.86p.c)	34(30.64p.c)
	3-4hrs.	0	0(0.00p.c)	(0.00p.c)	0(0.00p.c)

Table 12.10: Overall distribution of BMI values in relation with television watching among females

Television time per /day	*Number*	*Underweight*	*Normal*	*Overweight/ Obese*	χ^2 *(p-value)*
≤2hrs.	183	54(29.50p.c)	95(51.91p.c)	34(18.57p.c)	31.63 ($p<0.05$)
3-4hrs.	17	15(88.24p.c)	1(5.88 p.c)	1(5.88p.c)	

The distribution of different BMI values in relation with physical activity among children, adolescents and adult Khasi females of Saiden village is shown table 12.11. This table shows that the frequency of overweight/obesity (12.50 percent) was higher among children who exercised one hour and below in a week. The frequency of underweight (100 percent) was found among children who exercised four hours and above. Underweight 90.47 percent and 75.00 percent was found among children who exercised between two to three hours and one hour respectively. Among adolescents, the higher frequency of underweight (33.33 percent) was found among those who exercised one hour and below. The frequency of underweight 28.57percentand20.00 percent was reported among those who exercised between two to three and over four hours respectively. In adult females, the frequency of overweight/obesity (32.07 percent) and underweight (15.09 percent) was found only among those who exercised for one hour and below.

Table 12.11: Distribution of different BMI values in relation with physical activity among children, adolescents and adult females

Age group	*Physical activity per/week*	*Number*	*Underweight*	*Normal*	*Overweight/ Obese*
6-13	≤1hr.	8	6(75.00p.c)	1(12.50p.c)	1(12.50p.c)
	2-3hrs.	21	19(90.47p.c)	2(9.53p.c)	0(0.00p.c)
	≥ 4hrs.	14	14(100p.c)	0(0.00p.c)	0(0.00p.c)
14-19	≤1hr.	18	6(33.33p.c)	12(66.67p.c)	0(0.00p.c)
	2-3hrs.	21	6(28.57p.c)	15(71.43p.c)	0(0.00p.c)
	≥4hrs.	5	1(20.00p.c)	4(80.00p.c)	0(0.00p.c)
20+	≤1hr.	106	16(15.09p.c)	52(52.83p.c)	34(32.07p.c)
	2-3hrs.	7	1(14.26p.c)	6(85.74p.c)	0(0.00p.c)
	≥4hrs.	0	0(0.00p.c)	0(0.00p.c)	0(0.00p.c)

Table 12.12: Overall distribution of different BMI values in relation with physical activity among females

Physical activity per week	*Number*	*Underweight*	*Normal*	*Overweight/Obese*	*χ^2 (p-value)*
≤1hr.	132	28(21.21p.c)	69(52.27p.c)	35(26.51p.c)	19.37 (p<0.05)
2-3hrs.	49	26(53.06p.c)	23(46.94p.c)	0(0.00p.c)	
≥4hrs.	19	15(78.94p.c)	4(21.05p.c)	0(0.00p.c)	

Table 12.13: Distribution of BMI values in relation with intake of non-vegetables among children, adolescents and adult females

Age group	*Non-vegetables*	*Number*	*Underweight*	*Normal*	*Overweight/ Obese*
6-13	1-2 times	10	100(100p.c)	0(0.00p.c)	0(0.00p.c)
	3-4 times	25	23(92.00p.c)	1(4.00p.c)	1(4.00p.c)
	5+ times	8	6(75.00p.c)	2(25.00p.c)	0(0.00p.c)
14-19	1-2 times	15	9(60.00p.c)	6(40.00p.c)	0(0.00p.c)
	3-4 times	23	4(17.39p.c)	19(82.60p.c)	0(0.00p.c)
	5+ times	6	0(0.00p.c)	6(100p.c)	0(0.00p.c)
20+	1-2 times	30	7(23.33p.c)	15(50p.c)	8(26.66p.c)
	3-4 times	48	6(12.50p.c)	29(60.41p.c)	13(27.08 p.c)
	5+ times	35	4(11.42p.c)	18(51.42p.c)	13(37.14p.c)

Overall overweight/obesity frequency (26.51 percent) was found higher among females who exercised for one hour and below (Table 12.12). The frequency of underweight among females who exercised for four hours and above was 78.94 percent. This was higher than those who exercised between two to three hours (53.06 percent) and one hour and below (21.21 percent).

The relationship between the intake of non-vegetable food and nutritional status among Khasi females of Saiden village is given in table 12.13. The table shows that the prevalence of overweight/obesity (4.00 percent) was found among children who eat non-vegetables three to four times a week. The frequencies of underweight 100 percent, 92.00 percent and 75.00 percent were reported among children who eat non-vegetables between one to two times, three to four times and over five times respectively. Again, among the adolescents, the frequency of underweight (60.00 percent) was found higher among those who eat non-vegetables one to two times than three to four times (17.39 percent). Among adult females who take non-vegetables more than five times, the frequency of overweight/obesity was 37.14 percent. Whereas, those who eat non-vegetables one to two times a week, the frequency of overweight/obesity was 26.66 percent and among three to four times group, the frequency of overweight/obesity was 27.083 percent. The frequencies of underweight 23.33 percent, 12.50 percent and 11.42 percent were found among adult females who eat non-vegetables between one to two times, between three to four times and over five times respectively.

Table 12.14: Overall distribution of different BMI values in relation with food intake of non-vegetables among females

Non-vegetables per week	*Number*	*Underweight*	*Normal*	*Overweight/ Obese*	χ^2 *(p-value)*
1-2 times	55	26(47.27p.c)	21(38.18p.c)	8(14.54p.c)	31.63 ($p<0.05$)
3-4 times	96	33(34.37p.c)	49(51.04p.c)	14(14.58p.c)	
5+ times	49	10(20.40p.c)	26(53.06p.c)	13(26.53p.c)	

Overall study on nutritional status in relation with the intake of non-vegetables shows that the higher frequency of overweight/obesity (26.53 percent) was found among females who eat non-vegetables over five times a week (Table 12.14). The frequency of overweight/obese (14.58 percent) and overweight/obese (14.54 percent) was found more or less the same among females who eat non-vegetables between three to four times and between one to two times. The frequencies of underweight 47.27 percent, 34.37 percent and 20.40 percent were reported among women who eat non-vegetables between one to two times, three to four times and over five times respectively.

Discussion

The Khasi society is matrilineal, and women play a major role in the work force in this tribal community. The health and nutrition of the entire family rests on their shoulders as tribal women make all decisions related to family nutrition. For this purpose, it is essential to know about the existing food habits, beliefs, and trends that contribute to the nutrition and health of these women. The present research provides the socio economic factors influences on nutritional status among the Khasi women of Saiden village, Ri-Bhoi district of Meghalaya. The distribution of underweight and overweight in relation to different socio-economic conditions, lifestyles and food habits are discussed in the present study. The mean height, weight and mean BMI values are found higher among the adult females. Further, it was observed that the mean height, weight and BMI increase with increasing age groups. The differences in the distributions of these values in the different age groups are highly significant. The study further indicates that the adult females show the higher frequency of overweight/obese. However, the prevalence of underweight is significantly higher among the children.

The prevalence of overweight/obesity is positively associated with high income among children and adult females in the present study. The frequency of underweight shows fluctuation among children, adolescents and adults in the different income groups. However, the overall prevalence of overweight/obesity shows significantly higher among the higher income family. The study further indicates that the frequency of overweight/obesity tends to increase with increasing the level of income. Whereas, the overall frequency of underweight increases with decreasing the level of income groups. Higher income family can afford and get easy access to food, better lifestyles and better health facilities as compared to the lower income family.

The frequency of underweight is found higher in the primary level of education among children, adolescents and adult females. However, the frequency of overweight/obesity shows fluctuation among the adult females. The overall frequency of overweight/obesity found significantly higher among the higher educated females. The frequency of underweight is recorded higher among the primary level of education. The prevalence of tends to underweight decrease with increasing the levels of education of the females. The higher educated people spent more of their time on reading, writing, and in front of computer, that is more of sedentary lifestyles.

Marital status of women in association with household and other socioeconomic status affects their nutritional status (Grima and Genebo 2002). Married women show higher frequency of overweight and lower frequency of underweight than the unmarried women. The overall distribution of overweight/obesity is higher among the government employees and housewife in the present studies. A study by Ulijaszek and Lofink (2008) shows that people who work in the farm had low BMI values as compared to those who work anywhere.

The distribution of different BMI values in relation with television time shows fluctuation among children, adolescents and adult Khasi females of Saiden village. The prevalence of both underweight and overweight/obesity is found higher among children who spent more time on watching television. The frequency of underweight is higher among the adolescents who spent more time on television. However, among adult females, the prevalence of both overweight and underweight is recorded higher in those who spent fewer hours on television. The overall distribution further reported that the higher frequency of overweight is found among Khasi females who spend fewer hours on television. The overall prevalence of underweight is found among women spending more hours on television.

Physical activity plays an important role in maintaining the nutritional status. The present research found that the higher frequency of overweight/obesity is inversely associated with physical activity among children and adult females. However, the frequency of underweight shows fluctuation among children, adolescents and adult females. But, the overall result indicated that the frequency of overweight/obesity is significantly higher among females who spend less hours in exercised. The overall frequency of underweight tends to increase with increasing times in physical activities, which means less physical activity is associated with overweight or obese. Inactive physical activity means there is no movement of body and more fat is accumulated resulting overweight/obese. If a person is doing more physical activity means body burn more calories which result in less chance of being overweight/obese.

Most of the families in the study population are non-vegetarian. The more frequent consumption of non-vegetables is positively associated with increasing prevalence of overweight/obesity among children and adult females. The frequency of underweight shows higher among children, adolescents and adult females who eat non-vegetables fewer times a week. Further, the present study among females of Saiden village indicated that the overall prevalence of overweight/obesity is positively associated with the consumption of non-vegetables. Whereas, the overall frequency of underweight increases with reducing the consumption of non-vegetables per week. Therefore, the study indicates that those who consume more non-vegetable foods are associated with overweight/obese and those who consume less non-vegetable foods.

Conclusion

The present study highlights the nutritional status of Khasi females of Saiden village, Ri-Bhoi district of Meghalaya. Study shows the distribution of different BMI values among children, adolescents and adult females in relation with different socio-economic conditions, certain lifestyles and food habits, particularly the consumption of non-vegetable foods. The prevalence of overweight/obesity among Khasi females of Saiden village is influenced by certain socioeconomic factors like family income, occupation and inactive physical activities. Food habits specially the consumption of non-vegetable foods also plays an important role determining the nutritional status in the present research.

References

Bjorntorp P 2001. Do stress reactions cause abdominal obesity and co-morbidities? *Obesity Review,* 2(2):73-86.

Census 2011. Meghalaya profile. http://www.census2011.co.in/census/state/meghalaya.html (accessed on 15 May 2015).

Dikshit R, Dikshit K, Jutta K 2014. North East India: Land, People and Economy. New York, Springer.

Engel J 2007. Neurologic consequence of malnutrition. New York, Demos Medical publishing.

Fidanza F 1991. Nutritional status assessment: A Manual For Population Studies. London, Springer.

Grima W, Genebo T 2002. Determinants of nutritional status of women and children in Ethiopia. Calverton, Ogc Macro.

Jeejeebhoy KN 1987. Assessment of nutritional status. *Journal of Parenteral and Enteral Nutrition,* 11(1): 8-1.

Juan PMFS 2006. Dietary habits and nutritional status of school aged children in Spain. *Nutricion Hospitalaria*, 21(3): 374-378.

Lapang EK 2010. Project work on the packages of the integrated child development scheme (ICDS) with special reference to Saiden Aganwandi centre-I-Ri-Bhoi district, Meghalaya (unpublished).

Rao S 2001. Nutritional status of the Indian population. *Journal of Biosciences*, 26(4):481-489.

Stettler N, Shelly S 2009. *Living With Obesity*. New York, Facts on File Inc.

Ulijaszek JS, Lofink H 2006. Obesity in bio-cultural perspective. *International Migration Review.* 35:337-360.

Unicef 2103. Improving Child Nutrition: The achievable imperative for global progress, United

WHO 2000. International association for the study and International obesity task force, the Asian Pacific perspective: Redefining obesity and its treatment. Geneva, World Health Organization.

WHO 2010. Country profile indicators interpretations guide. Geneva, World Health Organization.

WHO 2012. Supplementary food of moderate acute malnutrition in infant and children 6-59 months of age. Geneva, World Health Organization.

13

Strategies for Contraception, Bodily Effects, and Speculations Related to Contraceptive Methods: A case Study of the Tangkhuls

Singtitla Vashum, Soibam Jibonkumar Singh

The value of children outweighs the life of a mother till recently in many societies. It is evident from the way the people of the society treated the barren woman and the fertile woman. Numerous women had died during child birth and the cause of their dead being injury from too many child births. The desire for children to sustain and prosper the family line, security for inheritance and as power in the society made the wife bear as much children as she can conceive. There is no health care at any stage of gestation and lactation period. Most of the women go to the paddy field after a week of child birth, in some case when the woman give birth during agricultural season especially planting season and harvest season the women go for work after three days. There is no child spacing plan. They do not care whether the mother's health is fit to conceive and give birth to a child or not. For this reason there are many spontaneous abortions. The application of contraception comes at this point of time. If the married women did not give birth to a child the women is always blamed without scientific diagnosis of the cause whether it is of the husband infertility or her infertility. The concept of contraception can be traced back to the primitive simple society. No doubt the discoveries of the methods are trial and error method mostly accidental. The knowledge is passed down orally through generations. Women in general would use various contraceptive methods available around her settings to prevent pregnancy. Contraception is used not only to control population explosion but it is used for various reasons such as pregnancy complexity, mother's critical health condition, and socio-economic conditions.

The people under study

Tangkhuls are one of the major Naga tribe inhabited mostly in the north eastern region of Manipur and spread through the Somra tract in Myanmar. Many Tangkhuls have settled at the foothills and in Imphal valley recently. Except valley dwellers, they built their abode on hill top for defense purpose because of frequent inter-village war. They are one of the oldest inhabitants of Manipur.

The Tangkhuls are agriculturist and have subsistence economy. They make handicrafts like weaving, basket making in their leisure time for their own use. Hunting and fishing is an occasional entertainment.

Every village has their own dialect which is different from others. The village is governed by the village chief with his council members. They give judgment in all issues by customary law.

Materials and Methods

The present paper is the result of studies carried out in eight villages of Tangkhuls in Manipur. The information data is primary and are collected through one to one interview with 515 married women within the reproductive age group of 15-55 years. An interview schedule with both open and close ends is used to collect the actual information.

Results and Discussions

The Tangkhuls used various contraceptive methods of both natural and pharmaceutical for different reasons but for one goal that is to prevent pregnancy or keep from giving birth to a child. The common natural contraceptive methods like rhythm, abstinence, and corpus-interruptus are used age old method and are still the most popular method used. Advancement in medical science and technology has invented different devices such as Copper-T, contraceptive pills, injection contraceptive, vasectomy, tubectomy, D&C, etc. and now easily accessible.

The promotion of family planning policy with common slogan "A small family happy family" has taken a rapid pace even in rural areas. The degree of contraceptive usage differs according to the accessibility of healthcare centre and facilities. The traditional methods are mostly used for induced abortion.

Table 13.1: Family size planning

Plan	*Frequency*	*Percent*
NA	1	0.2
Yes	230	44.7
No	284	55.1
Total	515	100.0

Married couples hardly plan family size before they started their family. About 44.7 percent couples plan family size before they started having children. Whereas 55.1 percent do not plan together how many children they would like to have. While inquiring as to why the subjects does not plan before having children they responded that most of them did not think about planning, others said they do not know how many children they are going to bear unless they have the sizable number of children they wanted, while others said children are a gift of God and human being should not put limitations to the child birth meaning it is sin to limit God's gift by human. About 76.1 percent are aware of family planning and the rest do not know anything about it.

Table 13.2: Device Known

No. of device known	*Frequency*	*Percent*
Zero	90	17.5
One	55	10.7
Two	61	11.8
Three	54	10.5
Four-six	227	44.1
More than six	28	5.4
Total	515	100.0

About 10.7 percent knows at least one contraceptive method. Around 44.1 percent knows four to six contraceptive methods and 5.4 percent informants know more than six contraceptive methods which is the highest number yet only 26 percent used the methods. 17.5 percent does not know any contraceptive methods. In educational qualification wise 44.39 percent woman who had completed secondary knows four to five contraceptive methods followed by elementary with 29.59 percent .

Table 13.3: Channel of knowledge about Contraception

Channel	*Frequency*	*Percent*
NA	108	21
Govt. agency/nurse	24	4.7
Govt. agency & friends	5	1.0
Relative	7	1.4
Relatives, friends & physicians, books	1	0.2
Friends/users	192	37.3
Friends and books	1	0.2
Physician	75	14.6
Rumours	23	4.5
Friend & physician	45	8.7
Govt. agency & physician	13	2.5
Books/media	15	2.9
Religious institutions	6	1.2
Total	515	100.0

The data shows that 21 percent are not aware of contraception. They get the knowledge of contraception through friend or a user which is also the maximum 37.3 percent . There is no awareness programme about how they can control child birth, what kind of health care facilities are available and can be used, the effects of the contraceptive methods, and options available and accessible at the local or nearest health care centre. The information directly received from the government health agencies such as ASHA and professional physicians and nurse accounts for only 21.8 percent .Other channels of information is relatives 1.4 percent , friends and books .2 percent , Books or media 2.9 percent , religious institutions 1.2 percent , and rumours 4.5 percent . About 10.1 percent women get the information from multiple sources.

Table 13.4: Used Birth Control Methods

Used	*Frequency*	*Percent*
NA	8	1.6
Yes	134	26.0
No	373	72.5
Total	515	100.0

Only 26 percent used different kinds of birth control methods for various reasons. About 72.5 percent do not used any contraception. When asked why they didn't use contraception some responded that they don't know about it, some do not want to use it, and some does not need to use because they want more children and others have already cross the fertile period. About 1.7 percent does not used because of religious restriction. Most of the individuals used after the third child which amount to 18.9 percent but 1.7 percent used after the first child for spacing and 7 percent used after second child. Those who used after the second child are of two categories the first are those who want to go for family planning and the second are those who maintain spacing between the children.

Table 13.5: Interval of Using Contraception

Interval	*Frequency*	*Percent*
NA	368	71.5
0.0	4	0.8
First child	9	1.7
Second	37	7.2
Three and above	97	18.9
Total	515	100.0

Primarily most of the women use one contraceptive method. When the method is incompatible or ineffective or inconvenient then they used two or more or changed the method. The methods used by the Tangkhul women are as follows:

Table 13.6: Primary Strategy Method Used

Name of the Method	*Frequency*	*Percent*
NA	379	73.6
Condom	6	1.2
Rhythm/traditional method	29	5.6
Pills	29	5.6
Abortion	7	1.4
D&C	1	0.2
IUD	22	4.3
Hysterectomy	13	2.5
Tubectomy	3	0.6
Injection	2	0.4
Coitus interruptus	1	0.2
Rhythm & Coitus interruptus	9	1.8
Condom & pills	1	0.2
Condom & Rhythm	2	0.4
Condom & IUD	2	0.4
Condom & Abortion	2	0.4
Pills & Rhythm	1	0.2
Pills & IUD	3	0.6
IUD & Abortion	1	0.2
IUD & Tubectomy	1	0.2
Rhythm, Abstinence, Abortion	1	0.2
TOTAL	515	100

Using Condom: About 1.2 percent women used only condom as contraceptive method.

Using Pills: About 5.6 percent used pills alone which is also the highest rate of Contraceptive used along with Rhythm or traditional method.

Using IUD: The second highest contraceptive method used prevalence is IUD accounting 4.3 percent .

Using D & C: Only 0.2 percent used D & C method for contraception.

Using DMPA: Among the users only 0.4 percent of know and used contraceptive injection.

Hysterectomy: About 2.5 percent go through hysterectomy after they had the desired number of children and some because of pregnancy complexities.

Tubectomy: Tubectomy, one of the sterilization methods was performed by 0.6 percent women.

Combinations of contraceptive methods are also used in the studied population. About 4.6 percent used two or more contraceptive methods combine together. Sometimes when one method alone does not give the desired result they used another method which they consider is more effective than the other. However, it is not solely determine by its effectiveness but also more of convenience.

Switching from one Methods to other

Some women used more than one contraceptive method. About 4.4 percent used two kinds of methods switching one method to another for convenience sake, for effectiveness, and in search of compatibility. The two methods that they change commonly from one after another are Condom and rhythm, condom and pills, condom and IUD, IUD and pills. Rhythm method does not work for some woman so they have to use condom. Some users cannot use condom consistently because of their working nature they forget to carry with them and so their partner have to use pills too; some changed to IUD, for some IUD is not compatible so they change to pills, and some find pills make them weak so they change to IUD. Among the users 15.3 percent were still using by the time this data was collected and 10.5 percent quit. When they cross the fertile reproductive period they quit using contraception but some quit because it is not compatible to their body. The shortest period of using contraception is 1-3 months representing 5.4 percent and 6.6 percent have been using for more than 5 years. The studied population has high rate of abortion both induced and spontaneous. But the paper shall deal with induced abortion only which is non-plan and unwanted pregnancy that is 3.5 percent.

Table 13.7: Continuation of Contraception

Still using it	*Frequency*	*Percent*
NA	382	74.2
Yes	79	15.3
No	54	10.5
Total	515	100.0

Bodily Effect

All pharmaceutical contraceptives have side effects. The commonly used methods like contraceptive pills cause general weakness, headache and moody to the user, a symptom of side effect. It also makes them thin, due to these symptoms those of women whose occupation is agriculture cannot continue to use as it affects their daily work. The intra-uterine device (IUD) is incompatible to many. It cause bleeding, and many users complained that they have painful lower back and abdomen so they have to discontinue using it. "Depo" injection caused the user fat and it stops menstruation for about 6 months to a year. This ceasing of menstruation much short temper and worried. They are worried because when a woman stops menstruation before menopause it is considered abnormal. When one method is not effective or suitable to the body the users stop that method and shift to another method.

Table 13.8: Opinion about Contraception

Opinion	*Frequency*	*Percent*
NA	16	3.1
Good	217	42.1
Bad	241	46.8
Good as well as bad	41	8.0
Total	515	100.0

Speculations about contraceptive methods

The hormonal changes in the user's body are visible because of the symptoms the experienced. About 46 percent have an opinion that contraception is bad, and 7.8 percent says it is good as well as bad. Seeing and hearing the side effect symptoms of the users 44.8 percent says they do not want to use contraception especially pharmaceutical methods.

Conclusion

With increasing educated women the knowledge of family planning and contraceptive use penetrates in the Tangkhul population. About 76.1 percent are aware of family planning yet only 26 percent used contraception of different kind. The knowledge about contraception is transacted through different channel among which 37.3 percent received it from friends or users which is the highest. Advanced medicine, pharmaceutical and technology open more option of contraceptive methods to use their own choice according to the user's convenient. The About 9 types of contraceptive methods are used by the studied population. Contraception is used for various reasons such as spacing, pregnancy complication, mother's health risk, and for family planning. Most women used it between the interval of three and more children that clearly indicates that people use contraception after they got their desired number of children. They use one method at the time in the beginning but gradually proceed to use two or more when the first method is not effective. Only 15 percent continue to use contraception and 10 percent ceased to use it. The incompatibility and effect of contraception is the reason most of the women ceased to use it. Different kinds of symptoms such as headache, nausea, amenorrhea, physical weakness were reported. In pulling the opinion about the contraception about 42 percent says it is it is good and 46.8 percent negate it. Hearing the effect of modern contraceptive methods some women refrain from using it. However, the younger generation married women shows desire to use contraception after they bear the number of children they want.

References

Adler, N.E. (1992). Unwanted pregnancy and abortion: Definitional and research issues. Journal of Social Issues, 48 (3), 19-35.

Ankole, A., Darroch, J.E., & Singh, S. (1999). Determinants of trends I condom use in the United States, 1988-1995. Family Planning Perspectives, 31 (6), 264-271.

Bongaarts, J. T. & Bruce, J. (1995). The causes of unmet need for contraception and the social content of services. Studies in family planning, 26 (2),, 57-75.

14

Ageing Change in Body Composition among the Tangkhul males of Manipur

H. Sorojini Devi and Zimic Urapum

Introduction

The science of body composition is an important aspect of health. The proportion of these components is different in males and females. Body composition, generally, refers to 'the make-up of the body in terms of absolute and relative amounts of adiposity, muscle mass, skeletal mass and internal organs" (Bogin, 1999). All such differences in the tissue components of individuals and sexes are reflected through the functional changes in the body. Body composition can be determined by indirect method using anthropometry. Two compartment model of body composition consisting of fat mass (FM) and fat-free mass (FFM) have been adopted widely. FFM composes of all nonfat tissues and is commonly used as an indirect marker for skeletal- muscle mass. Most of the researchers studied in the two compartment model without separating muscle and skeletal mass as two distinct components.

Research has shown that body composition is directly related to health. A normal balance of body fat is associated with good health and longevity. Excess fat in relation to lean body mass, known as altered body composition, can greatly increase our risks to cardiovascular disease, diabetes, and more. Although excess body fat is associated with poor health, some fat is actually necessary for overall good health as it can help to protect internal organs, regulate hormones and provide us energy. The National Institute of Health of United States of America recommends that a healthy adult male's body should have between 6 percent - 24 percent of fat and a female should have 14 per cent- 31 per cent. Levels above these amounts may indicate excess body fat. Measurement of body composition is essential for studying human variation and adaptation, and is being used increasingly in the assessment of growth and nutritional status, fitness, work capacity, disease and its treatment.

The aging process brings about many changes in body composition. In general, as individuals become aged, percent body fat increases and lean mass and bone mineral density decreased (Onge, 2005). Several anatomists in the early 20th century noted that amount of muscle appeared to increase during middle ages (Frantzell and Ingelmark, 1951). Forbes (1991) noted that during senescence, development of discordant changes in LBM and soft tissue component were found leading to low muscle mass in the presence of high level of body fatness. This disorder is called sarcopenic obesity (Baumgartner, 2000). Body composition is influenced by a number of factors such as physical activities (Devi and Singh, 2012) altitude (Surks et al., 1996; Bhasin and Singh, 1992), nutrition (Mayer, 1995 and Jolk, 1962) and age (Brozek, 1952). Devi and Singh (2012) reported that rural women had greater lean body mass than urban women. Its relative development is dependent upon the environmental influences, sex, socio-economic conditions, occupation, genetics, nutrition and exercise (Sodhi,1991). Various Scientists have conducted their research works in the aspects of body composition among different population groups all over the world. Therefore, the present paper aims at studying ageing change in body composition among the Tangkhul males of Manipur.

Material and Methods

The present cross sectional data was collected from 200 (two hundred) Tangkhul males of four Tangkhul inhabited villages namely, Nagaram, Tangkhul Avenue, Duelalalen and Feryland and in Imphal East district, Manipur. Tangkhul adult males ranging in age between 20-70 years were randomly chosen for studying ageing change in body composition among the Tangkhul males of Manipur. Ten anthropometric measurements viz., height, weight, biceps skinfold, triceps skinfold, sub-scapular skinfold, supra-illiac skinfold, abdominal skinfold, medial calf skinfold, wait girth and hip girth were measured following Weiner and Lourie (1969). Body composition of each subject was computed using the equation of Yahnz (1962).

Statistical methods

Statistical constants such as mean, standard deviation and standard error of mean (SE) were computed using SPSS version 16. One way Analysis of variance was computed using Excel software.

Results

Table 14.1 highlights mean values of anthropometric measurements of Tangkhul males of different age groups. While observing the various mean values, it is found that the highest mean stature (165.5 cm) is found among the males of 20-29 years, and gradually decreased with increasing age of individuals to 158.0 cm at age of 60-70 years. Body weight increases to 62.0 kg with other highest mean values of sub-scapular (12.44mm), supra-illiac (12.86 mm), abdominal (11.36 mm) and medial calf skinfold (8.25 mm) and decreased with increasing age of the individuals in between 40-49 years, but biceps skinfold (4.90 mm), triceps skinfold (6.91 mm), waist girth (83.23cm) and hip girth (90.31 cm) increase at the maximum levels between 50-59 years. Comparison of various mean values by one way analysis of variance indicates that there are significant differences in all parameters except in body weight (F-ratio=2.21, P>0.05).

Table 14.1: Mean values of anthropometric variables of Tangkhul males of various age groups

		Age groups					
Sl. No.	*Variables*	*20-29 years*	*30-39 years*	*40-49 years*	*50-59 years*	*60-70 years*	*F ratio*
1.	Stature	165.5	164.7	162.9	162.0	158.3	5.73*
2.	Weight	59.5	60.0	62.0	59.0	55.1	2.21
3.	Biceps skinfold.	3.69	4.36	4.73	4.90	3.31	8.70*
4.	Triceps skinfold	5.75	6.52	6.86	6.91	5.46	9.31*
5.	Sub-scapular skinfold	8.98	10.79	12.44	11.32	10.31	3.55*
6.	Suprailliac skinfold	10.69	11.21	12.86	12.22	10.0	10.65*
7.	Abdominal skinfold	9.43	11.07	11.36	10.32	9.38	7.23*
8.	Medial calf skinfold	7.06	7.84	8.25	7.49	6.08	5.95*
9.	Waist girth	77.69	81.13	82.82	83.23	80.85	7.03*
10.	Hip girth	87.61	89.98	89.75	90.31	84.46	4.44*

Note: Height and girths in cm, weight in kg and skinfold in mm.

Table 14.2 indicates mean values of body composition components of various age groups. It is apparent that age group 20-29 years shows the highest development of fat percent (26.47 percent) and body fat (17.81 kg). No increment has been observed further in the following age groups of males. However, in case of lean body mass, its highest mean (48.91 kg) is in between 40-49 years, thereafter, lean body mass declined due to ageing factors. However, analysis of variance indicates no significant variations among the different age groups (all P>0.05).

Table 14.2: Body composition components of Tangkhul males

Body composition	*20-29 years*	*30-39 years*	*40-49 years*	*50-59 years*	*60-70 Years*	*F ratio*
Fat %	26.47	22.38	21.05	20.94	19.18	0.379
Body fat	17.81	13.46	13.17	12.57	10.51	0.408
Lean body mass	41.78	46.62	48.91	46.46	44.60	0.564

Table 14.3 represents comparison of body composition of the present males with the data of Purum males. While comparing the internal tissue components, it is observed that among the Tangkhuls, the highest mean fat percent (26.47 percent) and body fat (17.81 kg) occur in the youngest age group of 20-29 years, which indicates the maximum development of fat in the young age then suddenly falling down in the succeeding age groups, while among the Purums the highest development of these two components are found in the subsequent age group between 30-39 years with 15.40 percent and 9.23 kg respectively. Moreover, it also revealed that Purum males exhibit lower fat percent and body fat as compared with Tangkhul males. The maximum development of lean body mass is at the same age group of 40-49 years in which 48.91 kg for Tangkhuls and 51.09 kg for Purum males.

Table 14.3: Comparison of Body composition of present study Tangkhul males and Chothe/ Purum males

	Body composition	*20-29*	*30-39*	*40-49*	*50-59*	*60-70*	*F ratio*
Tangkhul	Weight	59.5	60.0	62.0	59.0	55.1	2.21
Purum	Weight	58.15	58.12	60.33	57.54	53.22	1.004
Tangkhul		26.47	22.38	21.05	20.94	19.18	0.379
Purum	Fat %	14.38	15.40	15.07	14.88	14.52	0.416
Tangkhul		17.81	13.46	13.17	12.57	10.51	0.408
Purum	Body fat	8.51	9.23	9.22	8.78	8.10	0.560
Tangkhul	Lean body	41.78	46.62	48.91	46.46	44.60	0.564
Purum	mass	49.64	49.88	51.09	48.76	46.83	1.28

Discussion

From the above result it is observed that peak body height (165.5 cm) of the present study males is observed among the young adult stage of 20-29 years and gradually decreases and the lowest is found among old aged 60-70 years. Body weight increases to 62.0 kg at age group 40-49 years with other highest mean values of sub-scapular (12.44mm), supra-illiac (12.86 mm), abdominal (11.36 mm) and medial calf skinfold (8.25 mm), but biceps skinfold (4.90 mm), triceps skinfold (6.91 mm), waist girth (83.23cm) and hip girth (90.31 cm) increase at the maximum levels between 50-59 years. It means that increased in skinfolds and body girth measurements continue till 50-59 years with advancing age of the individuals. Comparison of various mean values by one way analysis of variance indicates that there are significant differences in all parameters except in body weight (F-ratio=2.21, P>0.05).

Comparison of body composition components of various age groups highlights that men aged 20-29 years show the largest fat percent (26.47 percent) and body fat (17.81 kg), thereafter, there are marked changes in both parameters in the succeeding age groups in a decreasing trend. In general, the present younger generations are more confined to sedentary life with more food intake containing fats and proteins among the urban settlers. Therefore, their fat percent and total body fats are more than other later age groups. However, in case of lean body mass, its highest mean (48.91 kg) is in between 40-49 years, thereafter, lean body mass decline due to ageing factors. However, analysis of variance indicates no significant variations among the different age groups (all $P>0.05$).

Further comparison of body composition components of two population groups has revealed that that among the Tangkhuls, the highest mean fat percent (26.47 percent) and body fat (17.81 kg) occur in the youngest age group of 20-29 years, which indicates the maximum development of fat in the young age, then suddenly falling down in the succeeding age groups, while among the Purums the highest development of these two components is found in the later age between 30-39 years with 15.40 percent and 9.23 kg respectively. Moreover, it also revealed that Purum males exhibits lower fat percent and body fat as compared with Tangkhul males, but the highest development of lean body mass is at the same age group of 40-49 years in which 48.91 kg for Tangkhuls and 51.09 kg for Purum males. As reported, physical activity/ exercise can increase muscle and skeletal mass at the expense of body fat (Sodhi, 1991). Since the Purum males are actively engaged in manual work, therefore, their lean body mass are higher than the Tangkhul males, who live in the urban setting with sedentary life style. On the other hand, the decreasing trend of fat percent , body fat and lean body mass of both the comparing groups is due to natural process of ageing.

Conclusion

With ageing process, reductions in the metabolic rate with functional decline of all organs contribute to a reduction in RMR (Resting Metabolic Rate) that in turn promotes changes in body composition. It has been well documented that as individuals aged, body composition changes, even in the absence of changes in body weight. However, such age related changes in body composition may be varied, which is influenced by many factors such as nutrition, life style, occupation and income.

References

Baumgartner, R. N. 2000. Body Composition in Healthy Ageing. *ANNALS Academy of Sciences* Vol. 904: 437-448.

Bhabini Devi and S. Jibonkumar Singh. 2012. Body Composition Variation between Urban and Rural Women of Meitei Manipur, *Frontier Anthropology Vol1: 1-4.*

Bhasin, M.K and I.P Singh. 1992. Body Composition of Two High Altitude Populations- Bodhs and Baltis of Ladakh, Jammu and Kashmir, India. *J. Hum. Ecol, 3: 39-42.*

Brozek, J. 1952. Changes in Body Composition in Man During Maturity and Their Nutritional Implications. *Fed proc., 11: 784-793.*

Bogin, B. 1999. *Patterns of Human Growth,* Cambridge University Press.

Forbes, G. B . 1991. Exercise and Body Composition. *J. Applied Physiology*. Vol 70(3): 994-997.

Frantzell, A. and Ingelmark, B.E. 1951. Occurrence and Distribution of Fat in Human Muscle at Various Levels. A Morphogenic and Roentgenologic Examination. *Ups Lakeref Forh.* 56: 59-87.

Jolk, E. 1962. *Nutrition, Exercise and Body Composition* Springfield: C.C Thomas.

Mayer, J. 1955. Physiological Basis of Obesity Leanness. *Nutritional Abstracts and Reviews, 25: 875-879.*

Onge , M.P. 2005. Relationship Between Body Composition Changes and Changes in Physical Function and Metabolic Risk Factors in Aging. *Curr Opin Clin Nutr Metab Care.;8:523–8.*

Sonia Aimol. 2016. Assessment on Health Status of Purum Men and Women. Unpublished Dissertation , MU.

Sodhi.H.S.1991. *Sports Anthropometry*. Anova Publication, Mohali.

Surks, I.K.S., and L.O. Matoush.1996. Alteration in Body Composition in Man after Acute Exposure to High Altitude. *J. Appl Physiology. 21: 1741-1746.*

Weiner, J.S. and Lourie, J.A., 1969.*Human biology- A guide to field methods,* International biological programme, Handbook no. 9, Blackwell scientific publications.

Yahnsz, M.S. 1962. The effect of sports training on body fat in man with prediction of optimal body weight. Unpublished Doctoral thesis. Univ of Illinois, Urbana, III. C.f. Indera P Singh and M.K. Bhasin: *A Manual of Biological Anthropology,* 245.

15

Opportunity for natural selection in Relation to Age at Marriage and Household income among the Kom Tribe of Churachandpur District, Manipur

Leivon Khamnu Kom and Prof. R. Khongsdier

Introduction

Darwin's natural selection is the process by which nature rewards individuals better adapted to their environments with survival and reproductive success. Natural selection occurs when individuals of the different genotypes in a population are different from one another in their fitness know as Darwinian fitness, or genetic fitness. Darwinian fitness is defined as the "reproductive capability of an individual or class of individuals, in terms of the number of offspring they contributed to the next generation" (Johnston, 1973). It is well known that demographic variables, like fertility and mortality are the fundamental events of natural selection. In fact, from the demographic point of view, "differences in rates of reaching maturity, mating, fecundity, fertility, mortality and emigration are the raw materials of natural selection" (Sphuler, 1973). Several studies have shown that natural selection is operating through differential fertility is more effective than differential mortality among modern population. This effectiveness occurred due to good facilities of modern health care system and quality of life in this global era (Cavalli-Sforza and Bodmer, 1971).

Crow (1958) proposed an index which is known as index of total selection intensity (now called the index of opportunity for selection) in terms of differential fertility and differential fertility. The method was modified by Johnston and Kensinger (1971) by taking into consideration the embryonic deaths as well. Both the methods have been widely used by anthropologists and population geneticists to estimate the intensity of natural selection in human populations (Reddy and Chopra, 1990). However, the methods failed to delineate the types of selection (whether it is stabilising, or directional, or disruptive). The methods simply assume that some phenotypic variation in reproduction has a genetic basis and fitness is heritable (Sphuler, 1973). That is, the methods ignore the role of socio economic factors in bringing about Darwinian fitness. As a matter of fact, many studies have revealed that the indices of total selection or opportunity for selection, calculated according to the methods by Crow (1958) and its modified version (Johnston and Kensinger, 1971), seemed to be negatively associated with socio-economic development (Reddy and Chopra, 1990; Kapoor and Kshatriya, 2000; Sikdar, 2008; Gautam, 2009). Several works has been done on the selection intensity of human populations throughout the world including India and have noted variation of selection with regards to economic conditions (Frisancho*et al.,* 1976; Bharati, 1981; Sikdar, 2012), cultural practices (Sphuler, 1962; Livinstone and Sphuler, 1965; Johnston and Kensinger, 1978; Mukhopadhyay, 1982; Sengupta and Begum, 1998), education and social status (Reddy and Chopra, 1990, Kapoor *et al.,* 2003; Das and Sikdar, 2010, and Altitudes (Cruz-Coke et al., 1966; Gupta, 1980; Kapoor et al., 2003; Gautamet al., 2009).

The problem is that the indices are actually estimated for one generation (i.e., by considering only women of completed fertility at the time of survey), thereby indicating the socio-economic development that takes place during the last 20 years or so before the survey.

Therefore, more studies are needed to test whether the indices can also be used to measure the recent socio-economic development in human populations.

The main objective of this study is to estimate the index of selection intensity among the Kom population of Churachandpur District Manipur as well as to analyze the intensity of natural selection in relation to age at marriage of the mothers and household income by using Crow's formula (1958) as well as the modified method suggested by Johnston and Kensinger (1971) and to make the present findings comparable with some related findings from other Northeast Indian population.

Materials and methods

As far as the study is concerned, the present study was conducted in nine Kom villages under Churachandpur District in Manipur, namely, Keirap Khunkha (lower), Keirap Khunthak (upper), Sempangjar, Khoirentak (lower), Khoirentak (upper), Moirang mantak, Kangkathei, Sagang khopui, and Keirap khullen (Haotak). A total number of 235 ever married mothers who had completed their reproductive stage (generally aged 40 years and above) at the time of investigation are taken into consideration and were interviewed to get the relevant information for this study as well as for calculation of the indices. An interview schedules was designed and was used to get the detailed reproductive history of these women. The entire demographic data were collected through in-depth interview using structured schedule for getting the required information WHO (1964, 1968) and Mahadevan (1986), which includes data on (a) individual and household records which include name, age, sex, marital status family members, birth order, place of birth, place of residence, religion, occupation, education, income and expenditure of the household, etc., (b) Reproductive records which include pregnancy history of each married women, present age of the mother, age at marriage, approximate age at each conception, age at menopause, total number of live births, birth order, name, age, sex, marital status of each children, number of death children, sex, date of birth, age at death, cause of death, number of reproductive wastage (spontaneous and induced abortion, stillbirths) etc.

The formulae proposed by Crow (1958) and its modified version by Johnston and Kensinger (1971), were used for estimating the index of selection intensity among the Kom Tribe of Churachandpur District in Manipur.

Results and discussion

Table 15.1 shows that there are 235 mothers who have completed their reproductive stage (generally aged 40 years and above). The average number of live births to such mothers was found to be 3.03 with the corresponding variance of 1.977. The proportion of child mortality before reaching the reproductive age and the proportion of embryonic death was 0.019 and 0.041 respectively.

Table 15.1: Parameters used in calculating selection Intensity

Total mothers who have completed their reproductive age (40 years and above)	235
Total number of pregnancies	751
Total number of live births	697
Number of death before 15years of age	13
Number of embryonic deaths	31
Proportion of child death (death before 15 years) P_d	0.019
Proportion of embryonic death (P_{ed})	0.041
Average live birth per mother who have completed their reproductive age ($\bar{x}$)	3.03
Live births variance (V_f)	1.977

Table 15.2: Indices Selection Intensity

According to Crow (1958)			*According to Johnston and Kensinger*			
I_m	I_f	I	I_{me}	I_{mc}	I_f	I
0.019	0.215	0.238	0.046	0.019	0.215	0.287

Table 15.2 shows the index of total selection intensity calculated according to Crow's formula (1958) and the modified methods suggested by Johnston and Kensinger (1971) for the present population. It was found that the value

of I, I_f and I_m calculated using Crow's formula (1958) was 0.238, 0.215 and 0.019, respectively. On the other hand the value of I_{me}, I_{mc}, I_f and I calculated according to Johnston and Kensinger was 0.046, 0.019, 0.215 and 0.287 respectively. Thus it shows that the value (I) calculated according to Crows formula is lower than that calculated according to the method suggested by Johnston and Kensinger. This is due to the fact that in the case of Crow's formula, we have not taken into consideration the embryonic deaths (still-births and abortions) as done in the case of Johnston and Kensinger formula. However, considering both the methods, the index due to fertility seems to contribute more towards selection than the index due to mortality. In other words, the opportunity for natural selection in the Kom population of Churachandpur District seems to be operating more through differential fertility as compared to differential mortality.

According to Khongsdier (2000), if the value of Crow's index of total selection intensity falls < 0.340; 0.340-0.470; 0.470-0.600; 0.600-0.730; 0.730-0.860; and > 0.860 for Indian populations, then it may be classified as low, moderate, mild, average, high and very high respectively. Therefore, following this classification, it indicates that the opportunity for natural selection to operate in this population is low.

Table 15.3: Selection intensity indices of the Kom population with other population of Northeast

Population	*According to Crow's (1958)*			*According to Johnston and kensinger (1971)*				
	Im	*If*	*I*	*Ime*	*Imc*	*If*	*I*	*References*
Kom population	0.019	0.215	0.238	0.046	0.019	0.215	0.287	Present study
Khynriam Khasis	0.198	0.158	0.387	0.012	0.198	0.158	0.403	Khongsdier (1990, 1994)
Pnar	0.236	0.134	0.401	0.202	0.236	0.134	0.681	Khongsdier et al. (2001)
Marngars	0.133	0.231	0.395	0.043	0.133	0.231	0.455	Devi (2001)
Hajongs	0.443	0.131	0.631	0.032	0.443	0.131	0.684	Barua (1993)
Pnar of Nangbah village	0.055	0.141	0.241	0.024	0.055	0.141	0.266	Gangte (1993)

In comparison with the other populations shown in Table 15.3, the total index (I) according to Crow's (1958) of the present population (0.238) was found to be similar to that of the Pnar of Nangbah village (0.241), but lower to that of the other populations of Northeast. With respect to the index due to fertility the present Kom population (0.215) seems to have a similar trend with the Marngars (0.231), but was found to be higher than the other populations in Northeast India. Similarly, index due to mortality (0.019) appears to be similar to that of the Pnar of Nangbah village (0.055) though it was lower in comparison to other northeast populations.

Table 15.4: Estimated indices of selection intensity with income and age at marriage

Characteristics	*No of mothers*	*According to Crow (1958)*			*According to Johnston and Kensinger*			
		I_m	I_f	I	I_{me}	I_{mc}	I_f	I
Income group								
LIG	107	0.028	0.247	0.282	0.056	0.028	0.247	0.338
MIG	71	0.013	0.243	0.259	0.046	0.013	0.243	0.301
HIG	57	0.012	0.102	0.115	0.017	0.012	0.102	0.131
Age at marriage								
≤ 19	124	0.011	0.224	0.2360.	0.053	0.011	0.224	0.306
20 years and above	111	0.019	0.110	131	0.031	0.019	0.110	0.161

*LIG-Low income group, MIG- Middle income group, HIG- Higher income group

Table 15.4 shows the estimated indices of selection intensity calculated according to Crow's formula (1958) and the modified version by Johnston and Kensinger (1971) with the mother age at marriage and income of the study Kom population. Among the income group, it is seen that the total index of selection (I) calculated according to crow's (1958) was higher in the LIG (0.282) as compared to MIG (0.259) and HIG (0.115). Similar trend is also found in the case of the index due to fertility (I_f) and mortality (I_m) which was higher in the LIG than in the higher income groups. Hence it is seen that the opportunity for natural selection to operate is greater in the low income group than in the higher income groups. In the case of the age at marriage of mothers, the corresponding figures for the age at marriage ≤ 19 and 20 + years with respect to the total index of selection intensity (I) calculated according to Crow's (1958) are (0.236) and (0.131) respectively. It is seen that the total index selection intensity (I) for the mother whose age at marriage is ≤ 19 appears to be higher than the corresponding age group. The index due to fertility (I_f) is also found to be higher among the mother whose age at marriage is ≤ 19 as compared to the age group 20 + years respectively. But in the case of the index due to mortality (I_m) the mothers whose age at marriage is 20 + years appears to be higher than the mother who married earlier. Thus, it is seen that among the mothers age at marriage the total index selection intensity (I) appears to be higher among the mother whose age at marriage is ≤ 19 years and it decreases with the increasing age at marriage of the mothers. This shows that higher the mother age at marriage lesser is the chance for the selection and is found to contribute more towards fertility than mortality.

These findings depict a number of possible reasons. Fertility and mortality performance of a population depends largely on various socioeconomic factors. Cavalli-Forza and Bodmer (1971) reported that among agrarian and tribal societies, mortality contributes more towards selection rather than fertility. Many studies, especially among the Indian population have found that mortality plays greater role in contributing more towards the process of natural selection. The reasons for these changes may be due the differences in the mean number of live-births, which is inversely proportional to selection intensity. But in the case of the study Kom population, as per Crow's formula the index due to fertility (0.215) was found to be higher than that of the mortality (0.019). This condition is mainly due to better accessibility to public health facilities.

Conclusion

Selection intensity is one of the major evolutionary forces that bring about changes in the genetic make-up of a population. From the result it is seen that selection plays a major role in bringing changes in the genetic make-up within the Kom population. From the findings it indicates that the opportunity for natural selection to operate in this population is low and contributes more towards differential fertility as compared to differential mortality. Similar trend is also seen while estimating the indices of selection intensity with age at marriage of the mothers and income. Among the age at marriage the mothers whose age at marriage is $\leq$ 19 years has the greater concentration of selection intensity as compared to the mothers whose age at marriage is 20+years and is seen to be contributing more towards fertility than mortality. Similar trend is also found among the income groups, which was higher in LIG than in the higher income groups and also contributes more towards differential fertility than differential mortality. From the result it is seen that among the Kom population opportunity for selection calculated according to Crow's as well as the modified method by Johnston and Kensinger is found to be negatively associated with the age at marriage of the mothers and income groups and contributes more towards fertility than mortality. The reason for the higher contribution of fertility component among the study population with respect to the total index may be due to better living standard, health care and other modern facilities which give a positive outcome on the lower contribution of mortality. Hence, fertility is seen to be more important as compared to mortality in the manifestation of natural selection in the study population.

References

Barua, S. (1983). The Hajong of Meghalaya a bio-demography study. *Hum. Sci.*, 32:190-200.

Basu, S., Kshatriya, G. and Jindal, A. (1988). Fertility and mortality differentials among the tribal population groups of Bastar District, Madhya Pradesh, India. *Hum. Biol.*, 60:407-416.

Bharati, P. (1981). Economic condition and demography among the Mahishyas of chakpota village, Howrah district, west Bengal. *J. Biosoc. Sci.*, 13:345-356.

Cavalli- Sforza, L. L. and Bodmer, W. F. (1971). *The Genetics of Human Populations.* W.H.Freeman: San Francisco.

Crow, J. F., (1958). Some possibilities for measuring selection intensities in Man.*Hum. Biol.*, 30:1-13.

Crow, J.F. (1966). *The quality of people*: Human evolutionary changes. Bioscience; 16:863-7.

Cruz- Coke, R., Christoffanini, A. P., Aspillaga, M. and Biancani, F. (1966). Evolutionary forces in human populations in an environmental gradient in Arica. Chile. *Hum. Biol.*, 38:421-438.

Das, F. A. and Sikdar, M. (2010). Opportunity for natural selection among some selected population groups of Northeast India. *Indian J. Hum. Genet.*, 16:61-66.

Devi, B. (1975). A note on the reproductive life of Kond women. In: *Bio-Anthropological Research in India, Calcutta:* Anthropological Survey of India.

Downhower, J. F., Blumer, L. S. and Brown, L. (1987). *Opportunity for Selection: Anappropriate measure for evaluating variation in the potential for the Selection ?* Evolution. 41:1395-1400.

Frisancho, A. R., Klayman, J. E., Matos, (1976). Symbiotic relationship of high fertility, high childhood mortality and socio economic status in urban Peruvian population. *Hum. Biol.*, 48:101-111.

Gautam, R. k., Kapoor, A. k. and Kshatriya, G. K. (2009). Natural selection among the Kinuara of the Himalayan highland : A comparative analysis with other Indian and Himalayan populations. *Indian J. Hum.Genet.*, 15:125-136.

Gupta, R. (1980). Selection intensity in the Sherpes. *Curr. Anthropol.*, 21:136-137.

Johnston, F. E. and Kensinger, K.M. (1978). Fertility and mortality differentials and their implications for micro evolutionary change among the Cashinahua.*Hum. Biol.*, 43:356- 364.

Johnston, F. E. and Kensinger, K. M. (1971). Fertility and mortality differentials and their implications for micro evolutionary change among cashinahua. *Hum. Biol.*, 43:356-364.

Jorde, L. B. and Durbize, P. (1986). Opportunity for natural selection in the Utah Mormous. *Hum. Biol.*, 58:97-114.

Kapoor, A. K., Kshatriya, G. K. and Kapoor, S. (2003). Fertility and mortality differentials among the population groups of the Himalayas.*Hum. Biol.*, 75:29-747.

Khongsdier, R. (1990). The Pnar of Sutnga and Moopala Villages: A study on selection intensity. *J. Ind. Anthrop. Soc.*, 25:182-184.

Khongsdier, R. (1994). Opportunity for natural selection among the war Khasi of Maghalaya, *India. J. Hum. Ecol.*, 5:307-310.

Khongsdier, R. (2000). *The Semas: a population genetic study. In: contemporary research inanthropology.* New Delhi: common wealth publishers.

Livingtone, F.B, Spuhler, J. N. (1964). Cultural determinats in natural selection. In: UNESCO expert meeting on the biological aspects of race. Paris: France.

Mahadevan, K. (1986). Fertility and Mortality: Theory, Methodology and Empirical issues.*Sage Publications.*, New Delhi.

Morton NE. (1968). Problems and Methods in the genetics of primitive groups.*Am. J. Phys.Anthropol.*, 28:191-208.

Mukhopadhyay, B. (1982). Selection Intensity in the Lepchas of Kalimpong, West Bengal.*Curr.Anthropol.*, 23:577-578.

Reddy, B. M. and Chopra, V. P. (1990). Opportunity for natural selection among the Indian populations.*Am. J. Phys. Anthropol.*, 83:281-296.

Sengupta, S. and Begum, S. (1998). Index of opportunity for natural selection among the Sayed Muslim of Assam.*Hum. Ecol.*, 9:95-97.

Sikdar, M. (2012). Socioeconomic Covariates and their impact on the opportunity for natural selection in a riparian Tribe of northeast India. *Anthropol.Anz.*, 69:273-287.

Spuhler, J. N. (1962). Empirical Studies on quantitative Human Genetics. In: proceedings of UN/WHO Seminar on the use of vital and Health Statistics for Genetics and radiation Studies. NY, USA.

WHO (1964). Research in population Genetics of Primitive Groups.*WHO Technical ReportSeries No. 279*. Geneva: WHO.

WHO (1968). Research in human population genetics.*WHO technical report series No. 387*. Geneva: WHO.

16

Reproductive and Child Health: A Comparative Study between the Koms of Khoirentak and the Chothes of Purum Tampak Village, Manipur

Lorho Mary Maheo, Pourinliu Kamei and Menaka Devi

Introduction

The concept of health occupies different meaning in different societies. With the conceptualization and measurement of health and quality of life, the health services are increasingly gaining due attention. One of the major issues in the health status measurement is the health seeking behaviour of the community which governs the morbidity and mortality pattern. The health seeking behaviour of a community again cannot be studied in isolation from the social network of a community. It is deeply interwoven into every event of social, economical and biological aspects of a population (Basu *et al*, 1994).

India being rather a big developing country still has to strife hard to bring its population at a respectable place. Population welfare programmes have been undertaken from time to time and one such welfare programme is that of the reproductive and child health (RCH). The major aim of this programme is to improve the survival status of mothers as well as children of the community and the nation at large (Jain and Visaria, 1998). As rightly pointed by Amin, it is the women who are a particularly vulnerable segment of a society. They suffer from social economic and nutritional deprivation to a far greater extent than their male counterpart (1995).

In India, reproductive child health programme was launched in 1997 to improve the ante-natal care, institutional deliveries or deliveries with trained health worker and also post-natal mother as well as child health care services (NIHFW 1999-2000) and later on the National Population Policy (2000) has set a goal to save motherhood empowering women for improving health and nutrition. A few research works has been conducted on different aspects of reproductive and child health among specific tribal communities in India which showed poor reproductive and child health status (Basu and Kshatriya, 1997; Reddy et al, 2001; Pandey et al, 2001; Narahari and Rani 2002, Chandraker et al, 2009).

One of the important elements in reducing health risk of mother and that of the child is to increase the proportion of babies delivered in places having proper health infrastructure, which will ultimately reduce the risk of infections of both mother and new born (Mitra et.al 1997). Therefore, increase number of health care centres would definitely be a blessing particularly in the rural region.

The present paper is an attempt to compare the reproductive and child health of the Koms and Chothes settled in two pockets of Manipur with a view to understand the pregnancy related women reproductive health along with infant and child care practices prevailing in the area. At the same time socio-cultural and other population characteristics are also taken into consideration to see if there is any correlation. The study was confined to women of these two villages currently available then during the study period.

The village & the people

Manipur lies on the extreme North-Eastern corner of the Indian sub-continent with total area of 22,327 sq. km and a total population of 2,855,794 according to 2011 census record. There are about 34 recognised scheduled tribes in the state of Manipur. The present study is based on the Koms from Churachandpur District and the Chothes from Chandel district, Manipur. Both the Khoirentak Khuman and Purum Tampak villages are located at a distance of about 43kms and 59 ½ kms respectively away from Imphal.

There is a primary health centre named as Khoirentak Primary Health Sub-Centre (KPHSC) established in 1978 under the government of Manipur with five staffs. In Purum Tampak village too, the health centre which was established in the year 1975 has four staffs. There is no doctor in both the PHSCs and the nurses carried out most of the home deliveries in the said villages. Some of the important health facilities provided by the PHSC include immunization, pre-natal and post natal check up if required and provide first aid medicine as and when needed.

Materials and methods

The study was conducted among the Koms of Khoirentak and the Chothes of Purum Tampak villages of Manipur. A sample of 121 married women along with 80 children (47 boys and 33 girls of $\leq$ 5 years). Mothers in their reproductive age group (15-49) years comprising 60 Koms and 61 Chothes along with their respective children (≤ 5 years) were randomly chosen. The present data was collected adopting an indepth interview schedule. Information on age at menarche, menopause and age at first marriage, pre-natal care, delivery practices of the last childbirth and also on birth control practices were collected as per the scheduled. The anthropometric measurements on height and weight of women and weight of the boys and girls were recorded as per the recommendation (Weiner and Lourie, 1961).

Nutritional anthropometric indices of children were calculated using reference medium NCHS and classified according to Jelliffe classification of weight for age and mothers' nutritional was assessed through body mass index (Jelliffe, 1966) and classification done according to thinness of mother (WHO, 2003).

Results and Discussion

Table 16.1: Age at menarche, marriage and 1st conception

Variables	*Kom*	*Chothe*
Age at menarche	13.56(Mean)	14.32(Mean)
Age at marriage	21.35(Mean)	21.00(Mean)
Age at 1st conception	21.55(Mean)	21.90(Mean)

The mean menarcheal age was found to be13.56 among the Koms and 14.32 among the Chothes. Similar findings are also found in some of the earlier studies on the tribes of Manipur (Chakravartti, 1986). The mean age at marriage for Kom and Chothe women were found to be 21.35 and 21.00 respectively. In the present survey most of the married women of Khoirentak and Purum Tampak villages are found to have conceived in the first year of their married life. The earlier the first conception, the higher is the fertility which may increase the average fertility as compared to those who had its first conception at a higher age.

Mother and child health status

Maternal and child health services play a vital role in achieving improved reproductive outcomes in various societies, particularly in rural settings (Bhatia and Cleland, 1995). Both mother and child health care practices ought to begin right from the time of conception i.e. the mothers should be properly protected against disease and have proper nutrition or balanced diet which is necessary for maintaining good health both for the mother and for the foetus. Specifically, women's quality of life with her children as well as family and community is largely influenced by pregnancy related health and nutritional problem of the women. Hence, the reproductive and child health programme is focussed in improving the survival status of both mother and the child.

Table 16.2: Distribution of the number of antenatal check-ups

Group	*No. of woman*	*Number of antenatal check-ups*		
		At least twice	*At least 3 or more*	*None*
Kom	60	7(11.7)	48(80.0)	5(8.3)
Chothe	61	7(11.5)	48(78.7)	6(9.8)

Both Kom and Chothe mothers show similar results pertaining to antenatal check-ups with a high percentage of mothers attending the regular checkups. Further it is less than 10 percent of both the mothers from two different communities not attending the antenatal checkups for the simple reason that they did not face any problem or did not go for any pre-natal care due to lack of medical facilities while in Chhattisgarh reports have shown that mothers of 42 percent of children did not receive any ante-natal check during the last child (NFHS-II 2000).

Health problems during pregnancy

There is an increase tendency of health problems during pregnancy. Many of the pregnant mothers have experienced different degree of health complaints in the early stages with morning sickness and frequent micturation and at the later stages from anaemia, backache, gastritis, constipation, etc. In the present studied women too, many of them encountered similar health problems.

Table 16.3: Distribution of prevalence of reproductive health problem during pregnancy

Group	*No. of women*	*Prevalence of reproductive health problem*			
		Morning sickness	*Paleness/ giddiness/weakness*	*Body pain, breathing problem, anaemia and gastritis*	*No problem*
Kom	60	9 (15.0)	15(25.0)	23(38.3)	13(21.7)
Chothe	61	8(13.1)	1(1.6)	11(18.1)	41(67.2)

About 87 percent of the Kom mothers experienced various health problems during the last pregnancy as observed from the table. An interesting observation is that about 67.2 percent the Chothe mothers had no problem faced during the last pregnancy.

Medical facility availed during pregnancy: Available of medical facility coupled with its easy accessibility of maternal and child health services play a crucial role in achieving improved reproductive outcomes in various societies. A look into the place of delivery of the last pregnancy, persons who assisted or conducted the delivery would further highlight the health status of the people.

Table 16.4: Distribution of delivery practices

Age Group	*No of women*	*Place of delivery*		*Assistance in delivery*	
		Home	*Hospital*	*Trained (doctors and nurses)*	*Untrained (elders)*
Kom	60	26(43.3)	34(56.7)	51(85.0)	9(15.0)
Chothe	61	36 (59.0)	25(41.0)	58(95.1)	3(4.9)

It is observed that home delivery is more common among the Chothes however, delivery assisted by trained personal was found to be higher in this community compared to that of the Koms. Higher percent of trained personal assistance could be attributed to availability of the two trained nurses from the said village itself. Further it is worth mentioning that the type of post natal care rendered to the mothers at the time of childbirth varies between the two studied populations. The Chothes have a similar pattern of post-natal care like the Meeteis which is not observed among the Kom mothers. They are made to rest for a period of three months where all services are rendered freely. This could be one of the reasons for a better state of health at a later period or for the next pregnancy.

Immunization of the children (≤ 5 years): Immunization being a regular government programme has been emphasised to be carried out at regularly. Staffs working in this field are compelled to reach its target.

Table 16.5: Distribution of immunization programme& type of medical facility availed for children ≤ 5 years

Group	*Frequency*		*Immunization programme*			*Type of medical facility availed*			*Total*
	Male	*Female*	*Fully immunised*	*Partially immunised*	*Not immunised*	*Traditional*	*Modern*	*Mixed*	
Kom	27	17	37(84.1)	7(15.9)	-	-	34(77.3)	10(22.7)	44
Chothe	23	18	30(73.2)	10(24.5)	1(2.4)	1(2.4)	30(73.2)	10(24.4)	41

From the above table, it is observed that no Kom child was left out for immunisation programme while among the Chothe immunisation programme was then not initiated to a child at the time of data collection owing to the child's ill health. Further it is learnt that if the previous visit fail owing to non-availability of medicine or on account of strikes/bandhs, the same is carried out in the successive visit. With regard to the type of medical facility availed only the ethno-medicine alone was not administered to the Kom children. If the children become ill modern treatment with or without traditional medicine is generally resorted for quick response in almost all children.

Present state of mother's health: Assessment of one's health and type of medical facility availed during the previous year was also taken into account which will further highlight their health status in general.

Table 16.6: Distribution of assessment of mother's health & type of medical facility availed during the last 1 year

Group	*No. of women*	*Mother's health*			*Type of medical facility availed*		
		Normal	Healthy	Sickly	Modern	Traditional	Mixed
Kom	60	23(38.3)	28(46.7)	9(15.0)	54(90.0)	3(5.03)	3(5.0)
Chothe	61	57(93.4)	1(1.6)	3(4.9)	56(91.8)	5(8.2)	-

The response obtained can be regarded as positive for most of them considered themselves to be either healthy or just normal during the last one year while only 15 percent & 4.9 percent of mothers assessed themselves to be of sickly type. Further, pertaining to the type of treatment resorted to it is seen that about 90 percent of mothers received modern treatment while 5 percent of mothers resorted to traditional or mixed treatment.

Nutritional status of mother: The nutritional status of these mothers was assessed using body mass index. BMI has a good relation correlation with fatness. It may also be used as an indicator of health risk.

Table 16.7: Distribution of body mass index classification (WHO, 2003) of the Chothe & Kom women

BMI (kg/m2) Gradation	*Classification (WHO for Asian)*	*Chothe*	*p.c.*	*Kom*	*p.c.*
<18.5	Underweight	1	1.64	-	-
18.5-23.0	Normal	12	19.67	23	37.7
23.1-27.5	Overweight	35	57.38	30	49.2
>27.5	Obese Class I	10	16.39	5	8.2
>32.5	Obese Class II	3	4.92	2	3.3
>37.5	Obese Class III	-	-	1	1.6
Total		61	100	60	100

The distribution of BMI (kg/m2) among Chothe show that 1(1.64 percent) woman is underweight while none of the women of the presently studied community falls under obese class III. The reverse is true for the Kom mothers. In general it is observed that both the communities have more women placed under the overweight and above category which might lead to various health problems in the near future if not taken care of.

Nutritional status of children

Table 16.8: Distribution of sex wise population of the children (1-5 years)

Age	*Kom male*		*Female*		*Total*		*Chothe Male*		*Female*		*Total*	
	N	*%*	*N*	*%*	*N*	*%*	*N*	*%*	*N*	*%*	*N*	*%*
Total	24	61.5	15	38.5	39	100	23	56.2	18	43.8	41	100

There are 39 Kom children in the age group 1-5 years, of which 24 (61.5) are males and 15(38.5) are females. While in case of Chothe children the total number is 41 of which 23(56.2) are males and 18(43.8) are females.

Table 16.9: Distribution of weight for age of the Kom and Chothe children (1-5 years)

Grades of malnutrition Indian Academy of Paediatrics (IAP)	*Weight for age percentage of the reference population*	*Kom*		*Chothe*	
		N	*p.c.*	*N*	*p.c.*
Normal	>80	21	61.6	35	85.4
Grade I: mild malnutrition	70-80	10	29.4	5	12.2
Grade II: moderate malnutrition	60 – 70	3	8.8	1	2.4
Grade III: severe malnutrition	50-60	-	-	-	-
Grade IV	<50	-	-	-	-
Total		34	100.0	41	100.0

Most of the children studied are within the normal grades of malnutrition on the basis of weight for age index with 21 Kom children and 35 Chothe children having a percentage of 61.6 & 85.4 respectively. None of the children of the present studied populations suffer severe grades of malnutrition as compared to high prevalence of under nutrition reported in Maria Gond (Rao and Rao, 1994) and Gond (Rao et al., 2005) among tribal pre-school children of Madhya Pradesh. From these one can draw an important inference that children of both the villages enjoy a comparatively good health.

Conclusion

An increasing trend of reproductive health care delivery among both the Kom and the Chothe women has been observed from antenatal check up attendance. Immunization of the children is also done regularly. This shows the awareness and high literacy rate among the women, although some lag behind. The women are also fully aware of the modern treatment facilities. However, due to financial constraint coupled with lack of health care infrastructure that generally hinders them from taking appropriate modern treatment. Maternal health status of the Chothe is comparatively better than the Koms. They have similar Meetei traditional house type and also practised similar pattern of child birth. This could be attributed on account of its close proximity with the valley people by the Purum Tampak villagers. However, keeping in view of the similar environmental and social conditions no significant variation has been observed between the two studied communities. Hence, it can be concluded that similar reproductive and child health prevailed in both the communities. For the present studied populations there is still the need for giving proper and adequate information regarding the importance of antenatal care, safe delivery, importance of immunization against preventable diseases, the advantages of a small family and adequate child spacing. All the presently studied women are aware of the birth control measures. One important finding in these two populations is the lack of importance attributed to traditional health care system. Hence awareness can also be undertaken in that line as well.

No doubt Mother and Child Health (MCH) services have been created, strengthened and expanded over the years yet; their output in terms of their utilisation has not reached its target in the rural areas. Hence, MCH promotional activities need to be intensified and the benefits of these services be properly explained to mothers in the far flung areas for the overall betterment of the community' health. As the tribal groups are deeply associated with community involvement guided by the clan elders and also the church leaders in the present context, constant effort is also required on the part of the leaders of the community to bring about change in the traditional perception particularly in the health sector. Data presented in this paper are truly primary in nature. Hence, the findings of the present study may provide base line information to both the Kom and the Chothe women.

References

Amin, S. 1995. The Poverty- Purdah Trap in Rural Bangladesh: Implications for women's roles in the family. The population Council Research Division, *Working papers series* 75, New York: Population Council.

Basu, S., Jindal, A; Kshatriya, G. 1994. Perceptions of Health and Pattern of Health seeking Behaviour among the selected Tribal Population Groups of Madhya Pradesh and Orissa. In Basu, (ed.), Tribal Health in India, Manak publications Pvt. Ltd. Delhi. pp.26-39.

Basu S, Kshatriya GK 1997. Fertility and mortality trends in the Kharia tribals of Orissa. *Soc Change*, 27: 114-128.

Bhatia JC, Cleland J 1995. Determinants of Maternal Care in a Region of South India. *Health Transit Rev*, 5: 127- 142.

Chandraker R, Chakrabarty S, Mitra M, Bharati P 2009. A Study of Reproductive and Child Health among the Dhur Gond Tribal Community of Mahasamund District, Chattisgarh, India. *Stud tribes tribals,* 7(2): 97-103.

Chatterjee M 1991. *Towards Better Health for Indian Women*. South Asia Country Department II. Washington DC: World Bank.

Chakravartti, R. 1986. *People of Manipur: Anthropogenetic study of four Manipuri Population groups*. B.R. Publishing, Delhi.

Goswami Monali i, Bijayalaxmi Dash &N.C. Dash 2011. Traditional method of reproductive health care practices and fertility control among Bhumija tribe of Baleswar, orissa; *Ethno-Med*,5(1):51-55.

Jain AK, Visaria P 1998. Infant mortality in India: An overviewed. In: AK Jain, P Visaria (Eds): *Infant Mortality in India: Differentials and Determinants.* New Delhi: Sage Publications, pp. 23-64.

Jelliffe D.B 1966. The Assessment of nutritional Status of the community, Monograph series No. 53, geneva; WHO.

Mitra SN, Al-Sabir A, Cross AR, Jamil K, 1997. Bangladesh Demographic and Health survey 1996-1997. *Main Report.* National Institute of Population Research and Training (NIPORT). Mitra and associate, Dhaka, Maryland: Macro International, Inc.

Narahari S, Rani DS 2002. Habits and reproductive performances in a food gathering tribe of Andhra Pradesh, India. *J Hum Ecol*, 13: 255- 56.

NFHS 1998-99. *National Family Health Survey* (NFHS- II). Institute for Population Sciences (IIPS), India, Mumbai: IIPS.

NIHFW *Report* (1999-2000). National Institute of Health and Family Welfare, India.

Pandey GD, Roy J, Tiwary RS 2001. Socio-cultural aspects and health care in Pando tribe of Madhya Pradesh. *J Hum Ecol*, 12: 391- 394.

Rao DH, Rao KM 1994. Levels of malnutrition and socio- economic conditions among Maria Gonds. *J Hum Ecol,* 5: 185-190.

Rao V.G, Yadav R, Dolla C.K, Kumar S, Bhondeley MK, Ukey M 2005. Under nutrition and childhood morbidities among tribal pre-school children. *Indian J Med Res*, 122: 43-47.

Weiner, J. S and J. A Lourie. 1969 Human Biology- a guide to Field Method, Blackwell, London.

WHO 1981. *Research on the Menopause* (Report of a WHO Scientific Group) WHO. Tech. Report Series sec. 670:1.

WHO 2003. *South east region* (Regional Health Forum) Vol. 7 (2) 31.

SECTION - II

Ethno-Medicine

17

The role of Traditional Medicine in Primary Healthcare: A study among the Karbis of Assam, India

Kh. Narendra Singh

Introduction

WHO has defined traditional medicine as the sum total of knowledge, skills, and practices based on the theories, beliefs, and experiences indigenous to different cultures, whether explicable or not, used in the maintenance of health as well as in the prevention, diagnosis, improvement or treatment of physical and mental illness (WHO, 2001). This worldview recognises good health as a complex system involving interconnectedness with the land, recognition of spirit and ancestry, and social, mental, physical and emotional wellbeing both of the individual and the community (Wilson and Richmond 2009). World Health Organisation (WHO) estimated that about 80 percent of the world's population depends on traditional medicine for their primary health care needs. In his book WHR Rivers *Medicine, Magic and Religion,* argued that indigenous medical practices, which might seem irrational to Westerners, were rational when placed in the wider context of local beliefs and culture.

Anthropological studies of health and medicine as a social institution have shown that every known human society has developed, according to premises implicit in its own culture, a system of values regarding health and disease, as also methods of coping with them. Studies in ethnomedicine are the pioneer natural attempts to combat human problem. Their history itself witnesses how they paved their way to classic medicine. Through the ages, the knowledge, practices and innovations of worldwide ethnic communities, has been turned into traditions, whether written or oral. Medicine is one such manifestation of traditions.

In recent times, with the increased knowledge of life and culture of the tribal communities, the social scientists are taking interest in ethno-medicinal studies. Many works have been reported, specially from among the rural and tribal communities of India (Bhadra and Tirkey 1997; Sharma Thakur 1997; Choudhury 2000). The knowledge and practice of ethnomedicine have been orally transmitted over centuries. It includes both magico-religious and herbal remedies for treatment of various diseases and illness. The ethno medical system has two universal categories of disease etiology- natural and supernatural causes. Ethnomedicines form the major source of healing among the tribal communities. Tribal communities often depend on local available ethnomedicinal plants and animal products. The traditional knowledge practitioners or ethnomedicinal practitioners often serve as their healthcare service providers.

Early studies on indigenous medical systems were mostly limited in focus on witchcraft and illness caused by super-natural forces, and on specialists such as folk healers, and shamans (Evans-Pritchard, 1937; Turner, 1967; Fabrega and Silver, 1973). During this period, the emphasis was on the meaning of the illnesses and on the symbolism of the curing rituals performed by the folk healers with the result that scholars mostly overlooked empirical aspects of indigenous medical cultures (Waldstein and Adams, 2006). In view of the importance of traditional medicine which provides health services to 80 percent of the world population, increase demand of herbal drugs by the pharmaceuticals and depleting natural plant resources, it is high time to document the medicinal utility of less known plant available in remote areas of the country (Zaidi and Crow 2005). The present paper envisages describing the significance and role traditional medicine in health care practices among the Karbis of Assam, India

Methods

Field survey was conducted in the selected villages of Lumbajong area of Karbi Anglong district of northeast India. Information was collected following interview methods and focus group discussions. Secondary data were collected from research journals, edited volumes and reports. Field study was undertaken during the period from March to June 2015. A total of 75 informants were selected from five villages and the selection of the respondents was done from the head of the households having knowledge traditional medicines.

The Karbis

Karbis represents one of the prominent indigenous tribes of Northeast India, Racially, Karbis belong to the Mongoloid group and linguistically belong to the Tibeto-Burman group particularly the Kuki-Chin subgroup of languages. Karbis follow patrilineal system of family and socially divided into five major *Kur* or clans *viz., Lijang, Hanjang, Ejang, Kronjang* and*Tungjang*.

Clans are further divided into many sub clans. These clans are exogamous, which means marriages between members of the same clan are not allowed.

Discussion

Northeast India is the homeland of many precious medicinal plants and most of the communities rely on ethno-medicine for their health care practices. The local people utilize different parts of plants to cure disease and illness. Most of the traditional medicines are prepared from fresh leaves which are used both for topical application of wound healing, skin diseases etc, and oral administration for health problems like stomach disorder, diarrhoea, fever etc.

There is an increasing focus on the importance of medicinal plants and traditional health systems to solve the health care problems of the world. Northeast India represents an extremely unique eco-system rich in medicinal plant wealth associated with folk medicine, Ayurveda, Siddha, Unani and Homeopathy system of medicines. The medicinal plants also have traditionally engaged an important position in the socio-cultural, spiritual and medicinal arena of the people in the region. Medicinal plants play an important role in supporting rural healthcare system.

Traditional health-care practices of the Karbis

Among the Karbis, disease or illness is called *Keso* and its treatment is called *seh-kelang*. The latter involves various practices such as therapies, charms and rituals. *Kapherem* involves incantation of holy verses related to concerned deity to cure minor ailments such as*Ingthum* (Boils), *Methan Kekor* (Dog bite), *But Pharo* (Acute gastroenteritis), *Me Kapherem* (Burn), *Inghai* (lymphadenitis), *Han Kangri* (vegetable poisoning), *Mek Aur*(sore eye), *Thengkur* (Poisoning) and *Furui Karchu* (Snake bite). Therapies or prescription prepared from plants, animals or minerals are also used; for a few ailments, therapies may be accompanied with *kapherem* or charms before being given to the patient. *Kachehi* (local therapy) involves the application of concoction locally, which may or may not involve *kapherem*. *Kecho* (oral therapy) involves administration of traditional medicine orally. For some ailments ritual involving blood-sacrifice (*seh karkli*) is done for recovery of the patient. Traditional medicine is not only source of healing, but the practice is also an important part of Karbi religion and culture.

Traditional knowledge considered as a body of information and set of skills developed by a group of people over time, which is based upon their necessity, observation; and in a constant state of change. The information about folk medicine of northeast India are still not gathered in systemic way or not documented in old literature, these are generally passed over generation vocally. In order to consider the "preservation" of traditional knowledge, perhaps it need documentation of those old and useful literature and to explore the nature of this system, how it evolves over time, and identify some of the forces involved in its destruction. The documentation of traditional knowledge is useful to address the intellectual property right issues and for evidence based research work. Multidisciplinary research and development work using the traditional folk medicinal plants based upon their traditional knowledge can provide deep motivation for identification of new pharmacophores. Multidisciplinary approach in combination with established traditional health principles may be useful in understanding health culture behaviour as well as improving community health.

The customary use of fish (*toman*) during the ritual of *nihu kachingtung* for curing mental depression-like symptoms is still prevalent. Traditional health-care practices of the Karbis are based on religious beliefs and therefore, are an important driver for continuation of their culture. During *chojun* ritual, the supreme deity of Karbi pantheon *Arnam Kethe* is offered live fish namely *nune* (*Amblypharyngodon mola, Danio aequipinnatus*). Fish and crab for this purpose are collected a day ahead of ritual and stored in a bamboo tube.

The Karbis have rich tradition regarding medicinal uses of plants and are quite knowledgeable about locally available medicinal plants and depends on the ethno-medicinal plants naturally grown in the forest for treatment of most of their common ailments and diseases. They also consume some wild varieties of plants both as vegetables and medicine on a regular basis.

The knowledge medicinal uses of plants have been passed from generation to generation through the oral tradition. A large number of medicinal plants have been reported from this region and the Karbis still follow the tradition of indigenous health care. Many medicinal plants in the region are becoming endangered due to over-exploitation. However, attention is being paid to preserve and expand the locally available medicinal plants that may also help in providing primary health care to the local community. The safety and effectiveness of natural medicines and the regulatory environment should accompany the incorporation of the traditional systems of health care into the national health care (Bodekar 1994). The local cultivation and production as well as utilization of such medicinal plants need to be addressed scientifically. The Bio-diversity cum Recreation Park at Diphu (Karbi Anglong) managed by the Department of Environment and Forest , Karbi Anglong Autonomus Council, Diphu harbours varieties of medicinal plants endemic to the region and about 560 species of medicinal plants are available.

Recent decades have seen significant changes occurring within several aspects of ethno-medicine as a result of environmental degradation and tremendous changes in modern, social, and economic systems (Anyinam, 1995). The understanding of indigenous knowledge and practices in relation to natural resource utilization and management is one of the key issues for achieving sustainable development communities of the region. There is a need to strengthen the forest conservation measures based on the traditional knowledge and value system.

The following table provides list some medicinal plants and its usage.

Table 17.1: Medicinal plants used by the Karbis

Sl.No.	*Local name*	*Botanical name*	*Used for the treatment*
1	Chuselok	*Abrus precatorius* Linn.	Cough
2	Bapchuki	*Acmella paniculata*	Stomachache
3	Jok –an-kelok	*Adhatoda zeylanica*	Dysentery
4	Phrikangnek	*Alpinia galanga*	Bronchitis
5	Raeaba	*Alternanthera sessilis*	Skin disease
6	Hen saiku	*Amorphophalus bulbifer*	Piles
7	Ingchum	*Antidesma acidum*	Appetizer
8	Chamua	*Arisaema tortuosum*	Piles
9	Bengali dido	*Beta vulgaris*	Jaundice
10	Pri	*Calamus rotang*	Vitality
11	Bapduli	*Cassia tora*	Jaundice
12	Churu	*Chenopodium album*	Dysentery
13	Repichingthun	*Cissus quandragularis*	Joint pain
14	Phelang-riho	*Clerodendrum serratum*	Wound
15	Kurveng	*Commelina benghalensis*	Earache
16	Tharmit tharve	*Curcuma amada*	Gastritis
17	Or –oh	*Cycas pectinata*	Gastritis
18	Kur-vengso	*Drymaria cordata*	Sinusitis
19	Ok hi atehang	*Homalomena aromatica*	Joint pain
20	Lopong brik	*Lippia geminata*	Conjunctivitis
21	Hewali	*Nyctanthes arbor-tristis*	Malaria
22	Nopak ban	*Oroxylum indicum*	Intestinal worm
23	Pharchingki	*Solanum nigrum*	Intestinal worm
24	Thebongkang	*Physalis peruviana*	Stomach pain
25	Rikang menthu	*Paederia foetida*	Gastritis
26	Vorke abap	*Vitex negundo*	Malaria
27	Parok hanthor	*Xanthium strumarium*	High blood pressure
28	Phrilangdung	*Zingiber zerumbet*	Blood dysentery

Source: Field study 2015.

Conclusion

Health care behavior is an integral part of culture and understanding of the ethnomedical practices of the various communities is of great importance to promote the health status of a community. Tribes of northeast India possess a vast traditional knowledge on effective ethno medicines, which was acquired through the experience, are usually passed on by oral traditions. Thus, the potentialities of ethnomedicinal studies in northeast India should be given the importance as it can provide us a lead to discover of more and potential useful chemical compounds. A detailed scientific study is required to document all those rare species of medicinal plants and protection of such traditional knowledge and their practices will be significant important for future research. A comprehensive research studies needs to be carried out to identify, document and study ethhnomedicinal plants for planning of sustainable resource management of the northeast region of India. Scientific approach for their exploration, utilization, conservation and value addition may be the key points for entrepreneurship development by exploiting the traditional technology knowledge. Undertaking research studies on such ethnomedicinal plants would be helpful for conservation of rare plant species as well as environment. Rapid changes in traditional lifestyles and cultural practices due to modernization, globalization and reliance on modern medical care have put this age-old traditional knowledge under threat. This calls for preservation of the knowledge and conservation of the plant and animal biodiversity of medicinal value.

Traditional medical system still plays an important role in health care behaviour among the Karbis. In most cases, causes of an illness and healing system are found to be associated with the magico-religious beliefs. Along with herbal treatment, magico-religious practices are still occupying a significant position in their indigenous methods of treatment. The analysis reveal that factors like age, sex, education of the patient, types of illness, severity of diseases, health care facility, beliefs regarding the cause of diseases and previous experiences effect selection of different ways of treatment.

The use of traditional healing practices seems to have an influence on their healthcare-seeking behaviour and treatment of illness. The link between the tribal healers and the Karbis is strong and well-established, since healers are, to a large extent, the only source of advice on good health and provision for treatment and cure. Modern medicine and state health service making in-roads into these remote and far flung villages have been a rather recent phenomenon. Observations indicated an interesting and intricate pattern of health behaviour and health communication among the Karbis. It is evident that the communication skills of the tribal healers are excellent and their trust, credibility and accessibility can go a long way in co-opting them as 'agents' of change for health practices. In order to be effective in the implementation of any health programme, effective communication among health providers, health seekers, and traditional healers is essential.

For effective implementation of any health programme, effective communication among health providers, health seekers, and traditional healers is vital. An in-depth study using anthropological methods and approaches is essential to get to understand the indigenous health seeking behaviour from emic perspective.

References

Choudhury S 2000. Indigenous beliefs and practices of herbal medicine among the few Arunachalis. Resarun, Govt. of Arunachal Pradesh, Department of Cultural Affairs 26: 72-81

Evans-Pritchard EE. 1937. Witchcraft, oracles, and magic among the Azande. Clarendon Press, Oxford.

Fabrega H, Silver D. 1973. Illness and shamanistic curing in Zinacantan: an ethnomedical analysis. University Press, Stanford.

Foster G. 1976. Medical Anthropology and international health planning. Medical Anthropology Newsletter 7(3):12-18.

Kleinman A., 1980 *Patients and Healers in the Context of Culture*. Berkeley: University of California Press.

Rivers WHR, 1924 *Medicine, Magic and Religion*. London: Routledge

Ronghang R, Teron R, Tamuli AK, Rajkhowa RC. Traditional zootherapy practiced among the Karbis of Assam (India) The Ecoscan. 2011;1:161–6.

Singh, Narendra and B.C Agrawal 2009. "Role of Magico-Religious Healers in Community Health: A Study of the Tribal Communities of Chhattisgarh". In Binod C. Agrawal (ed.), *Media for Health Planning, programmes and Practice.* New Delhi Concept Publishing Company.

Waldstein A, Adams C. 2006. The interface between medical anthropology and medical ethnobiology. Journal of Royal Anthropological Institute N.S.:95-118.

Wilson K, Richmond C: Indigenous Health and Medicine. International Encyclopedia of Human Geography. Edited by: Kitchin R, Thrift NJ. 2009, Amsterdam; Boston: Oxford: Elsevier Limited

Winkelman M., 2009 *Culture and Health,* San Francisco, John Wiley and Sons.

Zaidi MA, Crow SA 2005. Biologically active traditional medicinal herbs from Balochistan, Pakistan. J Ethnopharmacol, 96: 331-334.

18

Ethnomedical Practices of Lepchas: A Case Study of Tingshim Village in Sikkim

Tenzing Zangmu Lepcha

Anthropology of medicine or medical anthropology is one of the newest and the most active sub disciplines of the anthropology. It is about the learning of human health and disease, health care systems, and bio-cultural adaptation. In order to examine and compare the health of regional populations and of ethnic and cultural areas of both contemporary and prehistoric, the discipline draws upon the four fields of anthropology. The field is highly interdisciplinary, linking anthropology to sociology, economics, and geography as well as to medicine, nursing, public health and other health professions (Ember et al. 1996).The wellbeing of human is the matter in which every society is interested. Every society has its own separate way of describing and promoting good health and curing the ailments from which people suffer (Sikkink 2009). Medical anthropologists research these cultural variances and involve themselves intensely in the cross cultural matters surrounding health, illness, and health care.

Ethnomedical Approach of Medical Anthropology

The earliest ethnomedical research was confined to the study of non western societies and exotic cultures and was generally subsumed under the comparative study of religion, ideas about sickness and therapeutic rituals were analysed as a window on underlying cosmological beliefs and cultural values. As the close relationship between the concepts of illness and the social organization were recognized, ethno medicine became a common focus of ethnographic research. Fabrega (1975) defined this approach as 'the study of how members of different cultures think about disease and organize themselves toward medical treatment and the social organization of treatment itself'. Classic ethno medical studies focus on the classification and cultural meaning of illness (both somatic and mental), the health seeking behaviors of the people suffering from illness, and the theories, training and practices of healers.

Defining Health and Disease

Health is "not merely the absence of disease and infirmity but complete physical, mental and social wellbeing" - World Health Organization. Many medical anthropologists consider health to be a cultural construction whose meaning differs considerably from society to society or from one historical period to another (Bradby 2009). In all societies humans perceive disease as a disruptive event that in one way or another threatens the flow of day to day life. Disease differs from society to society, in some part because of climatic or geographical settings but in large part because of the ways productive activities, resources, and reproduction are organized and carried out. Disease is not just the direct result of a pathogen or physiological disorder. Instead, a various social problems such as malnutrition, economic insecurity, occupational risks, industrial and motor vehicle pollution, bad housing, and political powerlessness contribute to susceptibility to disease (Baer et al. 1994).

In the field of health and healing, pluralism has always been part of all cultures and at all times. In India the pluralistic nature of the medical system is crucially linked with its inherent heterogeneous character and its long history of medical tradition (Mishra 2010). In the officially renowned alternative system of health, India has a very long, safe, and continuous usage of many herbal drugs viz, Ayurveda, Unani, Siddha, Homeopathy, and Naturopathy, etc. As stated by Venkat Subramanium, these systems have rightfully existed side by side with allopathy and are not in domain of obscurity. There are more than 500,000 non allopathic practitioners, who are trained in the less than 400 medical colleges of their respective health system and are registered with the official councils which monitor professionalism (Nagori 2011).

In part IV of Article 47 of the Indian constitution, it is stated that it is a "duty of the state to raise the level of nutrition and the standard of living and to improve public health" (Mehta 2011). Around the world as culture change speed up, and more people get closer with each other, health care system has undergone vast change, sometimes losing treasured resources such as elder' s knowledge of herbal remedies (Sikkink 2009). Since the last decade, India has been undergoing health transition. Improved investments are being made into health and family welfare sector; newer forms of health care delivery through NGOs are being encouraged; business management practices are being increasingly applied; private public partnerships are emerging and community centered approaches to health care delivery are taking the forefront (source: Administrative staff college of India, Hyderabad).

In case of Sikkim, it has two big hospitals – STNM Government Hospital and Manipal Central Referral Hospital which provides their services to the people of Sikkim. Along with it there are numbers of Primary Health centers (PHCs) in rural areas which provides basic health care to people. Diverse benefits under various programmes and schemes of health care are benefiting people of Sikkim. Some of these programmes and schemes are Janani Suraksha Yojna, Mukhya Mantri Sishu Suraksha Avum Sutkeri Sahayog Yojana, Janani Shishu Suraksha Karyakram, Mukhya Mantri Jeevan Raksha Kosh Scheme, Mukhya Mantri Shrawan Shakti Samridi Yojana, Sikkim State Illness Assistance Fund, Chief Minister's comprehensive Annual and Total Health check up for Healthy Sikkim (CATCH) Programme (Source: Health care, human services & family welfare department, Govt. of Sikkim).

The aim of the present study is to look at the health care system among Lepchas of Tingshim village in North Sikkim. It focuses on common health problems, health care practices, magico religious practices and modern health care practices among the villagers.

Figure : Map of Tingshim Village, Phensong, North Sikkim

Methodology

As the purpose of this exploratory study was to study the health care system and practices, both primary and secondary sources have been used for this research. Secondary data has been gathered from various books, articles and journals. The study is empirical in nature, qualitative rather than quantitative data has been collected. Sample includes health care practitioners (both traditional and modern), women, men and children of the village. Anthropological methods like participant observation, interview, schedule and case study were used to accrue empirical data. Technological aids such as audio and video has been used to record information.

Ethnography of Tingshim Village

Tingshim is a village under Phensong GPU. It lies just above the renowned Phensong monastery with a distance of approximately 1 km. Phensong is 25 km away from capital town Gangtok. The whole villagers are Buddhist. The total number of house is 43, total population is 191, out of which 102 are male and 89 are female.

Flora and Fauna

Zye reep (Rose), *Sechek reep* (Sunflower), *Sungde kung*, *Heektee reep* (Marigold), *Sorong bee* (Urtica dioica), *Kolpoth* (Walnut), *Pa am* (Sugar cane), *Nasi poth* (Pear tree), *Tuko poth* (Plum tree), *Kundong poth* (Passion fruit), *Lenji* (Cardamom), *Hing* (Ginger), *Mong* (Millet), *Kuchong* (Maize), *Kukyo* (Wheat), *Fompot* (Avacado), *Prukuchae, Chinabryu* (Physalis), *Ambi poth* (Guava tree) *Aetok Koong* (Rhododendron), *Tik nyel* (Artimisia vulgaris Linn), *Pushyor* (Thysanolaena Maxima), *Kusim poth, Ko ol poth, Taptap, Kendum Pa am, Nokrul poth, Kunu poth, Simban, Kung chyo, Kumsel bee, Kushyo poth, Khoksi*, *Sulokon*, *Lingsyu*, *Bogdung*,.

Doto semu fo (Hoopoe), *Cuckoo fo* (Cuckoo), *Mungklyong fo* (Wood pecker), *Fudong* (Pigeon), *Tungpung fo* (Owl), *Beak* (Cow), *Mon* (pig), *Beu* (Snake), *Hamu* (Fox), *Suthum* (Hyena), *Bokrok* (Poky pine), *Sa-ar* (Goat), *Sana* (Bear), *Suku* (Deer), *Munchu mon* (Boar), *Keley* (Squirrel), *Suhu* (Monkey), *Kuzyu* (Dog), *Heek* (Hen).

Economy

Lepcha of Tingshim village practice agriculture along with domestication of animals like cow, bullock, goat, hen, pig. Beside cash crop Cardamom, all other products are produce only for consumption. But recently, few of them have started selling their agricultural products at nearby market.

Health

Phensong GPU has one Primary Health centre (PHC) in Safyong ward which looks after all seven wards including Tingshim. ICDS is there in village that provides educational, medical and nutritional facilities to children and pregnant women of the village.

Water Resources

Water is one of the main problems in this village. It has only one water source for entire village which is 12 km above from village at the top of hill. Since there is no road and in case of scarcity of water people of Tingshim village have to reach the source by foot. There is no water storage tank not even one sanction by the government.

Political Structure

The village has Panchayat raj system; Tingshim village is one of the wards out of seven of Phensong GPU. Other wards are Upper Paney, Lower Paney, Genzel, Safyong, Labi, Sardang. Every Monday Panchayats of all seven GPU meets and discuss at various matter. On this day Panchayats Public meeting is also held. Gram Sabha is conduct thrice in a year. 2nd October is fixed for one Gram Sabha and dates for other two are not fix. The panchayat of village is Doma Lepcha but her husband Mr, Choden Lepcha, ex-panchayat helps her in almost all phase in regard to her duty.

Education

The numbers of children are very less in the village as such the village school was closed in 2014. Now the nearest school for the children of the village is Phensong govt. sec, school which is at Safyong ward. The school was established in year 1946. The classes are from 1st to 10th standard. The number of students is 128. Out of which 80 girls and 48 boys. Number of teachers are 23. Subjects taught are English, Hindi, Lepcha, Science, Social Science, Nepali. Children are admitted at the age of 5.

Development Projects

Both the centre and the state has introduces certain development programs such as; Mahatma Gandhi Rural Employment Guarantee Scheme (MNREGS), Integrated Child Development Scheme (ICDS), CC foot path, Protective wall, REDRH, CHRHM and various health care programmes and schemes. Development project in the pipeline are sanction of roads and construction of new ICDS centre as the older one got damage due to earth quake.

Traditional Health Care Practices in Tingshim

Illness is culturally defined. Western world take illness in relative of germs, viruses and undertakes it to be a biological constant, a pathological state to be tested by laboratory tests or clinical examinations. From the cultural view illness is quite different; it is a social recognition that a person is not capable to fulfill her normal role appropriately and. she should be brought back to normalcy. World Health Organization (WHO) estimated that about 80 percent of the world's population rest on traditional medicine for their primary health care needs (Bhuyan 2015). W.H.R Rivers in his book Medicine, Magic and Religion argued that "indigenous medicine practices, which might seem irrational to westerners, were rational when placed in the wider context of local belief and culture" (Rivers 1924).

In the case of Lepcha of Tingshim village, there are various new initiatives that have been taken by the government with regard to health care, even though Lepcha like people in other part of the world for some cases prefer their traditional health care system such as in case of health problems (cold and cough, stomachache, B.P. problem, fever, nose bleeding, to heal wound, throat pain, breathing problem, vomiting, food poisoning etc.). Lepcha of Tingshim village also use few medicinal plants to cure health problem of their animals like marijuana for cow, pig and goat.

Medical Plants

India is a country where lots of medicine for various health problems are prepared and found at our home and its surroundings respectively. It is the heritage that has been transferred from generation to generation. K. P. Tamsang in his work titled "Glossary of Lepcha Medicinal Plants" has described more than 80 varieties of medicinal plants use by Lepcha (Tamsang 2004). There are some medicinal plants which are prefer by Lepcha of Tingshim village to overcome some health problems, some of them are *Mentha arvensis Linn* (Ausoodaong) commonly known as mint, for diarrhea, digestion; *Ammomum Subulatum* (Lenji), for stomach pain; *Zinziber officinale Rose* (Heng), for stomach pain and vomiting control; *Swertia chirata Haiu* (Rungkyen), for fever; *Entada scandens Benth* (Koolok poth), for swollen neck glands; (Tunghrel), for diarrhea ; *Cane shoot* (Rudung), for cold and cough, high blood pressure, diabetics; *Eupatorium cannabinum* (Nam nong muk), for healing wound and nose bleeding, *Urtica dioica* (Sorong bee), for high blood pressure; *Heracleum wallichii* (Syamben), for stomach pain; *Litsea citrata* (Ngemu poth), for stomach disorder; *Lindera neesiana* (Nokrul poth), For stomach disorder and vomiting control; *Artimisia vulgaris Linn* (Tik nyel), for control of nose bleeding and bleeding in case of injury. In case of animals, few plants are also use for medication like Marijuana for cow, goat and pig.

Besides varieties of plants for medicinal purpose, Lepchas of Tingshim also prefer animal products for some health issues like Deer skin (*Suku Kompu*) for mushroom poison; Monkey meat (*Suhu maon*) for high fever; Fox meat (*Homu* maon) for breathing problem or Asthma; Beer appendix (*Sinaha khepu*) for Tuberculosis and swelling; (*Chyakmongfo*) for diabetics; frog skin (*Tuluk*) for healing wound and diabetics.

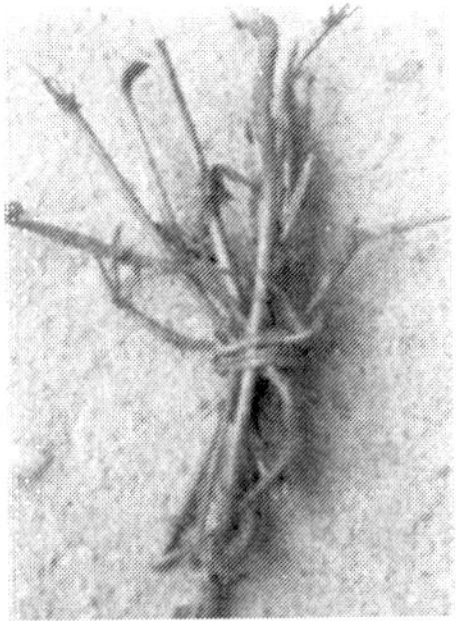

Swertia chirata Haiu (Rungkyen)-for high fever

Selek – for stomach pain and evil eyes

***Eupatorium cannabinum* (Nam nong muk), for healing wound and nose bleeding,**

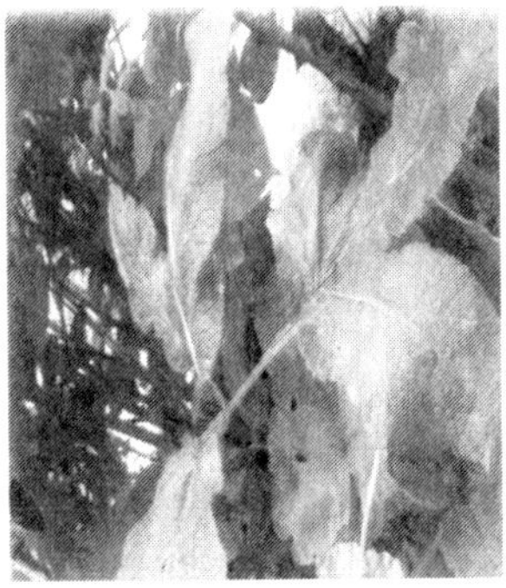

Heracleum wallichii *(Syamben), for stomach pain*

***Heracleum wallichii* (Syamben) for stomach pain**

Marijuana, for cow, goat and pig

Artimisia vulgaris Linn **(Tik nyel)-for control of nose bleeding and bleeding in case of injury.**

Parvek, for diabetics

Zinziber officinale Rose **(Heng), for stomach pain and vomiting control**

Herbalist

Name - Dhan Bdr. Mangar

Nick Name – Mangar Bajae, (meaning Grandfather Mangar)

Age- 84

Occupation- Herbalist and worked for Border Roads Organisation (BRO)

Religion - Christian

Permanent address- Udayapur, Nepal

Correspondence address - Phensong

Mangar Bajae is a prominent man who looks after patients from not only Phensong but from various distant places. People visit him in search of medicine for their health issues. He claim that he has medicine for almost all kinds of health problems. As state by him, he gain these knowledge about all those

medicinal plants for one of his book which he vaguely mention as "Baidang Kitab" by Jaisree Rana Mangar. Since the book is not with him because of his elder wife who threw it away in river because of irritation for his second marriage. He said that with the help of this book, firstly he cured himself, as he had suffered from Tuberculosis during his younger age. He claims that he did it by following all those procedure that were mentioned in that book for the cure of Tuberculosis. Later he shared that 27 items of various herbs and plants are needed for curing Tuberculosis. Along with it meat of black hen and local alcohol is also needed.

Jaundic

Some of the health problems which he claim that he can deal with – Bone setting, Jaundice, Gastric, Asthma, Snake Bite, food poisoning, Throat pain, Joint pain, Tooth ache, Cancer, Diarrhea, Epilepsy, Tuberculosis,

Some of the medicine plants use by him-Mango leaves (boil leaves and take bath with that water)-treats jaundice from outside.

Namley lahara – ***take juice or powder of it - cures jaundice from inside.***

Food Poison

Aconitum bisma (Bikmar) - after having it not to have sheep meat

Tooth ache and Minor fracture

Cancer

Urtica dioica (Sisnu) – root paste

Asuro – boil leaves and consume water.

Entada scandebs Benth (Pangra) – to apply the power of seed.

Leaves of Passion fruit – boil and drink it.

Throat Pain

Terminalia belerica (Barar) – dry bark – mix powder with water and drink it

Swollen neck glands

Diabetics

Snake Bites

Guava leaves – boil in water and take juice of it

Snake Bites

Kathyori ko moaha and *Putka ko moaha* - to eat and apply.

Schima wallichii (Chilowna) – powder of bark - only for applying not for consuming.

Asthma

Haraelo ko lahara – dry it and consume with water.

Bone setting

Paharae dabai

Sonam Regipo is the faith healer of the Phensong GPU. He is not known by his real name but people call him *Azyu Sangay*. *Azyu* in Bhutia language means Grandfather and *Sangay* as equal to Buddha, as he has knowledge of

Faith Healer

all. He is a wise man in his surrounding areas. He is very busy man and people hardly see him doing nothing. People come to him from far distant places. He is 63 years old.

Diagnosis

At first when a patient visits him he first evokes *Guru Rinpoche* (*Guru Padma Sambhava*), secondly to *Sangay Chevami,* as *Sangay Chevami* is a god of life. And thirdly, to *Cheraji* who is god of kindness and love.

In case of serious illness for instance, if the patient is seem to be in his or her last stage than he ask Sangay Chevami whether the patient has his time in this earth or not. He detects this from his *phaengpo* (rosary). As told by him, while counting if one or two beads left than it is bad. And which means patient does not have time in earth. For this he evokes Sangay Chevami and asks him the reason for the illness and whether the illness is curable or not. While counting if one or two beads remain that means not curable and the patient does not have time. So, for this he begs Sangay Chevami for long life of the patient. And recommend patient's family to perform *Tshep jung* rituals (recitation of mantras of Sangay Chevami). But in the case of three beads, which means the patient has a chance. He with the help of his rosary checks whether the illness can be cure by performing some rituals or by visiting hospital and according to it he recommend patient's family to do things further.

Folklore of Leprosy

Leprosy is caused by a slow growing type of bacteria called Myco bacterium leprae. This is what western medical practitioners believe. But according to Lepchas of Tingshim village its origin goes back to their ancestor. In ancient time some of their ancestors where hunters. Beside elephants, they use to hunt almost everything even tigers. After hunting their game they first use to pray god by saying I have live whole of my life hunting animals for survival and my descendant will also follow this tradition. If they do not then they will suffer from disease. Which is now they believe is Leprosy.

Food Poisoning

Food poisoning occurs when you consume food or water that has been infected with certain types of bacteria, parasites, viruses, or toxins. But in the context of Tingshim village it has very different meaning. Food poison in this society has nothing to do with contamination of harmful substances in food but is something that a person gives to some other by mixing it in their food. This is only oneside; people believe that there are different types of poison. According to Faith healer of the village Azyu Sangay, there are three types of *Ngeeng* or poison-

- Through mouth - People come in contact of poison that is through food. Symptoms of it is unremitting diarrhea and vomiting.
- Through clothes - In this case poison giver puts poison in victim's clothes. Symptom of it is with passing of time victim becomes weak and dull which not treat on time led to Tuberculosis and even death of victim.
- Through sitting on *Leelhop* (chair or other sitting places) – this type of poison is consider as most dangerous one and there is no medicine for the cure of it. In this case victim dies in short time.

Modern Health Care System in Tingshim

In part IV of Article 47 of the Indian constitution, it is stated that it is a "duty of the state to raise the level of nutrition and the standard of living and to improve public health". There have been multiple five year plans that address issues such as preventive medicine, communicable diseases, and health in rural areas (Mehta 2011).

Presently, India expenditure on health care is about $80 billion and is predicted to increase to $ 339 billion in 2023 (Mehta et al. 2008). This spending is about 6 percent of India's GDP, with over 16 percent of growth rate. Out of total health expense, the public sector contributes 26.2 percent with the remaining coming from private source. With such a lesser share of health care coming from the government, it comes as no shock that consumers go to private sector for health care is about 320 rupees per year. Of this number, 75 percent comes from individual input, 15.2 percent from state governments, 5.2 percent from the central government, 3.3 percent from third party insurance groups, and 1.3 percent from municipal governments and foreign donors (World Health Organization, 2005).

Integrated Child Development Services (ICDS)

With over 40,000 centres nationwide Integrated Child Development Scheme (ICDS) in India is the world's largest combined initial childhood programme. In 1975 since its initiation, the program has developed and extended, despite difficulties in adapting to the enormously different local circumstances found on the Indian subcontinent. UNICEF has helped to launch the ICDS programme and continues to offer financial and technical assistance along with the World Bank. Today the programme covers over 4.8 million expectant and nursing mothers and over 23 million children under the age of six. The purpose of ICDS is to advance nutrition, health and development of children. The program provides health, nutrition and hygiene education to mother, non formal preschool education to children of aged between 3 to 6, supplementary feeding for all children and pregnant and nursing mothers, growth monitoring and promotion, and relates to primary health care services like immunization and vitamin A supplements (UNICEF).In 1975, the government of India started the Anganwadi programme as a part of the Integrated Child Development Scheme (ICDS). It is a grassroots programme that reaches out to women in rural areas and urban slum, to teach them on the matters of elementary health and hygiene, nutrition, prenatal and postnatal maternal and child care and child rearing (Yadav 2012).

Tingshim village has one ICDS centre which is run by ICDS teacher Mrs, Lazay Lepcha and her co-worker Mrs, Doma Lepcha. The centre provides medical and nutritional facilities to children. Six days a week accept Sunday, the children of age group 3 to 5 years are provided with non formal preschool education. Meals are also given to these children that consist of rice, pulses, vegetables curry and milk. On every Thursday *kheer* (sweet dish made up of milk, sugar, rice and dried fruits) is given to children. The centre also provides iron tablet to pregnant ladies. It also provides nutritional powder to pregnant women that continue till their baby reaches the age of three. Money has been sanctioned for the distribution of dry fruits to adolescent girls of the village but has not started yet.

Problem of Leprosy

Leprosy is caused by a slow-growing type of bacteria called Mycobacterium leprae. It is an infectious disease that causes skin lesions and nerve damage in the arms and legs. Since the beginning of time, Leprosy has been around often surrounded by frightening, negative stigma and leprosy patients being shunned as outcasts. But it is to keep in mind that leprosy is completely curable and people suffering from it should not be discriminate. They need acceptance and support; as a result they will also become useful member of the society (NLEP).

According to the official report in Primary Health Centre (PHC), there is no single case of Leprosy in Tingshim village, and has been declared as 100 percent cure since 2004. But according to local people it is not. There are still good numbers of people who are suffering from it but suffer are not open about it. They hide their problem because of shame, as they feel that if people found it about them than villagers will dishonor them. As stated by Mr. Choden Lepcha, former panchayat , people suffering from Leprosy were suggested to visit hospitals or PHC in order to get proper treatments, but they get annoy and yell them back. So 100 percent leprosy cure has not been successful. Whenever there is counseling, suffers do not attend it in order to hide their truth. But if proper treatment is not done than later there suffering will get double. According to him, earlier the number of leprosy were decrease because of door to door visit by one of the multipurpose health worker but now he passed away. And with this, Leprosy number has grown up. So, again such door to door visits should be made by medical practitioners to take out leprosy from its root from the village.

Primary Health Centre

Phensong GPU has one Primary Health centre (PHC) in Safyong ward which looks after all seven wards including Tingshim. It is an important centre from where every activity related to health operates. Every month on 15th Village Health and Nutrition day program is organize in which free medical counseling is given to villagers. Medical mobile unit from main hospital arrives once in a month provides free tests for various health issues like sugar test, Anemia, etc. Free medications are also given to villagers. Multipurpose health worker, Gnawo Lhendup Lepcha visits village frequently to check health problems in the village along with ASHA worker Passangkit Lepcha. One of the strange thing to know about village is there is no midwife in Tingshim village. When asked to women about where and how they gave birth to their children, they reply it by saying that they went to hospitals earlier than their time of delivery or ANM came to home for delivery of child. And it is not with the women of infants who gave these reply but women with children of age 20-23. This shows that from more than a decade development in term of health is of good quality in Tingshim village.

Conclusion

There are various initiatives that have been taken by the government in regard to health. Even though, it has failed to cover many aspect of it. In case of Tingshim, leprosy cases still exist. Even after various measures taken by the government. The population is very less and there are no children of the age between 2-4 years, as such there are only four children in ICDS of which one is capable of reading and writing and other three are less than one and half years old. The same reason of less population or less number of children led to close of village school in 2014. Out of 191 populations, 48 are out of village for pursuing education and for job. One of the reason for population decrease is later marriage among present generation as the youngster are more focus toward better jobs and education which was not earlier. Another problem in this village is food poisoning. Because of it there is a negative impact on rural aspect of Tingshim village. People here always fear of food poison.

According to panchayat of village, the overall development of village lies in the coming of road which has been sanctioned but work has not started. Village has fertile soil. People in village grows good number of vegetables but they don't sell it out rather they waste it out. When researcher suggest about communal selling of vegetables at market, the panchayat of village state that there is no unity among villagers and one of the reason for it is food poisoning.

References

Baer, H. A., Singer, M., Susser. 1994. *Medical Anthropology and the World System*. Westport: Praeger Publishers.

Bajpai, N., Dholakia, R. H., Sachs, J. D. 2008. *Primary Health Services in Rural India: Public Investment Requirements and Health Sector Reform*. Columbia: The Earth Institute at Columbia University.

Bhandari, L. and Dutta, S. 2007. *Health Infrastructure in Rural India*. India Infrastructure Report.

Bhuyan, M. 2015. "Comparative Study of Ethnomedicine among the Tribes of North East India". *International Research Journal of Social Science*. Assam: North Lakhimpur College.

Bradby, H. 2009. *Medical Sociology*. New Delhi: SAGE Publication India Pvt Ltd.

Foster, G. M. and Anderson, B. G. 1978. *Medical Anthropology*. New York: John Wiley and Sons.

Kleinman, A. 1980. *Pattern and Healers in the Context of Culture*. Berkeley: University of California Press.

Mehta, N. 2011. *The Interactions of the Traditional and Modern Health Care System in Gujarat*. B.SC. thesis. University of Pittsburgh. School of Arts and Sciences.

Mehta, Rana, Baweja. G., Kejriwal, M., Sinha, A. 2008. *A Capsule on Healthcare Trends*. Technopak. Vol 1.

Mishra, A. 2010. *Health Illness and Medicine Ethnographic Readings*. New Delhi: Orient Blackswan Private Limited.

Multi-Hazard Risk and Vulnerability Assessment of North, East, West & South Sikkim. Sikkim: Sikkim State Disaster Management Authority, land revenue & disaster management department, Government of Sikkim.

Nagori, K., Sharma, M., Agrawal, A., Agrawal, A.K., Sharma, A., Verma, H., Tripathi, D. K. 2011. "General Awareness on Allopathic, Ayurvedic and Homeopathic System of medicine in Chattisgarh, India". *International journal of Pharmacy and Pharmaceutical science*. Chattisgarh: Rungta College of Pharmaceutical Science and Research.

National Coordination Committee, Jan Swasthya Abhiyan. 2016. *Health system in India: Crisis and Alternatives.* Retrieved from http://www.mumbaidp24seven.in/reference (Accessed on 9-02-2016)

Panda, A. K. 2012. "Medicinal Plants use and Primary Health Care in Sikkim". *International Journal of Ayurvedic And Herbal Medicine.* Sikkim. Retrieved from http://interscience.org.uk/index.php/ijahm

Rao, M. G. and Choudhury, M. 2012. *Health Care Financing Reforms in India.* National Institute of Public Finance and Policy.

Rivers, W. H. R. 1924. *Medicine, Magic and Religion.* London: Routledge.

Sherpa, M. T., Mathur, A., Das, S. 2014. "MEDICINAL PLANTS AND TRADITIONAL MEDICINE SYSTEM OF SIKKIM: A REVIEW". *World Journal of pharmacy and Pharmaceutical Sciences.* Gangtok: Sikkim University, Department of Microbiology.

Sikkink, L. 2009.*Medical Anthropology in Applied Perceptive.* Colorado: Western State College.

The Anganwadi Programme. Retrieved from http://www.chinh.in/2013 percent 20cikff/ (Accessed on 9- 04- 2016)

UNICEF. *India- Integrated Child Development Scheme (ICDS).* Retrieved from http://unicef.org/earlychildhood/files/ (Accessed on 11- 04- 2016)

World Health Organisation. 2005. *India Country Health System Profile.*

Yadav, R. 2012. *A Critical Analysis on ANGANWADI SYSTEM in Rural Bihar.* Patna: Indira Bhavan.

19

Ethnomedicine and its Significance in Meitei Society

Naorem Naokhomba Singh

Introduction

Ethnomedicine, also known as traditional medicine is indigenous art of medical treatment. It is an integral part of indigenous cultural system. World Health Organisation (WHO) described traditional medicine as "the knowledge, skills and practices based on the theories, beliefs and experiences indigenous to different cultures, used in the maintenance of health and in the prevention, diagnosis, improvement or treatment of physical and mental illness". Hughes (1968) defined it as, those beliefs and practices relating to disease which are the products of indigenous cultural development and are not explicitly derived from the conceptual framework of modern medicine. According to Foster and Anderson (1978), ethnomedicine denotes the totality of health knowledge, values, beliefs, skills and practices of indigenous people, including all the clinical and non-clinical activities that relate to their health needs. For Bhasin (2002) ethnomedicine refers to the long standing indigenous system of health care found in developing countries and among indigenous populations. It is a social institution which enables the members to meet their medical and health needs from a very early period.

During the very early period humans began to develop different ways of lessening pain and treating physical and mental problems in an effort to cope with their environment. "If there is a world's oldest profession besides hunter and gatherer, it is curer. The curer's role has some universal features" (Foster and Anderson, 1978). Many ways of treating these problems came through trial and error method over a long period of time. Over time, individuals within groups became more experienced, skilled and acquainted in helping the sick and injured. Some of them become responsible for carrying out healing practices and rituals. Thus, over time they became local curers or medicine man and other practitioners who are known by different names in different societies. Many of these methods of treatment have been passed down through families for generations.

The Meitei traditional medical system has a fully developed customary way of diagnosis and treatment. It is derived from local medicinal plants, minerals, different types of organic matters and spiritual belief. In this medical system *Maibis* (Female practitioner or priestess) and *Maibas* (Male practitioner or priest) have their respective significant roles. These local curers emerge through a culturally defined process of selection and training. Eventually, the curer is certified by older practitioners and that way acquires a professional image. They enjoy specified status in the Meitei society. This system is an integral part of the Meitei culture. Rivers (1924) may aptly be quoted here, "Indigenous medical systems are social institutions to be studied in the same way as social institutions in general and that indigenous medical practices are rational actions when viewed in the light of prevailing causation beliefs". In other words, medical systems can be appreciated only when they are construed as a part of the total cultural system.

The Meitei traditional medical system owes its origin and foundation to traditional Meitei religion. The Meiteis have their own system of religion which has its own myths and legends, gods and goddesses, priests and priestesses, rituals and festivals, etc. This religion centres around their belief in a supreme being, *Chingu Khoyum Yaibirel Sidaba* who is a formless divinity having myriad manifestations and also his two progenies-God *Sanamahi* and God *Pakhangba*. This primal religion of ancient Manipuris known as *Sanamahi* religion or *Sanamahism* after god *Sanamahi*. This ancient kingdom however, came within the fold of Hinduism since the beginning of the 18th century. *Charairongba* who ascended the Manipuri throne in 1697 was the first Manipuri king initiated into Hinduism. After the death of *Charairongba*, his son *Pamheiba* also known as *Garib Niwaz* ascended the throne in 1709. In the year 1717 he was initiated into Hinduism by Gopal Das (Nilbir, 2009). The zenith of Hinduism in Manipur was during the reign of *Bhagyachandra* (1759-1798), the grandson of Garib Niwaz.

During the reign of King Churachand (1891-1941) in the thirties a revivalist movement of the traditional religion popularly known as Sanamahi religion started in a Meitei village in Cachar. The leader of the movement was Naorem Phullo, popularly known as Laininghal Naoria. He formed a religious organisation known as "*Apokpa Marup*" along with his 7th companions on 12th April, Saturday 1930 for the revival of the Meitei traditional religion (Nilabir, 1991). He also wrote a number of books on different subjects to propagate traditional Meitei religion. He along with few of his companions worked hard for the revival of the traditional Meitei religion. They asked the Meiteis in

Cachar to renounce Hinduism. The orthodox Meitei Hindus of Cachar ostracised him with his friends from the Hindu society as unclean.

The news of the movement for the revival of the traditional religion reached Manipur valley in 1934. Takhellambam Bokul, popularly known as Sanamahi Bokul got the news from a friend who had returned from Cachar. As soon as he got the news, the anxiety of meeting Naoria grew in his mind. In 1935 he along with his two companions left Manipur for Cachar. In Cachar they met Naoria and listened to his talks on the importance of the revival of the traditional Meitei religion. Naorias talk on Meitei culture and religion was so convincing that Bokul and his two friends renounced Hinduism then and there. After one year and nine months with Naoria they came backed to Manipur. On May 14, 1945 a religious organisation known as '*Manipur State Meetei Marup*' was formed, Takhellambam Bokul and Ngasepam Manikchand as the president and secretary respectively for the revivalist movement (Nilabir, 2015).

The movement was not smooth in the beginning as it was against the will of orthodox Meitei Hindus. But slowly it began to spread in different parts of Manipur valley. During the period from 1975 to 1980 there was a new wave in the Sanamahi movement. It was organised and launched by educated youths. Their main objective was to take over traditional *Lais* (deities) *Laiphams* (worshipping places) from the hands of the Brahmins and Meite Hindus and restore them to the Meitei traditional religion followers. On February 6, 1974 a special functions was organised to free the Meitei community from the binding of the oath taken by their forefathers to follow Hinduism some two hundred and fifty years ago with the King Okendrajit. In another function organised on April 23, 1992 Okendrajit, the king declared, "*I open the Lubak Tabu and abandon Hinduism as state religion and recognition is hereby withdrawn by the Royal Customary Law of the country, instead the Royal Customary Law revives the Lainingthouism as state religion and do hereby give recognition as state religion*" (Cited from Nilabir, 2015). Thus, the Meiteis revived their cultural and religious identity. Today they are free to follow their choice of religion and there are Meitei traditional religion followers, Meitei Hindus, Meitei Christians and Meitei Buddhist.

Materials and Methods

The paper is based on data collected through interview, observation and case study method. The relevant data for this study were collected from the two Meitei villages namely *Uyal* and *Wangbal* of Thoubal district, Manipur. The villages are situated at a distance of 33 kms south east of Imphal. The data were collected from the *Maibas* (male practitioners), *Maibis* (female practitioners), and village elders who have got a good knowledge about Meitei traditional medicine that they have acquired from their parents and elders. Data collection was carried out from September to December, 2014. Semi-structured interview schedule was used to gather pertinent data. Necessary aids have also been taken for secondary data collection from the earlier monographs, books, journals, ancient Meitei texts and chronicles.

Findings

All societies have health care systems. These consist of beliefs, customs, specialist and techniques adopted to ensuring health and preventing, diagnosing and curing illness. The Meitei system of health care works in a set of juxtaposed natural and supernatural activities for an overall well-being of the people in which *Maibas* (male practitioners) and *Maibis* (female practitioners) play a vital role. The Meitei traditional medical system has a fully developed traditional way of diagnosis and treatment. It owes its genesis in the people's creation cosmogony. A mythical personality *Atiya,* figuring in the creation myth as the most important agent of creation is accredited in the creation story as the founder of the office of medical department (locally expressed as *Maiba Loishang).* The local medical practitioners are believed to represent this divine personage, thereby as the carriers of the traditions of this art of medicine laid down by him; as a matter of fact the *Maibas* and *Maibis* first invoke this high divine spirit for the efficacious results of all their healing practices. All the techniques of treatment are assumed to derived efficacy from the favour of this deity. Hence worship of this deity first before the application of any technique of treatment still prevails. The overall Meitei culture provides a unique place therein for medical culture; a separate medical department was instituted as an indispensable organ of the larger administrative system throughout the monarchical history of Manipur. The practitioners were selected and appointed by the kings as office holders of the department of *Maiba Loishang.* This profession was opened to both the sexes with some kind of sexual division of their jobs.

Another feature of the Meitei folk medicine relates it to the religious culture of the people as it is so revealed in the people's traditional lore of medicine and methods of treatment. Three cardinal directional deities, namely *Marjing* (presiding deity of the north direction), *Thangjing* (presiding deity of the west) and *Wangbrel* (presiding deity of the south) are at the same time identified as the divine authorities of the three traditional techniques of treating diseases and illness. They are (i) treatment by massage with hand on the belly of the patient *(puk-suba),* (ii) treatment by the application of medicine prepared out of herbs and other medicinal objects and (iii) treatment by application of oral magical formulae. In all cases of treatment pulsation of the patient is first read to diagnose the nature of the complaint. Pulsation is observed at certain specific points of the body, such as upper end of the index finger, wrist, armpit etc., according to the nature of the apparent symptoms of ailments. It is checked on the right hand if the patient is a male and on the left hand it the patient is female. All types of illness and diseases known to the people are recorded with names in the local folk medical vocabulary.

Diagnosis of illness and its etiological determination are conjointly resorted to while dealing with both the natural, supernatural approaches. The natural causes of diseases are attributed to the malfunctioning of the internal system of temperature in the physiological order of the organic body of the patient. Illness and diseases are treated with the indigenous medicines prepared mainly from plants. Such herbal medicines are very effective in curing a number of natural diseases and a number of herbal medicines may be applied for a particular disease.

Nongmangkha (Adhatoda vasika), *Nungsi Hidak* (Mentha arvensis), *Leipung Khangga* (S.Xanthocarpun Sch), *Peruk* (Indian pennywort), *Tulsi* (Ocinum sanctum), honey, *Yensil* (Oxalis Linn), *Kaphoi* (pomegranate), *Tera Paibi* (Gynura cusimbua), *Ekaithabi* (Mimosa dapndica), *Urik Sibi* (Vite Negndo), *Heigru* (Phylanthus emblica), *Chanam* (garlic), *Yaingang* (Curcuma longu), *Sing* (ginger), *Pullei* (Galangal), *Awathabi* (papaya), *Mukthrubi* (Zantrohylon Roxb), *Sing Khangga* (S. ndicum Linn), *Drita-kumar* (Aloevera), *Laipakngou* (Artemesia nilagirika pamp), *Urok-sumban* (Basella alba L), *Tera* (Bombax ceiba L), *Kongouyen* (Cissus aduata Roxb), *Tinghtou* (cynodon dactylon pers), *Pungphai* (dactyloctenium aegyptium), *Langthrei* (E. Biramanicum D.C) and *Tairel* (Tuna ciliata M.Roem) are some of the plants used in Meitei folk medicine. Of these, *Tingthou, Pungphai, Langthrei* and *Tairel* deserve special mention. They are indispensable ritual items of the religious life of the Meitei people too.

A number of diseases are treated effectively with the medicine prepared from these medicinal plants. A particular plant or its different parts are also found to be used for treating different diseases. Some of the diseases treated effectively with the medicine prepared from them are discuss as below:

1. Cold, cough and fever: *Nongmangkha* (Adhatoda vasika) - Fresh leaves are boiled and the decoction is given 3-4 times to the patient.

   -Fresh flowers are fried with little mustard oil and taken as food item for the cold.

   -Fresh leaves are kept below the pillow to cure cold in children.

   Leipung Khangga (S.Xanthocarpun Sch) - juice of fresh fruits with honey is given to the patient.

   -Ginger paste with honey is also used for the cold.

   -Juice of fresh *Tulsi* leaves with honey is also given for the cold and fever.

2. Dysentery: - Young tender 7 leaves of *Pong Heiton* (guava) 2-3 times per day is given to the patient.

   - *Kaphoi* (pomegranate) leaves is fried with egg and taken with rice.

3. Diarrhoea: - Decoction of *Peruk* (Indian pennywort) with honey is given 3-4 times a day.

   - Juice of fresh *Yensil* (Oxalis Linn) is also given.

   - Juice of fresh *Nungsi Hidak* (Mentha arvensis) with honey is also given 3-4 times a day.

4. Piles: -Powder of dried *Kambong* (water bamboo) is mixed with honey and made a paste. It is taken a teaspoonful in the morning on empty stomach.

   - Fresh leaves of *Urik Sibi* (Vite Negndo) are fried. A paste is made after putting *Meitei Thum* (indigenous salt) and honey to it. It is taken after food, twice a day.

5. Asthma: *Meitei Thum* (indigenous salt) with fat of snake (cobra) is given.

   - Bark of *Ashi Heibong* (Ficus hispida L) is boiled and decoction is given 3 times a day.

6. Burns: Honey is applied to the affected area.

   - Paste of fresh potato or egg yolk is also applied to the affected area.

7. Boils: Paste of cooked rice and charcoal is applied.

   - Paste of lemon juice and yolk is also applied.

   - Young shoots of *Nongmangkha* are smashed with ginger and little salt is added. The paste is applied on the affected area.

8. Small pox and other skin problems: Leaf decoction of *Nongmangkha* is taken bath for a week.

   - Decoction of fresh *Nongleishang* (Dandal, Xylosma longifolia) leaves is also used for taking bath twice in a week.

9. Diabetes: Leave and flower of *Nongmangkha* is taken as row or fried with food.

   - *Chanam* (garlic), Sitaphal (passion fruit), Torbot (Malabar gourd) and lemon are given as food items to the patient.

10. Arthritis and other bone problems: Paste of fresh garlic and mustard oil is applied.

    -Paste of fresh *Pullei* (Galangal) rhizome is also applied to the affected area.

11. Snake and dog bites: Paste of young shoots of *Yenthou* (Arundo donax) is applied over bitten area.

    - Fresh leaves paste of *Ureirom* (Bixa Orellana L) is also applied over bitten area.

    - Paste of fresh papaya is also applied over bitten area to neutralise the poison.

12. Cuts and wounds: Fresh *Terapaibi* (Gynura cusimbua) leaves are smashed and the paste is applied as antiseptic. It also stop bleeding and helps in fast healing.
    - Paste of fresh *Nongballei* (Lantana camara L) leaves is also applied to stop bleeding.
13. Jaundice: Decoction of *Lam Thabi* (Zehneria scabra L) is given 3-4 times a day.
    - Fruit of *Heikreng* (Celtis australis L) is also given.
14. Indigestion and stomach problems: Fresh *Ching Yensil* (Antidesma acidum) or Awa Phadigom (Eryngium foetidum) plants are smashed and a little salt is added to the syrup. The syrup is given 3 times a day.
15. Stone case: Decoction of *Kongouyen* (Ciccus adnata Roxb) is given 3-4 times a day. *Torbot* (Benincasa hispida) fruit is also given after boiling.

Treatment by massage with hand is another aspect of Meitei traditional medicine. It is called *Puk Suba.* In this method of treatment the *Maiba* or *Maibi* treat the patient by massaging on their belly (abdomen). The practitioner of this method have a very good knowledge of human physiology and anatomy. Muscle pain (*Hakchang Thindokpa*), back pain (*Khwang Naba*), pain in the abdomen (*Thajin Sougtpa*) and stomach ache (*Puk Naba*) etc., are treated with this massage therapy. This method of treatment is becoming very uncommon at present Meitei society. Lack of skilled practitioners for this method and people's preference to the modern methods of treatment are found to be the main factor of that.

Besides using herbal medicine and massage treatment the Meitei folk medicine also use magico-religious methods to deal with certain medical conditions. Incantation of spells, oracles, performing healing rituals, prayer, offering of food items, fruits, vegetables and flowers to the spirits are basic practices of this method. Spiritual belief is the key factor in achieving desire result in this therapy. *Hingchabi Changba* (possession of evil spirits), *Heloi Oknaba* (possess by the female spirit), *Potsem Jadu Touba* (witchcraft), *Maibi Changba* (showing symptoms of becoming a Maibi) and *Lai Oknaba* (contact with certain evil deities) are some common complaints treated with magico-religious methods. They are effectively treated by the *Maibas* and *Maibis.* It is also found that modern medicines have very little or no desirable effect in these complaints. On the contrary, modern or allopathic medicines give adverse effects in some cases. So the sole responsibility of treating these cases still lies in the hands of *Maibas* and *Maibis.* In fact, it is one of the most important role of folk medicine in contemporary Meitei society.

The role of *Maibas* and *Maibis* in treating those conditions cannot be replaced by modern physicians with all their advance tools and techniques. The symptoms of these conditions, locally known as *Laiokpa* are quite different from other medical problems. They exhibit some common features of symptoms in all cases. Sudden change in the behaviour of the patient is observed in most of the cases. Changes like excitement or depression, laughing or crying without any significant reason, keep murmuring to oneself are often found. Strange behaviours compared to their original personality are often found to be expressed by these patients. The patient is at their sub conscious state, they are unaware of their surroundings. Sometimes, the patient gets a kind of epileptic attack. If a patient develop these symptoms, immediately a *Maiba* or *Maibi* is consulted. After checking *Meehul Kanglon* (pulsation) and symptoms, the cause and way of treatment are derived by the *Maiba* or *Maibi*; which spirit is causing the harm, what is it they want from the patient, how to deal with it... etc. After deriving these necessary information the *Maiba* or *Maibi* make appropriate offering to the particular spirit to appease it and leave the body of the patient. In some other cases healing rituals like *Saroi khangba, Yelhing Thaba* etc., are perform to appease the spirits that causing harm. If the symptoms of *Laiokpa* develop to a patient who is undergoing treatment in the health centre or hospital, healing rituals or offerings are performed by the *Maiba* or *Maibi* and then her/his treatment in the clinic followed. While the patients are possessed, their body and actions are fully controlled by the spirits which dwell inside them. They claimed to remember nothing that happened to them while they were possessed.

Conclusion

In the present world of modern medical advancement ethnomedicine gains its popularity and is still in vogue in many societies including that of the Meiteis since it forms an integral and functional part of the whole culture. The Meitei traditional medical system has a fully developed customary way of diagnosis and treatment. Traditional Meitei healers locally known as *Maiba* and *Maibis* were found to play a significant role in the health care system of the people. Herbal medicines prepared from different medicinal plants and organic matters are used to cure a number of diseases. These medicines are easy to prepare and have very less or no side effects. It is also worth mentioning that there are certain medical conditions where modern medicine have very little or no desirable effect on them. And those conditions are treated very effectively by traditional practitioners. It is very much necessary to promote and preserved traditional healing practices for the future generations. It would help to conserved age old indigenous knowledge of medicine, practices, and valuable medicinal plants.

Acknowledgement

This work would not have been possible without the support of my key informants, traditional medical practitioners (*Maibas* and *Maibis*) and my respondents. I am grateful for their support.

References

Bhasin, V. 2002. Traditional Medicine among Tribals of Rajasthan. In *Journal of Social Sciences,* vol. 6(3). Pp. 153-172.

Foster, G. M. and Anderson, B. G. 1978. *Medical Anthropology*. Toronto: John Wiley and Sons.

Hughes, C. C. 1968. Ethnomedicine. In *International Encyclopaedia of Social Sciences, Vol.10*. New York: Free Press. Pp. 87-93.

Nilabir, S.1991. The Revivalist Movement of Sanamahism. In *Manipur Past and Present.* Vol.II. Ed. Naorem Sanajaoba. New Delhi: Mittal Publications. Pp. 109-126.

Nilabir, S. 2009. Sanskritization process of Manipur under king Garib Niwaz. In *New insights into the glorious heritage of Manipur*. Ed. H. Dwijasekhar Sharma. New Delhi: Akansha Publishing House. Pp. 239-270.

Nilabir, S. 2015. Laiyingthou Sanamahi Amasung Sanamahi Laining Hinggat Eehou. Imphal: G.M. Publications.

Rivers, W. H. R. 1924/2003. *Medicine, Magic and Religion*. London: Kessinger Publishing.

WHO. Web reference, retrieved from http://www.who.int/topics/traditional_medicine/en/

20

Indigenous Health Care Practices of The Vaiphei

Grace Mary Vaiphei and Arundhati Devi Maibam

Introduction

Indigenous people have an understanding of health as well being which is about the harmony that exists between individual communities and the Universe. The history of use of plants and animals as a source of medicine dates back perhaps to the origin of human race (Chopra et al., 1956; Kirtikar and Basu, 1975). Among many others, the importance of indigenous medicine has drawn the attention of Vidyarthi (1986), Mathur (1982), Banerjee and Jalota (1988), Rizvi (1991) and Dwivedi (2003). Tribal people, who are self-reliant and self-sufficient, have over centuries developed their own medicine system based on plants and other items collected from the nature processed locally (Tribedi et al., 1982).

The Vaiphei is one of the recognised hill tribes of Manipur under the schedule tribe order 1950. Their forefathers are believed to have lived in Mongolia from where a group migrated to Tibet and then to Burma. Still longing for a safer and better land for cultivation, a section of Vaiphei migrated to north eastern region of India in the year 1850 and 1891. The first group of migrants settled near Manipur and Mizoram and named the village as "*Maite*". In the year 1919, a section of people migrated from Maite to the place which is presently called Kangvai, with the consent of the Maharaja of Manipur. The first settlers of Kangvai were Mangtingkai who became the chief of the village. He was followed by three brothers namely: Khuplal Vaiphei, Thanglam Vaiphei and Vungkhosoi Vaiphei.

Aims and objectives

The study was undertaken with the following objectives:

i. to understand the beliefs associated with the causes of illness

ii. to recognize the classification of illness
iii. to document the curative measures adopted and herbal medicines used to cure diseases
iv. to investigate the current status of indigenous health care practices

Methodology

Qualitative data have been collected through interview with randomly selected elderly and knowledgeable men and women, healers and health professionals of the village. Data on the beliefs about the causes of illness, folk classification of illness, curative measures along with the application of herbal medicines and proscription of diet of the people were collected. The data were analysed taking all the common denominators and variations into consideration so that a conclusion may be drawn about the health care practices. Case study method was also employed to collect information from the people and healers.

Significance of the study

Specific research on indigenous medicine or indigenous health care practices among the Vaiphei have not been conducted significantly. The present study is an attempt to supplement to studies on traditional or indigenous health care practices among the tribal in general and those carried out among north eastern tribes of India in particular.

Limitations of the study

The present study was conducted in only one Vaiphei village. Local variations among the different Vaiphei villages in the state cannot be overlooked.

Beliefs related to the causes of illness

The Vaiphei do not worship any celestial body such as moon, sun and stars. They rather worship mountains, rocks and rivers as they are believed to be the dwelling places of innumerable spirits, good and bad. They also believe in the existence of one Supreme Being called *Nungzai* or *Pathian* and attribute to him the creation of all things and power over all things. The *Pathian* is invoked in times of need and offerings are made for his blessings.

Although the Vaiphei believe in one Supreme Being who is revered as the creator of the Universe and all living and non-living things, they also have strong belief in spirits which are capable of causing disturbances to their day-to-day life. Illness is regarded as a result of discontentment among the bad spirits. Offerings are therefore made to appease them in the form of sacrifices. *Chawmnu* is a female evil spirit which is believed to reside in hollowed tree trunks and caves deep in the forest and cause illness to human. *Thitha Gamngak* are spirits which restrict entry to or encroachment in territories where they reside. They cause sickness and even death to hunters and gatherers who wander into their territories knowingly or unknowingly. *Thalang* are spirits of those who died in accidents or in any unnatural manner. These spirits are believed to remain in and around the dwelling place where they once lived and often come into contact with relatives and family members thus causing them mental illness. To guard these spirits off, the Vaiphei offer sacrifices and perform rites and rituals to appease them. Any territory or object which is believed to be associated with the spirits directly or indirectly is avoided. Some of the objects and places which the Vaiphei avoid in fear are:

(a) *Thamphal* (swamp): Swampy areas are believed to be the abode of the evil spirits and are avoided to prevent illness.

(b) *Tuivamit* (eyes of a local aquatic bird): Two puddles formed under a tree after rainstorms which resemble eyes of a local aquatic bird are believed to be dwelling places of evil spirits.

(c) *Kawlhawm* (caves): Caves, especially those where strange noises are heard, are also believed to be dwelling places of evil spirits.

(d) *Thinggawphel* (bow-like tree): Trees which grow in the shape of a bow with the trunk dividing into two branches and joining again at the upper part at are taken to be war weapons or bows of evil spirits. It is therefore a taboo to cut such trees.

(e) *Phei Sam* (a kind of monkey): A monkey-like animal, with a leg shorter than the other is believed to be an evil spirit which lives in the deep jungle. This animal is usually sighted among packs of wild boars and is believed to be the guardian or keeper of the boars. It is believed that sighting of this animal brings bad omen to the one who saw it.

(f) *Kausia* (one with evil eye): Evil spirits are sometimes believed to enter human bodies. One distinct sign of such a condition is obsession for red meat. Persons suspected with this possession of evil spirits in their bodies are outcast from the society and all communications are terminated. They are forbidden to marry as it is believed that the children may inherit the evil spirit.

(g) *Kau mei Sel* (marsh gas): Unaware of the scientific characters of marsh gas, smoldering fires over swamps and marshes are taken as evil spirits roaming with torches.

(h) *Keimi* (tiger-man): Drinking water from a certain spring is believed to turn a human into a tiger which can cause great havoc to human and animal lives.

Case study of illness caused by evil spirit:

Name of the informant - Thangzasuan Vaiphei, Age - 72 years, Sex – Male

My informant says that he was born in the year 1940 at Singhat and migrated to Kangvai in 1978. He was a football player. He married in the year 1961 with the granddaughter of Mangtinkhai, the first settler and chief of Kangvai village. He is suffering from *Vun- Kang* (white patches on the skin) since 2005. He believed that it might have been caused by some evil spirits and may not be cured with allopathic medicine. So, he never consults any professional doctor but relies solely on the village *Thiampu.*

Classification of Diseases

Nine classes of illness are identified among the Vaiphei. They are:

i. Skin diseases: Skin diseases according to the people are caused due to ill effects of environment as well as evil eyes. It includes skin rashes and allergies.

ii. Pain and ache: Illness associated with painful symptoms like stomach ache, menstrual cramp, tooth ache, dysuria, back ache and dysentery.

iii. Fever: This class includes illness whose symptoms are always associated with fever. They include anemia, fever, weakness and jaundice.

iv. Cuts, wounds and bites: it includes cuts and wounds, dog bite, snake bite and bee sting etc.

v. Gynaecological problems: it includes miscarriage, infertility, white discharge, yellow discharge, menstrual cramps, and menorrhagia.

vi. Supernatural disease: This category of illness is believed to be caused by the intervention of supernatural of beings in their daily lives example mental illness.

vii. Associated disease: Those common ailments which are associated with one another.

viii. Most fatal disease: Illness which is considered to be most dangerous by the people like cancer and epilepsy.

ix. Seasonal disease: This class includes ailments which vary seasonally. Water borne diseases like diarrhoea, cholera, dysentery are attributed to summer, viral fever to rainy season and respiratory problems like cold and cough to winter.

Thiampu (priest or shaman)

The *Thiampu* plays a very important role in the socio-religious and political lives of the Vaiphei. He can be a member of any clan and enjoys an immediate subordinate position to the chief. He acts as the mediator between man and the objects they worship. He is believed to have knowledge about all sources of problems and illnesses and the type of sacrifices needed to appease the particular spirit to cure a sick or ailing person.

Animal sacrifices to heal a sick or to ward off evil spirits were common. The insides and tasty parts of an animal are placed along the path believed to be frequented by the spirits for consumption. Specific rituals are performed for specific spirits.

Curative measures using herbal medicine

A brief account of some commonly occurring illnesses and their curative methods is given below:

i. Diarrhoea (*ekkhaw*): Tender shoot or bud of guava plant is consumed in raw form. Children suffering from diarrhoea are made to eat banana.

ii. Dysentery (*santen*): The patient is made to eat eggs of duck cooked with *Theibufai dua* (pomegranate leaves) without oil.

iii. Flu, cold, cough (*hitang, kikhu*): Steam inhalation is done to expedite recovery. Another mode of treatment is drinking a solution prepared by boiling leaves of *Theidam* (*Adhatoda vasica*).

iv. Fever (*khawsik*): Leaves of *Theidam (Adhatoda vasica*) is boiled and the solution is consumed. Sponging the body with water in which some rice grains are added helps in cooling the body. And in case of Anaemic fever (*thisan tawm natna*), soup of eel with some ginger is consumed. Curry of pigeon (*vapaal*) with a pinch of salt is also given to the patient.

v. Headache (*luchangnat*): Leaf of mustard (*ankam*) is heated on fire till it becomes soft and it is then placed on the forehead.

vi. Tonsillitis: Gurgling with warm water with a pinch of salt added to it is a good remedy. Also solution prepared by boiling leaves of *Theidam (Adhatoda vasica*) is also another good remedy.

vii. Measles: Feathers of hen are heated till they become wrinkled or curly and then they are pasted all over the body so that the measles are fully expressed. Leaves of varnish fruit (*Khongma)* are crushed and boiled and the lotion is used for massaging the body to prevent scar marks after recovery.

viii. Cuts and wounds (*kiat liam*): Human hair or feathers of crane (*waking)* are placed over the injured area. Another remedy is application of crushed leaves of a local herb known as *Japan gui* on the cut or wound. Another local creeper called *Puklo* is tied near the injured area with the belief that the smell of the *Puklo* plant will suppress the smell of fresh blood which may attract any kind of evil/ bad spirit to harm the injured person.

ix. Scanty breast milk (*noitui tawm*): The patient is made to drink soup of local hen of black colour with ginger and a pinch of salt. Fresh juice of papaya, sugar cane and molasse are also believed to stimulate production of breast milk.

x. Irregular menstrual period and white discharge: Extracts of crushed root of silverberry (*Tau*) is mixed with molasse and sugar candy and consumed thrice after food. For white discharge leaves of *Theidam (Adhatoda vasica)* are boiled in a pot and the patient is made to sit on rim so that the vapour directly hits the vagina.

xi. Hypertension: Solution of boiled local herbs called *Anphuiche* and *Changkuangche* are consumed. Eating raw garlic is also another long term remedy.

Case study of a male midwife

Name of the informant- Paulianthang Vaiphei; Age – 54; Sex – Male

Paulianthang Vaiphei has been serving as *Naulai dawm* (mid-wife) since 1985 and has delivered 171 babies. According to him almost all the women deliver babies at home except a few complicated cases. They consult him for remedies for gynaecological problems such as irregularity of menstrual cycle, white discharge, and scanty breast milk and dislocation of foetus inside the womb as well as proscription of diet during pregnancy. According to him, consumption of honey, crab, bee larva, papaya during pregnancy causes still birth.

Present status of indigenous health care practices

As there is no health centre within the village, the villagers depend on the health centre located at Churachandpur for emergencies and other common illnesses. For serious cases, they visit the hospitals in Imphal city. However visits to these health centers often entail expenses and manpower which pose great problem. In such a circumstance the people prefer to consult the traditional healers. Women by and large avoid going to hospitals and depend on traditional medicines. They have great faith in the local medicine man and *dais*.

The traditional healer, on the other hand, is faced with the problem of procuring medicinal plants to meet the demand. His service is often interrupted due to non-availability of ingredients for preparing medicines. This is largely due to gradual disappearance of plants of medicinal value which are gathered from the wild. Forests which once housed these plants are reducing day by day due to spread of settlement. Aging is another factor which has handicapped the traditional healers. They no longer possess the stamina to wander in the wild to gather the plants. Knowledge of the plants and where they thrive lies with the healer and therefore has no scope of expecting others to do the job for him. Despite the fact that the knowledge is dying out, no one has shown genuine interest to keep it alive. Except for remedies for common health problems, knowledge of which have been passed on primarily through observation and experience, valuable indigenous knowledge on health care is declining.

Another important factor for the decline is conversion to Christianity which preached shunning of traditional life style and opting for the modern, with special emphasis on sanitation and health care. Modern medicines were found to be more effective despite the cost.

Conclusion

Every culture has its own medical culture to combat disease and sickness. The Vaiphei too have their own ways of treating the sick. The practices involve some kind of religious activities which have great social, psychological, and even physiological effects. They attributed health problems to the supernatural. To cope with various diseases they apply both supernatural treatment and traditional herbal treatment. The present paper highlights the indigenous knowledge pertaining to common ailments like fever, could and coughs malaria, diarrhoea, tonsillitis, urinary trouble, dysentery, and headache. Indigenous health care knowledge can make important contributions to the health sector of every society. Important compositions can be experimented to make wonderful discoveries in the arena of medical science.

References

Banerjee, B.G. & Jalota, R. (1988). (1977). *Folk Illness and Ethnomedicine*. New Delhi: Northern Book Centre.

Chopra, R.N., Nayar, S.L., & Chopra, I.C. (1956). *Glossary of Medicinal Plants of India*. New Delhi: CSIR.

Dwivedi, P. (2003). *Demographic profile and health care practices among the Baiga of Samanpur Block of Dindori district, Madhya Pradesh*. Unpublished dissertation, Department of Anthropology, Dr. H.S. Gour University, Sagar (M.P.), India.

Kirtikar, K.R. & Basu, B.D. (1975). *Indian Medicinal Plants*. New Delhi: Periodical Book Express Co.

Mathur, P.R.G. (1982). Anthropology of Tribal Medicine: disease and curing techniques among the tribal of North Wynad (Keria). *Man in India*, 62: 295-312.

Rizvi, S.H.N. (1991). *Medical Anthropology of the Jaunsaris*. New Delhi: Northern Book Centre.

Tribedi, G.N., Dayal, R.N., & Chaudhuri Rai, H.N. (1982). Some medicinal plants of Mayurbhanj (Orissa). *Bull. Bot. Survey India*, 24:117-120.

Vidyarthi, L.P. (ed). (1968). *Applied Anthropology in India*. Allahabad: Kitab Mahal.

21

Impact of Christianity on the Traditional Healing Practices Among the Angami Naga

Ketousienuo Kuotsu

Introduction

The traditional religion of the Nagas is usually described as "Animism" which is the worldview that non - human entities – such as animals, plants and inanimate objects possess a spiritual essence. The Nagas believed that every object both animate and inanimate, resides with a spirit which are malevolent in characteristics and so, appeasement was therefore an utmost necessity for them to pacify the malignant spirits from overcoming their wrath. No form of idol worship was prevalent among the Nagas and neither temples nor shrines or alters or definite cult objects were found. They basically worship unseen spirits and dieties without objects and material image. The traditional Naga religion was based on animism and theism, interwoven with extreme attachment to superstitious beliefs (Nshoga 2009).

The Nagas in the past were of the view that their gods and spirits visit them in the form of rain, lightning, thunder, heat, disease, death and natural calamities causing loss of lives and destruction to property. This perception instilled in them an impulse to please and pacify their gods by offering animal sacrifice to ward off the wrath of god to spare the lives and property of the people.

The Lothas believe that there are number of evil spirits whose abodes are rocks, springs, lakes and trees. All the evil spirits who are ill disposed with humans are collectively called *tsungrham* (evil Spirits). He makes human sick by detaining their souls and inserting foreign bodies in human bodies. Failure in timely propitiation results in death (Yanthan 2015). A Rengma, when sick, usually attributes his sickness to the malice of an evil spirit (*gejong*) who has either introduces some foreign matter, such as hair or a little stone, into his body or causes his soul (*aghamuo*) to desert him at a certain place (Kath 2005). Similarly the Angamis believe that *Rutzeh* (evil spirit) is the giver of sudden death. If a man dies unexpectedly, blood issuing from his mouth and nostrils, no illness having preceded it, his death is ascribed to *Rutzeh* (Hutton 2003).

With such superstitious beliefs and ritual practices found among the Naga society, it was almost impossible for them to part with their long followed culture and traditional way of life. However, through the ceaseless efforts of the pioneering missionaries from 1842 onwards, the light of Christianity reached the Naga Hills and it was only Christianity that tamed the tribals. By the end of the 19th century, Christianity invaded the traditional Naga religion and shattered their faith from supernatural belief and implanted instead the Christianity. Many social and religious practices were abolished or discontinued as a result of new faith (Nshoga 2009).

The growth of Christianity was a slow process in the beginning. There was much resistance and opposition from the people and those who embraced the new religion were persecuted by their own family members, relatives and villagers. The first Naga tribe to accept Christianity in large number was Ao, followed by Lotha and other tribes. Although more than 98 percent of the Angamis are Christians, they are one of the last Naga tribes having an animist population.

The Angami Nagas

The Angamis are one of the major Naga tribe native to the Nagaland state in North East India and are the dominant group in the district of Kohima. It is bounded by Wokha district in the North, Manipur state and Peren district in the South, Phek district in the East and Assam state and Dimapur district in the West. Kohima is located at 25°40'N 94°07'E 25.67°N 94.12°E. It has an average elevation of 1261 metres (4137 feet) and covers an area of 1,463 sq. km. Kohima town is located on the top of a high ridge and the town serpentines all along the top of the surrounding mountain ranges as is typical of most Naga settlements.

The territory of the Angamis is made up of the present Kohima district which is divided into four regions:

(1) Northern Angami (Kewhima, Chedema, Riisoma, Meriema, Zhadima, Nerhema, Chiechama, Dihoma, touphema etc.) in the North of Kohima.

(2) Southern Angami (Viswema, Khuzama, Kigwema, Phesama, Jakhama, Mima, Kidima, Pfuchama etc.) in the South of Kohima on the foothills of Mt. Japfii.

(3) Western Angami (Jotsoma, Khonoma, Sechiima, Kiruphema, Mezoma, Peducha etc.) in the West of Kohima.

(4) Chakhro Angami (mostly small villages around Dimapur district with large villages being Medziphema, Chumukedima, Sovima, Razaphe etc. other villages include Piphema, Tsiepama, Pherima etc.)

The former Eastern Angamis have separated and at present they maintain a separate identity recognised as Chakhesang under Phek district of Nagaland.

The Angami Nagas are hill people depending mostly on cultivation. They are known for terraced wet rice cultivation and because of this labour- intensive cultivation, land is the most important form of property among them. They practice wet- rice cultivation made on the hill slopes which allows them to cultivate the same plot year after year.

The traditional festival celebrated by the Angamis is known as *Sekrenyi*. It is a ten day festival usually celebrated in the month of February (*Kezei*). The term *Sekrenyi* literally means 'Sanctification Festival' (*sekre* – sanctification and *nyi* - fest). Few decades back, the festival was celebrated with great pomp and gaiety but as time elapsed, majority of the people converted to Christianity leaving ancestral practices behind. Today 99 percent have embraced Christianity and has also adopted a modern way of living.

Traditional Healing Practices

The Angamis, like the other Naga tribes also had their own elaborate set of ritual practices to ward off evil spirits. They had very clear idea on how to please and serve their gods. Animal sacrifices and offering of eggs, fowls or rice beer to the gods and spirits of the jungle, stone, tree, stream, mountain peak etc., were done on regular basis to avoid the wrath of god and also to avert epidemics, famines, diseases and natural calamities.

In the past, when the healing system of the Angamis was based completely on traditional beliefs and rituals, the shamanistic treatment was one of the most powerful and the most popular form of treatment sought by the people. Herbal medicines were no doubt extensively used by the people since time immemorial. Even today, a rudimentary knowledge of the curative aspect of few commonly found herbs is known to almost everyone in a community. The leaves of *Eupatorium adenophorum* (*Japan nha*) is commonly used for blood clotting, Guava (*moduram*) leaves are eaten raw to cure diarrhoea, *Centella asiatica* (*gara*) is boiled and taken for gastric problems, the fruit of *Solanum betaceum* (*si benganuo*) is eaten raw for blood cleansing, *Ocimum tenuiflorum* (*nyiechu*) is boiled and taken to lower high blood presser. These are some commonly found medicinal plants used by the people. Other common home remedies include the use of garlic (*ciimerie*), ginger (*kebvii*), lemon (*siihuo*), honey (*mepfi dzii*), pudina leaves and aloevera for curing illness such as cough, sore throat, headache and gastric problems etc.

In case a person is suffering from an unknown sickness and is not able to recover even after the administration of herbal medicines, then the shaman (*themoumia*) is consulted who begins his treatment by entering into a trance state where he mediate with gods or spirits (*terhuomia*) and suggests the task that should be done by the victim to get cured. As per the instructions given by the spirits, the victim will offer sacrifices and perform rituals in order to recover from his sickness.

If a person happens to fall sick after going on a hunt or trekking, it is believed that the soul (*ruopfii*) is captured by the evil spirits (*terhuo kesuo*) in the jungle, river, stream or any dreaded place where a person goes. In such cases in order to retrieve the soul, a shaman (*themoumia*) is arranged and he will proceed to those places where the sick man went early in the morning before anyone gets up. This soul loss of a person is known as *terhuo dzii* in Angami.

Sacrifices are performed for illness usually with fowls or pigs. In the former case the fowl's head is cut off with a dao in the middle of the village path and in the village burial places. Fowls are also killed in this way by a man who has had an unusually heavy sleep. For pains in the heart or chest, a live half grown chicken is impaled on a stake in the middle of the road. In cases of lasting illness, a man digs where there is no water visible on the surface until he finds water. This he fences over. He then kills an unblemished cock, washes it and cooks it with this water and when eating this also drinks off this water which he uses exclusively until well. A fractured skull is treated with raw eggs or with raw eggs and chicken's blood and it is believed that, provided the inner skin over the brain is not broken, the man will live (Hutton 2003).

Hutton also says that, for the Angamis, evil spirits and bacteria seem to be much the same thing. In any case they can be deterred from attacking the person by the device of carrying in the hand, or licking or sticking on to the forehead, a bit of wormwood (Artemisia locally known as *chena*) leaf which is apparently most obnoxious to the spirits of disease. Children are particularly susceptible to attack and a women travelling with an infant in arms protects it by carrying a reaping hook held in front of her to the haft of which a wormwood also is often tied as a sort of disinfectant. Disease may also be averted by offering a substitute in the form of old clothes, live chickens, eggs, etc. during the influenza epidemic of November 1918, which was very severe in the Naga Hills, the paths around Angami villages were littered with odds and ends of clothing and ornaments offered in this way and with many eggs laid in the path for the same purpose, while many chickens were turned loose in the jungle.

Introduction of Christianity

In 1878, Mrs and Rev. C.D. King, the first American Baptist Missionary to the Angamis arrived in Chiimukedima but they were forced to flee due to hostilities between the Angamis and the British. Two years later in 1881, after the revolt had been quelled, the missionaries returned with the Gospel of Christ. After the initiation of missionary work by Rev. C.D. King, Dr. S.W. Rivenburg succeeded him. The latter came to Kohima in the 1880's but his street preaching were not instrumental in the conversion process, but once he started to administer medicines to the sick, he found his patients and their families more receptive to his discourses on the Gospel. Seeing this as the way forward, Rivenburg went back to America in 1892 and studied medicine for two years. He returned back to Kohima in 1894 as a medical missionary and started prescribing medicines for different ailments and at the same time preached the Gospel. He printed for the first time booklets in Angami dialect with the help of educated Angamis for church use, opened a school and did medical relief work amongst the natives. Prayers were read for the sick people and medicines were distributed. Christianity then began to grow slowly in the region.

The Christian Angamis are known as *Kehoumia*, meaning 'those who gather to pray'. They believe in the existence of one Supreme God *Ukepenuopfii*, who dwells in the sky and according to the new religion, the souls of those people who have lived good lives on earth go to the sky after death and live with their Heavenly Father.

The Christians believe that disease is taken as a form of punishment inflicted when something is done wrong against the will of God. Any kind of adultery, drinking rice beer (*zu*), marrying without the consent of the church are likely to lead to illness. If a person speaks bad words, steals, beats up somebody or curses, he is punished in the form of disease.

Role of Church in healing

Joshi (1992) writes about how Church played an important role in the curing of the sick through faith healing and medicine. Mainly the curative aspect of Christianity has contributed to the spread of this religion. It has introduced the concept of 'divine healing' in the Angami system. This healing may be done in four ways:

(1) It is through the power of the Holy Spirit (*kemesa ruopfii*) that illness is cured. This curing is the will of the Holy Spirit and not because of the power in the religiosity of the elder.

(2) Through the faith of the patient in God and in his own prayers.

(3) Healing through the elders of the church, Pastor and Deacons, who pray to God and beseech Him to heal the patient.

(4) Healing of the patient might take place when his attendants pray for him i.e, through the faith of the attendants.

The effect of Christianity is also pronounced in the choice of a healer in the case of illness. Today, the shamans (*themoumia*) are no longer consulted by the Christians as according to the new religion, they are not supposed to believe in the existence of spirits and any healing done through ritual practices. This prohibition led to the acceptance of dispensary.

The Naga traditional religious ceremonies were supplanted by fasting and prayer in the church, animal sacrifice replaced by offering of coins and tithes in the church, taboos by Sabbath day while feast of prestige were replaced by Christmas and New Year celebrations. Sangyu 1996 says "They (Nagas) began to incline towards the concept of one God and Christ being the only Son of God. Their faith in old rituals began to disappear and Christianity "ushered in a transformation from animistic tradition based on superstitious practices to a more orderly society where the guiding principle was no longer that of natural human urges but based rather on the laws of God and love for one's fellow man".

Conclusion

Animal sacrifices and other offerings were made to the diety to supplant the impending misfortune of the people and to avert epidemics, famines, wars, diseases etc, which are believed to be the representation of an evil spirit's shadow and in the case of failure of appeasement is followed by utter destruction of the people. Regular appeasement to the diety was made in the form of offerings by laying an egg, pieces of meat, rice – beer and morsel of food in the field, outside the village, jungle and in the village gate to obviate the wrath of malevolent spirits. All the unnatural deaths, diseases, famines, plagues, natural calamities and misfortunes were believed to be the wrath of evil spirits.

Christianity was the product of the sermons and preaching of Jesus Christ where there is no room for any traditional faith of the tribal society. Christianity asked the new believers to part with all their old culture as well as habits and follow the new European or American culture in almost all aspects of life. Since the advent of Christianity nearly 90 percent villagers have embraced it. The converts do not observe the traditional practices and other rituals. The unremitting effort of the churches has removed the traditional beliefs and practices from the society. With the increase of Christian population and the expansion of the Christian ministry, the animist's religious ceremonies began to lose their importance. The traditional form of healing illness and the role of shamans began to decline and got replaced by dispensaries and health centres. Church has become an integral part in the life of the Angamis. Faith in the church has led to the acceptance of modern medicine as well as faith healing which does not demand the performance of various rituals. The traditional role of priests and shamans has lost much of their sanctity. Thus, we see that the introduction of Christianity in the Angami region played a commendable role in the life of the tribal population.

Reference

Hutton, J.H., 1921, The Angami Nagas, London: Macmillan & Co. Ltd.

Kath K. 2005. Traditional Religious Systems of the Rengma Nagas. Anshah Publishing House, Delhi

Nshoga, A. 2009. Traditional Naga Village System and its Transformation, Delhi. Anshah Publication House.

22

Traditional Healers of Khurkhul

Ngathem Pungfa Singh

Introduction

Traditional medicine plays an important role in primary health care in many developing countries.[1] It is defined as the sum total of the knowledge, skills and practices based on the theories, beliefs and experiences indigenous to different cultures, whether explicable or not, used in the maintenance of health, as well as in the prevention, diagnosis, improvement or treatment of physical and mental illness.[2]

According to the African traditional health practitioners Act 35 of 2004, the object of traditional health practice is therefore, the maintenance or restoration of physical or mental health or function or the diagnosis, treatment or prevention of a physical or mental illness: or the rehabilitation of a person to enable that person to resume normal functioning within the family or community: or the physical or mental preparation of an individual for puberty, adulthood, pregnancy, childbirth and death.[3]

The traditional healer, as defined by WHO (1976), is a person who is recognised by the community in which he lives as competent to provide healthcare by using vegetables, animals and mineral substances and certain other methods based on the social, cultural and religious background, as well as on the knowledge, attributes and beliefs that are prevalent in the community, regarding physical, mental and social well-being and causation of disease and disabilities.

Western medicine also known as biomedicine is often contrasted with the approach taken by traditional medicine practitioners. The former is usually associated with diseases of the physical body only, and is based on the principles of science, technology, knowledge and clinical analysis developed in North America and Western Europe.[4]

Traditional medicine and traditional healers form part of a broader field of study classified by medical anthropologists as ethnomedicine. In Khurkhul, most people associate traditional medicine with the herbs, remedies, treatments and advice imparted by the traditional healers along with strong spiritual components.

Khurkhul where the present study has been carried out is a small village located in Lamshang Sub-division of Imphal West district of Manipur state with a total of 1,344 families. As per population census 2011, it has a total population of 6,450 individuals of which 3,300 are males while 3,150 are females.[5] The village is located near the foothill of *Kounu* about 17km. from Imphal in between Pheidinga and Leimakhong. It is under the jurisdiction of Sekmai police station and has an area of 1, 75,666 acres with a gradual upward inclination towards west. The settlement area which has an elevation of 810 metres above the mean sea level is surrounded by Sekmai village on the north, Senjam Chirang on the south, Loitang on the east and the *Kounu* hill range on the west.

Khurkhul is inhabited by one of the Scheduled Caste (SC) communities of Manipur known as the *Loi*. The connotation of the term *Loi* has diverse versions. The term *Loi* cannotes not only the people who preserve the pre-hinduist traditions and customs of the Meiteis but also the people who were banished to the penal colonies in Sugnu, Ithing and Thanga islands.[6]

The *Loi* was included in the list of SC in 1956 and are distributed in several villages like Sekmai,Khurkhul, Phayeng, Leimaram, Tairenpokpi, Koutruk, Andro and Kwatha. These villages are quite distant from Imphal. They are, perhaps, the most hard working and useful class of people in the valley. All the men are employed in salt making. Silk manufacture and fishing belong to this class and appear to have a separate language.[7]

The objectives of the study are:

- To examine the traditional concept of health and illness.
- To study the age old traditional healing practices.
- To investigate the reason why they visit traditional healers

Methods and Techniques

As in folk medicine or ethno medicinal studies, the most reliable method is one involving field survey.[8] Therefore, the present study adopted standard techniques of modern ethnographic research such as observation, case study and interview. The relevant data of the present study were collected from the field site employing standard methods and techniques of anthropological research like, observation, interview, case study, etc. and also from such secondary sources as archives, records and libraries.

Traditional healers' approach to healing

The first approach of traditional healing process is to identify the cause of the illness. This is usually done by a *maibi*[9], who performs as a diviner by creating an order of supernatural divination rituals in which she transforms herself into a deep trance. She tries to find out if there were any *langjaba*, i.e violation of norms and duties while worshiping the supernatural divines or whether the patient is being *semjinba*, i.e bewitched by somebody or whether there was some *timu-laimu*, i.e evil spirits blocking the path.

A careful collection of patient history is the first step to treatment. This is followed by neutralization process known as *potsem louthokpa,* if suspicion of evil spirits acting upon the patient is detected. The treatment then starts by offering sacrifices to the acting spirit and conducting rituals to appease their anger by a *maiba*[10], the male traditional healer who also performs a traditional way of offerings known as *khayom lakpa* or *chaban thaba.* As a preventive measure, the *maiba* will then sprinkle holy water to ward off the evil spirits with leaves of red cedar locally known as '*tairen*' (*Cedrela toona, f: meliaceae*) and Crow foot herb called '*pungphai*' (*Dactyloctenium aegypticum, f: cyperaceae*). Prescription of medicines is the other alternative if the ailment is caused by some natural agents.

During the treatment, the family members are always involved and the healing process is facilitated by the broader involvement of several members of their community in the village, the *keirol leikai*. The patient is not considered as an isolated individual and the healer studies the patient as a whole and does not split the body and mind into two separate entities as they belief the interaction between the spiritual and physical well being.

Thus, traditional healers of Khurkhul treat all age groups, using and administering medicines that are readily available and affordable. Their treatment is comprehensive and has curative, protective and preventive elements, and can be either natural or ritual or both, depending on the cause of the disease.

Types of healers

The traditional healers of the Khurkhul does not all perform the same functions nor do they all fall into the same category. Each of them has their own field of expertise even though they are commonly designated as *maiba* or *maibi*. Following are some of the types of healers:

i. Diviner

A *maibi* (diviner) is the senior most women who define an illness and its circumstances by letting herself into a state of complete trance called *maibi laitongba* under which her spell or the prophecy called *laiphao* will be made about what went wrong in the past due to which the patient is suffering. She also diagnoses bewitchment by throwing ancient coins called *maibi sen hunba* and makes prediction. Such *maibis* are called *ema maibi* and they are highly respected in the community for their mystical power. She does not have direct contact with the patient. Any member of the patient's family may approach her for the diagnosis.

She may not have the knowledge of medicinal herbs. Her only specialty is divination where she operates within the traditions of spiritual contact by acting as a medium with the ancestral spirits, *ebudhou*, the male forefather and *ebendhou*, the female ones.

Training to become a *maibi* is not a personal choice but is a calling bestowed by ancestors (*ebudhou* or *ebendhou*) to a person who then gets apprenticed to a qualified *ema maibi* for several months during which she learns to control the trance-like situation of communication with the spirits. She also learns how to throw coins, i.e *maibi sen hunba* by maintaining proper conducts, dress codes, restriction of food items and relatives.

ii. Herbalist

The use of herbal medicine is common among the people of Khurkhul. It is old and started as home remedy for treatments ranging from small cuts and wounds to stomach pains. But when special attention is required, they would approach the village herbalist who is also called a *maiba*. This particular *maiba* is the one who is specialised in the use of herbal and other medicinal preparations for treating diseases.

He possesses an extensive knowledge of curative herbs and their applications. He does not receive a calling but chooses to become one through training and experiences. One of the *maiba*, in the village, relies on an ancient manuscript he had obtained from the *utra sanglen*, an apex body of the *maibas* of Manipur at the office of His Highness, the Maharaja of Manipur, at the Royal Palace Imphal in which he had been serving as an *irat langba* i.e preparation for rituals. The manuscript cannot be read by everybody as it is written in old Manipuri scripts.

The herbs are mostly grown in his courtyard or neighbouring houses or available in the vicinity of the village. Sometimes the herbs may be obtained from the neighbouring hills or bought from the *ema market* in Imphal.

iii. Faith Healer

The duty of a faith healer is to strengthen faith and will power in diseased persons. Healing is mostly done through prayer and offering to ward off *timu laimu*, the evil spirits. In order to please these spirits, the healer *maiba* prepares a kind of worship, the *khayom lakpa* or *chaban thaba*, for offering plantain leaves, rice, eggs and leaves of medicinal plant, *langthrei* (*Eupatorium birmanicum*).[11]

Sometimes another ritual known as *graha khurumba* is also performed for offering food items cooked by the patient's family. In this, the *maiba,* with his mystical power, forces the patient to spell out what the evil spirit really want to have. After hearing the evil's say, a feast will be arranged accordingly. It may be small or bigger depending upon the number of participants. But the numbers of participants are fixed in odds of three, five, seven, or nine including the *maiba* and the patient.

iv. Traditional birth attendant

Traditional midwife or birth attendant in Khurkhul are called *chabokpi* who are elderly women. They have no training in the field but possess skill through experience. Before the introduction of modern medicine, the *chabokpi* handled pregnancy related problems and deliveries. But today, the duty of the midwife or birth attendant has reduced to merely teaching behavioural avoidance among pregnant women, ritual bathing of the mother and child, ritual disposal of placentas and providing traditional massage after delivery. She also takes part in ritual purification of the house after child birth known as *yumsengba*.

v. Bone setter

The bone setters of Khurkhul develop specialty in treating bone fracture and dislocation of joints through experience. In the treatment process, despite the protests from the patients fearing the pain, they twist, pull and poke the arm or leg to locate the exact dislocation or fracture. In case of minor injuries of dislocation and fracture such as the fingers and the toes, the bone setter simply apply sesame oil or animal extract oil into the injury area to give a smooth massage so that the treatment is carried out painlessly in a relaxed condition.

To immobilize the area of injury, they tie up short piece of bamboo sticks with bandage. When the injury is in the arm or the hand, a sling around the neck is fixed to be used as arm rest. And in order to reduce the swelling and relieve muscular pain, they apply hot fomentation, *higa yeiba* by mixing the leaves of a common medicinal plant, *hanurei* (*Mussaenda roxbughii*).

Therapeutic process and methods

Diagnosis of a disease and seeking to discover the origin of the disease and determining what it is or who or what caused the disease and why it has affected a particular person at a particular time is the work of the traditional healers. After finding out the causes of the disease, traditional healers prepare healing processes. The types of healthcare offered by the traditional healers in Khurkhul can be classified into three categories:

Table 22.1: Comparison of traditional healers

Traditional Healers	*Skills*	*Method of service*	*Nature of service*	*Accessibility*
Diviners	-Called by spirits -Apprenticed to an expert *maibi*	-Essentially diagnostic -Throws and reads coins -Divination through trance -Contact with patient not needed for diagnosis -History, symptoms and nature of problem not revealed by patients	-Conflict resolution -Confirms patient's beliefs -Revelation of misfortune and illness -Recommends solution	-Freely accessible
Herbalists	-Individual choice to become one -Apprenticed to an expert/loishang -Medical skills acquired through training	-Knowledge of symptoms and patient's history necessary	-Curative and ritualistic - Prescribing healing herbs for different illness and mode of application with doses.	-Freely accessible
Faith Healers	-Individual choice to become one -Apprenticed to an expert *maiba*	-Essentially diagnostic	-Developing faith and will power to diseased persons in a ritualistic and symbolic manner	-Freely accessible
Traditional Birth Attendants /midwives	-Individual choice to become one -Medical skills acquired through experience	-Acts as birth attendant/midwives	-Assist during deliveries -Performs ritual bathing of mother and child	-Freely accessible
Bone setters	-Individual choice to become one -Medical skills acquired through experience and training	-Essentially diagnostic -Contact with patient	-Manipulating bone fracture and dislocation of joints -Application of ointment and bandages	-Freely accessible

i. Preventive

Most of the work of traditional healers concerns protecting patients from possible afflictions. This is achieved in various ways, for example by performing *tarpan katpa*, a regular ceremonial offering to the ancestors. Each and every lineage in Khurkhul observes *tarpan katpa* every year during the second half of *Langban*, Manipuri month coinciding with September to appease ancestral spirits for good health and wealth.

They believed the ancestors play a great role in the lives of the individuals in the society. Many of the diseases, illness and ailments are attributed to not satisfying their ancestors enough. So a large traditional feast is arranged by inviting old man and woman to eat the feast to their stomach's content. After the *tarpan katpa*, the souls of their forefathers are so pleased and showers blessings on their children for their filial deeds.

ii. Treatment for ailments

Herbal medicine is the most common therapeutic method of treatment by using plant's seeds, berries, roots, leaves, bark, or flowers. Variety of preparations or extracts in the form of powder, liquid, or paste by mixing herbs or with animal products may be prescribed or administered as and when applicable in treating and preventing disease. These recipes are usually a secret and are part of the knowledge that the healer will pass on to his apprentice.

iii. Warding off evil spirits

If the cause of the sickness is perceived to be that of an evil eye, known as *hingchabi changba,* in which the evil spirit, *hingchabi* enters into another person to give mental and physical harassments, then; a *maiba* will perform *graha khurumba* rituals for offering what the *hingchabi* wants to eat. The *Yelhing thaba*, is another form of such ritual in which a live cock is set free by a *maiba*. He also performs *ushin shinba* ritual, a process in which a specific live fish locally known as *meitei ngamu (Channa gachu),* is released in the water for health and longevity of a family member. Sometimes, instead of using the fish, the process of *ushin shinba* ritual is also done at the foot of an old Bo tree locally known as *Khongnang pambi (Ficus retusa Linn)* in which family members pray and seek health from the tree by offering rice, flower, fruits, etc. or by dressing up its trunk with white cloth.

The tying of a charmed amulet is also common preliminary act which serves two purposes: i. if the disease is caused by external agents, then the amulet may cure the disease. The charm also protects the individual against the demonic interference. The efficacy of the amulet is generally for a limited period. If disease is not cured, a bigger ritual may be required; ii. an amulet may act as a protective even if the cause is physical manifestation, for spirits can attack a person in a physically weak state. The charm or formula or the drawings are engraved inside metal cups which are reserved for this special purpose. It is locally known as *jantra*. The people of Khurkhul believe that wearing of a *jantra* will prevent external forces and will ward off evil spirits of sorcery called *potsem jadu*.

Reasons why people visit traditional healers

The people of Khurkhul depend on traditional healers as they are easily available within the village. Familiarity with the healers puts the ailing at ease during the course of investigation and treatment. The traditional healers do not address only physical problems. They also handle psychological and mental problems which are believed to be caused by evil spirits. In such cases modern medicine is not depended upon. It is also believed that illness arises either from supernatural causes due to displeasure of ancestral gods and evil spirits or is the effect of black magic. As the traditional healers are part of the society with good knowledge of culture and practices of the people, they have the ability to understand problems better and give better solutions in the form of medicines or performances.

Conclusion

Traditional healers hold an esteemed and powerful position in Khurkhul. Their role is that of physician, counsellor, psychiatrist and priest, and people visit a traditional healer, *maiba* or *maibi* for problems ranging from social uncertainties to major physical illness. They therefore, have a role to play in building the health system. As most of the illness and treatments are culture-bound, many areas are left untouched by the Western medical practitioners. In a village like Khurkhul, traditional healers can play an important and valuable role in helping their community to improve their health and quality of life.

References

1. Setswe, G. 1999. The Role of Traditional Healers and Primary Health Care in South Africa. *Health SA Gesondheid*, 4 (2): 56-60.
2. Traditional Medicine: Definition, World Health Organization 01-12-2008. Retrieved on 14-10-2016.
3. Republic of South Africa. 2004. *Traditional Health Practitioners Act, Act 35 of 2004*.

   Pretoria: Government Printers.
4. Richter M. 2003. *Traditional Medicines and Traditional Healers in South Africa*. Discussion paper prepared for the Treatment Action Campaign and AIDS Law Project. Available on the web: http://www.tac.org.za/ Documents/ Research Papers/Traditional Medicine briefing.pdf Retrieved on 10-10-2016.
5. http://www.census2011.co.in/data/village/270040-khurkhul-manipur.html
6. Hodson, T.C. 2010. *The Meitheis*. New Delhi: Akansha Publishing House.
7. Brown, R. 2001. *Statitical Account of Manipur*. New Delhi : Mittal Publication.
8. Jain, S. K. & Rao, S. 1969. *Field and Herbarium Techniques*. Jodhpur: Scientific Publisher.
9. Traditional priestesses of Manipur who are believed to be the spiritual medium since days of yore.
10. A man who performs rituals (priest),acts a medicine man, who can cure and acts aa shaman who performs magic that may be good or bad and performs a ritual for the benefit of family or person or community.

    A Critical Review of the Man in Biosphere:
11. Devi, L.Bino, 2002. *Lois of Manipur: Andro, Khurkhul, Phayeng & Sekmai*, p. 56.

Section - III

Socio-Cultural

23

A Critical Review of the Man in Biosphere: Khangchendzonga Biosphere Reserve Project of Anthropological Survey of India

Arup Bera

Khangchendzonga Biosphere Reserve (KBR)

KBR is one of the newest Biosphere Reserve established in February 2002. It has an expansion of nearly 70 percent of the land area of the Sikkim State covering the districts of North, South and West Sikkim. Its boundaries lie between Latitude 27"15' North Latitude and 88"02'40"' East longitudes. The core zone is extended on an area of 1784sq. km and is surrounded by four buffer zones of nearly 835.92sq. km. in the KBR the altitude varies from 1220 metres from the mean sea level.

Table No. 23.1: Geographical Area under Core and Buffer Zones

Sl. No.	*KBR components*	*Area (sq. km.)*	*Geographical Positions*
1	Core Zone (CZ)	1,784	Existing Khangchendzonga National Park
2	Buffer Zone 1 (BZ1)	154.48	Portions of Lhonak Valley
3	Buffer Zone 2 (BZ2)	55.29	Areas of West of Chungthang Valley
4	Buffer Zone 3 (BZ3)	29.37	Portions of Tholung Valley
5	Buffer Zone 4 (BZ4)	596.78	Along Indo-Nepal border, CZ and some reserved forests
	KBR Total	2,619.92	Falls in the North, West and South districts covering 36.92 p.c. of the state

The reserve covers mainly the two districts of State i.e., North and West district. In the North district Chung Thang is the subdivision office and in the West district Gylalsingh and Yuksam are the nearest places.

Main Features of KBR

The main features of Khangchendzonga Biosphere Reserve are as follows: It has the country highest peak. More than 70 percent of the Reserve is covered by dense forest. It has a wide variety of biomes from broad leaved forest of oak, castanopsis, temperate coniferous, rhododendron forest to dry alpine resembling cold desert of Asia. The KBR consists of Trans-Himalayan zone and the extension of Tibet plateau. It is home to various endemic and endangered flora and fauna, and the endangered red panda and Himalayan bear.

There are more than 5000 species of angiosperm, 4000 species flowering plants and 450-500 species of orchids and 300 species of ferns and allies. It also has over 400 species of butterflies and moths, 140 species of mammals and about 600 species of birds. It forms catchment areas to the tributaries of the two main rivers Tista and Rangeet. There are altogether 24 villages in the fringe area of the KBR of which 14 villages are in West district and 10 are in North district. There is one forest village – Tshoka – which is in the core of the KBR. It is also becoming important from tourist view point; both Indian as well as foreign tourist visit the Reserve regularly.

Biosphere Reserve as a Concept

The UNESCO's framework stipulates that Biosphere Reserves (BRs) should be representative of a bio-geographic province and should have appropriate zoning system with legally constituted and minimally distributed core zones. In addition, the site should contain unique and pristine biodiversity, ecosystems and landscape suitable to explore and demonstrate approaches to sustainable development and should be of appropriate size to serve three functions, viz., conservation, development and extension of logistic support. It is aimed to bring at least one representative site in the country within each bio-geographic province under the network of Biosphere Reserves.

The BRs are designated to deal with important questions of reconciling the conservation of biodiversity, the quest for economic and social development and maintenance of associated cultural values. Some important aspects of Biosphere Reserves delineates conservation of landscapes, ecosystems, species and genetic variation; economic development, which is culturally, socially and ecologically sustainable and extension of logistic support for research, monitoring, education and exchange of information related to local, national and global issues.

Launched in 1970, Man and Biosphere (MAB) programme covers different ecosystem types from mountain to the sea, from rural to urban systems as well as social aspects. MAB has proposed an interdisciplinary research and capacity building aiming to improve the relationship of the people with environment. In order to achieve the stated objectives it targets biodiversity from the ecological, social and economic dimensions.

In nutshell, the Biosphere Reserve (BR) is expected to fulfill three basic functions, which are complementary and mutually reinforcing:

(a) Conservation Function – to contribute to the conservation of landscapes, ecosystems, species and genetic variation;

(b) Development Function - to foster economic and human development which is socio culturally and ecologically sustainable;

(c) Logistic Function – to provide support for research, monitoring, education and information exchange related to local, national and global issues of conservation and development

The Ministry of Environment and Forests, Government of India has launched the Biosphere Reserve Programme (BR) since 1986. The specific objectives of this programme are:

(a) To conserve the diversity and integrity of plants and animals within the natural eco system

(b) To safeguard the genetic diversity of species on which their continuing evolution depends,

(c) To provide areas for multi-faceted research and monitoring

(d) To provide facilities for research and training, and

(e) To ensure the sustainable use of natural resources through most appropriate technology for improvement of economy and living standard of local people.

Issues Linked with Biosphere Reserve Development in India

In the context of India, human population living within the Biosphere Reserves has always been a matter of conflicting interests and debate. These considerations prompted UNESCO (1996) to move away from the earlier held view of concentric rings of core, buffer and transition zones, to a more flexible way of looking upon the local needs and situations. The flexibility and creativity in the Biosphere concept need to be seen from the point of view of both biodiversity as well as the cultural diversity. The benefits of cultural diversity at societal level are comparable to those accruing from the biodiversity. It is important to allude that, while the issues of biodiversity have been addressed at length and caught attention widely, the cultural diversity has not been touched upon and left to point of oblivion.

The BRs of India are also the abode of many traditional societies who have always been an integral part of the ecosystem functioning there, living close to the nature. Living in the areas rich in natural resource, traditional societies fulfill many of their livelihood requirements from the rich biodiversity around them. The ecosystems such as forest not only meets a variety of livelihood needs of the forest dwelling societies, through products such as timber and non-timber forest products, but also sustain traditional shifting cultivation and agricultural practices contributing to the food security of the people within the BRs.

So far the management efforts has largely been centered around protection of natural resources within BRs from the outside impacts, but at the same time restricting the use of these resources by the local communities residing in the BR. The concept of sustainable use of resources yet has not taken due to lack of location specific understanding on how the resources should be managed. Of late emphasis is laid on the aspect of that the eco-development should also combat problems of community participation in forest eco-system management and rehabilitation directly. What more is required for the management of natural resources is linkage with reinforcement of traditional system of land based activities based on the traditional value system of local communities.

The BR management, therefore, necessitates not only understanding of ecological issues but also the socio-economic and cultural issues linked with the former. Understanding societal perceptions of natural resources as a cultural resource – often seen through the conceptual framework of sacred species, sacred groves, sacred water bodies, sacred landscape or even sacred mountain system – and its relationship with conservation need to be integrated in the management strategy. In order to achieve this, conservation linked development strategy has to be based on a value system that people can understand, appreciate and accept. It, in turn, requires appropriate institutional arrangements for peoples' participation, through a 'bottom up approach', ensuring that each household takes part in the decision making process at the lowest level in the hierarchy keeping into consideration the gender sensitivities.

Anthropological Survey of India and the KBR

The growing conflict between man and his environment has forced the academia of our generation to think deeply on the issue of environment, its degradation and conservation. This problem has also become acute due to the various developmental programmes undertaken by different societies located in different geo-ecological and cultural zones of the world in general and India in particular. The conflict between man and environment reached to the alarming stage in the early part of the 1960's when the developmental process had accelerated to a great extent. Environment started degrading and a situation had arisen where the existence of human society appeared to be at stake. With this background United Nations Organization started pondering deeply and directed its sister organization UNESCO in the year 1970 to come out with detailed research programme on the concept of man and biosphere. Accordingly, Man and Biosphere Committee were constituted in the year 1972 to demarcate the Biosphere Reserves in different biographic zones of the world where the ecosystem was critical from survival point of view. Indian 'Man and Biosphere Committee' demarcated 12 sites at the first instance and later added two more sites. Thus, presently India is having 14 Biosphere Reserves which are spread all over the country right from the Himalayas to the sea of Andaman and Gulf of Mannar. This paper deals with the Anthropological

Survey of India's work on the biological and cultural diversity aspects of Khanchendzonga Biosphere Reserve, which is located in the three districts of Sikkim viz., North, South and West. The KBR is a new Biosphere Reserve with a unique ecological condition, which primarily varies from tropical climatic condition. Due to its varying altitude flora and fauna also vary along with other life support systems like soil, water. The development in the form of tourism and its impact on the conservation of the fragile ecosystem of KBR were also discussed. The Anthropological Survey of India undertook theme based research studies in three areas of KBR, which are Yuksum, Lachen, Dzongu and their adjoining areas. Ecologically and culturally also these three regions vary. There are only two traditional communities living in these areas namely the Bhutias and the Lepchas along with migrant Nepalese population.

They studied the ecological change in KBR has focused on anthropogenic pressures and tried to understand its impact on the ecology of KBR. Dependence of the population on forest is well visible because fuel and fodder resources are accessed from the forest. The study comes out with an interesting finding that people are willing to help in conservation efforts of the government provided their socio-economic concern are taken care of. In addition, the local NGOs are helping in the conservation efforts by creating public awareness. Another study is based on the cultural landscape of the fringe villages of KBR. The basic objective is to understand the changing cultural landscape in terms of economic resource management by the village population. It has been felt that both the areas have different pattern of cultural landscape. It has also been noted that transhumance as a system of livelihood is losing its importance and settled agriculture is becoming important economic occupation for the people of both the areas.

The economic life in the fringe villages of KBR is also studied. It deals with the primary and secondary occupations in these two villages. It also tried to explore the economic potentiality of the tourism industry in the context of declaration of KBR. The traditional form of art, craft, music and dance tries to understand the impact of tourism on material culture of the communities living in KBR. It may be mentioned here that tourism has created a demand for artifacts and the local community has responded in a big way because they see it as an area where there are enough economic opportunities.

The impact of tourism on KBR of North and West districts of Sikkim were also reported. Due to its unique natural setting, KBR is attracting substantial number of international and Indian tourists throughout the year. The local community has responded in a positive way and it has become a major source of income. No doubt there has been some negative impact of tourism. However, due awareness programme undertaken by different NGOs, environmental degradation has been arrested to a great extent. Report on the growth of urbanization tries to understand the process by which the village is getting transformed into an urban area. The place, Yuksum, which is historically an important centre in the political history of Sikkim, is slowly emerging as a nodal centre to support tourism and related activities.

Another report on nature, man and spirit deals with the interface between the symbols of human understanding taking into consideration of the local population. Living in close proximity with nature, the Lepchas and the Bhutias have developed a good understanding about the natural objects which is both benevolent and malevolent. Accordingly, they try to appease both forms of nature for better sustenance in the rugged terrain of Sikkim Himalayas. Studies on indigenous health practices of the communities living in KBR region have also there. The study shows as how people have developed their own indigenous method of health practices with the help of ethno-medicine, especially the Lepchas of KBR. The Lepcha community lives in close quarter with the nature which has helped them to develop unique system of ethno-medicine based on medicinal plants, which are practiced by the medicine man of the community. Another one has dealt with the community and their life cycle which revolves around various economic activities in KBR.

Summary

The Khangchendzonga Biosphere Reserve (KBR) was conferred the status of Biosphere Reserve on 7th February, 2000 by the Government of India. The Anthropological Survey of India have conducted study in three areas of KBR which are Yuksum, Lachen and Dzongu of North and West Districts of Sikkim. Ecologically and culturally these three regions vary considerably. The issues which have been covered by the Anthropological Survey of India focuses on ecology, change and conservation; cultural landscape and economic life in fringe villages; traditional art, crafts and performing dance; impact of tourism; growth of urbanization; general ethnography of the studied population; man-nature-spirit relationship among the studied population and indigenous health practices. All the work of the Anthropological Survey of India in the KBR region ultimately reflect the changing pattern of biodiversity and cultural diversity in KBR and analyze how different communities living in different locales have responded to the changes which they are witnessing.

References

Basnet, L. (1974). *Sikkim: A Short Political History*. New Delhi: S. Chand and Co. Pvt. Ltd.

Bhadra, M. (1992). *Sikkim: Democracy and Social Change*. Calcutta: Minerva Associates Pvt. Ltd.

Bhasin, V. (1989). *Ecology, Culture, Change*. Inter India Publications, New Delhi.

(1990). *Habitat, Habitation and Health in the Himalayas*, Kamla Raj Enterprises, New Delhi.

(1997) Social Dimension of Politics: The Case of Tribal Democracy in Sikkim. *Journal of human Ecology*, 4(1); pp. 63-78.

Bhasin, M. K. and Bhasin, V. (1995). *Sikkim Himalayas – Ecology and Resource Development*, Kamla Raj Enterprises, New Delhi.

Department of Forest, (2006). *Household and Population Structure of Fringe Villages of Khangchendzonga National Park*. Government of Sikkim. Gangtok.

Department of Forest, (2006). *Report of Khangchendzonga National Park and Biosphere Reserve*. Government of Sikkim. Gangtok.

Department of Forest, (2007). *Khangchendzonga Biosphere Reserve*. Government of Sikkim. Gangtok.

Gulia, K. S. (2005). *Human Ecology of Sikkim*. Kalpaz Publications. New Delhi.

Joshi, H. G. (2004). *Sikkim: Past and Present*. Mittal Publications. New Delhi.

Khangchendzonga Conservation Committee (2002). *Khangchendzonga: The Sacred Mountain – A Biodiversity Conservation Hand Book*. Published by K.C.C Yuksum Committee.

Khangchendzonga Conservation Committee (2002). *Brochure of Khangchendzonga and Its People*. Published by K.C.C Yuksum Committee.

Rai, S. C. and Sundriyal, R. C. (1997). Tourism Development and Biodiversity Conservation: A Case Study from the Sikkim Himalaya. *Ambio*, 26: 235-242.

Saeed, Taalat (1995). Cultural Heritage of Sikkim: A Survey. *Bulletin of Research Institute of Tibetology*, Gangtok.

Sharma, Ramesh (1983). *Images of Sikkim: The Land, People and Culture. Department of Tourism*. Government of Sikkim. Gangtok. Ringsum Publication.

24

Peril in the Harbor: Domestic Violence and Women's Autonomy in North-east India

Anindita Sinha

Introduction

Perhaps contrary to prevailing notion, domestic violence (DV) or intimate partner violence (IPV), i.e. physical and sexual violence or abuse within relationships, is the dominant form of violence experienced by women globally.[33] In fact, according to the landmark study on IPV conducted by the World Health Organization, around 60 percent of the surveyed women from 10 selected countries, who had ever experienced physical and sexual violence, reported that they had been abused by a partner (WHO, 2OO5). According to data from the third round of the National Family Health Survey (NFHS-3), that collected information on all forms of domestic violence including physical violence, sexual violence and emotional violence, around 40 percent of all ever married women in the reproductive age group (15-49) in India said that they had experienced at least one form of spousal violence in their lifetime. Physical violence seems to be more prevalent as compared to sexual violence and emotional violence according to the data (IIPS, 2007).[4]

While the experience of IPV has severe health consequences including long term physical, mental and emotional health problems, the distress is compounded in strongly patriarchal cultures such as most of South and South-east Asia including India, where women cannot move out of the relationship without paying a high price including social ostracism. Indeed, the agreed conclusions of the Commission on the Status of Women recognizes the historical and structural roots of all forms of violence against women (VAW) and calls for continued multidisciplinary research and analysis on the causes of, and cost and risk factors for, violence against women and girls, in order to improve the evidence base on IPV.

In this context and amidst concerns of changing gender relations and deteriorating women's status in North-eastern region of India (NER), the present paper is an attempt to critically examine the pattern and determinants of domestic violence in the region. Needless to say, gender based violence is a reflection of existing anti-female gender norms in society and as such nearly every society in present times exhibits anti-female social norms, though we find large disparities in terms of the extent of anti-female bias. The stronger the hold of traditional patriarchy and lower the status of women, the higher one can expect IPV to be. For instance, in a two-state community based survey, Jejeebhoy and Cook (1997) found that while IPV is high in both communities of India without exception, rates are higher in the Northern state of Uttar Pradesh (45 percent) characterized by a stronger hold of patriarchy and lower women's status, as compared to the Southern state of Tamil Nadu (37 percent). Interestingly, in the Indian context, it is widely recognized that tribal culture has been historically relatively more egalitarian as compared to mainstream culture and women enjoy a higher status in tribal societies. Thus, in the context of North-east India for instance, one would expect lower IPV among states that have a higher proportion of tribes in total population, *ceteris paribus*.

Perhaps surprisingly, given that women's agency and status undoubtedly has a major role in shaping individual experiences of IPV, research on the subject with a focus on women's status and autonomy, especially that which recognizes its multidimensional nature, is relatively recent and consequently evidence too remains rather limited. Autonomy, being a multidimensional concept has been defined variously by various researchers and scholars (that are not necessarily mutually exclusive). For instance, while Kabeer defines female autonomy or agency as "processes by which those who have been denied the ability to make strategic life choices acquire such an ability" (Kabeer, 1999: 437), Dyson and Moore define women's autonomy as "the ability-technical, social, and psychological-to obtain information and to use it as the basis for making decisions about one's private concerns and those of one's intimates. Thus, equality of autonomy between the sexes in the present sense implies equal decision-making ability with regard to personal affair" (Dyson and Moore, 1983: 45). Further, Jejeebhoy notes that there are five interdependent dimensions of women's autonomy- knowledge autonomy, decision-making autonomy, physical autonomy, emotional autonomy and socio-economic autonomy/self-reliance (Riyami et al., 2004). A common emphasis in these various definitions is that on the capability of women to make (relatively) independent decisions, and more broadly speaking, the power to break through traditional/patriarchal gender norms in some sense, in order to extend control over dimensions of their existence that hitherto remained dominated by others.

Intuitively at least, it is clear, why then, greater autonomy might lead to lower domestic violence- the former enabling the woman to extend greater control over her body and environment.

Recent theoretical developments that elucidate the role of autonomy in reducing IPV has been couched in terms of power and control within marital relationships and specifically, how (culturally sanctioned?) control over wives may precipitate domestic violence. As Grose and Grabe (2014) explain, "…the theory of gender and power proposes that gender-based inequalities are pervasive societal characteristics that result in men's disproportionate power and control over a number of areas, including women's bodies….Normative gender ideologies that assume masculine superiority and feminine inferiority…reinforce these structural inequalities. Specifically, these socially constructed ideologies perpetuate the belief that men are entitled to power over women and may discipline women for perceived insubordination or violation of gender roles (*ibid*, p. 973).

Here, it is important to distinguish between 'power to' and 'power over' in relationships. Simply put, the former refers to the capability to influence situations to improve personal well-being, without influence on others abilities to do so (Mosedale, 2005). On the contrary, 'power over' can be defined as the ability to control the behaviour of another person or dominate or another, or win in a conflict situation. Understood in this way and in the context of women's autonomy and IPV, women's age, education, and employment would be classified as 'power to' enhance her well-being, whereas spousal differences in resource contribution, differences in control over household decision making, and partner control of spousal behavior and mobility are indicators of 'power over' another individual in relationships (Grose and Grabe, 2014).

Interestingly, evidence on the subject remains mixed, especially in the context of the indices measuring 'power over' in marital relationships. For instance, several studies from various countries including India, have found that women who earn more or are better employed, or have higher levels of education than their partners also report greater levels of physical violence than women who do not report spousal differences on these indicators of power (Anderson, 1997; Atkinson et al., 2005; Flake, 2005). However, other research finds (e.g., India, Haiti) that differences in education favoring women lead to less physical, psychological, and sexual violence. Similarly, conflicting findings emerge from looking at other dimensions of autonomy reflecting 'power over' women, such as household decision making and mobility. While few studies note that higher decision-making autonomy and greater female mobility is associated with lower IPV, other studies find evidence to the contrary (Gage and Hutchinson, 2006; Jejeebhoy, 1998; Panda & Agarwal; WHO, 2005). In this connection, it is interesting to note that However, research by Sabarwal, Santhya and Jejeebhoy (2014), on the experience of physical violence within marriage in rural India, underscores the importance of context in shaping the relationship and points out that in more gender equitable settings (south India in the particular study), women's autonomy exerts a 'protective' influence on risk of marital violence. However, in more gender-stratified settings (north India), even higher individual autonomy of women might fail to reduce the risk of marital violence.

Material and Method of Analysis

The present study utilizes data from the individual women's and household questionnaires of the India National Family Health Survey, 2005-06. The analysis is restricted to women who are currently married, since most of the responses relating to women's autonomy were asked of them. Out of a total number of 6,552 cases for the eight states of North-east India (Assam, Arunachal Pradesh, Manipur, Meghalaya, Mizoram, Nagaland, Sikkim and Tripura in the data, our final sample size consisted of 1,925 cases, the sample size being reduced drastically mainly due to missing cases and non-response of many individuals in the data set, especially in the case of responses to the autonomy measures.

The dependent variable in the analyses is a dichotomous variable that assumes the value of 1 if the woman has experienced violence and 0 otherwise. We carry out three binary logistic regressions, for three separate cases defined by the nature of the dependent variable - (i) domestic violence, (ii) physical violence and (iii) sexual violence. (For definitions of domestic, physical and sexual violence, please see page 2, footnote, 2).

The set of independent variables remains the same in all the regressions, (please see Table 24.2 for the list of the independent variables included in the analyses). All the explanatory variables used in the regressions are categorical in nature. In most cases, we have collapsed the categories of the independent variables into fewer ones (mostly limited to two or three) for ease of analysis and exposition, as can be seen from Table 24.2.

We employ eight indicators of women's autonomy/status in the analyses. Woman's educational attainment and occupation measure the dimension characterized as 'power to' enhance well-being of self, based on the theoretical perspective presented earlier. Five indices measure five distinct dimensions of power and control in relationships, viz., women's decision-making capacity, physical mobility, financial independence, acceptance of subordination by men (reflecting internal acceptance of gender-specific traditional/patriarchal norms), and controlling behaviour of husband The five autonomy indices have been constructed through **factor analysis** on relevant items in the questionnaire. It is pertinent to mention here that the items to be included or excluded from each index were decided on the basis of theory, and validated by exploratory factor analysis (EFA). EFA proved to be useful in several cases. For instance, in the case of constructing the financial independence/ autonomy index, it was found that working for self (as against for husband or household), and having money for own use, capture a unique dimension of autonomy, and can be usefully combined to form the financial autonomy index.

It should also be perhaps mentioned here that the individual indicators forming the indices have been coded such that higher values denote higher autonomy for any particular respondent. For instance, in the case of household decision making, decision by respondent alone is given a value of 4, respondent with husband has been given a value of 3, respondent with another person a value of 2, and husband alone a value of 1. In general, a response where the woman shows greater self-reliance or does not accept harmful traditional norms has been given a higher value in the construction of the autonomy indices. We use regression scores from factor analysis for the construction of the four indices. After obtaining the factor scores for each woman, we recoded using it in *binary* form, with positive values representing higher scores and indicating higher autonomy, coded as 1 and, negative values depicting lower scores and therefore lower autonomy, coded as 0.

Thus, in the final analyses, the women's autonomy indices were included as categorical variables and multivariate analyses (**binary logistic regressions**) were carried out to assess the 'actual' impact of the women autonomy and status variables on contraceptive use, after carefully controlling for various socio-demographic, socio-economic status and socio-cultural factors, husband's education and occupation, standard of living, type of place of residence (rural/urban), religious affiliation, and son preference. The basic form of the logistic regression used is:

$$\log\left(\frac{p}{1-p}\right) = b_0 + b_1x_1 + b_2x_2 + \dots\dots\dots + b_kx_k$$

Where b_0 is constant, $b_1, b_2, \dots\dots\dots\dots, b_k$ are the coefficients of $x_1, x_2 \dots\dots\dots\dots x_k$

P is the estimated probability of experiencing domestic violence, physical violence or sexual violence as the case may be.

Results

Table 24.1 provides estimates of physical violence, sexual violence and domestic violence (defined as the experience of either physical or sexual violence or both forms of violence for the purpose of this study) for all the North-eastern states of India for the year 2005-06. We find strong correspondence between physical and sexual violence suggesting that these forms of violence concur. The average for the North-eastern region shows that domestic violence as well as physical violence is lower than the national average, whereas sexual violence (around 9 percent) is comparable to the all-India average. It is interesting to note that among the states of NER, all forms of VAW (especially sexual violence) are relatively lower in the tribal dominated states, viz. Meghalaya, Mizoram, Nagaland and Sikkim. It is alarming to note that all forms of VAW are abysmally high in Tripura and in fact, Tripura and Assam evince rates of domestic violence as well as physical and sexual violence much higher than the all-India average levels (Table 24.1). Overall, Meghalaya seems to be safest place for women as far as IPV is concerned and in fact, sexual violence (at around just 1 percent) can be considered to be practically non-existent in this state. Broadly, the pattern of IPV in North-east India supports the hypothesis that tribal cultural features continue to protect women from IPV.

Table 24.1: Rates of Various forms of Gender-Based Violence in Northeast India, 2005-06 (percentages) (relative ranking in parentheses)

State	*Physical Violence*	*Sexual Violence*	*Domestic Violence*
Arunachal Pradesh	23.2 [2]	7.3 [4]	24.9 [3]
Assam	21.9 [4]	16.1 [2]	28.7 [2]
Manipur	22.3 [3]	13.6 [3]	24.7 [4]
Meghalaya	7.9 [7]	1.04 [8]	8.8 [8]
Mizoram	10.6 [5]	1.6 [7]	12.1 [6]
Nagaland	10.0 [6]	3.6 [6]	12.2 [5]
Sikkim	7.5 [8]	3.7 [5]	10.2 [7]
Tripura	31.3 [1]	26.3 [1]	33.4 [1]
Northeast India	15.4	8.9	19.3
India	18.8	8.9	28.6

Source: Author's calculations from NFHS-3 data (IIPS, 2007).

Table 24.2 presents the main findings of the study. The first column of the table presents the results of binary logistic regression for domestic violence in NER. Among the indicators of women's autonomy that measure her 'power to' attain well-being, educational attainment, especially higher education (matriculation and above) has a significant effect in the predicted direction of reducing the odds of experiencing domestic violence. Woman's occupation does not affect the odds of experiencing DV. Also, women in the prime reproductive years (26-30 years old), are at the highest risk of DV/IPV.

Interestingly, all the indices measuring power and control in relationships, except the index of financial independence, turn out to be significant. Each index viz. Index of (household) decision-making, Index of mobility, Index of acceptance of subordination and Index of controlling behaviour of husband, reveals that women's power and control within relationships, (that is, women whose husbands do not exhibit decision-making dominance), has a protective influence against domestic violence.

Table 24.2: Determinants of Domestic Violence in North-East India: Main Results from Binary Logistic Regression Analyses

Dependent variable →	***Domestic Violence***		***Physical Abuse***		***Sexual Abuse***	
Independent Variables ↓	*Exp (β)* (1)	Sig. (2)	*Exp (β)* (3)	Sig. (4)	*Exp (β)* (5)	Sig. (6)
Women's Autonomy/Status Indicators						
Educational attainment of woman(Ref: no education)						
Literate but below Primary	0.868	0.451	0.654*	0.060	1.429	0.135
Primary but below Matriculation	0.778	0.123	0.729*	0.066	0.885	0.573
Matriculation and H. Secondary	0.513***	0.009	0.430***	0.003	0.556*	0.077
College and above	0.480**	0.040	0.355**	0.010	0.540	0.185
Occupation of woman(Ref: Not working)						
Primary Sector	1.382	0.455	1.165	0.738	1.600	0.388
Secondary Sector	1.709	0.153	1.531	0.273	1.352	0.532
Women's Autonomy Indices/ 'Power over' indices						
Index of Decision-making	0.701***	0.005	0.681***	0.004	0.678**	0.020
Index of Mobility	0.635***	0.001	0.661***	0.005	0.545***	0.002
Index of Financial Independence	0.970	0.841	1.074	0.655	0.982	0.927
Index of Acceptance of Subordination	0.667***	0.001	0.708***	0.009	0.638***	0.008
Index of Control in Relationship	0.313***	0.000	0.317***	0.000	0.319***	0.000
Dependent variable →	***Domestic Violence***		***Physical Abuse***		***Sexual Abuse***	
Independent Variables ↓	*Exp (β)* (1)	Sig. (2)	*Exp (β)* (3)	Sig. (4)	*Exp (β)* (5)	Sig. (6)
Household Structure (Ref: Nuclear)						
Joint household	0.927	0.569	0.857	0.285	0.944	0.747
Socio-economic status variables						
Husband's Education (Ref: No education)						
Primary	0.905	0.605	0.876	0.510	1.219	0.467
Secondary	0.928	0.676	0.821	0.293	1.504	0.101
Higher	0.547*	0.055	0.569*	0.096	0.858	0.714
Husband's Occupation (Ref: Agriculture)						
Manufacturing	0.900	0.554	0.837	0.359	1.026	0.911
Services and Others	1.172	0.294	1.180	0.300	0.990	0.962
Standard of Living Index (Ref: Low)						
High	0.614***	0.008	0.552***	0.002	0.774	0.314
Type of Residence (Ref: Urban)						
Rural	0.754*	0.068	0.597***	0.002	1.125	0.559
Socio-cultural variables						
Social Group (Ref: Non-tribe)						
Dependent variable →	Domestic Violence		Physical Violence		Sexual Violence	
Independent Variables ↓	*Exp (β)* (1)	Sig. (2)	*Exp (β)* (3)	Sig. (4)	*Exp (β)* (5)	Sig. (6)
Tribe	0.849	0.436	0.805	0.330	0.780	0.376
Not caste or Tribe	2.185**	0.014	2.133**	0.024	1.767	0.171
Religious Affiliation (Ref: Hindu)						
Muslim	1.369	0.235	0.993	0.980	1.816*	0.051
Christian	0.514***	0.002	0.616**	0.033	0.415***	0.003
Others	0.549**	0.020	0.610*	0.071	0.405**	0.013
Sex Preference (Ref: No son preference of husband)						
Son Preference	1.312**	0.043	1.428**	0.012	0.948	0.774
Women's Age Group (Ref: 15-20)						
21-25	1.781*	0.060	1.636	0.126	1.535	0.314
26-30	2.081**	0.015	1.842*	0.052	2.045*	0.084
31-35	1.656	0.107	1.365	0.346	1.779	0.180
35 and above	1.827*	0.062	1.737	0.102	1.343	0.517

Notes: *** 1% < p ** 5% < p * 10% < p.

We tested for the effect of alcohol consumption on all forms of violence and it turned out to be significant as expected.

In this context, it is interesting to note that partner control (index of control in relationships) has the largest effect on DV. Women who do not experience partner control are around *3 times less likely* to experience DV as compared to those whose partners exhibit such behaviour. Thus, in the case of North-east India, we find that there is a strong correspondence between the effects of various dimensions of women's autonomy on domestic violence and indeed, among the various indicators included in the analysis, women's autonomy seems to have the strongest effect on reducing IPV in NER.

Among variables measuring socio-economic status (SES), urban residence increase odds of DV, as does poverty or a low standard of living. Husband's education is significantly associated with lower IPV, but only when it is higher than secondary education. Partner's occupation, like the occupation of the woman, turns out to be insignificant in this context. Further, within NER, we do not find evidence of lower DV among tribes after controlling for all other factors. Also, there is no significant difference between Hindus and Muslims, although belonging to the Christian religious group seems to lower the odds of DV in NER. Further, son preference leads to almost 30 percent increase in the risk of experiencing DV.

Results for physical violence (column 3), are largely similar to that of domestic violence, with the exception that as against only higher levels of woman's education being significantly associated with lower violence, we find that education at any and all levels, including below primary, lowers the risk of physical violence against women in NER. All indices measuring power and control within marital relationship (except financial independence) turn out to be significant in the expected direction of lowering the risk of physical violence.

Remarkably, results from the binary logistic regression on sexual violence bring out the protective role of women's autonomy and power within relationships unmistakably. In fact, indices measuring control and power in relationships are the only variables that turn out to be significant and reduce the risk of sexual violence in marital relationships.

Conclusion

Various forms of violence have a strong cultural component associated with gender norms prevailing in the society. Policy interventions at the community level and sustained rises in women's autonomy and education seem indispensable for reducing domestic violence in NER.

References

Anderson, K. L. (1997). Gender, status and domestic violence: An integration of feminist and family violence approaches. *Journal of Marriage and the Family*, *59*, 655-669.

Atkinson, M. P., Greenstein, T. N., & Lang, M. M. (2005). For women, breadwinning can be dangerous: Gendered resource theory and wife abuse. *Journal of Marriage and Family*, *67*, 1137-1148.

Flake, D. F. (2005). Individual, family, and community risk factors for domestic violence in Peru. *Violence Against Women*, *11*, 353-373.

Gage, A. J., & Hutchinson, P. L. (2006). Power, control, and intimate partner sexual violence in Haiti. *Archives of Sexual Behavior*, *35*, 11-24.

International Institute for Population Sciences (IIPS) and Macro International (2007) *National Family Health Survey (NFHS-3), 2005-06, India (IIPS: Mumbai).*

Jejeebhoy, S.J. and R.J. Cook (1997). State accountability for wife-beating: The Indian challenge. *Lancet*.

Jejeebhoy, S. J. (1998). Wife-beating in rural India: A husband's right? *Economic & Political Weekly*, *33*, 855-862.

Mosedale, S. (2005). Assessing women's empowerment: Towards a conceptual framework. *Journal of International Development*, *17*, 243-257

Panda, P., & Agarwal, B. (2005). Marital violence, human development, and women's property status in India. *World Development*, 33, 823-850.

World Health Organization. (2005). *WHO Multi-country study on women's health and domestic violence against women: Summary report of initial results on prevalence, health outcomes and women's responses*. Geneva, Switzerland.

Notes

1. Though the term Domestic Violence is in common usage currently, it is now being gradually replaced by the term Intimate Partner Violence. Domestic violence is currently defined in India by the Protection of Women from Domestic Violence Act of 2005. According to Section 3 of the Act, "any act, omission or commission or conduct of the respondent shall constitute domestic violence in case it (1) harms or injures or endangers the health, safety, life, limb or well-being, whether mental or physical, of the aggrieved person or tends to do so and includes causing physical abuse, sexual abuse, verbal and emotional abuse and economic abuse; or (2) harasses, harms, injures or endangers the aggrieved person with a view to coerce her or any other person related to her to meet any unlawful demand for any dowry or other property or valuable security; or (3) has the effect of threatening the aggrieved person or any person related to her by any conduct mentioned in clause (a) or clause (b); or (4)otherwise injures or causes harm, whether physical or mental, to the aggrieved person."

2. NFHS defines the various acts of violence as follows: **Physical violence:** Any of the following acts of violence perpetrated by her husband: (i) Pushed her, shook her, or threw something at her (ii) Slapped her (iii) Twisted her arm or pulled her hair (iv) Punched her (v) Kicked her, dragged her, or beat her up (vi) Tried to choke her or burn her on purpose (vii) Threatened her or attacked her with a weapon **Sexual violence**: Any of the following: (i) Forced her to have sexual intercourse when she did not want to (ii) Forced her to perform sexual acts she did not want to **Emotional violence**: Any of the following: (i) Said or did something to humiliate her in front of others (ii) Threatened to hurt or harm her or someone close to her (iii) Insulted her or made her feel bad about herself.

25

Chirus, Purums, and How Social Changes in North East India Provided New Windows for T.C. Das*

Dr.Abhijit Guha

T.C. Das was born in January 1898 and earned his M.A. degree from Calcutta University in 'Ancient Indian History and Culture' and joined the newly founded Department of Anthropology at Calcutta University in 1921 as a research scholar and then he became a lecturer in 1923 and finally retired from the rank of Reader in the Department in 1963. (Ray 1974: 56 & Science and Culture 1941:26-27). Das conducted extensive field works in Chotanagpur in the then Bihar and in Assam. He also conducted field works to assess the impact of industrialization in Birlapur in West Bengal, wrote thought provoking articles containing anthropological and sociological analyses on Bengal dowry restriction bill of 1940 and Hindu code bill in the years 1940 and 1944 along with articles on the practical suggestions for the improvement of museums in India and an empirical article on the fish-gorge in Bengal in the prestigious journals like *Modern Review*, *Calcutta Review* and *Ethnos*. He was very much interested in the application of Anthropology and had a great reputation as a teacher and trainer in field methods.

One comprehensive available account of the list of publications of T.C. Das including a short life-sketch was prepared not by an anthropologist or a sociologist but by the Reference Librarian in the Central Library of the Anthropological Survey of India, Shyamal Kumar Ray, in his invaluable book *Bibliographies of Eminent Indian Anthropologists (with Life-Sketches)*

---

* After a whole day's labour of replying to my queries, a batch of Chirus started at nightfall from Bishenpur dak bungalow in Manipur for their home, 15 miles away through hills covered with dense jungle. They were completely oblivious of the hard task that lay ahead when they started from the bungalow. My anxiety over the trouble and risk only evoked a little surprise. With a smile they departed as if on an evening walk.

T.C. Das (1963). "Aspects of Tribal Culture under modern impact In Eastern India". In Anthropology on the March. Edited by Bala Ratnam. Madras: The Book Centre.

Application of such knowledge for the improvement of the people concerned is the ultimate aim of the modern ethnographer. He is no longer an academician like his compatriots of the other day. Study for study's sake is not his motive.

T.C. Das (1945) The Purums: An Old Kuki Tribe of Manipur (p.281).

published by the Anthropological Survey of India in July, 1974. The volume contains the list of publications and short life-sketches of 12 eminent Indian anthropologists including Tarak Chandra Das (Ray 1974: 56-60). It begins with L.K. Ananthakrishna Iyer (1861-1937) and S.S. Sarkar (1908-1969) is the last anthropologist covering a span of more than one hundred years if we take the year of birth of Iyer and the year of death of Sarkar at the two ends of the continuum. T.C. Das falls somewhere in the middle of the continuum.

The publications of T.C. Das spanned over a period of 41 years from 1922-1963. He began to write academic articles in Anthropology when he was 24 and wrote his last article in 1963, a year before his death. Das, of course was not a prolific writer like his illustrious contemporaries, viz., K.P. Chattopadhyay, Nirmal Kumar Bose, D.N. Majumdar and Irawati Karve, and he did not publish popular or serious articles in the vernacular in the newspapers and magazines.

Despite the institutional amnesia and obliviousness of the individual scholars about the social responsibility and commitment of T.C. Das to human welfare, he is still remembered for his ethnography on the Purum Kukis of North-east India. His brilliant monograph *The Purums: An Old Kuki tribe of Manipur* published in 1945 by the Calcutta University became one of the major sources of database in the acrimonious debate on descent versus alliance theories on kinship in Anglo-American Anthropology which involved mavericks like Claude Levi-Strauss, George Homans, David Schneider, Rodney Needham, Floyd Lounsbury and others.

The Indian anthropologists too continued their ethnographic enterprise on the Purum on behalf of the premier governmental institution of the country—the Anthropological Survey of India. A team of anthropologists were sent to the field area where Das conducted his ethnographic observations during 1931-1936 and a book was published entitled *Proceedings of the Symposium on Purum (Chote) Revisited* in 1985 as an outcome of a symposium in which about 20 anthropologists two educated members of the tribe participated and presented their views/papers on the Purums (Das Gupta et.al. 1985). The Indian anthropologists in the symposium seemed to have been preoccupied them in revisiting the keen interest of the series of Western scholars who wrote and debated on the marriage alliance pattern and rules of the Purum tribe. Thus, from the beginning to the end of the symposium volume we find the contributors harping on the theme of Western attention to the Purum case. None of the anthropologists pointed to one of the most significant chapters of the Purum book in which Das made an attempt to apply his own brilliant findings for the development and betterment of the Purums who according to him were surviving with a very low standard of living in terms of economy, health and education (Das 1945: 281-295).

Materials and Methods

From 1922 to 1940, that is about 18 years of his active academic life Das did not venture to write any significant article on the application of social anthropology for the welfare and improvement of the communities and cultures he had studied. His main research interest during this period was to record and study the different aspects of culture and social organisation of the tribal and non-tribal communities of the eastern and north-eastern parts of India. In this period he conducted field work and published on the Ho, Bhumij, Kharia, Chiru, Bathuri and Purum Kuki. His paper in prestigious international journals of Anthropology like *Anthropos*, *Man,* and *Ethnos* had been published during this period.

The year 1941 can be regarded as a major turning point in the academic career of T. C. Das. In 1941, he delivered the presidential address of the Indian Science Congress. The lecture was a 28 page full-length paper entitled 'Cultural Anthropology in the Service of the Individual and the Nation'. This paper can be regarded as one of the pioneering articles on applied anthropology in India, although neither L.P. Vidyarthi nor Surajit Sinha mentioned about this significant article in their works on the application of anthropology in the Indian context (Sinha 1969; 1971 & 1980 and Vidyarthi 1978).

In an earlier article 'Urgent problems for research in social and cultural anthropology in India: perspective and suggestions', in a book titled *Urgent Research in Social Anthropology*, published by the Indian Institute of Advanced Study in 1969, Surajit Sinha seemed to have fully engrossed himself with the contributions of his famous teacher Nirmal Kumar Bose whose five articles were mentioned by him as regards urgent research in social anthropology in India (Sinha 1969:162-169). Like his Presidential Address delivered in the Section of Anthropology in the Indian Science Congress in 1941, another very significant work of Das remained unnoticed by the scholars on Indian Anthropology. This work of Das was published in the prestigious international journal *Anthropos* as early as 1937 under the title 'Some notes on the economic and agricultural life of a little known tribe on the eastern frontier of India' (Das 1937:440-449).

Findings

Science Congress Lecture

The year 1941 can be regarded as a major turning point in the academic career of T. C. Das. In 1941, he delivered the presidential address of the Indian Science Congress. The lecture was a 28 page full-length paper entitled 'Cultural Anthropology in the Service of the Individual and the Nation'. This paper can be regarded as one of the pioneering articles on applied anthropology in India. In the address Das elaborately charted out the future path of Indian anthropology with a rich description of the social dynamics of the tribal and peasant societies in India in the context of the role of anthropologists in nation building.

In this lecture Das's major objective was to convince his readers about the immense potential of social-cultural anthropology as applied science for the overall development of the Indian population. In the five subsections of the lecture, Das dealt with the application of anthropology in almost all the important sectors of a modern nation, viz. trade, industry, agriculture, legislation, education, social service and administration. With the help of concrete empirical findings either from his own field experiences or from the ethnographic accounts of world renowned social anthropologists(e.g. Lucy Mair, Felix Keesing, Issac Schepera, H.I. Hogbin, B. Malinowski) Das justified the inclusion of anthropologists in policy making bodies and application of anthropological knowledge in every sphere of nation building(Das 1941: 1-29). In order to substantiate his arguments, Das had used rather unconventional sources of data, like Mahatma Gandhi's 1937 article published in *Harijan* about the adverse effects of the methods adopted by the Christian missionaries to convert the economically poorer classes of the Hindu population in different parts of India(Ibid : 17-23). One of the most vital sections in the Presidential Address of Das was on the role of anthropologists in building up a proper type of educational system suitable for the real needs of a particular community in the Indian context. The great anthropologist had the courage to write strong words regarding the colossal wastage of public money by the then colonial government for the establishment of schools among the tribal people. Das then narrated from his own rich field experiences in Manipur valley of North eastern India about the adverse social impact of the establishment of a network of primary schools and a few high English schools. I quote Das

The two schools I saw used to teach their students how to read and write Methei besides a little arithmetic, which they managed to forget within a few months after their departure from the school. It is difficult to understand how high school education will help Manipuri agriculture or textile industry. The employments at the disposal of the State are very limited and the students who pass out of these schools every year will increase the number of unemployed as they no longer think of going back to their fields. During the first few years they will be idolized by the community but this will soon pass away when they will be looked upon as parasites and it is not impossible that they will be a source of trouble to the State(Ibid 1941:15-16).

Consider this insightful observation of Das in connection with the active participation of the English educated youth in the ethnic and secessionist movements that developed in this region of India after the Independence. Das strongly advocated that in this type of situations the advice of the experienced and trained anthropologists is required in the Herculean task of educating the tribal and other underprivileged communities in a diverse country like India.

First, Das probably was the first Indian anthropologist to advocate the indispensable role of social-cultural anthropology in nation building by combining micro-level field observations within a macro framework which is still lacking among the majority of Indian anthropologists. We have a lot to learn from Das even today (Guha 2012: 40-46).

Purums

It is interesting to note that the whole discussion and debate on the Purums in Western and Indian Anthropology centered around the monograph of Das, did not take into consideration the final section of the book under chapter X. This chapter has two sections, viz. 'Acculturation' (section I) and 'The Future' (section II).

I would begin my discussion with L.P. Vidyarthi's reading of the Purum monograph, since he is the lone anthropologist who emphasized the applied dimension of Das'work on the tribe. Vidyarthi in the first volume of his book *Rise of Anthropology in India* described in detail about the findings of Das in the different chapters of the monograph with much admiration for its meticulousness and penetrating analyses. In the final part of his description, Vidyarthi discussed about the suggestions put forward by Das for the betterment of the Purums (Vidyarthi 1978:77-81). For Vidyarthi, with the publication of the Purum book T.C. Das 'set an example of a systematic presentation of ethnographic data' (Ibid 1978:80). He concluded the discussion on Das' monograph with the following comment:

His monograph, though not well known to Indian scholars, remains a piece of meticulous fieldwork and penetrative analysis. It will continue to serve as a model for ethnographic research in anthropology (Ibid 1978: 81).

We would now look more closely into the concluding chapter of T.C. Das' book on the Purum Kuki.In the first part of his concluding chapter Das laid emphasis on the dynamic nature of Purum society which had undergone changes through historical times and also on the different aspects of Purum culture under various kinds of external influences.

Secondly, Das was keenly interested to understand the nature of the 'productive system'(he did not use the Marxian term *means of production* but it was clear that by the term 'productive system' he did not only refer to technology and material culture) in a dynamic rather than in a functional framework.

Thirdly, without borrowing terms from the Western Marxist scholars mechanically Das made a very sincere empirical attempt to record the processes by which the new productive system, characterized by plough and plains-land cultivation had begun to influence the different sectors of the Purum society, viz., inheritance, marriage and religion. Apart from looking into the internal sociocultural changes brought about by the adoption of the plough cultivation among the Purums, Das was also aware of the wider politicoeconomic forces which were at work in the region where this small tribe inhabited. He stated at the beginning of the section I of his concluding chapter:

Though foreign merchandise has come to Purum home, it is still immune from the money-lenders of the plains. This is partly due to difficulties of transport and partly to the judicious laws of land tenure of the State as well as the nature of land-economy of the people. Investment is risky where there is no permanently cultivated land with a marketable value. Nobody would invest money against *jhum* fields and the Purums have nothing else from which the loan can be realized. The recent introduction of permanently cultivated fields will sooner or later change the situation and if the State also relinquishes the stringency of the land-laws the Purums will fall easy prey to the land-grabbers who are sure to flock to their home (Das 1945:273).

In section II of the concluding chapter Das put forward some concrete recommendations for the improvement of agriculture and health conditions of the tribe without introducing any quick solutions. Das was more in favour of slow and steady changes through employment oriented education among the tribal youth. He also spoke against the conversion of the members of the tribe to Christianity. B.K. Das Gupta reported in his revisit study that a good number of churches have been established in the Purum villages. (Das Gupta 1985:52-80). But how did it really affect the social and economic life of the Purums? How the wider market economy was influencing the tribe's social and political structures? There was virtually no attempt to explore into these vital questions in Das Gupta's restudy paper. If one reads the concluding chapter of T.C. Das' Purum book one would hardly find any evidence of his interest in the marriage alliance pattern of the tribe which fascinated the Western anthropologists and driven their Indian compatriots to conduct the revisit study.

Chirus

A very significant work of Das remained unnoticed by the scholars on Indian Anthropology and this was on the Chirus of Manipur. This work of Das was published in the prestigious international journal *Anthropos* as early as 1937 under the title 'Some notes on the economic and agricultural life of a little known tribe on the eastern frontier of India' (Das 1937:440-449). In this paper Das dealt with the relationship between the variation in technology of agricultural practices with the natural environment and the socioeconomic consequences of this variation within the same tribe. Chirus, like the Purums belonged to the old Kuki group of tribes of the north-east India. At the time of Das' field work during 1931-34, the Chiru population was 1272 and they lived in 11 villages, 9 of which were situated on the top of the hills and 2 were on the plains of the Manipur valley. Here Das first established the importance of agriculture particularly shifting hill cultivation among the Chirus despite the presence of hunting, fishing and gathering which were found to be subsidiary occupations among them. According to Das:

Agriculture forms the basis of Chiru economic life. All other activities, whether social, religious, or economic are directly or indirectly connected with this important food-producing work. Economic activities like hunting, fishing, rearing of domestic animals and trading are all subservient to agriculture' (Das 1937:441).

But how did he substantiate his claims made in the above statement? Without going into quantification, Das adopted the ethnographic methodology to prove his argument.

First, he described the methods and situations under which the Chirus engage them in fishing, hunting-gathering, domestication of animals and trading.

Second, he then described in brief the different rites and rituals connected with *jhum* cultivation and the role of traditional village officials in those communal festivals. The evidences put forward by Das revealed how the natural environment and the socio-religious practices of the tribe have made shifting hill cultivation as the main economic foundation of the tribe. Das then proceeded further to look into the sociological implications of this cultural ecological scenario of the Chiru society. In the words of Das:

Chiru society is composed of agriculturists only. As already shown, hunting, fishing and trading have not grown into independent occupations, but are practised along with agriculture and is subordinated to its interest. Thus, these avocations have failed to produce special socio-economic groups. The traces of stratifications found among them cannot be attributed to economic pursuits. (Ibid 1937: 443).

A careful reading of the paper reveals that the economic life of the Chirus which Das constructed is not a simple description of the methods of shifting hill cultivation and the associated religious rituals and rites. Neither it is an ethnographic report for the search of borrowed culture traits from the neighbouring tribes and Hinduised populations nor was it an attempt to put the Chirus in the classical scheme of social evolution. The ethnography of Das on the other hand is a penetrating analysis of the various socio-cultural dimensions of shifting hill cultivation in an environmental framework and the slow changes that had been taking place at the time of observation. Take for example, Das' method of dealing with an apparently simple ethnographic observation. He recorded that majority of the Chiru villages possess only 20-30 households and the biggest village did not contain more than 40 households. But what are the reasons and consequences of Chiru village size in terms of the households? It is better to quote Das:

The Chirus do not renew the fertility of an exhausted patch of land by means of fertilizers. It is left to nature which by accumulating the mould for years together makes it again fit for another period of cultivation. The effects of discarding exhausted patches of land are many and far-reaching. It has led to scattering of villages at considerable distance from one another. It puts a limit to the growth of population in each village.... Increase of population leads to establishment of new villages in order to relieve pressure on land. This type of cultivation does not help in the accumulation of wealth in individual hands and consequent growth of rank. On the other hand it has bred an extreme democratic spirit in their social and political life (Ibid 1937: 445).

The most interesting aspect of Das' work on the Chirus is about the changes that took place in their socio-political life due to migration of some sections of the tribe from the hills to the edge of the Imphal valley. Das' observations can be called pioneering in terms of its analytical strength. According to him a shift from *jhum* cultivation on the hills to wet rice cultivation on the edge of the valley is not only a techno-economic affair but it also entailed a whole gamut of socio-political changes in the life of the Chirus. That is why he began his observation by contrasting the ownership pattern of *jhum* land with that of the plains land. While the jhum land was not owned by any individual family but under the control of the village authority, the plains land could be owned by an individual family for which a rent had to be paid to a supra-local political authority. Since wet rice cultivation with the plough could be carried out I the plains, the crop output was higher and a section of the Chirus (though small in number during the time of Das' fieldwork) was found to have been adopting the plains-land cultivation. This shift has had immense socio-political consequences for the community. The analysis forwarded by Das deserves to be quoted in his unique words:

So long we had been dealing with jhum-land only. Besides this there is another kind of land which is gradually coming into prominence in Chiru economic life. This is the land at the feet of the hills where plough-cultivation is possible... The village community has no authority over the disposal of this type of land and it does not hold itself in any way responsible for its fortune. On the other hand it is a source of danger to the authority of the village community. The bachelors' house, marriage by service, equal right of every individual over the village jhum-land, and setting up of new houses soon after marriage, are institutions directed to the same end, namely undermining the influence of the family and setting up the village community as the only body to which one may look for help and succour. But the new type of land will set up the family over the village community and place the house-father above all (Das 137:446).

It is an irony that both Marxist and non-Marxist sociologists and anthropologists of India paid no attention to such an incisive analysis of the relationship between productive technology and the socio-political life of a tribal society in the context of the village. In this context, it is interesting to note that one of the earliest publications of Julian Steward in which he dealt with the relationship between productive technology and the other sectors of culture was published in the same year in *Anthropos* (Steward 1937: 87-104).If one compares the paper of Steward with that of Das, then certain important similarities become evident. Like T.C. Das, Julian Steward also gave emphasis on the importance of environment and economy in shaping the social organisational features of a culture in an era dominated by diffusionism. An interesting observation of Das made in the *Anthropos* paper regarding the close interrelationship of the social and economic life of the Chirus in the context of the role played by the women. Although he made this observation at the end of the paper, it was definitely a forward looking one during late 1930s. Let us hear from Das:

The wife helps the husband in all operations of the jhum-field. In the plains-field also she is of equal importance except at the time of ploughing and leveling.... The wife is in the sole charge of preparing the food of the family, drawing water and collecting fuel. Not only these, she supplies the whole family with clothes for all seasons, woven on her loom with yarns spun by herself from the cotton grown on the *jhum* of the family.. Thus women's contribution to Chiru economic life is more important than that of man. So, it is in the fitness of things, that a man has to serve for five years to secure a bride and most of them do not forget her value.' (Das 1937: 449).

Suffice it to say that Das' *Anthropos* paper which dealt with relationships between the productive system and other sectors of culture and the fact that it was contemporaneous to Steward's earliest paper on ecology (Guha,)

Conclusion

Tarak Chandra Das was one of the founders of professional and academic Anthropology in India who earned his international fame through his research on the Purums of Manipur. But both the Indian and foreign anthropologists viewed him only as a meticulous ethnographer of Purum life. His other important works and observations on North East India having contemporary relevance had largely gone unnoticed. These works have immense application value for making Anthropology useful for the country.Das' Science Congress paper and his incisive cultural ecological analysis of the Chiru society and even his socially committed observations on the Purums are not only important for North East India but also for the whole country. Undoubtedly, North East India provided Das with a new window to turn Anthropology towards application and nation building and he was really running ahead of his time.

Acknowledgements

I express my sincerest gratitude to the faculties of the Department of Anthropology, Manipur University for giving me the opportunity to present this paper in the 46th Annual Conference of the Indian Anthropological Society held during 8-10 Nov.2016 at the Dept. of Anthropology, Manipur University,

Imphal. I also owe my debts to the organizers of the Indian Anthropological Society and Manipur University for holding the Conference. Finally, I thank all my friends and colleagues who always inspires me to continue my research on the contributions of Tarak Chandra Das and many of them have provided me with the rare and unnoticed articles and books of Das without which this research would not have been possible. Last but not the least I would like to thank the authorities of Vidyasagar University for their continuous cooperation towards my research endeavours.

References

Das Gupta, B.K., Basu, A., Raychaudhuri, B., Gupta, P. (1985). *Proceedings of the Symposium on Purum (Chote) Revisited*. Anthropological Survey of India. Department of Culture, Govt. of India. Calcutta.

Das, T.C. 1937. Some notes on the economic and agricultural life of a little-known tribe on the eastern frontier of India. *Anthropos* 32: 440-449.

Das, T.C. 1941. 'Cultural Anthropology in the Service of the Individual and the Nation'.PP.1-29. *Presidential Address delivered in the Section of Anthropology in the Twenty-eighth Indian Science Congress*. Benares.

Das, T.C. 1945. *The Purums: An Old Kuki Tribe of Manipur*. Calcutta University. Calcutta.

Das, T,C. 1963. Aspects of Tribal Culture under modern impact In Eastern India. In *Anthropology on the March*. Edited by Bala Ratnam. Madras : The Book Centre.

Guha, A. 2011. Tarak Chandra Das: A Marginalised Anthropologist. *Sociological Bulletin*, 60(2):245-265.

Ray, S.K. 1974. *Bibliographies of Eminent Indian Anthropologists* (*WITH LIFE-SKETCHES*) Anthropological Survey of India, Govt. of India, Indian Museum, Calcutta. Roy Burman, B.K.

Science and Culture. 1941. Short Life-Sketches of the General President and Sectional Presidents: T.C. Das, President, Anthropology Section. 1941, 6:7, Science Congress Supplement.

Sinha, S. 1974. "Foreword". In *Bibliographies of Eminent Indian Anthropologists (WITH LIFE-SKETCHES)* By Shyamal Kumar Ray. Anthropological Survey of India, Govt. of India, Indian Museum, Calcutta.

Sinha, S. 1978. 'Introducing the seminar'. In *Field Studies on the People of India: methods and perspectives*. Edited by Surajit Sinha. Indian Anthropological Society: Calcutta.

Sinha, S. 1980. "India: A Western apprentice". In *Anthropology: Ancestors and Heirs*. Edited by Stanley Diamond. The Hague: Mouton.

Steward, J. H. 1937. Ecological aspects of Southwestern society. *Anthropos* 32:87:104.

Vidyarthi, L.P. 1978. *Rise of Anthropology in India: A Social Science Orientation*, Vols. I & II. Concept Publishing Company. New Delhi.

26

Emoinu Model in Contemporary Meitei Society

Chungkham Supriya Devi

Introduction

'Lai' is a term used to denote gods and goddesses by the Meitei, the major ethnic group of Manipur. The Meitei worship a number of deities and more than three hundred sixty deities exist in the society. The Meitei religion possesses elements of animism, fetishism, totemism, ancestor worship as well as Hinduism. Atiya sidaba or Atingkhok sidaba or Sidaba Mapu who created the universe is the supreme of all Meitei gods. He had three sons; Ashiba, Achiba and Konjintuthokpa. After creating the universe he ordered Ashiba to create mankind and other living things on earth. Ashiba created living things based on what he had seen from his father's abdomen and also created atmosphere, soil, sun, Khongjom Nubi (a constellation), rivers and so on. Atiya Sidaba then thought of giving his throne to his son, so he called his three sons and asked them to move round the universe seven times. He told them that the one who came first after circumambulating the universe seven times would be given the throne. Konjin Tuthokpa ascended the throne and came to be known as Pakhangba while Ashiba or Sanamahi became the king of every household residing in a shrine on the southwestern corner of every household. Leimaren Sidabi, mother earth, is represented by an earthern pot filled with water and is enshrined to the left of Sanamahi. Sanamahi together with Leimaren Sidabi reside in every Meitei household and are revered as the main god and goddess of the group. Therefore, Sanamahi is regarded as the religion of the Meitei before the advent of Hinduism.

The Meiteis believe in polytheism and their gods and goddesses can be categorized into four types:

(i) *Yum lais* - household deities includes Laininthou Sanamahi, Leimarel sidabi and Emoinu. They are worshipped every day in every household for the well being and prosperity of the family.

(ii) *Maikei ngakpa lai* - directional deities namely Koubru, Thangjing, Marjing and Wangbren. These deities reside in the hills and are worshipped to protect the people from disasters caused by evil spirits.

(iii) *Umang lai*- village deities. There are around 361 umang lais and are worshipped annually for 5-10 days at the time of Lai Haraoba for fertility, peace, economic well being and solidarity.

(iv) *Apokpa* - ancestors of seven clans. It was the most important features of Meitei belief. They are worshipped for fertility, wealth and to protect lineages or clans from misfortune.

(v) Lam lai - gods of country side

As mentioned above, the Meitei profess Sanamahi religion. However, during the reign of king Pamheiba, the religion took a turn. He introduced Hinduism to the Meitei people and those who refused to adopt it were exiled from the state. Though the Meitei became Hindus, they continued to worship the traditional deities and the practice is continued till today.

An important characteristic feature of the Meitei belief system is ancestor worship. Each and every clan has its own ancestral god to whom specific edible items and tools are offered during rituals performed on specific days and in specific months. Lai Haraoba (merry making of gods) is a notable worship of Umang lais. Formerly there were only nine Umang Lais but later the number increased to more than three hundred due to the expansion of lineages during the period of Nongda Lairel Pakhangba. Umang lai is the status assigned to administrative heads and functionaries of different areas in the state who rendered relentless and selfless service to the people. They are worshipped collectively at village level for the maintenance of peace and prosperity. Notable worships of these deities are Moirang Haraoba, Chakpa Haraoba, Kanglei Haraoba and Kakching Haraoba. These worships involve a series of rites and rituals, chanting of hymns, and giving oracles by Maiba (priests) and Maibis (priestesses) though the nature of worship varies from one Umanglai to another and from one village to another. Lai Haraoba is a social, cultural and political institution where the thoughts, art, literature and beliefs of Meiteis are reflected. It gives a platform for social gathering of the villagers to strengthen solidarity and proper functioning of the village.

The Meiteis have a firm belief in magical power, evil spirits, black magic, oracle, witchcraft and evil eyes. The concept of evil spirits and taboos also existed. Hellois (witches), Hingchabis(vampires) and Saroi Ngaroi(evil spirit) are elements which are believed to occupy the outside world. Due to this reason, the elders restrict movements on certain days and time to avoid unwanted happenings.

Rites and rituals are inseparable aspects of every religion. Various rituals, rites and ceremonies are performed by the priests and the priestesses to appease the deities and evil spirits to cure diseases, to increase productivity of food, to ward off evil spirits affecting the health both at household level and at village level. The role of the priests and the priestesses in Meitei religion is manifold. It is also through them that oral tradition is kept alive and stories of the past are relayed through generations. When Hinduism was adopted as the state religion, Hindu ceremonies became more popular. Brahmins who perform these ceremonies enjoyed better positions than the traditional performers.

Methodology

In order to understand the impact of modernization on Goddess Emoinu's codes of conduct on Meitei women and in Meitei society, anthropological methods of data collection like interview and case study methods have been employed. Case study method was carried out on 10 women, 5 each from working and non-working groups.

Case Study	*Name*	*Working Status*
1	Sumila	Non-working
2	Priyanka	Non-working
3	Bededa	Non-working
4	Shantibala	Non-working
5	Bijentimala	Non-working
6	Mrinalini	Working
7	Bidyarani	Working
8	Memi	Working
9	Radha	Working
10	Damayanti	Working

Interview was conducted with the help of an interview guide. Secondary information has been collected from books, articles and newspaper. Findings are analysed and discussed in four different themes.

Goddess Emoinu Ahongbi

Goddess Emoinu is the goddess of wealth. The goddess is one of the manifestations of goddess Leimarel Sidabi whom Atiya Sidaba, the supreme god, created from the left side of his body with an aim to procreate and establish mankind. On being directed by Atiya Sidaba to create another goddess to look after the human beings, Leimarel sidabi created Emoinu, the goddess of wealth. Emoinu resides in the hearth of every household called 'Phungga Lairu' (Phungga= hearth, Lairu= most important). The Phungga

Lairu is an important place in the Meitei household with great religious significance. It consists of a small hole dug in the western corner of the fireplace which has a tripod stand over it to support cooking vessels. The iron tripod feet of the Phungga should not be moved and fire in the Phungga should never be extinguished at dusk. Absence of fire in the hearth at dusk is considered a taboo. There may be a scientific reason behind this as smoke from the fire can repel mosquitoes and other insects. The hearth also has great social significance as folktales were narrated at night sitting around it as a means of recreation and enjoyment. The norms prevalent in the Meitei society are believed that such to have been framed by the Goddess Emoinu.

The goddess has many manifestations. Leithak Leikharol (manuscript of Meitei cosmology) mentions of Konjin tuthokpa (youngest son of Supreme god Atiya Sidaba) being surrounded by Lai nura Taret (manifestations of goddess Emoinu) Hipokpi, Yaipokpi, Hireima, Yaireima, Hikubi, Yaikubi, and Yaisna when Asiba (eldest son of Atiya Sidaba) tried to kill him. When the goddess comes to fishing, the deity takes the form of 'Ngareima' (goddess of fish), during agriculture as Phouoibi, during war as Lanleima, when it deals with salt producing practices as Thumleima, when it comes to book and work as Sinleima and in the hearth of the household, the Goddess takes the form of Emoinu Ahongbi. The Meitei people believe that Goddess Emoinu monitors the way of living and behavior of the members. If the Goddess is pleased, the family will be blessed with wealth and prosperity. Thus, the Goddess Emoinu occupies a very important place in shaping the behaviors of the individuals specially women folk who are assigned to look after the household. Khuman kangleirol (a manuscript) makes mention of Khayoiron Nganuthumbi, sister of Khuman King Yumoiba, being married to Meitei King Luwang Guru Punshiba as his ninth wife. They had a son named Senba Mimaba and got separated. When Senba Mimaba grew up, one day he went for hunting to his father's place and shot a deer in the King's court, which was a manifestation of Goddess Emoinu. This led to the identification of father and his son. Later his son begged for the Goddess which resides in the hearth of King's court. Senba Mimaba brought the Goddess to the Khuman place and thereafter was blessed with wealth. Therefore, worshipping of Goddess Emoinu started since the very early period before the small different groups merged into whole as Meitei. However, wide spread worship of Emoinu prevailed during the reign of king Khagemba (1597-1652) who took stern steps to popularize the teachings of the goddess. His son Meidingu Khakta Khoinai (Khunjaoba) followed his father's steps to maintain the popularity of the goddess as a result of which the state was blessed with wealth and prosperity.

Beliefs and values associated with goddess Emoinu

The Meiteis have a firm belief in worshipping household deity with devotion for well being, wealth and prosperity of the family. Goddess Emoinu prescribes certain codes of conduct to women to assume the ideal image. Though men are not much aware of the codes, women take the responsibility to impart the knowledge to daughters so that peace and prosperity remains in every household. While men remain busy in earning bread for the family, women look after the family by preparing food, cleaning and washing for all. The tasks performed by women are necessary for the smooth functioning of the family. And the codes prescribed by Goddess Emoinu help them to perform in an appreciable manner.

The Meitei traditional house has a separate room for keeping dried paddy called Kei. Before taking rice from it, they have to pray to the goddess Phouobi, a manifestation of goddess Emoinu, as a form of seeking permission for the act. The people believed that when buying vegetables or rice from outside, storing is to be done in their proper storing vessels before being cooked. The Meiteis pray to the household deities Lainingthou Sanamahi and Leimarel Sidabi before retiring to bed, before stepping out of the house, and after coming home to yield better result for the day's work.

Morning is considered as the most important phase of a day. It decides the fate of the day, thus bad and unwanted things are avoided in the morning. Before stepping down from the bed in the morning, one has to smoothen hair and clothes, offer salutation to mother earth by touching the floor and then the forehead three times. One should then step down from the bed by blowing through both noses and then choosing the unblocked side as the auspicious one to take the first step of the day. Prayer to the Korouhanba (Sun) before brushing and cleaning is believed to bring good fortune.

Behaviours of women prohibited by Goddess Emoinu

Meitei women use a wrapper called Etum-phi while taking bath. Entering the house in wet etum phi or changing etum phis frequently is prohibited. The goddess does not favour over makeup by women. Display of bad temper or anger by thumping on the ground is strictly prohibited. Habits of gossiping, laughing with open mouth, engaging in adultery, flirting with young boys, and countering husbands are not encouraged.

Cleanliness of the house and its surrounding is maintained by women. However sweeping the floor in haste or when someone is eating is not prescribed. Utensils that are used for dinner should not be kept unclean overnight. Softness and tenderness are believed to characterized women. They should not make sound while walking and cleaning inside the house, for it irritates the deity and sue away.

The Goddess does not appreciate women who scratch their head while talking, keeps secret for long time, express anger with murmuring sound and who do not give attention to personal hygiene. Women should not be rough while handling cooking utensils or taking out rice from Chengphu, a rice storing vessel. Tasting or smelling dishes while being cooked is not allowed. Leaving cooking vessels empty after serving meals is also strictly prohibited as it invites shortage of food.

Women are prohibited from disrespecting their husbands and in-laws, kicking children, cooking unwashed vegetables, eating meals on unclean floor, eating in concealment, touching wallets, cupboards and other household items prior to brushing teeth in the morning.

Behaviours of women prescribed by Goddess Emoinu

An ideal woman, as perceived by Goddess Emoinu, is one who regards her husband as god, can pacify her husband's anger, wakes up early and keeps the house clean, does not take meal before her husband does, who is pure and honest at heart, casual only to her husband, looks after children with love and care, remains faithful and loyal to her husband even in his absence.

Giving fire from the hearth at night is believed to be equivalent to giving away the goddess thus resulting in decrease in wealth and prosperity. Therefore denial to give fire to others at night is a must. However, no such restriction exists during the day though the frequency should not exceed more than three times; be it rice, vegetables or money. While lending, they should not let others to take the objects from the owner's wallet or containers by themselves. Rather the owner should make sure to hand over the objects to the borrower to ward off ill-luck as the goddess is believed to be insulted if not done so.

Women are expected to stay away from gossip or the habit of borrowing. They should not let neighbours influence their decision making. Wise use of resources is considered a womanly quality. Personal hygiene and purity of soul and body should be strictly maintained as the body is considered as a temple of god. Daily routine of offering prayer should always be treated with priority. Failure to do so is believed to result in misfortune and accidents.

Women as a home maker

Under the influence of modernization, women have greater participation in education and in public sphere. But the sole responsibility for the sustenance of the family such as cooking, cleaning and washing still rested on women. Men remain as the sole earner of the family. In comparison with working and non-working women; working women struggle more than non- working women in doing the household chores. They try to finish the household chores before leaving for work and continue doing it after coming back too. Comparing both groups, few husbands of both working and non-working women help in doing household work. Example can be stated from case 7 and case 10.

Case 7: Bidyarani (Private school teacher)

My husband is a mason and he usually leaves for work at 6 a.m. Before he left for work, he fetches water from the pond and sweeps the surrounding areas of the house. As my kids are small, it is hard for me to do all the household works. So when I am busy doing other household chores, he cooks food for the family. We both do the work co-operatively.

Case 10: Damayanti (Government School teacher)

My husband does help in doing household works. I am often in haste to do household works in the morning and then getting ready for school. When I am busy doing it, he prepares tea and makes breakfast for us. Most of the works that need muscular strength are done by him. In contrast to it, most men do not help in doing household work. Significant example can be cited from case 9.

Case 9: Radha (Government School teacher)

I leave for school at around 9:30 am. I try to finish household works before I leave for school but sometimes I left the work undone due to limited time. Though I want help from my husband, I have no means as he is unwilling to do. Rather he would always wait for me to offer tea in the morning, despite my hectic household work. His work in the morning is to do yoga, drink tea, read newspaper and then getting ready for office. When I asked help from him, he would end up comparing me to other women who could do all the works alone. The situation was worse during my early days when I used to go school at 6:30 am to 10:30 am and when my kids were small. I could not cook food for the family as I had class early. Most of the time I cooked meals after I came back from work and in addition to this, I had to look after kitchen garden, in-laws and help my children in studies. Because of this I kept helper to look after my children and to do household works.

Women in decision making and pacifying anger

The status of Meitei women is lower than their male counterparts. Despite such nature of patriarchy, they are given due importance in the society. They play a very important role in decision making. Their opinion are heard and considered by their husband. Decisions regarding small matters are taken by themselves but when it comes family oriented problems and monetary problems, both husband and wife discussed and take the decision together. Both working and non-working women depend on their respective husbands for making decisions. Interviewees gave different opinion in regard to decision making:

Case 1: Sumila (Non-working)

I do not take decision alone whether it is small or big matter. While doing something I always informed my husband and asked for his approval as he is taking main responsibility in earning. I keep my husband superior to me and I love to live my life under him.

Case 9: Radha

I can make my own decision but feel guilty when I do something without the consent of my husband. I cannot follow my own wish thinking what if my husband denies. I do not get freedom in making my own decision after entering married life. Our society is patriarchal and I consider it as the characteristic of it. So I discuss with him while making decision.

In case of an argument or quarrelling between husband and wife, it is the women who cool first in order to avoid further unwanted happenings. Comparing working and non-working women, both takes the initiatives to pacify the anger. Their opinions are:

Case 10: Damayanti

Men tend to get more angrier when his wife argue more with him instead of pacifying it which often leads to beating and other unwanted problems. So I try to cool down first.

Case 7: Bidyarani

I am the first to cool down when we argue or quarrel. Though he knows that he is wrong, he will never say sorry to me. I feel ashamed before my neighbours so I cool down first and explain the matter after pacifying him. He never compromise to me and in regard to this I have depression.

Meitei women and Goddess Emoinu

There is a close relationship between the Goddess and the Meitei women. Codes of conduct of Goddess Emoinu are believed to help the society in general and women in particular. Modernization has brought many changes in Meitei society and deviation from the prescribed behavior of women by the Goddess is observed in the study. But it does not imply total disappearance of traditional values and beliefs. Though there are some changes in contemporary Meitei society, some daily practices are still in vogue such as giving salutation to the mother earth before stepping down from bed and offering prayer to the Sun god in the morning. And it is evident from the following cases:

Case 6: Mirnalini (an employee of MSPDCL)

I wake up at 6 am in the morning and step down from bed after praying to mother earth. After it I take bath and directly cooks food as meals has to be ready before 8 am for my husband. When my husband is having meal, I offered morning prayer to the Sun God.

Case 5: Bijentimala (non-working)

I am a herbal life associate and I mingled with different kinds of people when I go for international trip. I wear jeans and Kurta too but I never forget my own origin and do not want to break the traditional norms of our forefather. So I try my best level to follow it. I wake up at 3:30 am daily and leave for my nutrition club along with my husband at 4 am.

Before I step down from bed I pray to the mother earth by touching the floor then to the forehead three times, blow through both the nose and step down choosing the unblocked side of the nose and goes out and pray to Sun God to shower blessings for my day's work. I also pray to Lainingthou Sanamahi and Leimarel Sidabi before going out for work and before going to bed.

While comparing working and non-working women, working women have little idea about the prescribed behavior of the Goddess Emoinu than non-working women. Although working women have idea about it they cannot follow it due to work.

Case 7: Bidyarani

Goddess Emoinu like religious, soft and tender women who is soft in speaking and in handling things and who cares for her husband. But I cannot follow all of it, in order to finish my household work in limited time I sometimes shout to my husband and throws tantrums which is dislike by the Goddess Emoinu.

Ways of worshipping the Goddess

Goddess Emoinu is worshipped every year as the Goddess of wealth and prosperity by the Meitei on the 12th day of the Meitei month of Wakching (December-January). It is believed to be a very auspicious day to worship the goddess of wealth to bring peace, prosperity and well being of the whole family. On this day every household offers fish (mostly white colored), fresh seasonal vegetable and flowers to the goddess. Lights are lit up around the homestead at dusk and offerings are made to the goddess. Now a days the traditional worshipping of goddess on 12th day of Wakching month is no longer confined to the household only rather it has become an activity of the whole locality associated with rituals and celebration which includes Pena performances (a traditional musical instrument), reciting the tales of the Goddess, chanting of hymns invoking the Goddess, folk dances and various cultural programmes. Local clubs take the initiative to mark the celebration by lighting candles at night in and around the locality. People prayed for the sustenance and peaceful co-existence of the community on the occasion. The bringing up of the celebration on the locality level was to preserve the importance of the Goddess.

The beliefs and ways of worshipping goddess have evolved over time. Modernity and increase in population are the two main factors. The Meiteis no longer live in kutcha houses with earthen floor. In the household of both groups, there is absence of Phungga and the concept of keeping Phungga is neglected in building a new house. Thus the place of the goddess is no longer restricted in Phungga Lairu but is depicted by the images of the Goddess and a tripod stand near it. Some household equated the place of Goddess Emoinu in rice storing vessels called Chengphu and offer prayer to it. Daily offering of small quantity of two cooked meals before having by the family members is still practiced. But keeping small quantity of food in respective cooking vessels after food is less practiced. However, it is done only when any member of the family is out or aboard for work for few days. Though there is a vast change in the traditional worship of the goddess, its significance and value is still maintained.

Conclusion

Modernization has brought various changes in traditional way of living of the Meitei society. It opens the entrance of women in education and in economic activities. Both working and non-working women helps in the economy of the family. Men are kept much higher in status than women; despite it women ideas are considered and have an important role in decision making. Modern Meitei women are less aware of the prescribe behavior of the Goddess Emoinu. Codes of conduct of the Goddess towards an ideal woman have led to the dilution under the influence of modernity. In this world where people are lost in a sea of opportunities and competition, deviation from the expected behaviour is on the rise. Crimes become normal features in the society. Law alone cannot eradicate such evils from the society. Deviation from the normative can be checked only when the society re-emphasizes the codes of conduct of Goddess Emoinu directed towards women as they are treated as carriers of culture. Further, popularization of the codes of conduct can be done by inculcating in socialization, through media and performing arts.

References

1. Ashokumar, Laiphrakpam.2000. Old Manipuri Literature(Medieval Period) 18th and 19th Century. Imphal: Iboyaima Printers.
2. Ashokumar, Laiphrakpam. 2016. Manipuri Literature before 18th Century. Imphal: G M Publications.
3. Buddhachandra, Yumnamcha.ND. Emoinu Imagi Tungnafam. Imphal. Publishers name not given.
4. Ceaser, Thounaojam. Chaningkhombee, Soyam. Sanasam, Reena.2012. Study of Myths in Literature and Socio-Religious Rituals. In A Journal of Humanities and Social Sciences. Vol- I(II).pp(271-283).

5. Chakravatti, Rama.1986. People of Manipur. New Delhi: B R Publishing Corporation
6. Devi, N Promodini.2011. The Cultural History of Early Manipur. Manipur: Times Publishing House
7. Goshwami, Hareshwar.2004. History of People of Manipur. Imphal : Kangla Publications
8. Hodson, T.C. 1908.The Meitheis. New Delhi: Akansha Publishing House
9. Lang, Andrew.2008. Custom and Myth. New Delhi: Cosmo Publications
10. Lowie, R H.2008. Primitive Religion. New Delhi: Cosmo Publications
11. Parratt, John. Ed. 1998. Notes on Meithei Beliefs and Customs. Manipur: Iboyaima Printers
12. Rabia-Queder, Sarab Abu.2006. Between traditional and modernization: understanding the problem of female Bedouin dropouts. In British Journal of Sociology of Education. Vol-27(I).pp(3-17)
13. Singh, Khomdon.2011. Encyclopaedia of Manipur. New Delhi: Kalpaz Publications
14. Sudhir, H. ed.2012. Social history of Manipur. New Delhi: Sunmarg Publishers and Distributers
15. Singh, Rajketan Chirom. Ed. 2016. Oral Narratives of Manipur. Manipur : Cultural Research Centre Manipur
16. Anonymous. ND. Leithak Leikharol. Chanam Hemchandra. Trans. Imphal: Bird Printers

27

Gender Inequalities as Key Driver of the HIV/AIDS Epidemic among the Tribes of Jaintia Hills, Meghalaya

Monsumi Barooah

Introduction

Today it has been estimated that 40 million people worldwide are carrying the deadly virus known as HIV. Despite the fact that the virus can affect men and women alike, an increasing proportion of people living with HIV are women and girls, and this proportion is continuing to grow. This writing is dedicated to explore the factors that drive the epidemic. The purpose of this paper is to explore the links between gender inequality and HIV/AIDS. The point of departure is theories of gender inequality, where the patriarchal structures and men's domination over women are explained. The result of this study is that gender inequality, the subordination of women and men's predatory behaviour are major contributors of the epidemic, the larger numbers of women with HIV/AIDS and the women's younger age. The HIV pandemic disproportionately impacts young women. Worldwide, young women aged 15–24 are infected with HIV at rates twice that of young men, and young women alone account for nearly a quarter of all new HIV infections. The incommensurate HIV incidence in young – often poor – women underscores how social and economic inequalities shape the HIV epidemic. Confluent social forces, including political and gender violence, poverty, racism, and sexism impede equal access to therapies and effective care, but most of all constrain the agency of women.

AIDS is the acronym for acquired immune deficiency syndrome. It is not a disease but rather a stage of HIV infection where the body's immune system is severely compromised, allowing for a variety of opportunistic infections to take hold (infections are considered 'opportunistic' if they cause disease when immunity is impaired). Globally there are more than 35.3 million people living with HIV today, 69 percent of which are in Sub-Saharan Africa and in the U.S. approximately 1.2 million people are infected. In India, AIDS has caused 36 million deaths in a year. HIV has reached epidemic proportion in many states of our country. Approximately, 2.40 million people are affected with HIV and out of which 39 percent (930, 000) are women (Kamath et al, 2003). In all races and ethnicities, the largest number of HIV/AIDS diagnosis during recent years was for women aged 15-50 years. The HIV epidemic impact upon women has been exacerbated by certain roles within society. The responsibility of caring for people living with HIV is an issue that has a greater effect on women. Additionally, millions of women have been indirectly affected by the HIV/AIDS epidemic through issues such as mother-to-child transmission (MTCT) of HIV. Some of the factors that influence the transmission of HIV to women are polygamy, and pregnancies, multiple sex partners, harmful culture and traditional practices, violence against women, stigma and taboos, religion, poverty, education, lack of access to productive resources. The movement of migrant workers from urban centres to rural areas might explain the increase in infection in some regions. The detection of HIV infections among pregnant women with migrant spouses points to the possible role of migration i fuelling the HIV epidemic (NACO, 2013).

"This epidemic unfortunately remains an epidemic of women" (UNAIDS, 2013)

In some societies, women have few rights within sexual relationships and the family. Often men make the majority of decisions, such as whom they will marry and whether they will have more than one sexual partner. This power imbalance means that it can be more difficult for women to protect themselves from HIV transmission. For example, a woman may not be able to insist on the use of a condom if her husband is the one who makes the decisions.

Marriage does not always protect a woman from becoming infected with HIV. Many new infections occur within marriage or long term relationships as a result of unfaithful partners. In a number of societies, a man having more than one sexual partner is seen as the norm.

Women typically have more frequent access to healthcare than men due to antenatal care. This means women often know that they are HIV positive before their partners. However, the imbalanced power in the household, and lack of education, can lead to men assuming their partner was infected first: this may cause friction that may lead to violence (Global Network of People living with HIV, 2010). The vital role of the present study is to highlight the effects of HIV/AIDS in the society/ the impediments faced by women in the HIV/AIDS epidemic due to gender inequalities.

Methodology

Type of Study

Gender inequalities as key driver of the HIV/AIDS epidemic among the tribes of Jaintia Hills, Meghalaya is a qualitative study. This type of research method involves describing in details specific situation using research tools like interviews, surveys and observations.

Study Area

The study was conducted at all the blocks of Jaintia Hills, Meghalaya.

Study population and sample size

The study population was women of Jaintia Hills, Meghalaya aged 15-35 years. The sample size of the study was 320 women (The sample size of 308 was calculated using online sample size calculator http://www. surveysystem. com/sscalc.htm, giving prevalence estimates with 95 percent confidence level and within 5 percent confidence interval for a total number of people living with HIV (PLHIV) in Meghalaya, which is 1,541(MACs, 2014).

Study Variables

Independent variables: Socio-demographic and economic characteristics (age, marital status, educational status, occupation and partner involvement and average monthly income), socio-cultural characteristics (marriage, religion, stigma and taboos, violence against women, inequality in relationships) are the independent variables of the study.

Dependent variables: Women's vulnerability to HIV, women's awareness on MTCT of HIV, the attitude of people towards women living with HIV/AIDS and their understanding of HIV/AIDS prevention are the dependent variables of the study.

Methods of data collection

Structured Interview schedules were prepared focusing on socio cultural factors like marriage, harmful culture and traditional practices, violence against women, stigma and taboos, religion, poverty, lack of education and access to productive resources, which facilitate HIV infection in women. Participant observation along with interview method was employed to interact with the women under study to develop a mutual trust with them, to understand the socio economic stresses, abuse and gender issues related to HIV infection. This was supplemented with living in the community, participating in its activities and constantly observing what the women actually do in specific situations.

Different State Health policies and programmes, availability of health related infrastructure in the district specific to women was taken into account and its implementation was looked thereafter.

Findings and Discussion

The society under study is matriarchal but there exists gender issues. One of the main causes of HIV infection among the women in Jaintia Hills is that most of the men do not work for a living which results in monetary problems leading to activities which are prone to HIV infection. There are many health care services for the women affected with HIV. But most of the women are unaware of the schemes as the men of the family do not want them to use these services.

Promoting and protecting women's human rights in the HIV/AIDS epidemic

In the study population there exist major inequalities between women and men in all aspects of living- from employment opportunities and availability of education, to power inequalities within relationships. These gender roles can confine women to positions where they lack the power to protect themselves from HIV infection. It is thought that promoting women's basic human rights will enhance their status within society and help protect them against the risk of HIV infection.

Transforming gender roles

Both men and women are affected by gender roles that define what it means to be a man or a woman. These gender based expectations can increase vulnerability to HIV infection. For example, in the present study women are expected to be innocent and submissive when it comes to sex, preventing them from accessing sexual health information and services. For many men, masculinity is linked with taking risks and being tough, which can increase vulnerability to HIV infection and discourage men from seeking HIV testing and treatment.

Recognising and challenging harmful gender roles is crucial to preventing the spread of HIV. Programmes that focus on men are equally important in protecting women from HIV, as they can transform men's attitudes and behaviours towards their partners, families and women in general.

How is The HIV/AIDS Epidemic Affecting Women?

Responsibility of Care

When a person develops AIDS related illness, the care is usually a woman's responsibility. This care giving is usually in addition to many other tasks that women perform within the household, such as cooking, cleaning, and caring for the children and the elderly.

Caring for ill parents, children or husband is unpaid and can increase a person's workload by up to a third. Women often struggle to bring in an income whilst providing care and therefore many families affected by HIV suffer from increasing poverty. In the present study population, where most of the families' livelihood relies in growing and maintain crops, the deaths of farmers lead to poverty.

The HIV epidemic also affects young girls and elderly women. Often in households, where both parents are ill from AIDS, the responsibility of main carer is taken on by a daughter, even if it means that she has to miss school. If both parents die then it tends to be the grandmothers, aunts or cousins who then look after the orphans.

Women and Children

Mother-to-child transmission (MTCT) is an issue that directly affects women and at same time increases the speed of HIV. MTCT occurs when HIV is passed from a HIV positive woman to her baby during pregnancy, labour and delivery, or breastfeeding.

Violence against Women

Women who are victims of sexual violence are at higher risk of being exposed to HIV; due to lack of condom use. A study concluded that women who were beaten or dominated by their partners were much more likely to become infected with HIV than women who were not. HIV transmission was much greater in abusive relationships, but also that abusive husbands were more likely to be infected with HIV than non-abusive husbands.

Conclusion

Gender based issues are the prominent reason for HIV infection in the study population. AIDS feeds on systems of injustice that existed long before HIV had considerable impact on human society. Ending the epidemic both exposes these systems and presents an historic opportunity for real change. It will involve a revolution in long-held cultural beliefs and intensely held personal norms for both men and women. Men will need to work hard to face their vital part in the pandemic. They will need to learn about and dismantle the parts of their gender conditioning that have resulted in the development of inappropriate power over women. Both sexes should recognize that men's efforts will bear most fruit in a climate of encouragement and understanding. Women need to be encouraged to continue to empower and protect themselves, as well as to speak and live their truths as autonomous sexual beings. They deserve help and support in standing up to male domination where that is the case. At the same time it must be remembered that women are powerful and not helpless victims of male oppression. They are proactive participants and full partners in the fight to halt the HIV/AIDS epidemic.

References

Bunnell, Rebecca, Ekwaru, John Paul, Solberg, Peter, Wamai, Nafuna, Bikaako-Kajura, Winnie, Were, Willy, Coutinho, Alex, Liechty, Cheryl, Madraa, Elizabeth, Rutherford, George, Mermin, Jonathan (2006). Changes in sexual behavior and risk of HIV transmission after antiretroviral therapy and prevention interventions in rural Uganda. AIDS: Official journal of the international AIDS soceity; 20(1):1-142.

Coovadia H (2004). Antiretroviral agents— How best to protect infants from HIV and save their mothers from AIDS. N. Engl. J. Med; 351 (3): 289–292.

Crepaz, Nicole, Lyles, Cynthia M, Wolitski, Richard J, Passin, Warren F, Rama, Sima M, Herbst, Jeffrey H, Purcell, David W, Malow, Robert M, Stall, Ron (2006). Do prevention interventions reduce HIV risk behaviours among people living with HIV? A meta-analytic review of controlled trials. Journal of the International AIDS Society; 20(2):143-315.

Dasgupta S, Patrick S, Sullivan, Dasgupta A, Saha B, and Laura F, Salazar (2013). Care Association of Providers of AIDS. Journal of the International Association of Providers of AIDS Care; 26.

http://en.wikipedia.org/wiki/HIV/AIDS#cite_note-pmid11396444-1

Harden, Victoria Angela (2012). AIDS at 30: A History. Potomac Books Inc. p. 324. ISBN 1-59797-294-0.

Holmes CB, Losina E, Walensky RP, Yazdanpanah Y, Freedberg KA (2003). Review of human immunodeficiency virus type 1-related opportunistic infections in sub-Saharan Africa; 36 (5): 656–662.

Lucy Platt, Emma Jolley, Tim Rhodes, Vivian Hope, Alisher Latypov, Lucy Reynolds, David Wilson (2013). Factors mediating HIV risk among female sex workers in Europe: a systematic review and ecological analysis. BMJ; doi:10.1136/bmjopen-2013-002836.

Ramjee G and Daniels B (2013). Women and HIV in Sub-Saharan Africa. Articles for AIDS Research and Therapy; 10.

Raman R. Gangakhedkar, Margaret E. Bentley, Anand D. Divekar, Deepak Gadkari, Sanjay M. Mehendale, Mary E. Shepherd, Robert C. Bollinger, Thomas C. Quinn. Spread of HIV Infection in Married Monogamous Women in India. JAMA; 278(23):2090-92.

White RG, Boily MC (2008). Systematic review of orogenital HIV-1 transmission probabilities. International Journal of Epidemiology; 37(6): 1255–65.

Zwelunmor J, Ezeanolue EE, Airhihenbuwa CO, Obiefune MC, Ezeanolue CO and Ogedegbe GG (2014). Socio-cultural factors influencing the prevention of mother-to-child transmission of HIV in Nigeria:a synthesis of the literature. BioMed Central; doi:10.1186/1471-2458-14-771.

28

Gender Socialization of Children among the Tangkhuls of Manipur

Rv. Khanchuila

The attitude that comes out in the practices of the people is linked with the concept of gender. It is culturally and historically specific. Gender, the product of social relations, is the outcome of how society constructs the categories 'women' and 'men'. Gender as analytical category resulted through time as biological differences fall short to define the social significance of those differences. This made Mead (1935) question the fixed relationship between biological sex and gendered character in the nascent stage of formulating theories of gender. The famous statement of Beauvoir (1949), "One is not born a woman but becomes one" thus made significant landmark in the development of gender studies.

The social definition and subsequent self identification of a child as a boy or a girl is significant for both the development of gender identity and learning of the way in which one's role performances is tailored to one's gender. In the words of Wharton (2005), "Gender socialization is the processes through which individuals take on gendered qualities and characteristics and acquire a sense of self" (2005:31).

Socialization takes place within the paradigm of the cultural set up. Children learn to fit into their own appropriate gender spaces sanctioned by the society. The data of the paper is based on the study among the Tangkhul tribe of Manipur. The structure of gender among the Tangkhul society is based on the patriarchy. The father is known as the *akhava* (head of the family). He is the authoritarian head and decision maker of the family. He represents the family in the *meiphung* (lineage group), the *shang* (clan) and at the village level (Ruivah 1993). Women, on the other hand, cannot take independent decision without the knowledge of *akhava*.

Patriliny is another core values rooting the gender structure of the Tangkhul society. The descent is traced through men. They carry on with the name of the family and inherit the ancestral immovable property (Ruivah 1993). In the line of succession, they follow the rule of primogeniture. The eldest son thus inherits the lion's share of the property. Women are not permanent member of their father's family. Their identity is subsumed with that of their men; as a daughter of her father and the wife of her husband. The main objectives of the present study is to examine gender socialization at different stages of childhood and to evaluate how gender values of the society is reproduced through socialization process.

Methods of Data Collection

Primary data for this paper were collected from the field (Somdal village) with the help of interview schedules and observation method. Secondary data related to the work were collected from various sources. The field is located in the western region of Ukhrul district and it is one of the biggest villages among the Tangkhuls.

Gender Socialization at Different Stages of Childhood

This paper focuses on three different stages of childhood; pregnancy and birth, 0-5 years and 6-12 years. It examines gender socialization against the patriarchal background of the society and elicits a fresh look on the symbolic representation of how femininity and masculinity is reproduced through gender socialization. It unfolds the entire gamut of an individual identity as a woman and man.

Pregnancy and birth: The concept of taking care of the child starts right from pregnancy. Restrictions and prohibitions are imposed on a pregnant woman to protect the fetus inside her womb.

Food prohibitions

(a) A pregnant woman is forbidden to eat crab and prawn, as they belief that the baby will dribble all the time.

(b) She is not allowed to eat bitter food items and papaya as they belief that these food items are harmful for the fetus.

Restrictions of movement and action

(a) A pregnant woman is not allowed to move out of the house after dark for fear of harm by the malevolent spirit to the baby.

(b) She is not allowed to attend funeral service for fear of affliction by the spirit of the dead.

(c) She should keep away from haunted places known as *ngalei kharar pam.*

(d) She is forbidden to kill snakes as they belief that the baby will have the habit of stretching out their tongue.

These restrictions imposed on the mother do not have any demeanor on the father. The strong adherence to these beliefs keeps a pregnant woman to endorse the societal norm and ensure safety for the baby.

The Tangkhuls believe in dreams to predict the sex of the unborn child. Wares, things and objects, associated with each gender, seen in dreams are believed to be revelation of the child's sex. Weaving materials, kitchenware, ladies attire, etc are related with a female child while axe, spear, men's attire, etc. are believed to be indicative of a male child.

Birth

As soon as a child is born, a therapeutic treatment known as '*nao khangalui' (*hot water therapy) to the infant is given by the midwife or the grandmother to ensure good health for the baby which indeed is continued for months. Relatives, friends and neighbours pay visit with gifts in the form of chicken and clothes. It is believed that the mother gets relieve from her delivery pain on the sixth day in case of a boy and on the fifth day in case of a girl child.

After a week, a ritual known as '*naoyan',* which literally means 'seeing the baby' for the first time is performed. This ritual is symbolical of exposing the baby to outsiders. It is customary for parents to keep away the newborn from outsiders prior to this ritual for fear malevolent spirits and from fear of harm from *mirai kakaza* (belief in the sadistic possession of a person by another person). A fat rooster usually gifted by the maternal uncle or grandfather for the ritual is cooked and distributed to neighbours and relatives known as '*naoyansa'*. Killing of the rooster symbolizes their wish to let the infant grow up to be a dutiful person to awaken the people as the rooster does.

The ritual marks the arrival of a new member. However, this ritual is mostly celebrated with intensity in case of the first born son. In case of a girl child, the ritual may even be given amiss. Even if the ritual is performed for a girl child, a strict rule of gift in the form of rooster from the maternal uncle is not maintained which is characteristic of the interference of their patrilineal system.

0-5 years

This is the stage where children spend most of their time within the home environment. The mother and the grandmother are the most important persons for the infant.

A baby is given a name few weeks after birth as they have a belief that evil spirits harm the unnamed baby. This occasion is known as '*naoming kaphok*' (name giving ceremony). In the past a feast is given for the occasion. Today, the baby is christened in the church ceremony where the pastor/priest prays for the child. The name giving ceremony for the eldest son is usually celebrated with a feast. The baby is named signifying certain things to the family or the society. In giving names to children, the prefixes '*la*', '*phy*', *or* '*won*' is added at the end of a girls' name but no such prefixes are added to the name of boys.

Before a child could accurately label themselves as a girl or a boy, they receive a range of verbal clues. Elders handle a baby boy saying, 'boys do not cry' (*mayarnao kachap mangacha mana*) and soothe the girl infant by saying 'who makes my girl cry' (*Ishi nao ngalavali khipanada*). The underlying connotation is that boys are nurtured to be strong while girls are cared for and protected. The verbal clues recounts the values associated with femininity and masculinity.

Toys, dresses and other materials which a child possesses tend to emphasize male and female attributes. Boys play with *kari* (toy cars) and *sayur* (animal figurines usually made out of clay). Girls, on the other hand, play with *thang thang* (kitchenware toys) and *ngangangnao* (dolls). The response to such gender stereotyping comes from parents and elders where toys are categorically purchased for a boy and a girl child.

Internalization of gender values by the child, at this stage, can also be observed in the role imitation. Boys take the role of a carpenter, miller, or a driver while girls take the role of their mother or aunt as nurturer and homemaker. The role they imitate reflects the role of their adults and the gendered division of labour of the society.

At this stage, the child is taught to pronounce kinship terms. Kinship terms to female members like *ava* (mother), *achon* (elder sister), *azarva* (boys to a younger sister), *akatuiva* (girl to a younger sister), *ani* (aunt), *avakatui* (mother's younger sister), *avakharar* (mother's elder sister), *ayi* (grandmother), etc are taught to them. Likewise, kinship terms to male members like *ava* (father), *awo* (grandfather), *amei* (elder brother), *akato* (boy to a younger brother), *apa* (girl to a younger brother), *awo* (uncle), *avakato* (father's younger brother), *avakharar* (father's elder brother), etc are taught to them.

6-12 years

Gender once assigned, the society expects individual to act as men and women. It is in the practices of everyday life that these expectations are fulfilled and reproduced. The role imitation in the early years now becomes role learning. A boy of six years starts to run errands and learn to assists older men of the family in their works. Girls of this age group are expected to learn household chores, and attend to the younger siblings. Simultaneously with role learning, they learn responsibility appropriate to their own gender. In the process of imparting roles and responsibilities, the older members of the family take the growing child of one's own gender under their supervision.

The children at this stage venture beyond their courtyard and begin to internalize values beyond the home environment. Gender segregation is observed among children of this age group. This is apparent in the games they play. Girls play games like *Saotheila* (Throwing Knuckle Bones using a seed called *saothei*), *Kotla* (Five Stones with small pebbles), etc. Boys, on the other hand, play more daring games like *mahar kapai* (high jump with sticks of a plant locally known as *maharthing*) or ride *thing kari* (a tri-cycle or bi-cycle made out of wood). Girls play games which are more of indoor type whereas boys have fun with outdoor games.

Children at this stage conceptualize and understand the meanings of kinship and their terms, the utterance of which was insensible at the younger stage. Elders verbally elucidate on why they should refer to people by different terminologies. This way, children learn to locate their place in their kinship network and this is how they internalize the customary practices of patriliny where men uphold the tradition of the family. In the same way, women learn to accept the societal norm of shifting their identity after marriage.

Conclusion

It is evident from the data that abstract gender values are reproduced and expressed through concrete utterance and practices. Gender streamlining among the Tangkhuls starts right from the time the child is conceived. The prediction of sex, names given to the child as a girl or a boy, dresses, the toys, or games each gender plays, are indicative of such gender differentiation.

The values of femininity depict patience, caring attitude, understanding nature, and a homemaker which is manifested in the way they assign duties, the nature of their games, etc. The values of masculinity portray men with a daring character, protector, etc. It is apparent in the games boys play, in the way they console the small baby boy and in manners of mending their character.

The values of patriliny and patriarchy interfere in all the process of socialization. The *naoyan (*baby exposure ceremony), the *naming kaphok* (name giving ceremony), kinship teachings, etc., are all indicative of reinforcing their patiliny. The value of patriarchy is also clear in the way elders soothe the girl child protectively which indicates men as the protector of their women.

Literature cited

Beauvoir, Simone de. 1972 (1949). *The Second Sex*. Harmondsworth: Penguin Books Ltd.

Mead . M, 1935. *Sex and Temperament in Three Primitive Societies*. New York: Morrow.

Ruivah, Khashim. 1993. Social Change Among the Nagas (Tangkhul). Cosmo Publication.

Wharton, Amy S. 2005. *The Sociology of Gender: An introduction to Theory and Research*. Oxford: Blackwell Publishing Ltd.

29

Influence of Modernity and Christianity on the Status of Tangkhul Women

Shangpam Kashung

Introduction

'Modernization' according to M. N. Srinivas (Upadhyay and Pandey, 2002: 438) is a popular term for the changes brought about in a non-western country by contact, direct or indirect with a western country. In the light of this meaning on modernization, the present paper will be based on studying the changes taking place concerning the status of Tangkhul women. Modernization in Tangkhul society began when they first came into contact with the western Christian missionaries (few years after the imposition of British administration). In other parts of North East India modern period begins with the imposition of British administration. For the Tangkhuls, Christianity played the most important role in the process of modernization. Thus it is more appropriate to bring modernity and Christianity together (than to take either modernity or Christianity alone) in understanding the changing status of women. The last quarter of the 20th century marked the period between pre and modernity/Christianity. Tangkhul culture was indigenous in its characters before the introduction of Christianity along with modernity. Ultimately, their culture change and thus change the status of women. The present paper attempts to understand how much the status of women has been improved under the influence of modernity and Christianity.

Materials and Methods

The most meaningful way to measure the status of women in a society is through a comparison of their status with that of men in the same society. In order to understand the changes on the status of women, an in depth study was done based on the pre and post modern /Christian era.

The data were collected on the basis of secondary and primary. Secondary data consists of published and unpublished materials in the form of books, reports, journals and periodicals, related to women. Primary data were collected with the help of a comprehensive questionnaire along with interview schedule and by making observations.

Pre-modern/Christian status of women among Tangkhuls

In Pre-modern/Christian Tangkhul society the status of women was low. The Tangkhul family system is patrilineal. They trace their descent through the male lineage exclusively which gives in the patrilineal character. The rule of residence after marriage is based on patrilocal (a woman leaves her parental home and joins the husband's family after marriage) principle. Thus the women after marriage live with the husband's families. The basic family structure of the Tangkhul Nagas remains unchanged.

Attitudes towards women

The preference for male children is apparent in patrilineal society. A male child is perceived as a continuator of the lineage. Besides, another reason is that, in the olden days when war and hunting were the essential aspects of communities survival, physical strength and courage were essential ad therefore preferred a male child over a female child.

Tangkhul view woman as a perilous creature in many ways that can bring ill luck to the entire society. A Tangkhul woman cannot live a life she wants. Her life is bound with a bundle of taboo/restrictions. For instance, a woman is restricted to sit cross-legged. She is not allowed to eat sacrificial meat. She should not yell in the public. She should not climb over roofs, trees etc. She should not go for hunting games. A woman should not visit her parents' house at particular times etc. Her movement is restricted in several ways. In the past, it was considered inauspicious for men setting out on wars to have any contact with women before leaving. Women were considered polluted at particular times. Woman's life is compared with mist because her life is short in a family. A family that has many sons is regarded as a good family and a family without a son is look down by the society. (Kashung, 2012).

Division of Labour

In traditional Tangkhul society all the household chores were done women. Agricultural works were done together by both (male and female). A Tangkhul woman is busy from dawn to dusk. She is the first one to get up in the morning. Before leaving for the fields in the morning, she draws water from the water source (river or streams) for the entire family, husk the grain, cooks and feeds the family, animals and poultry. After a busy day at the fields, she must collect firewood from the jungle; gather all the livestock continue the process of cooking, feeding etc. She is fully responsible for caring child, aged person, and for supplementing inadequate food by growing vegetables, collecting edible roots and tubers from the forests, and by raising poultry, dogs and pigs. It is her responsibility to take care of the food grains and if any person in the family goes hungry, it is treated as her lapse. In addition to households chores and heavy involvement in cultivation, she should provide clothing for her entire family. Besides, it is her duty to groom her daughters to become responsible persons.

Contribution of Christian missionaries on the status of women

Among the Tangkhul it was Christian missionaries who introduced education as they felt it necessary to impart Christianity. One of my informants said, "the Christian missionaries were the pioneers in giving the modern type of education to Tangkhul. They felt the need for education while propagating Christianity. They felt that unless they were educated they might not be in a position to understand Bible and encourage their children to embrace Christianity." Basically, the first converts were all educated and gainfull employed.

The first task taken up by William Pettigrew was to start constructing school building and to learn the language of the people. A lower primary school was accordingly opened at Ukhrul in the month of February 1897 with an enrolment of 20 boys. Thus, modern education had its root in Ukhrul under the guidance of Pettigrew. Moreover they helped them to raise their standard of living by teaching them various other skills. He was, later on, assisted by Major Maxwell (the then British administrator) by all possible means (Singh, 1996). In an account of the work of Rev. And Mrs. William Pettigrew prepared by Mr. Pettigrew, it is written, "There was no written language, almost every villages had its own dialect, and not a soul in the whole tribe knew anything of even the rudiments of education. Any old piece of paper was grabbed and looked upon as a curiosity. The majority of the people had never left their mountain in fastnesses, even to visit another tribe or the people of the valley. They were completely ignorant of the outside world... The Pettigrews' first task was to win the confidence of the people, to convince them that they were not the paid agents of Government, planning to remove their young men to the outside world. Mr. Pettigrew set about learning and reducing to writing the dialect used at Ukhrul."(cited in Solo and Mahangthei, 1986).

In regards to education of girls, he writes, "If the people looked with suspicion upon any attempt to educate their sons, how much more strongly did they oppose the education of girls. Girls were meant for a life of drudgery in the home and in the rice fields. It took Mrs. Pettigrew fourteen years to make any appreciable impression upon that attitude of mind, even when the parents had become Christians. Later Mrs. Pettigrew persuaded nine girls to come in from the villages to Ukhrul. Here they were not only taught to read and write, but living in small dormitory, learned to keep a home sanitary and clean, to sew and knit; they did gardening, worked at cultivation, weeding and harvesting in the rice fields in short all the things that they would have to do when they returned to their own homes." (ibid.)

Until recently, most Tangkhul parents were quite apathetic towards their daughters' education and often withdraw them from schools after completing the primary stage. When there were 57 boys enrolled in school in 1903, there was not a single girl allowed to go to school. (Keishing Byrne, 1996) Mrs. Alice Pettigrew persuaded the parents to allow the girls to read and write in night schools after the girls had done their daily chores. The parents yielded to this arrangement and ultimately Mrs. Pettigrew persuaded some girls to come and stay in dormitory where they were taught not only how to read and write, but also the home sanitary, cleanliness, how to sew and knit and kitchen gardening. The first batch consists of nine girls from different villages. And so by 1910, there were 9 girls enrolled as students who stayed in the dormitory.

Here, I have the privilege to quote Shining Keishing's (Ex-M.L.A) narration, who knew Mr. and Mrs. Pettigrew. She was small and young when she first met them. She was one of the students of the school started by William Pettigrew's students. She wrote, "She was never tired of talking to children. She would explain to us how to wash our face, how to clean our mouth and teeth. In those days, our hair was full of lice. She would tell us to wash our head once in every two days. To keep the children clean was her first lesson to us. Then Mrs. Pettigrew would visit our houses. Our mothers would follow her as she visited from house to house. She would instruct the mothers to wash the utensils and plates before cooking and serving food. She told the mothers to sweep the house every morning.

Mrs. Alice Pettigrew was also a medicine lady- a lady doctor like. She would attend to all types of sickness in the village, treated their cuts and wounds and scabies. She instructed them how to look after the patients and so on. Another remarkable thing about this lady was that her hands were always busy. This was the first time we saw what knitting was. Even if she was talking to someone, her hands were busy knitting wools. During such a short stay at Bungpa, she demonstrated how to use knitting stick to the womenfolk." (ibid.)

The contribution of Christianity is therefore massive to women's development in particular and community's development in general in the field of education, health care, economy and literature prior to the present day governmental (state and central) efforts.

Perception of change and the influence of Christianity and modernity

Women's position in Religion

The adoption of Christianity and spread of modern education are believed to have created greater awareness among the Tangkhuls regarding women's inferior traditional status. Traditionally, women played no role in religious activities except in chumpha phanit[1] . The priests are always men and sacrifices can be performed only by men. Women started participating in religious activities after their conversion. When we go to Church we can see women taking choir seat, reading Bible, preaching from the pulpit, conducting service, song presentation and so on. Some mothers take the lead in family prayer, women service etc. This way, everybody gets a chance to participate and get exposed to social activities. Camps, seminars, revival crusades, conference, etc. are organized every year to expand their horizon. Such a practice sharpens one's personality. It widens a person's worldview, changes her/his way of thinking and is more exposed through different programmes and activities of the church. The church trains a person to become a leader through its programme of leadership training. The church services and the weekly family worship service give various spiritual lessons from the Bible. But not all the Christians are sincere and committed. There are many who have converted just in the name only. There are many young girls and adult who live lives that are against the norms and doctrines of Christianity.

Women's position in Education

With the coming of Christianity and the subsequent introduction of formal education the role of the parents is also assumed different kinds of responsibilities. Today the duty and role of the parents towards their children has taken a new direction. The parents have geared their interest and priority towards providing education to their children unlike the traditional parents who emphasized more in training their children on how to become good agriculturists. Increasing number of parents is giving equal opportunity in regards to education to their sons and daughters. Literacy rate of women therefore increased. According to the government of Manipur census 2011, the literacy rate of male and female in Ukhrul district is 85.52 percent and 76.95 percent respectively.[2] The status of women raised with the adoption of modern education.

Women's position in Economy

Furthermore adopting Christianity kept them away from ritualistic demands of *Hau* involving "unprofitable" expenditure of time, labour and money. Today, wealth is invested for other things like children's education.

The introduction of education by Christian missionaries also paved away the economic burden to a large extent. Traditionally, their economy was purely based on agriculture. Now they take up salary jobs (employed in professional and higher administrative positions). Some mothers also supplement family through their earnings as daily wages, weavers, business, clerks in offices or schools and teachers etc.,

One of my aged lady informants who is well educated said, "If we look at the traditional days, when the Tangkhul were not educated, they were mostly confined to agricultural works and household chores. Because of modern education and changes that are taking place in the society, many of us have gradually stopped doing work in agricultural fields and have engaged in government and private jobs."

Women's position in Decision making

The Tangkhul family, being patriarchal, the father assumes the headship of the family even today. The father continues to carry the greatest authority. In any decision making the men take almost all the major decisions. However, this scenario has undergone some changes in the modern times due to women gaining confidence and information about various issues with the help of modern education. Qualified women and employed in respected jobs have a greater say in important family decisions, e.g. those related to children's education, marriage and men tend to be more favourable towards sharing household and child care tasks.

Findings and Conclusion

Among the Tangkhuls it is the Christian missionaries who introduced modernity. With the adoption of Christianity and modernity a lot of changes have been taken place among the Tangkhul in general and Tangkhul women in particular. Today, the position of Tangkhul women has risen to such an extent that they become part and parcel in the various aspects of society. They take part in religious activities though not equally with men[3]. It has been found that a large number of Tangkhuls today are aware of the importance of women's education. This has increased the number of educated women. The status of an educated woman is found higher than that of an uneducated one. They made better homes than those with no education. Education prepared women to take a more active role in the leadership of society. To some extent educated women are discussed and consulted in decision making. With the increase of qualified and employed women, the negative attitudes towards women receded and consequently their economy enhanced as they no longer depend only on agriculture for economy. Division of labour is not as distinctive as in the olden days. There is a change in division of labour. For example, the more intellectual parent teach lesson to children. Meantime the spouse whether the husband or wife takes up household chores. Women have more leisure time.

Tangkhul women had no place in the field of traditional administration. Today, the trend has changed and with the introduction of a modern political system, the Tangkhul women along with their male counterparts have equal political rights and freedom guaranteed under the Indian Constitution. Tangkhul women now enjoy adult franchise and participate in the voting process for election of the members of the District Council, Legislative Assembly, Parliament etc.

But the question of gender equality remains, and it will continue to do so until the family structure of the Tangkhul remains unchanged. They remain patrilineal, patriarchal and patrilocal. As a tradition till today, the eldest son gets the lion's share of the ancestral property such as land, terrace fields, forest etc. as he is the head among all the sons. There is no picture of women inheriting immovable properties. There are very few lucky women inheriting the immovable properties but those are outside the Tangkhul domain (such as in Imphal). Despite gender inequality, the influence of Christianity and modernity proved beneficial in many ways.

References

Governtment census of Manipur. 2011.

Kashung, Shangpam. 2012. Continuity and Change on the Gender Relations of the Tangkhuls of Manipur. *Global South (SEPHIS e-megazine)*. Vol. 8, No. 1.

Keishing Byrne, Shining. 1996. Rev. William Pettigrew as I knew him. In Gangmumei Kamei *et al.* (eds.), *Rev. William Pettigrew (a pioneer missionary of Manipur)*. Imphal: Fraternal Green Cross.

Singh, Leiren. 1996. Reverend William Pettigrew and Modern Education in Manipur. In Gangmumei Kamei *et al.* (eds.), *Rev. William Pettigrew (a pioneer missionary of Manipur)*.Imphal: Fraternal Green Cross. Pp. 7-13.

Solo, Jonah M and K. Mahangthei.1986. *Forty Years Mission in Manipur*. Imphal: Christian Literature Centre.

Upadhyay, V.S and Gaya Pandey. 2002. *History of Anthropological thought.* New Delhi: Concept Publishing Company.

Note

1. *Chumphu* phanit: It is the festival to mark the beginning of taking out newly harvested paddy from the granary. On this day women offer prayer to the Supreme Being to have sufficient food throughout the year. It was considered inauspicious for women performing rituals to have any contact, even accidental, with men. Therefore, male members spend their night outside the village gate.
2. It is the Ukhrul district census as there is no tribe wise census available. Tangkhuls are predominantly settled in Ukhrul district and thereby it is considered reliable.
3. So far women are denied their ordination as a priest.

30

Modernisation and Change: Transition of Youth Organisation among the Kukis

Jangkhomang

Introduction

Modernisation is a total transformation of a traditional or pre-modern society into the type of technology and associated social organisation that characterised the advanced economically prosperous and relatively stable....society (Moore, 1965:89). Another aspect of modernisation is described by Lerner (1958), "Modernisation is the current term for an old process- the process of social change whereby less developed societies acquire characteristics common to more developed societies..... Modernisation therefore is the process of social change in which development is the economic component" (cited from Encyclopaedia of Social Sciences: 386-387).

In the words of a major proponent of the modernisation field of study, "Historically, modernization is the process of change towards those types of social, economic, and political systems that have developed in Western Europe and North America from the seventeenth century to the nineteenth and have then spread to other European countries and in the nineteenth and twentieth century's to the South American, Asian, and African continents" (Armer & Katsillis, 2006).

In North East India, Modernisation was the result of the colonial rule and Christianity, which is almost true for all the tribes inhabiting the region. In this respect T.K.OOMMEN said, "While change has been occurring always an appropriate point of departure for North East India is the colonial period and the advent of Christianity. After Independence the Indian state and latterly market and civil society also played significant roles. But all the change are occurring within the framework of Indian polity, globalisation notwithstanding, as i have observed at the very outset" (T.K.Oommen 2009: 7).

Methodology

The present paper is an attempt to understand how the traditional youth organisation of the Kukis, particularly *Lawm* and *Sawm* underwent changes with the arrival of British raj, followed by Christianity and modern education. Here, attempt shall also be made to highlight the importance the of these youth organisation in the traditional Kuki society. In what form do they exist in present day context? As such most of the material to be elicited will be secondary and nature.

Youth Organisations

The tribal world of the Kukis was egalitarian and uncomplicated; far removed from the norms of social stratification or caste rigidities. The village economy was primarily elemental, organized around production and consumption of food grains, domestication of livestock, hunting, fishing and food gathering. Consequently, the level of wisdom and skill set necessary for survival was rudimentary and easier learned in relative freedom and through adaptation with the natural environment.

Youth clubs or youth organizations are modern concepts. Just like any other tribe of the region, the Kukis follows village based youth organisational set up known as *Lawm* and *Sawm (*also spelled *Lom and Som).* Since time immemorial the two institutions had been a very integral part of the society in term of socio-economic development. Of the two, *Lawm* was concerned mostly to the economic welfare of the community. While on the other hand, *Sawm* is concerned with the safeguarding of the village from external dangers such as attacks and invasion from enemies as well as internal dangers such as conspiracy and disputes, fire, theft, gambling and other unwanted incidents which may bring disintegration in the village (KIM 2003: 39)

Lawm

Lawm has been defined in many ways by different scholars. Lawm literally means 'corporate labour' or Labour in rotation (Pudaite Rochunga 1963: 45). According to T.S Gante, "the word *Lawm* means an informal labour organisation in a simple and corporate village life of the Kukis, where in all the able-bodied young boys and girls are member" (Gangte 1993: 132). He further elaborated it as an organisation where young people learn a sense of duty and dignity of labour and learn in the process the basis of leadership. Tarun Goswami, a noted scholar working on the same tribe described *Lawm* as, "the youth corps of the village" (Goswami 1985: 95).

Lawm consisted generally of representatives, both male and female from each household. The *Lawm* member use to work by turn in each other field regardless of the capacity of each individual. According to Haokip, *Lawm* was a traditional form of youth club. It was an institution in which young people were engaged in social activities for the welfare of the individual as well as the community. As a traditional social institution it was a source of traditional learning. It was a source of imparting technical and practical knowledge to its members, especially economic activities as well as sports. It also provide environment for love and affection, respect and obedience, and help for the weak and the poor (Haokip, 1998: 7). *Lawm* as a part of the life of the young people served as one of the most important factors of unity in the village. It also keeps the village economic growth in good health. Thus Lawm was an important tradition around which the village social life revolved.

In every Kuki village Lawm is practice. The number or types of Lawm however varies from region to region depending on the size of the village. T.S. Gangte gave four types of Lawm among the Kukis- *Lawmpi, Lawm-Lai, Lawm-Neo, Lawm- Changpah* (Gangte 1993: 132-133). The Lawm official consists of *Lawm haosa, Lom u-pa, Lawm becha, Lawm tucha, Lawm nungah,* each two in number (Helthang Kilong 2012: 48). *Lawm Lhangva* is another important official of the Lawm organisation.

T. Lhuntong Doungel (1992: 132) listed the purpose of Lawm as follow:

1. To bring about development and welfare of the village,
2. To balance economic inequality,
3. To help the poor and needy,
4. To maintain unity and fraternity in the village,
5. To help and to support the chief and his council of ministers, and
6. To safeguard the village from external and internal danger.

Sawm

Sawm literally means dormitory. It is the name of the other youth organisation which concerns only able- bodied young boys of the village. It is a bachelor's dormitory in which all the young boys of the village sleep together at night. T.S Gangte (1993, 133) puts, "the nature of hostility and practice of tribal raids necessitate the existence of this organisation; so that in times of emergency, the service of all the able-bodied men might be available in short notice". This is an organisation responsible for mobilisation of the services of the young men to meet the exigencies of the society. In this Roy (1918: 218) describe the bachelor's organisation as:

> ......archaic from of economic, social and religious organisation. It must have been its times and effective economic organisation for purpose, a useful seminary for training young men in their social and other duties, and an institution for magico-religious observances calculated to secure success in hunting and to augment the preventive power of the young men so as to increase the number of hunters in the tribe.

Besides, its main aim purpose of defending the village from external and internal dangers, Sawm, in times of peace renders every possible service to the village community whenever required. It is also an organisation for recreation of the young boys . The younger boys also learn social customs and manner besides obedience to elder. The young people receive non-formal traditional education like (1) Handicrafts (2) Technique of war (iii) Traditions (iv) Stories (v) songs (vi) Dance (vii) Discipline (viii) Social etiquette etc (Nemminthang Lhouvum, 2014, p.1590). Thus, it was a centre wherein young people were shaped into responsible adult member of society (Varghese and Thanzawna 1997: 18)

The dormitory system of the Kukis was peculiar. Unlike most of its neighbouring tribes, the Kukis do not a separate dormitory house. As a custom young boys having attained a certain age were not allowed to sleep in their parent house. So, the young and unmarried boys of the village form several groups. Each group selects a potential and capable person to be the leader of the *Sawm*. The selected leader is called *Sawm-upa* (Lhouvum 2014: 1590). The *Sawm upa* serves as a guide and teachers to its Sawm members (Haokip 2013 :183).This system of sleeping together in the house of another person is known as Sawmgie (Goswami, 1985: 98).

From the above discussion, it can be said that the traditional youth organisation of the Kukis forms the basis of not only the socio-cultural life but also the economic and political life of the people. The whole set of the village life centre around the proper working of the two institutions. Many scholars defined *Lawm* and *Sawm* as two separate institutions. But in my opinion, they are inseparable. In the words of Goswami (1985: 97), he said, Sawmgie also comes under the organisational framework of the Lawm. Both the two were institution of traditional learning, though, differences may be observed. Traditional values and customs are spread by both the institution.

Christianity among The Kukis

Christianity came to North East India in the beginning of the 19th Century. Different area witnessed the growth of Christianity in different period of arrival. Between 1836- 1840, the American Baptist Mission Society as well as the Welsh Calvinistic Methodist Foreign Ministry, suggested by Rev. Jacob Tomlin, a Former missionary of London Missionary Society already made attempt to enter the soil of Manipur. But, the unsettled political situation of the state prevented it from entering. However, when Manipur was occupied consequent upon the Anglo-Manipur War of 1891, William Pettigrew went to Imphal, the capital city of Manipur, in 6 February, 1894 (Lal Dena 1991: 105).

Christianity was brought to the Kuki people of Manipur by two separate missions, the Baptist in the North and the Independent Non- Denominational Mission in the south. William Pettigrew, the first American Baptist Missionary came under the auspices of a private society called the Arthington Aboriginese

Mission Society, named after Robert Arithington, a millionaire at Leeds near London. While waiting for the opportunity to go to Manipur for three years (1891- 1894), he had ample time to learn Bengali and Manipuri. When Manipur was occupied consequent upon the Anglo- Manipur war of 1891, William Pettigrew went to Imphal, in 6 February 1894. He began his work by opening a school for which he was granted permission by A. Porteous, the Acting Political agent during the absence of Maxwell. But due to the resentment of the Hinduised Meitei's, he was not able to continue his work any longer. But Major Maxwell, the political agent who was friendly with Pettigrew, came to the rescue by suggesting that it would be possible for the missionary to remain in the state if he would go to the hill areas that were under the direct British administration, but at "his own risk"

But just as he was about to start the work in Ukhrul, Pettigrew was asked to leave the place for another field or to go home. Having no other alternative, he thus applied for membership to the American Baptist Missionary Union in Assam. Accordingly he was formally redesignated as a Baptist missionary to Manipur. Thus, the Arthington Mission transferred the Manipur field to the American Baptists in February 1896, and Pettigrew took up work at Ukhrul under the auspices of the American Baptist Missionary Union.

In fact, on 10 February 1897, the first school in the hill was opened at Ukhrul with 24 boys, whose age ranges from 7-14 years. But, till 1912, no Kuki or Anal boys entered the Ukhrul Mission School (Lal Dena 1991: 112). In 1910 it was reported that two Kukis were seeking admission to the Ukhrul Church but their names are not given. In 1912, nine students were baptised, the first Christians among the Kukis of Manipur (Downs 1969: 168). The names of 5 of them are, Lungkhobel Kom, Teba Kilong, Sheijalhut, Helhup and Jamkithang (Lal Dena 1985: 113 and Down 1969: 186).

The first convert among the Kuki Baptists was Nehseh Chongloi, a Thadou from Makui who had accepted Christ in the hand of Angami Christians while in Nagaland followed by Ngulhao Thomsong who was also from Nagaland. Both came to Manipur in 1910 to assist the mission work at Ukhrul centre. The mission began to expand to the Kuki areas and Tujangwaichong became the first Christian village among the Kuki Baptists in 1914 largely through the work of Ngulhao Thomsong (haokip, 2008). According to Downs (1969: 167) he was said to have converted 85 persons in this village including the chief and 70 others from the neighbouring villages. The first baptisms were conducted by U.M. Fox (an American Baptist missionary who had served for several years in Manipur during the absence of Pettigrew who was on leave) in December 1914 while on his way from Imphal to Kohima for furlough. Altogether 26 were baptized on that event.

Rev. U.M. Fox also pronounced the establishment of the Church among the Kuki Baptists on 12th Dec.1914 and also laid his hand (consecrated) on

Lhingkhosei and Letlam as pastor and deacon respectively at the wishes of the members. Those who came late on that day but wished to be baptized by the missionary at Karong River went after him and took baptism at Maram the next day (Haokip 2008). The Church was formally organized by Pettigrew in 1916 to become the third baptist church in Manipur after Ukhrul and Keishamthong village churches near Imphal and the first baptist church among the Kukis followed by Tongkoi and Chaljang in 1919, Karakhun, Songphel Khulen, Gelnel, Kachai Kuki all in 1920 and Lhongchin in 1922.

The whole of Manipur was claimed to be the exclusive mission field of the American Baptist Mission. Though, it technically belong to the American Baptish Mission, yet, it could not cover the south districts practically. This vaccum so created was filled in by another mission called the Indo-Burma Thadou-Kuki Pioneer Mission (IBTKPM), an independent non-denominational mission started by Watkin R. Roberts.

Watkin R. Roberts was born in 1886 at Caernarvon. He was converted by R. A. Torrey's sermons but continued to work as a quarry man. The 1904 revival made a still deeper impression on him and he decided to serve overseas. He was a close friend of Dr. Peter Fraser who was his senior by some years. Roberts apparently came to Mizoram at Fraser's expense and with the intention of helping him in his work. He was a Presbyterian and organized the Churches he later established on Presbyterian principles but without any denominational attachment. Travelling en route to Calcutta, Roberts went on with Fraser to the British out-post in Aizawl in the Lushai Hills where Dr. Peter Fraser opened a medical clinic and appointed Roberts as his assistant. Roberts then learnt the Lushai language and began visiting programmes of evangelism apart from the clinic works.

In the south, while assisting Dr. Fraser in this way and engaging in evangelistic works, some young men having slightly different outlook came to the clinic. These young men could not speak Lushai properly. They were Hmars from Senvon village of Manipur. Robert's heart was greatly touched and wanted to give them something so that they learn about the gospel. He gave them a copy of St. John gospel which had been translated by Rev. Savidge and J.H. Lorrain, the Arthington missionaries in Mizoram. One copy was sent through some students to the chief of Senvon, Mr Kamkholun. Mr Kamkholun was believed to be the same chief who had earlier refused entry to the Baptist missionary Rev. William Pettigrew. He was happy and profoundly impressed by the booklet, so much so that he apparently invited Watkin Roberts to establish a school in his village and also tell him about 'that book' and 'his God'. He sent three messengers with the same copy of the gospel and an appeal written on the flyleaf: "Sir, come yourself and tell us about this book and your God" (Lal Dena 1985: 109). This appeal was taken as a 'Macedonian call' and accepted. Accordingly, Roberts set off for Manipur with his two Vaiphei students, viz. Thangkai and Lungpao, as his porters.

The parties arrived at Senvon on 5th February 1910. No sooner had he reached than he preached the Gospel to them and visited the neighbouring villages preaching the good news. Six of them, including the chief, were converted to Christianity on that day. Since then regular meetings were held day and night. People from the neighbouring villages also came to hear the word of God with deep interest. Thus, the church was established at Senvon in 1910, which was the first Kuki Christian village in Manipur followed by Leisen, Khopibung, Malte, Bualtong and Chawngkhozo.

Christianity and Its Impact

Christianity has come in a big way as the formidable agent that has brought about transformation in the socio-cultural and political life of the people (Barnes Mawrie 2009: 132). Socio-political consciousness among the tribal communities in North east India has been a result of the ongoing process of enlightment brought about by education in particular. In spite of its educative value and social relevance, the institution of Lawm and Sawm had completely disappeared today. Certain factors have contributed to the disappearance of such institution which had once played a very important role in the socio- cultural and economic life of the people. As discuss above, mentioned may be made on the impact of British colonial rule, followed by Christianity which in turn brought about revolutionary change by introducing modern education among the Kukis. In the modern Kuki society, the institution of *Lawm* and *Sawm* do not exist in the actual sense as they were in the primal Kuki society. With change in the Kuki society brought about by the coming of Christianity accompanied by wave of modernisation and development, people felt it more and more inconvenient to put them into practice. Here School and college going youths can no longer participate in group cultivation works. They can also no more sleep together in the same houses. In this context, Paokhohao Haokip puts: "Today the traditional *Sawm* has disappeared as it is not practicable. However, it can be contended that it has now been replaced by the modern formal education institution like schools, colleges, universities, boarding houses and hostels" (Haokip 2013: 183). The same is also applied for the discontinuance of *Lawm.*

Here it may be noted that Christianity was opposed to the various institutions that support the practice of inter-tribal warfare and headhunting (Downs 1983: 2007).Christianity also paved the way modernisation. And due to modernisation and consequent changes in habits and tastes, these institutions had been abandoned as impractible or irrelevant institutions. Thus, the emerging new culture, modernisation and education owing to the coming of Christianity led to the abolition or put an end to the remarkable institution of Lawm and Sawm (Thanzauva 1989: 102).

Some of the student organizations formed in their post Christian dispensation are: Gangte Students' Organization (GSO), Hmar Students' Organization (HAS), Kom-Rem Students' Organization (KRSO), Kuki Students'

Organization (KSO), Paite Students' Association- Siamsinpawlpi (SSPP), Simte Students' Association- Khangthah Zun Pawl (KZP), Thadou Students' Association (TSA), Vaiphei Students' Association (VSA) Zillai, Zou Students' Association- Zomi Sangnaupang Pawlpi (ZSP), etc. These student organizations primarily focused on the educational uplifting of the Kukis.

Some social organizations for various areas were also formed in Manipur. They are: Singngat Area Kuki Inter Sports Association (SAKISA) in Churachandpur District, Lonpi Area Games and Students Association (LAKSA) in Chandel District, and South Eastern Kuki Youth Organisation (SEKYO) in Ukhrul District, etc. These organizations have a concern for maintaining their customs-cultures and unity among them by having an area wide conference once in awhile. They also have philanthropic organizations such as the Kuki Khanglai Lawmpi (KKL), Young Paite Association (YPA), and Hmar Youth Association (HYA). In this way, the Kuki people maintained their oneness since the dawn of Christianity among them (Haokip 2009).

Conclusion

Today many changes had been observed in the age old traditional institutions of the Kukis. The institution of *Lawm* and *Sawm* which had been the centre of village social life have now been replaced by modern youth organization like the youth clubs at the village level and students organizations at the students level. Yet, it is important to note that just as the traditional institutions fulfilled the need of those times, the modern day youth organization fulfilled the demand of the present time. The modern day youth organizations are well structured and well organized. The youth clubs' which function at the village level still follow certain aspects of the traditional institutions, like working for the welfare of the village, helps the poor and the aged people, guarding the village in times of trouble etc. Thus comparing the similarities between *Lawm* and the modern day youth club, Haokip described *Lawm* as a 'Traditional form of youth club'. But, in my opinion the youth club of present day may be decribed as representing both the tradition institution of *Lawm* and *Sawm*, as it fulfilled certain criteria of both, while keeping in mind that the education work being carried out by modern educational institutions. One of the main objectives of these organizations is to preserve and protect the traditional culture and customs. They mobilize the youths and take any actions as per the need of the situation. They also take active part in the political front and fight against any issue that is harmful to the society.

References

Downs, F. S. 1969. *The Mighty Works of God*. Guwahati: Lakshmi Printing Press.

Downs, F.S. 1983. *Christianity in North East India*. Delhi: ISPCK.

Dena, Lal. 1991. Christian Proselytism. In Lal Dena (eds), *History of Modern Manipur* (1826-1949). New Delhi: Orbit Publishers-Distributors.

Goswami, Tarun. 1985. *Kuki life and lore*. Assam: Sreeguru Press, Haflong.

Gangte, T.S. 1993. *The Kukis of Manipur- A historical analysis*. New Delhi: Gyan Publishing house.

Haokip, P. S. 1998. *Zale'n Gam*. Kuki National Organisation.

Horam, M. 1998. *Nagas Old Ways and New Trend*. New Delhi: NP.

Haokip, Paokhohao. 2013. Reinculcating Traditional Values of the Kukis with Special Reference to Lom and Som. In Thongkholal Haokip (eds), *The Kukis of North East India: Politics and Culture*. Delhi: Bookell.

Kilong , Helthang. 2012. *Khul Piengho Chonna Khanna in Thadou-Kuki*. Imphal: Creative Compu Print.

KIM. 2013. *Kuki Customary Law*. Imphal: Kuki Inpi Manipur.

Lhouvum, Nehminthang. 2014. *Educational Status of the Thadou- Kukis of Manipur* in International Journal of Research, Volume 1, issue 11.

Mawrie, Barnes. 2009. Christianity and socio-political consciousness in North East India. In T.B. Subha et al (eds), Christianity and Change in North East India. New Delhi: Concept Publishing Company.

Oommen, T.K. 2009. Cultural change among the tribes of North East India. In T. B. Subha *et al* (eds), *Christianity and Change in North East India*. New Delhi: Concept Publishing Company.

Verghese, G. G and Thanzawna, R. L. 1997. *A history of the Mizos*. Vol.1. New Delhi: Vikas Publishing house Pvt. Ltd.

Haokip, Thongkhosei. 2009. *Overcoming Church division in Manipur: Kukis' perspective* .kuki international forum.

http://kukiforum.com/2008/02/overcoming-church-division-in-manipur-kukis-perspective-2/. Accessed on 12/10/2016.

Armer, J.M., & Katsillis, J. 2006. *Modernisation Theory*. Retrieved 10 10, 2016, from Macmillian Rfernce USA:

http://find.galegroup.com/gic/infomark.do?&idig est=fb720fd31d 9036c1ed2d1f3a05 00fcc2&type=retrieve&tabID=T001&prodId=GIC&docId=CX 3404400243 & source = gale & user Group Name=itsbtrial&version=1.

31

The Role of Women in Traditional Institution among the Jamatia of Tripura

Mariam Jamatia

Introduction

Traditional institution may be difficult to define and categorize it into social, cultural, political and economic institutions since tradition in any given society is a composite whole of it (Synniang, 2010). Traditional institution is synonymous to traditional leadership which is defined as including "those political, socio-political and politico-religious structures that are rooted in the pre-colonial period, rather than in the creations of the colonial and post-colonial states. Traditional leaders can include kings, other aristocrats holding offices, heads of extended families, and office holders in decentralized polities, as long as their offices are rooted in pre-colonial states and other political entities" (Ray, 2003: 2). In traditional institution men played an important role in decision making in the society.

Materials and methods used

Data has been collected from the field sites that represent the three tiers of the *Jamatia Hoda*. Observation as a tool of data collection is employed. A schedule was also prepared for data collection. Interviews, both structured and non-structured had been carried out with executive members of *Hoda* as well as the general populace. Fieldwork will also include the key informants interviews and case studies. Fieldwork has been carried out in village called *Kuar Kami,* district Gomati, Tripura. Mechanical aid was also used such as camera, tape recorder, etc. Secondary data will be collected from available literature in books, journals, research report, etc.

Findings

In undertaking fieldwork, it has been found that women's participation in the socio-political and religious level is both numerically and substantively insignificant. The reservation quotas for the women's development in the socio-political administration of the *Jamatia Hoda* were pursued to certain extent. Jamatia society is a patriarchal society. The Jamatia Hoda works in a three tier system. On the highest level is *Hoda*, on intermediary level is *Moyal*, which composite of 18 villages and on the lowest level is the Luku which is a village council. Only married women who is above 35 years of age participate in the traditional institution. The traditional institution among the *Jamatia* of Tripura are very much influence by the modern system of adult franchise. Most of the women are seen doing the household chores and the cultivation. Even within the household and outside the family all the decisions are made by the male.

Agriculture: The Jamatia practice both jhum and paddy cultivations but mostly paddy cultivation. The heavy work such as cutting trees, ploughing the field etc. are done by man. Women carry out most of the agricultural operations such as preparation of nursery beds, sowing seeds, transplanting, weeding etc.

In decision making: When it comes to decision-making in society, women have no voice. In all three tier system of Jamatia Hoda women participation and decision-making is still negligible. Even though with the advancement of education the outlook of people has become broader. However women decision-making in the traditional institution is not encourage. I decision-making man lead the role where as women was left behind.

Economic position of women: The economic position of Jamatia women is at the low level because it is always believed that men are the bread-winners of the family. They are confined to the four walls of their house and do the agricultural activities. Even though the Indian Constitution State that there should be no discrimination to any citizen of India on the base of gender. However in reality there is discrimination in the payment of labour wages, men are paid more than women.

Conclusion

In the olden days women had no share or role in the political and administrative set-up of the *Jamatia* society. However, with the introduction of the adult franchise, women got the opportunity to raise their voice and some of them even become the executive members of the *Jamatia Hoda*. Even though women are given opportunities in the field of socio-political and religious but they could not utilised it without their male partner. But with the development in education women are no longer confining to their four walls of house.

Reference

Ray, Donald I. 2003. Rural Local Governance and Traditional Leadership in Africa and the Afro-Caribbean: Policy and Research Implications from Africa to the Americas and Australasia.: In D. I. Ray and P. S. Reddy, eds., Grass-roots Governance? Chiefs in Africa and the Afro- Caribbean. Calgary: University of Calgary Press.

Synniang I.R. 2010. Traditional Institution in Khasi Hill: A Study of Mawphlang Lyngdohship., An unpublished Ph.D thesis submitted to North Eastern Hill University, Shillong.

32

Rituals of Harvest: A Study on Paddy Harvest Rituals and Change among the Angami Nagas of Kigwema Village, Nagaland

Vilhousienuo Neli

Paddy or Rice (*Oryza sp.*) has been an identity of the Southeast Asian countries for ages, and the agricultural way of life, centered around rice, has played an important part in their history. Rice, often referred to by scholars as "Grain of Gold" or "Essence of Life", has become deeply embedded in the cultural heritage of Asian societies, and is the life, heart, and soul of the people (Keizrul bin Abdullah, 2006). The cultivation process of Paddy has shaped the landscape, culture and character of thousands of people all over the world. When one looks closely at the fields and terraces one finds societies whose customs and rituals are inextricably tied to the rice they grow. Wherever rice is planted, festivals, traditions, rituals and languages celebrate its importance even for those for whom rice is an everyday sight, and something magical, more like spiritual, still radiates from the depth of the green fields (Gomez, 2001). Thus, in many of the Southeast Asian countries, including South, East and Northeast India, rice serves not just as food but rice-centered agricultural life has given a deep influence on their society, economy, politics and ideological activities. From this sense, these societies can be termed as rice-centric, with rice permeating in all aspects of their culture.

Nagas practice the traditional form of agriculture - the jhum and terrace. These two methods of cultivation have traditional knowledge systems connected to it which are still passed on from generation to generation. Jhum cultivation, though at a lesser degree, is found among the Angami Nagas. The life of Angami Nagas revolves around terraced Paddy cultivation, and this paddy forms a significant part of all social, religious, and other cultural activities.

This method is interwoven into their culture and traditions. Terraced paddy fields are the prized property of the Angami Nagas and the customary laws and ethical values play an important and significant part in shaping the agricultural sustainability. Their food, shelter, firewood, daily agricultural works etc. are all supplied to them by nature. So, their belief, customs, rituals, taboos and *genna* help them shape and organise their agricultural activities (Yano *et al.*, 2013).

A religious aspect of paddy has lived on throughout the ages and festivals revolve around the agricultural cycle mainly with the paddy cultivation as in the case of the Angami Nagas. Every stage of the paddy cultivation of leading from preparing the terraced field to harvest has its specific rituals. The present paper will discuss specifically on the traditional harvesting of paddy and the various harvest rituals practiced by the Angami Nagas of Kigwema village and the modification it has gone through ages.

Methods

For the purpose of the present study ethnographic fieldwork was conducted in Kigwema village situated 9kms away from the state capital Kohima. The primary occupation of the people of Kigwema village is still agriculture. Rice is the staple food of the people and thus terraced paddy cultivation is majorly practiced here along with potato cultivation. Primary data was collected by using structured and semi structured interviews.

Findings

The Angami Nagas of Kigwema village usually start harvesting paddy by the end of September and goes on till first week of November. Before harvest when it is almost time for harvest all the paddy stalks are kept ready for harvesting by binding three or four stalks of paddy together in order to make it easier and faster to harvest. Harvesting of paddy is usually done by women with sickle and carrying the Angami traditional bamboo basket called the *Khodi* on their back they carefully place it one after another after cutting. When it is filled they bring it to where the mat is spread for threshing. Threshing is usually done by men which are piled up in the bamboo mat. First they beat it a bamboo stick and followed by stamping on the piles by foot. After this is done the threshed paddy is winnowed with a bamboo winnowing fan with both men and women participating. The paddy is then carried home or to the granary manually in paddy baskets *Khodi* by women and men in their traditional shawl which is tied on their back in such a way that they hold the grains.

Harvest ritual

Scott (1994) while studying the Philippines food and farming noted that harvesting of paddy was accompanied by strict religious taboos. In Sri Lanka, paddy cultivation took deep root and the ritual associated with the activity of threshing the paddy has over the generations acquired sanctity of its own (Samara, 2013).

In Kigwema village the harvest rituals were performed for the whole village by the *Leidepfii* (first reaper) who is an elderly woman and who has knowledge about the rituals of the *Kriinamia* (traditional religion). When the paddy in the terraced fields starts to ripen the *Leidepfii* (first reaper) gets ready to do her rituals. On the day she appoints to do her rituals she goes to the field early morning to perform the ritualistic harvest of paddy. On her way to her field even if she meets anyone she does not greet or talk to anyone. Also on the way to the field she finds earthworm feces. On reaching the field this earthworm feces is carefully wrapped with the paddy leave inside- out into a ball like structure and she selects few stalks of paddy and bind it together with the leaves of the paddy even now the leaves are placed inside- out. After this is done she brings two stalks of grains back home and place it in the bottom of the big paddy baskets stored in the granary. After this ritualistic harvesting is done by the first reaper that is the Liedepfii anyone can go to respective field and do the same ritual as she did in her field. The same ritual is especially done by the woman however it is not restricted to woman alone even man can perform this ritual. In case a person owns two or three terraced fields in every field before the harvesting starts the same ritual is performed and then only the rest of the paddy is harvested. This ritual which is performed early in the morning when nobody has woken up she brings back two stalks of paddy and placing it in the bottom of the paddy baskets says "may you fill up fast". After this ritual is performed then only the whole family or the peer group *(Peli Kro)* who will be helping for the paddy harvest can go to harvest.

In the field during harvest when they spread the traditional mat to thresh the paddy the first stalk of paddy is brought in the middle of the mat and with bare hands rub it together and let the first grains fall on the mat uttering some prayers that they may not leave good grains behind while threshing. After this all of them can bring in the harvested paddy and start threshing. Also it is not allowed for anyone who has fed the hens and cocks with his or her bare hands with paddy on the day of harvest to harvest paddy because it is believed that those which they have harvested will finish in no time since hens and cocks are considered greedy and can keep eating whole day. Therefore on the day of harvest if somebody has to feed the hens and cocks with grains they are told to take the grains out with a small bamboo baskets and without touching it with bare hands and throw it directly from the basket.

After the harvest of paddy is done in one terraced field those stalks which were tied together before the harvest are harvested and placing it on top of the other entire paddy it is carried home. Even when transferring the paddy into the paddy baskets *(Tshii)* the paddy stalks which were used to perform the rituals are placed on the very top of the paddy in the paddy basket. The same is done for the rest of the other terraced fields also. This was how harvesting was done by the *Kriinamia* in the earlier times when all the villagers practiced the traditional religion.

Changes in the Harvest Ritual

With the passage of time and with the coming of Christianity almost all the people in the village have converted to Christianity with only a few of them practicing the traditional religion and all of whom are men. Thus there has come about modifications in the all the rituals and practices and the harvesting ritual is no exception to all these modifications. With all the women in the village converting to Christianity there was no one to take up the responsibility of the *Leidepfii* and thus the ritualistic harvest which was performed before any harvest is not practiced anymore however those men who still practice this religion still does their own personal first harvest rituals in their respective terraced paddy fields before the harvest is carried out.

Now instead of the traditional rituals performed in the paddy fields before harvest the Christians pray to God in church for fruitful harvest and hold special prayers which are especially seen evident in the case of the Roman Catholics. When the time of harvest approaches i.e., when the paddy has started to ripen the church appoints a specific day to bless the harvest. Thus on the day appointed all the members of the church brings two or three stalks of paddy from their field and place it on the altar of the church for the priest to bless it during the holy mass. This is done so that the harvest will be a fruitful one. Also when they have brought in all the harvest of that year one tenth of the total harvest is given to the church as tenth tithe.

Other Changes

The traditional way of harvesting and threshing has remained the same as practiced over the years however the major change that has come about with development in the villages is construction of roads for better connectivity and availability of vehicles. In the earlier days there when the harvesting was done the villagers had to carry everything back home by foot and as such those who had their terraced field in far off areas sometimes had to walk 9-10kms to bring home the harvested paddy. However with the availability of vehicles and connectivity it has reduced the workload to minimum when it come to carrying the paddy back to the village as their terraced fields are now all either connected with big roads or falls nearby. Thus after harvest they only had to carry it and place it in nearby roads which are all transported to their respective homes through vehicles by paying minimum amount. Also with the availability of sacks, the entire harvested paddy are stored in sacks and tied carefully in place of traditional paddy baskets.

Conclusion

Social change in a society is inevitable and continuous. Modern amenities, development in various sectors and spread of Christianity in Kigwema has resulted in certain changes and modification in relation to the harvesting of paddy and connected rituals were witnessed. With women all having converted to Christianity and only a few men practicing the traditional religion modifications in the form of performing the first ritualistic harvest is witnessed in the present scenario. A kind of acculturation is seen when it comes to harvest by the Christians as in place of performing the first harvest ritual the first ritual before harvest is brought in the church to be blessed by the priest.

Through this it is evident that rice being the staple food of the people of Kigwema village is revered and its cultivation plays an important role in their life. Thus at every stage of its cultivation rituals and festivals are conducted for a bountiful harvest and the harvest ritual is no exception to this. With changes in the socio- economic aspects these harvest rituals are not as complicated as it was before it has still continued on with certain modifications.

References

Gomez, Kwanchai A. 2001. Rice, the Grain of Culture. *The Siam Society Lecture Series.*

Keizrul bin Abdullah, D. 2006. Rice Production and Paddy Irrigation in the Asian Monsoon Region.*Symposium on the International Network on Water Ecosystems and Paddy Fields (INWEPF).*

Samara, Daleena. 2013. The Rice of Life: Paddy Cultivation forms the Heart of Sri Lankan Culture. www.srilankan.com. DOA: 9/10/16.

Scott, W.H. 1994. *Barangay: Sixteenth-century Philippine culture and society.* Quezon City: Ateneo de Manila University Press.

Yano K. and T. Lanusosang. 2013. Globalisation and its Impact on Agriculture: An Overview of Kohima District, Nagaland, India. *International Journal of Bio-resource and Stress Management.* 4(4): 651-654.

33

Pakan: A Historical Nomenclature of Ethnic Affinity

Romeo Bungdon

PAKAN was once a conglomeration of tribes like Annal, Chothe, Lamkang, Maring, Moyon, Monsang, Mara {Mizoram}, Nambasi, Kashung, Irong, Poirou [Tangkhuls] and Tarao which are easily identical by their distinct common adoring nicknames for their sons and daughters. For sons, they name in order of precedence by birth as Mote, Kopu, Bepu, Angpu, and Thumpa; and for their daughters, they call them in order of precedence by birth as Khinu, Tonu, Shangnu, Penu, and Thumnu. This tradition of naming is not found among other ethnic tribes in the world. PAKANs also have linguistic affinity and similarity even though their past lingua franca had diminished due to their new social assimilation to modern socio-linguistic mosaic.

The term PAKAN is possibly derived from IKAN which is a majestic feast very much similar to banquet that a rich man who cultivated a huge size of mountain slope and reaped abundantly offers to his community. PAKANS had a strong belief that if a group of hornbill fly encircling above a village, it was a good omen that nature shall bestow upon someone in that village to have a bumper harvest and shall endow IKAN feast. The feast IKAN is very much traditional for the PAKAN tribes, which is normally celebrated with ritual drumming with folk songs, folk lore and cultural dances associated with servings of rice brew [beer], meats of mithun (Bos-fontalis),buffalo, pork, river fish, venison or wild animal meats [if the game is hunted luckily in time of the feast] and delicious steamed rice. Rice beer/brew is a non toxic and has low percentage of alcohol yet contains high amount of amino acid (protein), glucose, iron, traces of citric acid (vitamin C) and calcium, which is a healthy drink unlike the modern toxic alcohols.

In fact, the PAKAN tribes, an ancient brave warrior originated from Yunnan province of China who are then scattered in countries like Myanmar, Borneo

Photo 33.1: Ancient Pakan Naga Head hunters of Manipur (Source:)

Photo 33.2: Nanga Pakan head hunter (Malaysia) (Source:)

Island [Malaysia], Chittagong [Bangladesh], NE of India and other Southeast Asian countries. They have a common tradition of erecting Stone Menhirs in honour of the spirits of demised heroes, brave warriors, rulers and rich individuals who accomplished a tradition of offering the IKAN feast seven times, wherein, seven wooden Y shaped big posts are erected at frontal courtyard of a host depicting each event of the feast. Stone Menhir erecting is not done by other ethnic tribes often in those historical period though some do now. The PAKAN tribes also used sepulchre and a properly dug out closet as a common tomb exclusively for each separate clans. The PAKAN tribes predominantly living in Manipur and NE India are not accessible on internets as they don't pload any information under PAKAN nomenclature but had embraced new tribal nomenclatures as a separate recognized tribes of India since 1956 A.D. For instance, when the British Ethnologist reached one PAKAN village, the Anal khullen village sometime in 1931 A.D. and when he asked the villagers to which ethnic tribe they belong to, due to English language misunderstanding they answered the wrong way saying that the village was established by Angnal, thinking that the British officer was asking of the village. Whereas, PAKANs living in some other countries can be accessed on internets.

Since then, PAKANS in Chandel district of Manipur were ethnically recorded as ANAL not even as ANGNAL (a typical PAKAN name) which was stated by the then villagers. Until 1956, most of the PAKAN tribes from Chandel district like Anal, Lamkang, Moyon, Monsang were clubbed in as Anal by the British Indian Government in Census, Army recruitment and other employment. To prove these ethnical genealogy information anthropologically, clinical research like DNA and Dental Morphometric can be experimented.

Photo 33.3: Stone Menhirs in Vangchhia, Mizoram (Source:)

As published in 2015 A.D. by the Archaeological survey of India (ASI), it had declared Vangchhia which is abode to 200 Menhirs and was declared a heritage site of national importance in 2014 A.D. The exact site located near Vangchhia village in Champhai district near the Myanmar border is known as Kawtchuah Roupui (the great passage way). The menhirs have puzzled both common people and experts alike. Even though the embossed figures in the menhirs depicted some Mizo cultures, cross cultural dating suggested that they belong to the period of 1200-1400 A.D. which was long before Mizo forefathers arrived from Burma. Archaeologist said that the menhirs are unique to India's North-Eastern region. No one is certain what these carvings are supposed to represent, but experts said they may be akin to the" heroic stones" found elsewhere in the sub-continent - commemoration stones that carry images of games of or warriors hunted or killed by chiefs or warriors of a particular clan, tribe or community.

Supplementing on the above paragraph which was published by Archaeological survey of India (ASI), the PAKAN tribals were the first to settle in Mizoram after escaping the devastating war of Mongols led by Kublai Khan around 1281 A.D, where the PAKANS migrated from ARAKAN valley (Ara= Migrate -Kan = PAKAN) and crossed Irrawaddy (Are you migrating?) River and led a nomadic period of life through Chittagong mountain jungle ranges in Bangladesh. PAKANS lived and flourished for long period of years in Aizawl which they name it in their Pakan dialect which literally means (Ai=reddish brooke crab, zawl =base/buttock) which is still in used. In Mizo dialect Ai Means Crab which is similar to that of the Pakan dialect whereas, Mizos do not have a term zawl which they could interpret literally, which is obvious that the Pakans lived there and name some places and left behind some physical structures. The PAKANS along with HMARS left Aizawl or Mizoram when Mizos invaded them in the 15th Century and settled at Thanlon which literally means "grave hill" in Churachandpur district. Cluster of stone menhirs erected still exist there. Another similar subject to ponder upon is that the Zeliangrongs who predominantly settled in Assam, Manipur & Nagaland called themselves indigenously MAKAM which is quite similar terminologically as PAKAN and both have some linguistic and cultural affinity with close nature of food habits and living manner.

Socio - Religious tradition as their administrative System

Even during ancient times PAKANS have a high faith on the existence of one almighty God. They propagate and worship Him along with the belief of animism and venerations of dead parent's spirits. The highest sanctified status was that of the High Priest (KHOLPU) followed by scribe (thimpu), Hero/ war commander (phetha) and smith man (tholpu). Maintaining and strictly abiding the set up protocol, they systematically administered their community. The foremost task is the high priest or the prophets consulting of gods and conducting a séance (consulting spirit of dead people) and would prophesised fortunes, taboos and dangers ahead. Thus, accordingly the other ranks would rule and lead sustaining such prophecies. As such, there was no chaos in the past as everything was spelled out initially by a prophet which were strictly obeyed as a Devine rule since they had great fear of God. Such instincts prevailed for peaceful customary administrations easier & simpler efforts even in times of war and calamities. After they embraced Christianity and other religion in which the concept of God's forgiveness and to forgive others enthralled liberal faith of complex social custom of modernity emitting socio-cultural confusions rather, between religious doctrines and social customs or traditions.

Skill Activities

PAKANS were and are still skilful in cultivation, hunting and fishing as these were their means of survival. Tools they used are technically designed so that less efforts are exerted but with high efficiency. They hunt with bows and arrows with poisoned tips, spears, different types of laying traps according to the size of animals. They used barks of trees and other climber plants to poison fish and catch them in summers. They also uniquely can construct a raft dam across rivers in dry season and lay big cruver traps in monsoon floods to catch huge river fishes, which other tribes seldom do.

Ancient Ruins in India May Be Lost Civilization of Mizoram

Researchers in the Indian state Mizoram recently made an exciting discovery – the remains of what may be a lost civilization. According to The Times of India, the general director of the Archaeological Survey of India (ASI) visited the city of Vangchhia, located in the Champai district of Mizoram, India in November 2015. His visit led to an excavation of the area, which revealed an important archaeological find. Over the following months, researchers came to the area to try to uncover the secrets of the city that may have once existed there. According to the Assistant Superintending archaeologist at the Archaeological Survey of India Delhi, Sujeet Nayan, the discoveries at the site may reveal previously unknown information about Mizoram, and the Northeast.

"We were exploring what lay beneath the bushes and thick foliage. The entire site could hold traces of a lost city or a greater lost civilization. It is amazing to stumble upon so many things. We need more time and research to reach a final conclusion," said Nayan. While more research is needed, the excavation team has gleaned some interesting and helpful information from the area already. They found more than 50 structures and nine terraces or retaining walls. The structures contain depictions of human, animal, and floral life. The terraces are constructed with large stones, and range from 10 to 25 feet tall. Upon exploring eight of the nine terraces, the team has concluded that they may have served as burial sites. They also discovered what appears to be a water pavilion, similar to those found in Mughal structures like the Taj Mahal. Further studies are planned in the area, in hopes of learning more about the lost civilization. For example, fragments of charcoal were removed so scientists can conduct scientific testing, such as carbon dating. This testing may be the key to learning more about the ancient civilization that may have lived there. Mizoram is located in north-eastern India, and is bordered by Myanmar to the east and south, Bangladesh to the west, and the states Tripura, Assam, and Manipur to the north. It is also known as "Land of the Mizos." It is a hilly area with many forests and a great deal of foliage. Modern Mizoram is populated by Scheduled Tribes, although it is one of the more sparsely populated states in India. The discovery of the lost city in Mizoram may reveal significant information about the ancient civilizations that lived there and in surrounding areas, which would have been influenced by the topography of the area and the climate, as well as provide insight into the origins of the modern-day tribes in Mizoram.

As Nayan and other researchers continue to explore the lost city in Vangchhia, and testing commences on the items found in the area, they are hoping to learn more about the people that lived there, when and why they came to the area, what type of structures they lived in, what they ate, and why they left. This information will be a significant contribution to the history of Mizoram, and to India.

Well, to be honest, I have been enlightened and inspired by the column of Dr.Irengbam Mohendro Singh of United Kingdom, which was published on 27th May 2012 "OBJECTIVE BURMA-I" through which he quoted the PAGAN(now Bagan in Burmese). His writings authenticated my perceiving and intuitions of my belonging to the Pakan tribe nomenclature as often was narrated as legendary historical facts by my forefathers. I do acknowledge him for his vast knowledge of search through travels and firsthand information collection of data such as the Burmese chronicles and inscriptions with English, Dutch and Portuguese sources and Chinese chronicles in the book History of Burma from early times to 1824 A.D.

It is possible that most of the tribal mongoloids who settled in Manipur and North East India might have dispersed and migrated from China; escaping the great labour force for constructing the Great Wall of China. They possibly escaped through certain cave-like passage/tunnel/unfinished structure of the wall beginning from 220 B.C. The event might have begun during the reign of the first ever emperor of China Shi Huangdi who ruled from 259-210 B.C. It was under his iron hand dynasty the name Qin which is pronounce as Chin got its name thus it is now as China thereafter.

I do not intend to manipulate this primitive history; however, it is possible that after the mass exodus of the escapees, they established kingdoms soothing their well being perhaps after much struggle against scarcity of various livelihood materials. It is learnt in the Chinese history that various ethnic communities of different seven kingdoms were annexed together by this emperor Qin (Chin) under one single empire China from 259-210 B.C. So, it is possible that some different mongoloid stocks presently living in the region descended from it while evading the labour force or through war expedition.

Well, coming back to the nomenclature Pakan (Pagan Baan) it is true that this kingdom was established near Irrawaddy River at its fertile valley, sometime from 849 A.D. as according to the British ethnologist who said that the Pakans/Pagans/Bagans came down with horse riding from the Nanzhao kingdom of the present Yunnan province of China raiding a war at this region. The Nanzhaos went back after collecting the war booties but the Barmars/Burmans (some are found in Assam) stayed back and established the Pakan/Bagan Empire with their common language which is now called Burmese. It is now the lingua franca of' Myanmar. The ruins of this empire with its two thousand pagodas and temples have become the modern tourist attraction. The pagodas were first constructed when they propagated their indigenous religion of worshiping nature god before they embraced Buddhism. However, these pagodas had been renovated by the Buddhist shrine of the habitation as it was converted. It is also presumed, Pakans/bagans/pagans were not escapees or migrant deserters during the Qin labour force between 220 B.C and 210 B.C. The reason is that they remained in Yunnan province of China till 849 A.D. and reached Irrawaddy region of Myanmar in war expedition the same year. Thus, they were ancient horsemen warrior tribes loyal to China. Unfortunately, they abandoned the use of horses after the collapse of their kingdom invaded by Kublai Khan after which they had to lead a nomadic life for a period of years living initially in caves. They changed living in caves to a very high stilt wooden houses made of wooden planks and posts. The planks were made by splitting a single trunk of a tree that would be trimmed down to get only two pieces of thick planks by using iron axe as there was no saw blade in those days. This very high type of stilt house was so designed to evade wild predators and enemies.

Photo 33.4: Very high stilt Pakan house with a ladder (Source:)

Their summarily living in caves must be the reason why they called themselves or were known to others as caveman (Kholmi). During the process of such natural lifestyle in wilderness, they tamed their very revered wild mountainous animal called banteng in Southeast Asia which is commonly known as mithun (bos fontalis). This mountainous cattle are still reared as a majestic animal and is called charhimsal in local dialect.

Around 1281 A.D. the empire was again destroyed by another Mongols of Kublai Khan. The Mongols left but the Shans remained and established many separate Shan states in the entire northwest through central to eastern Burma. So, in the process of this invading war, groups of Pakans/bagans migrated further for safety while the majority assimilated to the new kingdom

Photo 33.5: (a) Ancient Pakan Traditional Costume

(b) Modern Pakan Traditional Costume (Source:)

of Shans. The migrated group of the tribe' might have settled in the Arakan valley near the sea shore as sea shells like sea cowries and conches are still kept and treasured with much cherished as traditional ornamental dress of wealth. The ornaments are worn only on special occasions of cultural or traditional events. After the Arakan settlement, they migrated to upper lands for some reasons which are still to be researched, wherein folklores, epos, epics and epochs still were being passed on orally, generation to generation which depict the events of settlements, peace and wartimes. Some of the sub-tribes of the Pakan tribe, Annal, Lamkang, Moyon, Monsang, Maring, Tarao and Chothe tribes settled in (Kankhulon as indigenously known) Chandel district of Manipur. In the course of migration from one place to another perhaps with limited utensils, the Pakans/Bagans invented the use of semi ovoid-shape bamboo creed (Ngaan) for steaming rice or any other foods which is uniquely delicious. The apparatus is only used by the Pakan tribe which is now being replaced by kindled clay type traded to them by popular Meitei clay potters mainly from Chairen village of Thoubal district where some Pakans converted there and embraced the caste during devastating wars. In very recent years, aluminium type of the said ngaan is being minted. We indeed need to explore and launch research more of the tribe Pakan to ascertain facts of its historical traces. Yet, there are also many other tribes having close affinity with Pakans. But due to separation of elongated thousands of years as they took different mountain ranges in different directions, they adapted various segregated anthropological social life and lingua franca by environment influences. Some tribes certainly belong to this historical clan which is now naga sub-tribe after the term Naga was coined. Pakans of Malaysia too have Nanga region similar to the term Naga. If broader anthropological research is minutely taken up, many more affinities to this ethnical tribe could be discovered.

Summary

Having expressed and quoted some essential glimpse of outlines on the PAKANs who have been living with much unsung recognition, the writer's intention is to attract new challenges of anthropological deeper research on such thousands of years lapsed study fields. It is never too late yet and it is believed that anyone who is striving and has such solace of thirst on new discoveries shall venture wisdom to re-integrate the fragments of such consunguity for paving higher achievement of natural historical facts in the North East region of India. It is a humble yet resilient appeal that such Anthropological and ethnological research must never be compromised just relying on British research documents; which rather were constricted and limited of information data due to lingual (English) communication gaps between those researchers and questionnaire tribal respondents, while collecting such firsthand information data. Thus, it is emphasized for deeper research and analysis with such clinical experiments to accumulate genuine data through appropriate field studies.

References

Sir, Charles Brooke who visited PAKAN NANGA of Sarikei, Sarawak, Borneo island (Malayasia) on 30th April 1845

Archaeological Survey of India (ASI) journal 2015 & 2016

An article "Objective Burma I" by Dr. Irengbam Mohendro Singh (U.K)

Chronicles of China, Yunnan Province.

Chronicles of Burma (a) Pagan Kingdom 849 - 1297 A.D. (b) Early Pagan Kingdom 849 - 1044 A.D.

Souvenir article of golden Jubilee, Thungcheng village, by Romeo Bungdon.

34

Socio-Economic and Cultural changes among Hmar from pre-Christian period to Present: A Comparative studies

Esther Lalremkim and Soibam Jibonkumar Singh

The Hmars: Mapping of People

The Hmars are one of the tribes of North East India belonging to the Chin-Kuki -Mizos ethnic group. They are found today in Cachar and North Cachar Hills of Assam and the adjoining states of Manipur, Meghalaya, Mizoram and Tripura in India and Bangladesh and Myanmar (Dena: 2008: 3). They are a distinct community with respect to their traditions, culture, and social customs. The Hmar people are united by common tradition and customs (Barooah: 2007). Regarding the origin of the word 'Hmar', there are diverse opinions. Scholars are of the opinion that the term Hmars have been clubbed as Kuki by the colonial rulers and the Bengalees, and used the term Mar, Mhar to refer to the Hmar (Dena: 2008; Grierson: 1904; Pudaite; 1963). Grierson (1904) in 'Linguistic Survey of India Vol. III Part III' writes, 'the word Kuki is, more especially, used to denote the various tribes who have successively been driven from the Lushei and Chin Hills into the surrounding country to the north and west (2). He further classified Kuki into two groups: Old Kuki and New Kuki. He refers to the Thados, Jangshens and their off-shoots as New Kuki while to the Old Kukis he refers to the tribes who were driven out of the Lushei land (2). He placed the Hmar under the Old Kuki but spelt it as 'Mhar'. Lt.Colonel John Shakespear (1912) in 'The Lushei Clans' also included Hmar (north) in the Old Kuki clans and used the term *Khawtlang* (western village) interchangeably to differentiate them from the Lushai and the Kukis. (185). According to the scholars and Hmar historians, there are two opinions with the origin of the term 'Hmar'. The first group of scholars suggests that the term have originated from the word 'hmar' which means 'north' or 'northerners' (Gierson: 1904; Shakespeare: 1912). This implies that the term came into use only after the Hmars settled down in Mizoram (Thiek: 2013). The second group of scholars contends that the term Hmar is derived from '*hmerh*' which means 'tying of one's hair in a knot on the nape of one's head' (Pudaite: 1963; Thiek: 2013). In support of the second group, the local informant reveals that there were two brothers- the elder because of a sore on the nape of his neck, tied his hair in a knot in his forehead and was called Hrunsawm, and the younger tied his hair in a knot on the back of his head was called Tukbemsawm, a synonymous word of *hmerh*. It is, therefore, quite possible that the word Hmar originated from the word *hmerh* as all the descendents of the Tukbemsawm are now known as Hmars. From examining several historical data's, it is most satisfactory and credible to say that all the Hmar's originated from '*Sinlung*', but the location of which is hotly debated. They claimed that Manmasi was their ancestor. The Hmars have as many as 22 major clans namely Biete, Changsan, Chawnthei, Darngawn, Faihriem, Hmarlusei, Hrangkhawl, Khawbung, Khelte, Khiengte, Khuolhring, Lawitlang, Leiri, Lungtau, Neitham(Also included under Zote clan), Ngente, Ngurte, Pautu, Rawite, Thiek, Vangsie and Zote and a numbers of sub-clans or lineages. About the physical appearance of the Hmar, Rochunga Pudaite (1963) gives a detail description. He wrote as, "In general, the Hmars have cultural and physical resemblance to the rest of the mountain peoples of northeast India and Burma. They are generally a short and sturdy race of men with godly development of muscle. Their face is broad and round and their cheek bones are high, broad and prominent. Their eyes are small and their nose flat and short. Though they are of Mongolian origin, their skin is not yellow. It is rather dark-yellowish-brown".

Focus and Area of Study

The advent of Christianity brought about far reaching affects on the Hmars society of Manipur, pervading all spheres of activity, outlook, culture, custom and way of life. It brought anew awareness as well as concern leading the society to move toward modernism. Christianity, an imported religion played an important part and considered a main factor responsible for the changes and development among the Hmars. However, If compare the present condition in all aspects of Hmars with that of other civilized tribe, we may be much impressed with the inefficiency of its administration and the lamentably low stages of its development. But if, on the other hand it contrast the present with the period of the time of yore. So, the present paper is to see the continuity and changes among Hmars by comparing the culture of past i.e. pre-Christian period and present- modernity and western influences. The past culture is based on secondary sources while the present culture is collect through scientific and systematic fieldwork carried out at Saikawt Village. The village covers a vast area where majority sections of the society are still engaged in agriculture as a main source of living. As such, poverty and backwardness still looms over some section of the society. But, notwithstanding that, majority of the youth accept modern culture and modern education system to improve their social strata, personal well-being and enhance quality of life. Being its close proximity to the District Headquarter, mixed society and diversified cultures resulted in adoption of modern trends, change in lifestyle and traditional traits. Hence, the village can also act as an intermediate link that can represent both urban and rural people of Hmar as a whole making it a perfect field site for a systematic documentation and recording the prevailing Hmar society. Thus, socio-economic and cultural aspects that continue and undergo changes which is taking place and clearly noticeable among Hmars are discussed as follows.

Settlement patterns

The Hmars once lead a nomadic life. They mostly live and earn through the hills and forest areas. After they give up, they started to live in a village living a settled life. In the past, they prefer to live in hills then in the plains for providing protection for the village against the attack of wild animals and their enemies. Their houses were constructed in similar patterns and were laid in regular rows of the rows facing each other. The traditional Hmar houses were constructed with wood and bamboo (Hmar: 2013). It is usually divided into four parts: *sawngka* (the open porch), the enclosed veranda, the main room and the *namthlak* (Pudaite: 1963). In contrast, the present Hmars prefer to live in the valley (though many people still live in the hill) for economic opportunities, better health care and many social factors such as better educational facilities, better standard of living, need for status, etc. Houses are scattered and constructed with wood, mud wall and brick that face any direction as per the owner liking and taste. However, it generally faces toward the village main road. The houses of mixed type, traditional, slightly modern type as well as modern type are observed.

Youth Dormitory (*Zawlbuk*)

Lal Dena (2008) wrote, *Zawlbuk* 'served as a sort of military wing of the village organization by imparting strict discipline and vigorous training in the art of tribal warfare and defence to youngsters (except women) above fifteen years old' (71).From this, it is clear that *Zawlbuk* is an important social institution of Hmars society. It was a place where young boys spent the night by sleeping together in a group. It was also a place where they learnt every type of informal education, art, history, folktales and songs which shaped their moral and ethical conducts. Despite its advantage, it had lost its status and importance in the present Hmar society. Today, the people of Hmar were trained and shaped into responsible adults and much of their lives were mould through formal education at schools, church and at every household since birth. Though the disappearance of *Zawlbuk* resulted in the extinction of a unique indigenous practice however modern education and the advent of Christianity help them to achieve goodness in moulding and reforming human behaviour and so behave well based on Christian principle. Culture, tradition and custom were passing down through oral tradition generation after generation.

Economy

Agriculture was the main source of livelihood for the people (Dena: 2008; Hmar: 2013; Pudaite: 1963). The economic life of the people depended on *tlang lo* (jhum cultivation or slash and burn method of agriculture). The main cultivated crop is rice. Apart from this, they also cultivate different kinds of vegetables and fruits and red chilly (Pudaite: 1963). After the seeds began to sprout, weeding is another important task. Between the sowing and the end of the rains in October the crop requires constant weeding, a duty which falls on the women folk (Shakespeare: 1912). After all the crops were harvested in the month of November, the jhum land is left behind and for the coming year, they have to look out for new land where the same process continues (Hmar: 2013; Pudaite: 1963). Besides these entire tasks, in pre-Christian period, the Hmars had certain feast and sacrifices associated with their harvest which are no more prevalent in the present Hmars society. The festivals are *Tharlak* (sacrifices of early harvested crops), Threshing and *Fangko (Fang* means grains, *ko* means call, so *Fanko* literally means calling grains), *Thuoite Ko* (calling *thuoite*) and *Pawl Kut* (Feast of harvest). At present, such festival related to harvest were no more to be seen. Generally, they practice both shifting (farm) and wet cultivation as their mean of economic life. However at present scenario, they are not emphasizing much on the former cultivations but mostly emphasizing in wet or settled field based on field study.

Food habits

Rice is the staple food of the Hmar. The main food is rice while meat and vegetables were taken as supplements to garnish his rice. As their 'jhums and kitchen gardens cannot supply them with all the food requirements, they constantly go to the forest for wild vegetables' (Pudaite: 1963: 46). But at present time, the Hmars purchase from the nearby market. Many plants and plant parts are eaten as food and numerous number of plant species are cultivated for food. These include root vegetables (potatoes and carrots), bulbs (onion family), leaf vegetables (bean leaf, pumpkin leaf, mustard, spinach and lettuce), stem vegetables (bamboo shoots), and inflorescence vegetables (broccoli and other vegetables such as cabbage or cauliflower). The people of Hmars are also fond of eating meat of different kind like beef, pork, chicken, duck, etc. a direct product taken from an animal, which comes from muscle systems or from organs. The Hmars eat lots of chilly. Some of the popular traditional dishes of the Hmar are *chartang* (mixture of meat, vegetable, spices, and hot pepper), *hmepawk* (stew rice), and *changal hme* (vegetable or meat cooked with hot pepper and soda from the ashes and fermented meat).

Dresses

Dress reflects culture of the people. Women weave and designed all the requirements of clothes for the family from the family looms. The dress of the Hmar women consist of a single piece of cloth about six feet long and four feet wide (Sanate: 2012). One corner of the cloth is 'grasped with the left hand and the cloth is passed over the left shoulder behind the back. Then it is brought under the arm across the chest and the end thrown over the shoulder' (Pudaite: 1962: 47). But men wore a tunic-like shirt and *hrenpereng* (loin cloth of five by two feet around his waist) (ibid). It was also very common for the men to wear hats made of bamboos and canes which were generally flat and circular in shape (Sanate: 2012). But the Hmars of present days has been deviating from their traditional sense of dressing to that of modern style due to the influence of Christianity along with formal education, westernisation and modernisation. They therefore, wear latest design like jeans, pants, skirts, mini-skirts, shirts, kurta, coats, etc. Wearing of modern dresses with latest styles of design has become a common trend among them. The young as well as old generation prefer modern dresses against traditional ones which immensely affect traditional cloth and its way of dressing. However, within an attitude towards the wearing of traditional attires, women are seen preserving the culture of the traditional dresses by wearing the traditional wrap-around and shawl especially on special occasions and days. Similarly, men also uphold such tradition by wearing waistcoat, tie made from tradition cloth or hanging small piece of traditional clothes around their neck.

Festival

The Hmars Festival experience transformation to a great extends. In the past, the Hmars celebrated a number of festivals where men and women, young and old participate together for merry making. There are two kinds of festivals-festival organized by family and festival organized by whole Village. The former one is also known as Inchawng which means festivals organized by the rich and well to do family as part of their family worship. Some of the common festivals were *Siel-Sun* (pierching mithun), *Khuongchawi* (festivals organized by the Chief and *mi neiung*[5] (rich), *Sahlang Dawm*, *In-Ei* (festivals of celebrating success and victory of their hunting expedition and victory in the war). *Hranglam Hla* (Hero Dance) and *Sikpui Ruoi* (winter festival) are included in the later type festival organized by the whole village. At present, the Hmar has a love of song and festival. They celebrate few numbers of festivals only though people in the past celebrate various kinds of festival though out the year. It is due to the traditional religious practices involved in the celebration which forbids the festivity according to the Christian religion.

However, they try to maintain their custom by modifying it in a desirable way based on Christianity traits. Sikpuiruoi, Kut, Christmas etc. are some of the existing festivals related with their traditional system and religion. Hmar population being converted wholly to Christianity no longer observed most traditional festivals as they were in the days of yore. In fact, traditional cultural dances today have become items only in the cultural functions and few others occasions only.

Prohibition of *Zu* (locally brewed rice beer)

In the time of yore, drinking of *zu* (locally brewed rice beer) was very common among the Hmar. It plays an important part of their culture and tradition being served and drank at any social gathering and as a courtesy to guest and visitors at home. In times of mourning, it was obligatory for the *pu* (maternal uncle) to serve *zu* at the condolence meeting of his *Tupa* (Sister's Son) and *Tunu* (sister's daughter) known as *Pu-Zu* (Sanate: 2012). It was the responsibility of the women to prepare and serve *zu* and to have it ready to serve at any time (Lalhmuoklien: 2009). However, with the advent of Christianity, the missionaries, simultaneously with their evangelical task, took steps for social reformation in the Hmar society by prohibiting consumption of *Zu* to the new converts since *Zu* as a common drink was very closely linked with the animistic sacrifices and other Hmar customs which belonged to their old pagan life and an atmosphere of such revelry was uncongenial to Christian spiritual growth (Crossthang Sanate: 2013). This step was taken and continuous by the missionaries, the Churches and even Village Authority of the present days. Thus resulted and make it disappear as a common drink in all occasions which is substituted by '*Thingpui*' (tea).

Priest *(Thiempu)*

Another important official next to the chief and his councilors is the *thiempu* (Varte: 2010). There are various complicated methods of sacrifices and the person who could master all these methods eventually emerged as '*thiempu*' (priest)' (Dena: 2008: 28).In the days of yore, priest is the keeper of the health of the masses, the sickly are referred to the priest who is expected to identify the cause of illness. It is believed that all the ailments are the handiwork of evil-spirit and the priest is expected to cast it out. Patients are treated by the priest with indigenous herbs and magical invocations. So long as the incantation or spell is not revoke from the patients, they are not allowed to socialize with the rest of the society. In brief, Crossthang Sanate (2010) elaborates the responsibilities of the priest as "His service was required in almost all walks in life. He therefore, became the obligatory intermediary between the people and god or gods in the society. His power, especially on religious matter was beyond challengeable. In his priestly capacity, while performing religious sacrificial on behalf of the whole village community, even the *Lal* would bow to him for his blessing. He also performs all sacrifices for the sick and the dead, offers prayer for the prosperity of the crop, and sanctifies the village from the influence of demons and evil spirits. For performing those connected with cultivation, he received a basket of rice, but for some it is not expected to take payment, and the fees depend chiefly on the position of the person who had to pay him (69)".

Today, the role of priest was taken over by Pastor[6] owing to the adoption of Christian faith and belief. Sick or patients are not referring to pastor instead used modern medicine facilities, consulted medical expert at hospital. However, Pastor also prays for healing illness and sickness through the Lord Jesus Christ. Everything related to life cycle ceremonies such as naming of child, baptisms, wedding and funerals were perform by a pastor.

Naming of Child

Earlier, before the coming of Christianity, on the day for naming the child, the family used to offer *zu* (rice-beer), which everyone drank to their heart content called '*Nau zu dawn*'. On such occasion, they first offer *zu* to the woman whose first born child is alive and then to others. The first born child is name by the child paternal grandparents and the second child by the child maternal grandparents. For the third child if the parents wish to let anyone name their child, they are free to do so. However, for the first and second daughter such pattern is followed. The child is named mostly 'before the completion of seven days counting from the day of the child's birth' (Riengsete: 1986:23 in Sanate: 2010). Children were name in remembrance of the name of their grandparents. Some were name in remembrance of the achievement of the child grandparents (Thuomte: 1997: 73-74). But in the present Hmar society, Timing and name of the child is decided as per family desire. Tea or small feast was prepared for all the attendees and well-wishers. The most important part is blessing prayer by Pastor. He dedication the name of child to God and prays for the child health and wellbeing.

Marriage

From the past until now, traditionally practice marriage form monogamous is evident and polygamy is permitted though not encourage. For selection of mates both endogamy and exogamy are prevalent, they are free to choose or merry within and outside the group except consanguineous marriage (blood relation). Cross-cousin marriages which may be of mother's brother's daughter or father's sister's daughter are allowed though not compulsion, but marriage between parallel cousin is forbidden. *Sawngpuia Innei* (Marriage with the approval of the parents), *Chawngmolak* (child marriage), *Arasi hnuoia Innei* [7] (eloped marriage) and *Tlun* (Marriage by Intrusion) are the types of marriage prevalent in the earlier time period. At present, the primitive form of child marriage (*Chongmolak*) and *Tlun* (Marriage by Intrusion) has totally disappeared. The traditional form of arranged marriage has been replaced by Hmar Christian marriage known as *Dan a innei (marriage by rule)*. But the practice of marriage by elopement is still prevalent in the present Hmar society as *Danlou a innei* (marriage not by rule). Thus, considered only two types of marriage exist among contemporary Hmars. One remarkably point is that the traditional norms and social obligations do not undergo change in the process of marriage negotiation. However, the part once played by *Zu* during marriage negotiation was now replaced by tea.

Death

In situation of death, the Hmars extended their help to the bereaved family since time memorial. They observed such day as *um ni kham* (spending the day with the bereaved family and not going for work). Elderly people stayed in the house of the *lusun* (bereaved) family to console them. Close relatives of the departed family wrapped the corps by cloths while relatives, friends, and neighbours extend *mithi ralna* (material help for the family) by giving money, firewood, sugar, rice, etc. They sang the dirge called '*Semruk Hla*' or '*Lamkhozo Hla*' with the main intension of consoling the bereaved family. Young women engaged in collecting firewood and rice from every household[8] in the village and served *zu* [9] (rice beer) to everyone who has come to console the bereaved family. Though there was no compulsion with rendering such help, however everyone consider it as their duty to extend their help in whatever ways they could (Keivom: 1982; Sanate: 2012). The Hmar practiced a burial system. If a person dies before noon, the burial was conducted on the same day. However if a person dies in the afternoon or at night, the *mithi-vui* took place the next day. In the past, those who die a natural were buried near the house where as those who died of some other causes were buried outside the house. However, in the present days, dead is not be classified as per the condition of the dead. It has been treated equally both natural and unnatural. Child died before 60 days of being born is buried separately by their family. But if the child is above 60 days, he/she will be accorded normal condolence burial. In such situation, village authority elders play great role in leading youth in digging grave, making coffin, carrying death body to cemetery, buried and condolence service at night. Delivering a funeral sermon and conducting a graveside service is done by Pastor or depending on the family wishes and church tradition. After the burial, night condolence program for the youth will go on for two nights and *tlawmngai* young men would sleep with the bereaved family for not more than three days so as a sign of comforting the bereaved family.

Family

Among Hmars, family includes members who are related by blood (consanguineous) and marriage (affinal). The family functions under the leadership of the father. The father or husband is the head who supervised all the matters related to the family. He is known as *in khat pa* or *in nei pa* which means head of the family or owner of the house. The honour, prestige and the success of the family solely depend on him (Sanate: 2010: 47-48). He represented the family and its members in any important public meetings and social work as representative of the family (Dena: 2008: 21; Hmar: 2013). The Hmars practiced joint family system. The members of the family comprised of the grand-parents, husband and wife, married and unmarried children and grand children. The number of the family members ranges from eight to fifteen or more (Hmar: 2013).

When the son gets married, he takes his newly wedded wife into his father's house. The couple received guidance from the parents so as to make them capable of taking on the responsibility as they consider 'family as the most important and effective learning centre' (Hmar: 2013: 100). The Hmars also practiced neo-local type of marriage, where the eldest son or whoever gets married first moved out from the ancestral home and constructed a new house nearby (Sanate: 2010). They moved out from the ancestral home after having their children (Baroah: 2007). However the stability of the extended family depended on the nature of relationship and interaction between the male members of the family (Dena: 2008). Variations in the form of family are quite natural in the present Hmar society. At present, both join and nuclear types of family prevail.

Village Administration

Before the coming of Christianity i.e. at the time of yore, Village Administration was run under the leadership of Chief, *Muolkil mitha / khawnbawl upa* (chief councilor) and *Khawnbawl* (councilors), *Thiempu* (Priest), *Thirsu* (blacksmith), *Tlangsam* (village crier) and *Val- upa* (Youth Commander). The chief is the supreme head of the council (Darliensung: 2013) and other officials were appointed by him. The chief along with his councilors discuss and decide all matters connected with the village and adjudicate disputes (Darliensung: 2013; Pudaite: 1963). Though the councilors may advice the chief, however the chief has the authority for the 'final say in all matters within his jurisdictions '(Vanlalhnghak: 2004: 157). In the 'absence if the *Lal* (chief), the '*khawnbawl upa* takes the place of the chief and presided over such meetings' (Dena: 2008: 19).

As discussed, the village council administered both judiciary and administrative power (Dena: 2008) including power of life and death. Both civil and criminal cases were heard and settle by the village council at the chief's house (Thuomte: 1997). H. Thuomte (1997) further notes that, 'with regard to complicated cases, without giving the final decision at its first meeting, the *Lal* and his *Khawnbawl* prefers to discuss it the 'next morning with fresh mind'(6). Before it heard any dispute, the one who filed the case was under obligation to pay 'court fee in the form of *zu* (rice beer) to the chief and his councilors' (Thuomte: 1997: 6). If he wins the case, the other party 'reimburses the expense of the *zu*' (Pudaite: 1963: 52). After the case is decided, whosoever is found to be guilty has to pay *salam* (fine) in the form of pig to the village council (Dena: 2008). However Rochunga Pudaite (1963) is of the view that '*salam* is paid as a fee for trying cases' to the village council by the complainer and not as fine (52). In support of both, Darliensung Hmar (2013) writes that, 'the culprit was fined a pig as a fee and punishment for his guilt and this is known as *salam* (93). There were certain fines imposed depending on the nature of the crime committed. Apart from such power, in cases where the chief and his councilors could not decide who is innocent or could not come to final conclusion of the disputes, there were certain methods applied by the chief to check, proof and give the right decision. Such methods includes boiling rice, *tui li lut* (water immersion) and *sakei ha ret* (chewing the teeth of the tiger) (Keivom: 1982; Songate: 2013). Everyone respect and obey the orders of the village council. Any individual or family who disobeyed the orders of the village council or who in the opinion of the Village council were considered as troublesome for the village, and the *Lal* and his councilors had the right to declare them as '*Khawtlang Ensan*' (social ostracize).

Similar pattern of Chief position and his Village Authority members (Councillors) is still continued and observed in the present Hmars society. But, there is a great change in power structure. The absolute power of the Chieftainship degraded considerably. The reasons may be due to the changing trend from authoritarian to democratic system of administration, lack of knowledge, political consciousness and lack of awareness of individual and legal right among the people. Today, the Chief and his Village authority members are like developmental committee for the welfare of the village. Besides carrying out the developmental works, they give great emphasis on smooth administration, welfare and protect the village from anti-social activities. Some of the other functions of the village authorities are implementation of Schemes made by Government for poverty eradication, recognising beneficiaries for poverty alleviation schemes, receive grants and utilised the same for public works, etc. In the mean time, Village Priest and Blacksmith lost its importance. With the advent of Christianity the former is replace by respective church pastor and the later Blacksmith is taken up as business line by those having skill and talent. The authority lost power of judiciary in life and death. District court is the only competent court to punish a person committing non bail able offence at this time. Therefore, to improve and develop the situation of administration at grass root level, it is necessary to make them aware of their right and duties relative to democratic system of local self government.

Religion

The change in the whole tone is apparent in the sphere of religion among the Hmars from traditional religion to Christianity. L. Hranglien Songate (1996) listed as much as four types of *Pathien* (God) that the Hmars believed in the past viz: *Pathien tak* [10](supreme God), *Khawzing*[11], *Khuonu-Khuopa*[12] and *Vanhrit*[13]. It is obvious that the Hmars religion was animistic and believed in a variety of gods and spirits. They believed that the gods and spirits have caused misfortune or any illness to the people. Therefore, bloody sacrifices were done to appease them. At present, almost cent percent or cent percent of the Hmars population accept Christianity. They believed in one supreme God '*Pathien*' who created heaven and earth. They considered him to be a beneficent being that dwell high above in heaven, loving and kind who blessed people and punish wrong doer. Their general belief is that the soul of the dead who accept Jesus Christ as God goes to heaven whereas the other goes to hell. Thus, they worship him to find a place in heaven after death.

Health Care

In the pre-Christian period, the health conditions of the people were miserable and pathetic. To heal the sick, the common practice was by offering bloody sacrifices to the evil spirits by the village *Thiempu* (priest) (Crossthang Sanate :2013) . In fact, the Hmar people did not believe that they could be cured of sickness or diseases by any means other than sacrifices performed by the *Thiempu* since it was their belief that diseases was closely associated with powers of a spirit or a wizard (ibid). On one hand, some diseases/illnesses are healed by using herbs or animals/insects as medications. Practitioners of traditional medicine have solid knowledge of herbs and of their effects in healing. But such knowledge is not sufficient with the continuous appearance of new diseases. Using the knowledge missionary imparted about the important of health care and modernisation, People of Hmars view on health no matter where you are, what you do and prefer the best treatment for living. Thus, the Hmars have given up their age-old traditional practice of curing diseases preferring modern treatment over indigenous medicine. They are adapted to modern beliefs, values and scientific-based medicine due to the impact of modern forces though modern medical amenities are hardly accessible. However, due to non-availability of modern medicines and physicians in some areas, the traditional method of curing diseases by using herbs, insects or animal to the patient is still practiced.

Conclusion

Today, the people of the Hmar caught in between two contemporary cultures – the traditional and the western influences. It is impossible to accept both cultures and many unique cultures and ways of life were at high risk. Various traditional customs and practices are given up in the name of Christianity while in certain spheres of activities and ways of life it shows impressive results. For this, the Hmar society is no longer static; it has change and is changing. If this continued, the rich traditional cultures and indigenous systems may be lost. We could see some indigenous customs and practices are too fast disappearing from the society without any replacement set in. It is highly necessary and recommends that cultures and traditions, languages, dresses, folklore and songs, fashion, indeed the totality of Hmar life style should be regularly and with passionate practiced, properly recorded and preserved and proudly and widely promoted. Without culture, people are as good as extinct, erased and existence without dignity or recognition. It because there is part of one identity rooted in the tradition and culture. Most importantly, it is important to the future of our children and to our nation as culture ensures a history, a past, present and certainly a future. Thus, the finding and documentation on the changes of life among Hmars people in all spheres of activities shall be of substantial help and useful to the planners, administrators and future researchers. Further study on different communities on similar approach must be continued to know and understand the status and changes taken places within their communities.

References

Barooah, Dr. Jeuti. 2007. *Customary Laws of the Hmars of Manipur. With Special Reference to their Land Holding System*. Guwahati. Law Research Institute.

Darliensung 1987. *The Hmars*. Churachandpur: L&R Printing Press.

Dena, Lal. 1990. 'Social and Political Institutions of the Hmar' (134-144), in Jaynanta Sarkar & B. Datta Ray ed. *Social and Political Institutions of the Hill People of North East India*. Revised version of papers read in a seminar in Shillong on 4th-5th July 1977, Organized jointly by Anthropological Survey of India and North-East India Council for Social Science Research. Calcutta.

———. 2008. *In Search Of Identity: Hmars of North-East India*. New Delhi: Akansha Publishing House.

Grierson, G.R (ed.). 1904. *Linguistic Survey of India. Vol III Tibeto-Burman Family. Part III Specimen of the Kuki-Chin and Burma Groups*. Calcuta: Office of the Superintendent, Government Printing India.

Hmar, Darliensung. 2013. *The Hmars*. New Delhi: Akansha Publishing House.

Hmar, Lalthakim. 2013. Role of Women in the expressive behaviours of the Hmars of Assam. Ph D. Thesis submitted to Department of Cultural Studies, School of Humanities & Social Sciences, Tezpur University.

Keivom. Louis L. 1982. *Hmar Pi le Pu Dan (The Hmar Customary Laws)*. Manipur: Published by the Author.

Lalhmuoklien, Rev. Dr. 2009. *Gospel through Darkness. History & Missionary work of the North East General Mission (ECCI) 1010-2004*. Manipur. Smart-tech Offset Printers.

Parry. N.E. 1976. *A Monograph on Lushai Custom and Ceremonies*. Aizawl: Tribal Research Institute.

Pudaite Rochunga. 1963. *The Education of the Hmar People. With historical sketch of the people*. Manipur. Indo-Burma Pioneer Mission.

Sanate, Crossthang. 2010. *Social Change Among the Hmar in Manipur*. Unpublished Ph.D Thesis. Department of Sociology. School of Social Science. Shillong: North Eastern Hill University.

Shakespeare, J. 1912. *The Lushai Kuki Clan*. London: MacMillan & Co Ltd.

Songate, L. Hranglien. 1996. *Hmar Chanchin (Hmar History)*. Manipur: H. C. Lawma & Son's Press.

———. 1956. *Hmar History, Hmar Chanchin*. Imphal: Mao Press.

Thiek, Hrilrokhum. 2013. *History of the Hmars in North East India (with special reference to Assam)*. Published by the Author.

Thuomte, H. 1997. *Hmar Nunhlui*. Manipur: Published by the Author.

Vanlalnghak. 2004. 'Tribal Value System and Leadership Issue' in Miri Sujata (ed) *Rationality and Tribal Thought* (155-160). New Delhi, Mittal Publication.

Varte, Immanuel Zarzosang. 2010. *Impact of Development on the Hmars of Tipaimukh in Churachandpur District, Manipur*. Unpublished Ph.D Thesis. Shillong: North Eastern Hill University.

35

Socio-political and Cultural Existence of Monsang Naga Tribes: Retrospective Outlook

P. Dhaneshwari Devi

It is fact that Monsang Naga Tribes have been living in the Chandel District of Manipur since long back. The name of the tribe itself is the derivative of the name of the village 'Monsang' where the Monsang tribes are located in a large number. These Monsang tribes love to call themselves as 'Sirti' or 'southerners', mainly speaking languages alike to that of other tribes of the region like Tangkhul, Marings, and Thadou.[1] Socio cultural norms too are quite ennobled as depicted in its plethora of festivals and joyful functions. They have their own mythical origin, distinct life-style, culture, customs, traditions, festivals, and language inherited from their forefathers and preserved in folksongs, folktales, etc. As an indigenous community, the Monsang Naga Tribe was recognized as one of the scheduled tribes of India Vide Notification No SRC 2477 dated 29th September 1956. Nature has endowed the Monsang villages with rich vegetation and natural landscapes. The rivers, streams, fields and forests around them have been a source of sustenance for people's livelihood in one way or the other. Shifting cultivation in Monsang society continued for many years.[2]

Methods and Data

Qualitative and quantitative methods along with empirical and observational analysis are the methods through which this study came to make a successful ending. The universe of the study is Chandel district exclusively where Monsang Naga Tribes dominate in six villages, which includes Liwa Changning, Heibunglok, Liwa Khullen, Liwa Sarei, Japhouo and Monsang Pantha Village, etc. information and required data were collected through structure questionnaire and informal interview from the villages. The population and sample size of the study covers 383 families (Table 35.1). For more understanding on the socio-cultural activities of the people, both the participant and non-participant methods were also employed. The key-informants include village leaders, politicians, family heads and elite groups of Monsang tribes.

Table 35.1: Distribution of village population with household

Sl. No.	*Name of Villages*	*No. of House*	*Population*					
			Total	*P.C.*	*Male*	*P.C.*	*Female*	*P.C.*
1.	Monsang Pantha village	82	504	25.10	254	25.58	250	24.63
2.	Japhou village	113	564	28.09	276	27.79	288	28.37
3.	Liwa sarie village	58	287	14.29	139	14.00	148	14.58
4.	Liwa khullen village	43	203	10.11	94	9.47	109	10.74
5.	Heibunglok village	25	140	6.95	65	6.55	75	7.39
6.	Liwa changing village (Komlathabi)	62	310	15.44	165	16.62	145	14.29
	Total	383	2008		993		1015	

Total no. of population = 2008 (Male=993, Female = 1015)

Table 35.2: Distribution of age and sex composition

Sl. No.	*Age group*	*Total*	*P.C*	*Male*	*P.C*	*Female*	*P.C*
1.	0-15	731	36.40	362	36.46	369	36.35
2.	16-30	529	26.34	267	26.89	262	25.81
3.	31-45	426	21.22	204	20.54	222	21.87
4.	46-60	194	9.66	98	9.87	96	9.46
5.	51-70	96	4.78	46	4.63	50	4.93
6.	76-90	30	1.49	15	1.51	15	1.48
7.	91+Above	2	0.10	1	0.10	1	0.09
	Total			993		1015	

Family

In the social of any society or community, the family is organized and it is true that the Monsang Maga tribes of Chandel district recognized into number of families. There are 383 total numbers of families into the six different villages. The number of persons composing a family / household determined as the size of family. The size of the family varies from 1-13 numbers of a family. As shown in table No. 35.3, the size of family varies from very small (V.sm) to very large (VL). Medium size of family 4 to 5 and 5 to 6 persons is the highest frequency (17 percent and 22 percent) which is follow by small size (Sm.) 3 to 4 with a frequency percentage of 13 percent. Very large family comprising above 10 persons has a frequency percentage of 0.5 percent. The figure No. 1 shows most of the families i.e. about 56 percent are composed of the father, mother and their unmarried sons and daughters. This table again shows that there are different type of families- (i) Nuclear family (277), (ii) Joint family (79), (iii) Extended family (19), (iv) Unmarried family (3)and (v) Single family (5) etc.

The people of Monsang Naga tribes are more preferred nuclear type of family than the other types. They are successively being patrilineal society with dual organization, exogamous and male dominated society. After the marriage most of the person prefer to set up of his own.[3]

Table 35.3: Village Family size frequency distribution

Sl. No.	*Size of the family*	*Frequency*	*P.C.*	*Category*	*Cumulative frequency*
1.	0-1	6	1.57	V.Sm	6
2.	1-2	18	4.70	V.Sm	24
3.	2-3	47	12.27	Sm	71
4.	3-4	51	13.32	Sm	122
5.	4-5	67	17.49	M	189
6.	5-6	85	22.19	M	274
7.	6-7	44	11.49	A.M	318
8.	7-8	37	9.66	A.M	355
9.	8-9	15	3.92	L	370
10.	9-10	9	2.35	L	379
11.	10-11	2	0.52	L	381
12.	11-12	1	0.26	V.L	382
13.	12-13	1	0.26	V.L	383

Total no. of family = 383

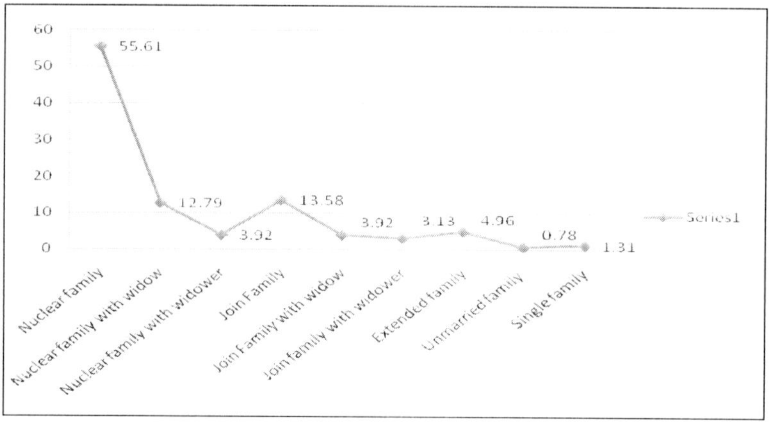

Fig. 35.1: Family type distribution

Clan

The society is composed of various social groups based on kinship and locality. On this kinship based, groups are more important in all spheres of life. The Monsang Naga tribal society is a part of larger Naga society in term of kinship nomenclature. This Endogamous tribe is divided into two major exogamous clans - (i) *Rinnheti* (Luwangcha) and (ii) *Simputi* (Ningthoucha). The families of a clans are related through an assumption of common blood ties i.e. affinal kin. They are supposed to have descended from a common ancestor. Because of this relation, parents and children, brother and sister and marriage between individuals belong to the same clan is considered incestuous; therefore marriage among the same clan is strictly prohibited in this Monsang society. The *Rinnheti* and *Simputi* clans are divided into 13 sub-clans shown in table No. 35.5, out of the 13 kin groups of Monsang, *Sherbumti, Hranglumti,* and *Enhla-Bungjir* are not found.

Table 35.4: Monsang sub-clan

***Rinnheti* (Luwangcha)**		***Simputi* (Ningthoucha)**	
1	Thesongti	1	Ngoroti
2	Wanglarti	2	Koroti
3	Rohinsti	3	Thumhliti
4	Shongsirti	4	Charahti
5	Hongmti	5	Sherbumti
6	Khartu – Bingpich	6	Hranglumti
7	Enhla – Bungjir		

However, their homeland and agricultural areas are found even today. Wanglarti is the highest frequency family included (17 percent) which is followed by The Songti (16 percent), Thumhliti (15 percent), Ngoroti (14 percent) and Shongsirti (12 percent) etc. the smallest clan having only 0.52 percent is Charahti.

Table 35.5: Exogamous Kin group distribution

Clan group	*Sub-Clan group*	*Family included*	*P.C.*
Rinhreti	Thesongti (Ts)	64	16.71
	Wanglarti (W)	67	17.49
	Rohineti (R)	6	1.57
	Shonngsirti (Sh)	46	12.01
	Hongamti (H)	14	3.66
	Khartu – bingpich (Kh)	35	9.14
Simputi	Ngoroti (Ng)	57	14.88
	Koroti (K)	34	8.88
	Thumhliti	58	15.14
	Chahliiti (Ch)	2	0.52
	Sherbumti	0	-
	Hranglumti	0	-
	Enhla – Bungjir	0	-

Marriage System

The history of Monsang Naga tribe shows that the first marriage system was established at the time of Thumpungpa. Following pie chart shows engagement and love marriage are practiced by the Monsang per customary laws. However engagement marriage which the parents and elders of prospective groom and decide matter was much preferred in the olden times. Nowadays traditional forms of marriage are becoming less frequent. Marriage by mutual consent is more common this day. As mention above, the Monsang society has two major clans *Rinnheti* and *Simputi.*

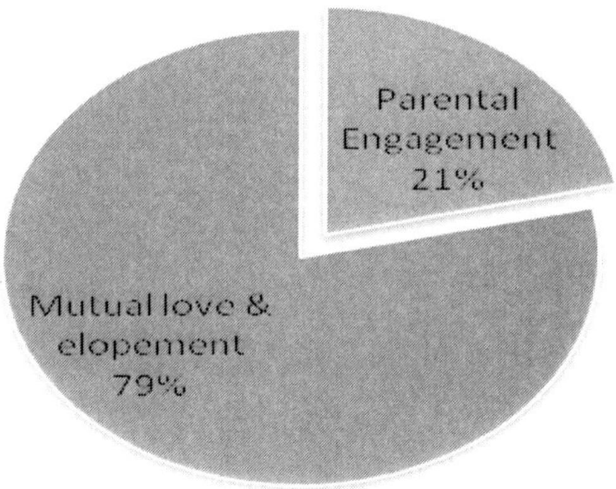

Pie Chart 35.1: Types of marriage distribution

A boy from Simputi can marry to a girl from Rinnheti, thus a boy from Rinnheti is also can marry from Simputi. The Monsang customary law allow marriage between two main clans but intermarriage among the same clan is strictly prohibited. If sometimes, the same clan is married, elders separated them, "Even the child, if born to them, is murdered since this killing is illegal it is no long in practice". However nowadays intermarriage between certain sub clan with same clans are allowed by the village authority according to there declaration of 1998 reformed rule at *Liwa Khullen.* Forexample - marriage between *shongsirti* and *wanglarti* is now allowed. There is a patrilocal marriage residence. And polygamy is also not practice in the Mongsang society. If a person is found having any concubine or extra marital relationship with any female, he has to pay a fine - a Pig and a pot of wine to his in-laws.

From the census operation table No. 35.6, the Monsang Naga tribal society recorded as 729 persons are marriage both male and female. Male are commonly marries 20 -25 years whereas female are marries commonly 15 to 20 years of age that is boys does not encourage early marriage. Marriage above 30 years is not regular feature among the boys and girls.[4]

Irregular marriage

The Monsang customary laws do not allow the following irregular marriage such as capture, intermarriage between members of same sub clan (e.g.- Wanglarti - Wanglarti), adulterous marriage with other wives, advanced secret marriage before engagement and widow re-marriage (Now allowed freely). However, this form of irregular marriage of occurs very often. For such cases are imposed punishments according to their light and heavy degree of guilt.

Table 35.6: Age at marriage distribution

	1	2	3	4	5
Male	0.55	16.94	36.89	29.23	16.39
Female	6.61	39.39	33.06	13.5	7.44
Range of Age	10-15	16-20	21-25	26-30	31-above

Divorce

Divorce is prevalent in the Monsang society. If it happens, heavy penalty is inflicted upon the person who is responsible for the separation. Thus in Monsang society there two type of divorce- (1) *Divorce from male's side* - If a man does not accept the girl as his wife after being seduced, the male shall pay a fine of rupees Rs.150/-. Over and above, he has to pay the unavoidable fine in the form of a Pig which measures 5 wais. In the case of non-convert, a jar of wine shall be accompanied with other fines. If in the case of separation just after marriage - all the article given to her at the time of marriage should go to her; she received half of their earnings; and if the couple have children the man received those children.

(2) *Divorce from Female's side* - If a marriage woman during the life time of her husband gets herself remarried to another man, she should give Rs. 1000/- to her previous husband, and one Pig and a jar of wine to the village. Following the divorce of this nature, she is not entitled to any property from the previous husband, she has no right to claim over the return of her bride price paid during her marriage.

Mating Patterns

The customary law of Monsang Naga tribe allowed to marry between two main clans but inter marriage among the same clan is strictly restricted. However, nowadays inter marriage between certain sub clan with same clan are allowed by the village authority. Although some sub - clans like *Thesongti, Hongmti,*

Roheneti, wanglarty, Sherbumti, Charahti, Thumhti, Hraylumti and *Ngoroti* etc. -Such sub clans are not allowed to marry among themselves even today i.e. marry among themselves is strictly prohibited. Because they consider such, sub clans as their own nearest or closer relationship.

The finding shows that the Monsang population strictly represents a Mandelian population. The Mendalian population refers to a population that is interbreeding without major restriction and are sharing a common gene pool and sufficiently well defined geographically and in other ways for meaningful sample to be taken from it and within which we study different characters. Although deviations from random mating are seen with respect to certain social factors etc. these population chosen for present study truly represent the Mandelian populations and thus each has its own identity. They strictly follow the rule of Indogamy. Although in literature, it is said that they follow the clan exogamy. Thus among the Monsang Naga tribe, we get the sub cash exogamy.

Inheritance of Property

According to the Monsang custom the eldest son, receive the granary whereas youngest one receives the house constructed by their father. The youngest son lives with the old father up to his last days. If the property include landed property and other transferable property those are distributed equally to all the sons. In case of the person who does not have any male issue, the properties may be transferred to female children. Despite this fact, the properties were distributed among the consanguineous male relative. Women are deprived of all the rights, some portion of the father's property was given in the form of bride - wealth to all the married female children.[5] As soon as eldest son get married, they construct a new house for themselves and live separately. In the same manner, other children are also separated from their parental families. Thus youngest son remain with the father at the latter's house.

In the olden time, the Monsang has depended solely on shifting cultivation. Every household *had* separate jhum fields of their own. In case of person who has not left behind any male issue, I: the jhum field are distributed among the person belonging to the deceased person's clan. In the village if there is no any blood relative, those field are distributed among the villager. Nobody can alienate any piece of paddy field to any person. However, he can alienate with the consent of the villager. Again, if any person cultivate at another clan's field, he has to pay some sort of reality in the form of wine or cash money.[6]

At the time of distributing the father's property to his children, they are singing the following songs:[7]

When my father distributed property, I was not given gong. Your father sheds tear on his in ability to give you a gong. Daughter: Your mother has not given any cattle from her stock. Mother: Your mother sheds tears when she thinks for you.

Political Organization

The meaning of the word 'politics' or 'political Institution' is often uncertain because of varying usages. Political organization has been defined structurally by reference to institution that regulates the use of force and functionally within the reference to social co-operation and leadership. Political organization can be described in terms of the processes of decision-making found in a given population.

The Monsang Naga tribe is a peace loving community, keeping their own integrity of the traditional and customary law. That is every Monsang villages has their own administration of traditional village councilors headed by a chief of village called *Irungpa.* This village councilors are not heredity i.e. they are selected as the wisest and most able man by the villagers. They are the law makers and responsible for maintaining law and order in the village and implementation of all the welfare and development programmes of the village. In 1938, the Monsang community firstly brought direct National Political Organization. Before this year, there is no nature and function of the traditional village councilors i.e. there is the institution of *Khulakpa* (hereditary chieftainship). In fact, village authority is only additional little designing by the Government because the traditional village councilors and the village authority members are one and the same person functioning under a combines title. In the view of village and their population, the Monsang village was governed by a village council headed by the traditional leader called 'Irungpa' and 13 number of other elected counselors which belong to the Monsang Naga tribe as follows -

(1) ***Eruwng* (Chief):** He is the head of the village. His main duty was looks after the administration of village. In every field of development programmes of the village, his subordinates execute the works with his prior approval.

(2) ***Senapati* (Secretary):** He is next to the chief, some time if the chief is not present in the village, he acted as the Head of the village.

(3) ***Khula* (Member):** He is the third number of member in the village council. He is incharge of the whole village society. Particularly he looks in the field of development programme.

(4) ***Lula* (Member):** He is the fourth No. village council and has a officer rank. His main responsibility work is to maintain co-operation and harmony among the villagers.

(5) ***Mantri*** **(Member):** He is also a member of the village council and his main duty is assist the Khula.

(6) ***Pakhangla*** **(Member):** He is next to Mantri. His main duty is in-charge of the youths, train them to build up their good careers.

(7) ***Chingsangla*** **(Member):** He is also a member of the village council. His main work is incharge of inter community relationship between one another in a village.

(8) ***Meitei Lampu*** **(Member):** He takes an important role in their society that is he controls the social relationship with the valley people and looks after the outsiders in the village.

(9) ***Jupanba*** **(Member):** He takes incharge of the collection of any tax in the village.

(10) ***Nharak*** **(Member):** He is also a village council member and mainly looks after the child welfare of the village.

(11) ***Wangkherapa*** **(Member):** He is mainly responsible for the arrangement and the collection of information during social festivals and meetings. He also looks the delegates providing lodging and fooding etc.

(12) ***Lanching*** **(Member):** He always supervised the village common feast or meeting as to serve the village councilors according to their social status.

(13) ***Selung and Keirung*** **(Lowest member):** They are the lowest post in the village council. They look after the councilors during the meeting and act as servers.

The above mention village councilors, there is no fixed term from the offices. Any officials can enjoy the leadership as long as people find tenacity on him. Any vacancy caused in the event of death or resignation the next smaller officer fills and his place is again filled up in like manner. A majestic feast follows the enrolment of person to village council. Thus, all of the village councilors look after the administration of the village, maintenance of law and order, punishment of lawbreakers according to customary laws, management of the distribution of the agricultural land, collection of house taxes and construction of roads and bridges.

Social Structure

The Monsang Naga tribe has their own identity dialect as the name of family member, days, months, and numerical etc. In a family, the naming of the child is done by the parent and have systematical in born names for male and female. These inborn names are always used in addressing one another in the society.[8] Here the names would bring in lines with English:

Naming system of family: ***English to Monsang***

Male (Pashar)		*Female (Nepene)*	
Grand-Father	*Apu*	Grand-Mother	*Api*
Father	*Apa*	Mother	*Enna*
Eldest Son	*Momo (Moti)*	Eldest daughter	*Titi (Tinu)*
Second Son	*Koko (Koti)*	Second daughter	*Toto (Tonu)*
Third Son	*Bebe (Beti)*	Third daughter	*Pepe (Penu)*
Four Son	*Angang (Angti)*	Four daughter	*Shangshang (Shangnu)*
Youngest Son	*Thumpa*	Youngest daughter	*Thum Thum (Thumnu)*
Uncle	*Apati*	Aunty	*Anati*

Name of Days, Months and Numerical in Monsang dialect

Name of days:		*Name of months in Monsang dialect:*	
Sunday	*Rhingnei*	January	*Thatuwrbuw*
Monday	*Tharnei*	February	*Meneitha*
Tuesday	*Ngamnei*	March	*Khosaammhotte*
Wednesday	*Pwarnei*	April	*Ttepuw*
Thursday	*Lernei*	May	*Minchiim*
Friday	*Minnei*	June	*Phurwa*
Saturday	*Khamnei*	July	*Diipa*
		August	*Yiengmour*
		September	*Jeingpuw*
		October	*Aeram*
		November	*Mintang*
		December	*Pherveh*

Numerical			
One	*Ingkhe*	Twenty	*Sumnhii*
Two	*Enhii*	Thirty	*Sumthum*
Three	*Enthum*	Forty	*Sumnellii*
Four	*Mellii*	Fifty	*Sumnga*
Five	*Ronga*	Sixty	*Sumruw*
Six	*Kuruw*	Seventy	*Sumsarii*
Seven	*Sarii*	Eighty	*Sumeriih*
Eight	*Eriih*	Ninety	*Sumekuw*
Nine	*Ekuw*	Hundred	*Chama*
Ten	*Suwm*	Thousand	*Lishing ingkhe*

Educational Composition

When we study the demography of any place, the educational condition of that peoples are also very important. Here we accept literacy as ability to read and write, it is clear from the record of the sample survey that the illiterate section of the population occupies about one-fifth (1/5) of the total. The No. of illiteracy of male is lower by margin of 80 than that of female.[9] The level of illiteracy is pushed upward in the children age-group i.e. 0-5 perhaps late schooling might be one of the reason. Most of the literate adult population is found between std. VI - std. X. There are 84 males graduate degree holder as against 70 females graduate.[10] However, female largely cannot move beyond to quality herself for master's degree. There is only 2 females in this category as against 14 males holding the same standard. By a large by the Monsang take interested in their children's education. These may be due to presence of good educational institution and having a well family economic condition.

Occupation

The people are generally agriculturist, cultivating paddy in the flooded field. Both male and female participate in the cultivation in their capacity at various stages. Ploughing and sowing is however done mainly by male while transplantation and weeding is done by female section. About 20 percent of male population is directly employed in the activity as a primary occupation whereas 64 percent of male population is engaged as cultivation of paddy as secondary occupation. And 18 percent of female population is directly employed in the activity as a primary occupation whereas 86 percent of female population is engage as a cultivation of paddy as a secondary occupation. Among them other subsidiary occupation, salaried person engaged as government employed, private employed, health volunteer and business etc. This shows that both male and female of this society, are interested in outdoor activities. A part from cultivation and government employee the main activities of female—housekeeping, weaving, firewood collection and business (vegetable) etc. And other activities of male accounting for only 10 to 20 person became village community administration service, basketry, fishing, driving of vehicle, mason mistry, carpenter, business (shopkeeper) and rice mill keeper etc. But now-a-days, in Monsang society government service are more interested due to increase of literacy as well as good communication and information.[11]

Festival

The Monsang Naga tribe has a rich of traditional festival. Most of the festivals are related with the socio-religious function. The important festivals are briefed bellows -

***Ekam*:** Ekam is the festival of remembering their own custom or culture. It is one of the important and biggest feasts of Monsang Naga tribes. It is not celebrated every year. This festival is offered by only rich man. It has celebrated into five stages or five day and man who performs these five stage is regarded as a rich man. Within this festival, the people of Monsang and other neighboring villages will wear their customer dresses and ornament as well as they will dance and singing a song with happily. After the dancing, all the people will take their lunch with tea, meat, and Wine etc.

Harvesting Festival (Bohrin-Esha): It is the festival of harvest celebration. It is the one of the most important festival among the Naga tribes of

Manipur. In Monsang it is known as *Bohrin-Esha.* Every year 23rd October, when the harvesting comes, all the villagers were celebrated follows by a public feast. The main theme by the harvesting festival was pray to God with a ritual service for the village to have good harvest of the year. It is under practice till now and this day 23rd October was given holiday all the schools, colleges and other government offices of the Chandel District of Manipur.[12]

Nakathengba (Yakhanthin): It is the festival of inauguration celebration of a newly build house. This festival mainly celebrated in the inauguration day of newly build house. In this day the house owner can be held *a* public feast if the hosts can afford. This festival is practice continuously still today.[13]

***Good-Friday*:** It is the remember celebration festival of Jesus Christ's death and birth. In this day all the villagers of the Monsang Naga tribe were enjoyed, they have bring various kind of vegetable and animal as they have can at Church in the morning. Then all the villagers were pray to God with happiness and they have taken feast all together. Thus the festival was closed. Every year this festival was celebrated.

Mangla Thaba or Abaar Enthtfic (Their chong): It is also a ritual festival of memorial stone erection. It is generally performed in the month of March. If the death occurs in the month of April, the ritual is performed in the month of March of the following year. If one is unable to celebrate this ritual it can be carried out through another alternative in which he offers one dog, two packets of tam, some arum maize, pulses and wine. These offers are made at the burial area. This day, man and woman can give feast or wine to the people. A stone will be erected in the memory of the man and woman.

***Christmas*:** It is one of the biggest and famous festivals of the persons who has Christianity. It was held annually on the night of 24th December upto 26th December. During this time, all the villagers-rich, and poor will be share all together. They will pray to God and enjoyed the whole day and night with dance and sing a song. During the day time, they will take feast all together at a particular place or ground with meat. After feast, they will play a no. of traditional games.

New year Celebration (Kum Ethar): Every year, after the harvest this festival was celebrated on the night of 31st December upto the evening of 1st January, On this day, all the Monsang Naga tribe considered it as holiday and no one was allowed to go out of village. On this occasion their houses will be cleaned and decorated. Then burnt the fire by friction of two pieces stone. The entire villagers light the fire and light rise upto heaven and that moment the people declares the Happy New Year. The next day the priest drove evils sprite with wine and piece of meat outside the village gate. Then the priest was also closed the New Year Celebration. He did not occupied any post in the village council.

Death

From the early time to even today, the Monsang Naga tribal people were not cremated the death body. They buried the death body in the local graveyard. This function is mainly conducted by the head of the family or by the chief of the clan. Women are not allowed to perform death ceremony. During the non-Christianity, the people of Monsang were not used coffin (A wooden box) but after they have Christianity, they were used coffin when they buried the death body. If a man has death, first of all, the death body was keep on the flat and washed with water. Then a white cloth will cover all across above the whole death body. After crossing the whole body, it will keep into the coffin and the coffin with death body will bring out to the local graveyard. A prohit who is the leader of the performed funeral rites over will come to the graveyard. Then he will perform ritual service according to their custom for the death body to get peace and he would buried the death body. Thus the prohit will be finished the death body ceremony, After the 15th days or sometime three or four months later, they have celebrated the memorial stone erection, in the memory of death Person. On this day, according to their custom man and woman can give the feast or wine to the people. During thenon-Christianity period, this memorial stone erection celebration was very important by after the Christianity it is not compulsory.

Summary

Socio cultural norms are quite ennobled as depicted in its plethora of festivals and joyful functions. The Monsang tribe has a rich of traditional festival. Most of the festivals are related with the socio-religious function. They have their own mythical origin, distinct life-style, culture, customs, traditions, festivals, and language inherited from their forefathers and preserved in folksongs, folktales, etc. The people of Monsang tribes are more preferred nuclear type of family than the other types. They are successively being patrilineal society with dual organization, exogamous and male dominated society.

The Monsang tribal society is a part of larger Naga society in term of kinship nomenclature. Marriage between individuals belong to the same clan is considered incestuous; therefore marriage among the same clan is strictly Prohibited in this Monsang society. However, nowadays inter marriage between certain sub clan with same clan are allowed by the village authority. The Monsang practices engagement and love marriage as per customary laws. However engagement marriage which the parents and elders of prospective groom and decide matter was much preferred in the olden times. Male are commonly marries 20 -25 years whereas female are marries commonly 15 to 20 years of age that is boys do not encourage early marriage. Divorce is prevalent in the Monsang society. If it happens, heavy penalty is inflicted upon the person who is responsible for the separation.

Regarding inheritance property, the eldest son, receive the granary whereas youngest one receives the house constructed by their father. The youngest son lives with the old father up to his last days. If the property include landed property and other transferable property those are distributed equally to all the sons. Village council headed by the traditional leader called 'Irungpa' governed the Monsang villages and 13 number of other elected counselors which belong to the Monsang tribe.

The Monsang tribe has their own identity dialect as the name of family member, days, months, and numerical etc. In a family, the parents do the naming of the child. Fishing is one of the most important subsistence practices in Monsang villages. The fact that all the Monsang villages are situated on the banks of the two important major perennial rivers i.e. the Chakpi and the Maha Rivers in Chandel district provides an ample opportunity to depend on this subsistence practices. Fishing is carried out both by males as well as females.

In Monsang villages, food gathering especially by women folks is still a living tradition. The hills and forests surrounding the villages abound in many types of wild fruits and plants.

The Monsang society has different types of traditional handicrafts. Being an agricultural society, the making of various types of baskets for different purposes is necessary. Apart from agriculture related baskets and tools, there are also other crafts for household and other basic needs for storage. Weaving is a traditional activity of women folk in the Monsang tribe. In earlier, during the existence of the dormitory system, the art of weaving was believed to be taught inside the dormitory house by the elder woman to young girl s. Even at present, it is commonly noticed that village girl s pick up the knowledge of weaving by giving a helping hand to their mothers or elderly women.

It is very clear that nature has endowed the Monsang Naga villages with rich vegetation and natural landscapes. The rivers, streams, fields and forests around them have been a source of sustenance for people's livelihood in one way or the other.[14] Shifting cultivation in Monsang Naga society continued for many years. With the adoption of wet-rice cultivation since the early twentieth century, the economy of the Monsang Naga was based on a mixed-economy. Most of the present Monsang Naga villages sprouted up on the foot-hills close to the Chakpi river and Maha river belts in the early decades of the twentieth century. Indeed the coming of Christianity sometime in the 1920s and conversion to the new religion brought-forth many changes in the socio-political and cultural existence of the Monsang Naga. Despite the many positive contributions of Christianity to Monsang Naga society, it has, at the same time dismantled some of the rich traditional practices.[15]

References

Northeast today, (Online) available at: http://www.northeasttoday.in/monsang-naga-tribe-celebrates-1st-monsang-cultural-exhibition/, accessed on 22 March 2016

Waanglar Somie, 2016, Material culture and subsistence practices of Monsang Naga society: Continuity and change, Sangai Express, 13 October 2016, p. 6

Majumdar and Madan : An Introduction to social Anthropology N.P.H. Delhi 1987

Ng. Mono, Monsana Naga History Seminar paper Manipur

DAS Tarakchandra, MA - "The Purum-An old Kuki Tribe in Manipur 1945. P. 179.

Interview with R. Konsam Monsang Village Chief Liwa Sarei 19th July, 2001

Interview with Sh. Bitin Monsang 23rd March, 2002

Japhou Women Fellowship, (Japhou Sanuw Ruhkhe Calender Manipur 2002

Census of village household survey of Monsang community for 4th, 5th January, 2001.

SA Answer - Manipur Tribal Demography and Socio-Economic Development 1991 - P. 91.

Ng. Molahring Monsang, "Church on the Rock Theological Seminary" unpublished Master of Divinety Thesis Manipuri University 2003. P. 23.

Waanglar Somie, 2016, Material culture and subsistence practices of Monsang Naga society: Continuity and change, Sangai Express, 13 October 2016, p. 6.

36

Status of Women Among the Khasi's of Saiden Village, Meghalaya

Rongnyoo Lepcha

Gender is a social construct as it is not something we were born with, and not something we have but something we do as explained by (West and Zimmerman,1987).Gender has been defined as "psychological, social and cultural aspect of maleness and femaleness" by (Kesseler and Makenna 1978: 7) or what we understand as the cultural understanding of how men ought to be and how women ought to be, the cultural characteristics taken up by males and females and the maintenance of gender depends on the reinforcement in day-to-day behaviour.

"Gender roles are embedded so thoroughly in our institutions, our actions, our beliefs and our desires, that it happens to us to be completely natural", (Eckert and Ginet 2013). These gender roles form the concept of status in the society. All genders have their status in the society.

Status of women refers to the position of women in the society compared to that of men. The main reason to pursue on women studies is also because women form an integral part of any society without women the society is not complete.

The North eastern region of India presents a picture of women enjoying a better status than their counterparts in the rest of the country, but everything that glitters is not gold, so a deeper understanding of the status of women in the North-East would shatter some of the myths regarding the status of women in the North-East.

This research concentrates not only the women in particular but also involves the men since it is hard to understand the whole scenario without understanding both puzzle pieces. This study also focuses on the various socio-economic activities that women are involved in so as to have a better understanding of their status.

The present study is based on field work conducted in the Saiden village of Ri-Bhoi District of Meghalaya. The population of Saiden follow the matrilineal system, one of the significant features of matriliny is that the decent, title, and inheritance is followed through the female line, and all the members of a clan (*kur*) believe in a common female ancestress called "*kalawbeitynrai*". This sure does elevated the status of women in the family to some level but as it a patriarchal society, the entire decision making lays at the hands of the men in the society.

Since birth the duties are acquired by a child. In the naming ceremony if it is a girl she is given '*da-koh*' a basket signifying that she has to bear the burden of the family, whereas if it is a boy he gets a bow and three arrows signifying the three important duties he has to do protect himself, protection of the family and protection of the community.

Women are considered to be important in the family. Women are considered to be life giver. A Khasi woman is supposed to perpetuate the lineage in turn by producing children. A daughter set up their own household (*ling*) and subsequently acquire the status of "*kalawbeikhynraw*" the young ancestress or as "*kakmietymmen*" the old mother.

Traditionally the property goes to the youngest daughter of the family. Sons have no right to it except in rare cases, if there are no daughters in the family. The position of women in the Khasi society becomes clear when we examine the role of the youngest daughter, who is the traditional heir to the ancestral property of the household. As the heir to the family property, the youngest daughter is not only expected to be closely guided by the counsel of the mother's brother who controls the property but is also obliged to look after her aged parents and other vulnerable members of the family. Hence the youngest daughter is expected to have high moral standards— standards set by the society which is directly or indirectly set by men, so much so that poor moral conduct or religious conversion could result in the loss of her rights. In contrast to the young daughter the elder daughter has more autonomy but due to the absence of ancestral property she is more dependent on her husband. Daughters except the youngest of the family have to start their own family and house after marriage with their husband from another clan.

Marriage holds importance in Khasi society. The research showed that the women are free to choose their spouse yet; marriages are still arranged by the elders. Both young men and women have the freedom in choosing their own spouses but never the less parental consent and especially of the *kni*have to be taken.For marriage it is important to inquire about the groom as it is crucial that he does not belong to the same *kur*. Both parties for marriage meet for a meeting known as *Ar-lyanKha* it is the passing of bill for the marriage called the *Pyn hair syn,* only after the bill is passed that the marriage takes place.

One of the major roles in a Khasi marriage is played by the *kni* he plays the role of a negotiator. The *knis*of both parties (bride and groom) act as negotiators, negotiating marriage terms between both the parties.

According to Gurdon 2010 (pg 76- 79), post-marital residence is matrilocal, with the husband and wife leaving the wife's mother's residence after the birth of one or two children. C. Nakane (1967) makes a further distinction between two types of marriages, the first being marriage to an heiress, the second marriage to a non-heiress. The type of marriage is, for Nakane, the determining factor in marital residence. This practice is the result of rules and regulations governing inheritance and property ownership. These rules are themselves related to the structure of the Khasi*ling*. In short, post-marital residence when an heiress is involved must be uxorilocal, while post-marital residence when a non-heiress is involved is neolocal. Khasi men prefer to marry a non-heiress because it will allow them to form independent family units somewhat immune to pressures from the wife's kin. A Khasi man returns to his *ling* upon the death of his spouse (if she is the youngest daughter. If she is not, he may remain with his children if they are not too young and if he plans to marry his wife's younger sister. Marriage to a deceased wife's elder sister is prohibited. This is the only form of the sororate found among the Khasi. The levirate does not obtain in Khasi society.

Polygamy does not exist among the kasis such a practice would naturally be against the norms of amongst the people who practice matriarchate; however there are instances of men having more than one wives or even extra marital affairs. As the clans are strictly exogamous a khasi cannot take a wife from his own clan. To do this would entail him to the most disastrous religious and social consequences.

By far the Khasi society is believed to be matrilocal in residence after marriage but the findings bring out that after marriage the residence will be matrilocal if a man marries the youngest daughter of the family who is considered to be the custodian of the family and if a man marries a women who is not the youngest daughter of the family then the residence after marriage will be a neolocal one.

When a khasi man marries a non-khasi woman the problem now is in giving a *kur*name to the children in conformity with the matrilineal principle of the descent. The children cannot inherit the *kur*name of their father. Since the mother is a non-khasi, she cannot start a new *kur*as per the khasi kinship norms the children born out of such a marriage are socialised into the khasi customs are traditions and these female children after marriage, starts new *khop*(branches of *kur*).

As far as the findings of this research go there were only a handful of people following the traditional marriage system as the village of Saiden is dominated by Christianity following the Christian ways of marriage though some of the customary laws remain same for instance the post-marital residence remains matrilocal. Today if a khasi marries a non-khasi then the children acquire the lineage of the father into the khasi society maintaining the community's solidarity. Due to various change in the society like education and increasing monetization of the Khasi economy and availability of jobs for men beyond village confines may alter the customary post-marital residence patterns of the society.

Divorce was not so popular though many women were deserted, divorced or mutually separated. Divorce is frequent with causes ranging from incompatibility to lack of offspring, adultery and easily obtainable. Both men and women are allowed to initiate divorce if they want to be separated. Parties who have been divorced cannot remarry one another, but they are at the liberty to marry into other families. A woman cannot be divorced during pregnancy.

In the study area there were many cases of divorce all cases shared the similarities that the husband had abandoned their wives.This research revealed that mostly indulging in extra marital affairs leading to divorce, out of the five samples I could collect three were cases of husband deserting their wives for another women. Many were not reluctant in sharing the information as this is a very sensitive and personal issue for them while I was lucky in getting how much ever they wanted give. The cases I have gathered indicate that women are abandoned by their husbands for other women. Also religious segregations are also responsible for many of the divorces that occur, inter-marriage among different denominations in the end lead to incompatibility of spouses and ultimately they end up getting divorce.one particular case related to alcoholism and domestic violence.

When asked, it revealed that they do not report adultery or domestic violence to the village councils or the village authorities as fear of shaming their own family names.

Status can be earned also due to control over economic access which leads to acquiring power and status. Whether a woman in a family or in the community at large is an earner or is dependent also is one of the factors that affect the status of women. Way back in 1930's the village was very poor and infected by various diseases like Malaria, Cholera, etc. But at present the village have tried hard to be self-sufficient. However 50 percent of the inhabitants are cultivators and 45 percent are the office goers, school teachers and those who have taken up other activities or related jobs.

Although the women in agricultural families perform many farm related activities, the division of labour between men and women varied greatly from regions and activities. Women are involved in most of the operations in agriculture, including subsidiary enterprises like diary, poultry, beekeeping, mushroom cultivation, sericulture.

In Saiden most indulge in agricultural production mostly cash crops and women had equal participation as the men in the society. Agriculture is carried using some of the primitive technology synchronised with some of the modern technologies suited for terrace farming. Broom plants, pineapple, turmeric, black pepper, *kwai*(beetle nuts), beetle leaves are some of the important economic crops grown in the study area and women take active role in the cultivation of these crops. Shops hold another important economic aspect of the village as there are few shops in the village all of them operated by women.

Broom plant cultivation is one of the most important sources of income during the dry seasons (winter). Jhum cultivation is deemed fit for the cultivation of this cash crop, people clear large area of vegetation and cultivate their broom plants in the area. Broom plants are cultivated in large quantities for economic purposes each family has their own plot of land which they clear and cultivate the broom plants, which when matured are plucked by the women folks, dried in the sun for a couple of days and then sold in the market.

Another important plant that is grown is the beetle nut (*kwai*), it not only is a source of income for many families but also holds cultural importance for the community. The folktale provides evidence of the importance of *koi* in the khasi society. It begins with the story of two best friends, one rich and the other poor, the rich friend one day invites his poor friend for dinner he lavishly spends for the dinner and when it comes for the poor friends turn he has nothing much to offer so he offer *kwai*to his rich friend and ashamed of his incapability to treat his friend properly he commits suicide. Form that day onwards *kwai* became of cultural significance to the khasi population, every one consumes *kwai* whether rich or poor and offers it to everyone from in and outside of the community. We rather had many people offering *kwai*to us every day in Saiden. Since it holds cultural importance among the khasi community *kwai*is grown in a certain cleared area under trees so that the trees provide support for the creeper. It is harvested and then brought to the weekly market nearby by the women folk of the community.

The local weekly market is one place where the true colours of gendered division of labour could be observed clearly. Once a week the market comes alive with people pouring in from neighbouring areas for selling and buying local as well as outside products. Women have important role in the local market as most shops were held by women. Selling groceries, garments, local products, local medicines, *Kwai* are all done by women folk of the community. The women also hold food stalls selling local cuisineswhile the men are more involved in selling agricultural tools, and butchery.

Another occupation adopted by the women folk of Saiden is shop keeping in the village there were all together sixshops in the village and all run by women. There are canteens run by women, grocery shops according to some of the shop holders the men of the community shy away from this kind of work and all other jobs are taken away, so the women have to take up these jobs. By running canteens the can earn for themselves and for their family.

Seri Culture is one field where women are required for their skilful hands. A huge manpower is required for sericulture activities throughout the year and the sericulture farmers utilize their family members particularly the aged persons and women folk in it.In saiden, the Ri-bhoi Silk Emporium an effort from the self-help group provides employment for the women folk in and around of saiden. Alongside it the government of Meghalaya have also funded for the handloom, the traditional style of looming and modern technology go hand and hand simultaneously. Handloom Research and Design Development Centre, Nongpoh is the industry where they make silk cloths for the people and some useful item like bags etc. it is founded under the scheme BRGF, Government of Meghalaya, So silk is an animal protein fiber produced by certain insects to build their cocoons and webs. Many different types of silk are produced by a huge variety of different types of insects other than moth caterpillars.

The commercial process of silk making is highly complex and labour intensive. Women were involved fully in all the activities related to silkworm rearing such as, disinfection of rearing house & appliances, incubation of silkworm laying, brushing, feeding of chawki& late age worms, bed cleaning, mounting care etc. in all the locations studied. Muga silk is the most famous of all varieties of silk produced in the state of Meghalaya. Muga silk is also one important material used to make the traditional garments of the Khasis. Women specialise in rearing of the muga silk worm and cleaning of the cocoons manually so that the silk fibres can be drawn out of it through machine later.

Women maintain the temperature of the rooms where the worms and cocoons are kept by not allowing sunlight into the room and this is done by painting the window glasses all black, this also maintains the humidity of the rooms. They look after the feeding when the moths were ready and quickly after the breeding only the female moths are kept in a separate room for laying eggs.

Women are also involved in the weaving and making a variety of finished products out of muga silk like shawls, bags, purses, muffler, cushions, half coats for men, the khasi traditional wears, etc. which are exported to neighbouring areas and also outside of the state.

Cultivation of the silkworm is known as sericulture. Although many insects produce silk, only the filament produced by*Authereaassamensis* or the muga silkworm is reared in most of the North Eastern states as the climatic conditions are very suitable for the rearing of this varierty of silkworm and production of Muga silk. The larvae of *Authereaassamensis*feed onthe leaves of the muga plant. Muga is famous for its natural golden coloured fabric and is used by the commercial silk industry. Hatching the Eggs; the first stage of silk production is the laying of silkworm eggs, in a controlled environment such as an aluminum box, which are then examined to ensure they are free from disease. The female deposits 300 to 400 eggs at a time.

The Feeding Period; Once hatched, the larvae are placed under a fine layer of gauze and fed huge amounts of chopped mulberry leaves during which time they shed their skin four times. The larvae may also feed on Osage orange or lettuce. Larvae fed on muga leaves produce the very finest silk. The larva will eat 50,000 times its initial weight in plant material. The silkworm is now ready to spin a silk cocoon. Spinning the Cocoon; Silkworm attaches itself to a compartmented frame, twig, tree or shrub in a rearing house to spin a silk cocoon over a 3 to 8 day period. This period is termed pupating.

After the cocoons have been fully formed it is again the job of the women folk to separate cocoons into good cocoons which are kept separately for taking out the silk fabrics, bad cocoons which are thrown away and the cocoons which they keep separately allowing the silk moths to come out of it and continue the silk cycle all over again. Reeling the Filament at this stage, the cocoon is treated with hot air, steam, or boiling the cocoons chosen for drawing out the silk are then boiled in water with soda and then the women clean the cocoons and draw out the very thin filaments. then the cocoons goes into the machine where the silk filaments are drawn out, at least 10 to 12 filaments are required to make up one silk thread. The silk is then unbound from the cocoon by softening the sericin and then delicately and carefully unwinding, or 'reeling' the filaments from 4 - 8 cocoons at once, sometimes with a slight twist, to create a single strand.

Types of Silk; Raw silk is twisted into a strand sufficiently strong for weaving or knitting. This process of creating the silk yarn is called "throwing," and prevents the thread from splitting into its constituent fibers. Four different types of silk thread may be produced from this procedure: crepe, tram and thrown singles, androgenize. Crepe is made by twisting individual threads of raw silk, doubling two or more of these together, and then twisting them again. Tram is made by twisting two or more threads in only one direction. Thrown singles are individual threads that are twisted in only one direction. Organzine is a thread made by giving the raw silk a preliminary twist in one direction and then twisting two of these threads together in the opposite direction, so that thread is use for making cloths and other articles.

Due to this mode of economy many in the village have opted for the cultivation of muga plant for the seri-culture factory based in *Mawpadang*. However the numbers of women working in the silk factory from saiden is considerably low.

Education is another field where women are trying to make their mark for centuries. Prior to the infiltration of the education system of the Indian government in the village many agreed to the fact that it was actually the missionaries who first started education system in the village and according to some the schools even had religious learning's as one of the subject. But in the very beginning it was only the men who pursued education and women were not so much encouraged later slowly the scenario changed and girls were encouraged to study but if the family economy was in a bad condition they would rather drop out.

There are three schools in Saiden village all co-education schools:

1. Government Upper Primary School
2. Saiden Senior School
3. Jubilee Presbyterian Upper Primary School, in*Mawpadang*.

In Saiden most women population have had the basic primary education, but many had failed to pursue further and higher education because poor economic conditions in the past. The present generation though are rapidly grabbing the modern education system. Most were happy to send their daughters to school and also outside for further studies.

The ICDS with all employees being women in the village also work for the education of women in the village, they provides non-formal education for children and mainly focus on girls. Non Formal Pre School education or Pre Primary School was set up in the village. Besides receiving salary from the ICDS office, the village also grants certain amount for the workers to run the school for children in the ages of three to six. Preparing the children for formal education by teaching alphabets, rhymes, reciting poems and so on.

Women though have great involvement in the social sphere of the village their status in the political is interesting, as under the sixth schedule most of the states of the North East region of India including Meghalaya have the privilege of Autonomous District Councils, the people are allowed to follow their own traditional political institutions and Saiden included has its own. The *DorbarShnong* at the village level headed by a *RangbaShnong*(the headman).

In Saiden village, headman is called as *Rongbashonong* which is not hereditary phenomenon, and village has unique way of appointing its headman. *Rongbashnong* means a Khasi male adult administrative head or village headman nominated unanimously by *u khun u hajar*(the citizens/ general mass) of the village *dorbar*, under the administrative control of the khasi *Hima* (s). Again here the citizens include only the male members of the village who is above 18 years, no woman is allowed for the election of the headman. The election of the headman is done by simply raising their hand, if they like the candidate. The elected headman has to work as voluntary service if he goes against the law and the rules of the village than villagers have power to dismiss them from their post as headman, which is for three years and elect another headman from the village. Headman in Saiden is voluntary service they don't get paid from the government like the Panchayat heads in other states of India. Though they adapt the rules of state government but they never neglect their own system. They give more importance and save their customary law, which is still prevalent in modern society today.

Women do not possess any significant role in the political sphere, they are not even allowed for the selection of their leader. Though the women are independent in many aspects they still have to be subordinate to the men. The main power lies in the hands of the men of the society which is clearly visible in the election of the headman which lowers their status eventually.

In the area of political hardly any women actively participate. Even the society does not allow women to participate in political decision-making. Till now any woman Headman of a Dorbar is hardly found. Also they do not participate much into political discourses. Only recently women are allowed on a very limited scale to participate in Dorbar meeting. Also they do not have any such programs that would help in the empowerment of the women folk, more strongly this is also because most women do not seem to be interested in politics.

There have been recent new about the changing political scenario in the villages of Meghalaya including Saiden. The women feel that they are being neglected in the field of politics they are now questioning their age old system of Headmanship just recently. This change now may bring the levels of the women status in the field of politics to an equal to that of the men.

Though having their own traditional way of governing body Meghalaya still comes under the Indian government as it is part of our country. In contrast to the traditional system of governing of the khasis democracy on the other hand is ruled by the people, now the question arisesas to who participates in the political decisions, which is one of the most fundamental questions of democracy. Men and women in Saiden take collective decision regarding which political party to vote. It is often that the KhasiStuden Union an autonomous political body mainly involving the youths of the community, who tell the people whom to elect.

The Women Organisation

What the women lost in the political sphere of the community they gain in the women organization of the village, established in 1977 for the betterment of the village especially the women population of the village. It consists of women member but who are already married. There are fifteen members who work for the betterment of the women of the village. They provide help for women who are in need of it. But the members have not been working intensely for the development of the women rather they focus more on the betterment of the village, they work for the cleanliness of the village, every Saturday, and it was their efforts and the vision of the village headman Saiden won the 'Clean and Green village' award in 2013, a sum of 2 lakh from the government of Meghalaya which was kept by the headman to be used for needs of the village.

By women organization one thinks it's an all women organization but the members include:

- K. Namsaw -the president from Saiden (female),
- R. Lyngdoh- vice president (female),
- T. Marsing- the secretory (female),
- P. Tham- assistant secretory (female),
- G.H. Kharsanlor- the advisor (male),
- T. S Syngkli- the financer (female),
- B. Lyndoh- the treasurer (female).

The other members include M. Kharshandi, B. Thankew, BinaSyiem, S.A. Synkli, Wan Sunday Lapang, A. Synkli, D. Lyndoh, P. Ranee, all female members.

When asked to the headman about the advisor of the women organization being a man he explained that women are rationally weak in taking decisions and get emotionally involved so it'll be difficult for them to take strict and rational actions and they find it hard to handle situations. This is also the reason why the headman explains there are no women leaders in the community.

The women organization play active role in maintaining and taking part in the socio-cultural sports club where both boys and girls of the village are encouraged in taking participation in sports. One of the members of the women organization, Please-meeRanee is an athlete herself, running in marathons for which she has won numerous awards.

The women organization plays an important role controlling the village and its rules. the members of the women organization patrol the village regularly and strictly at nights and during special occasions like at times of festivals or any programs in the village and catch those defying the public rules and norms, like fighting, intoxication and if anyone caught indulging in such acts are summoned to the headman where they are given warnings at first and if they repeat their action again they are punished by handing them over to the police.

The women organization of saiden provide counseling for women, who are in need of it especially the ones victims of domestic violence. Though the women organization do not provide any particular schemes to provide health awareness or health programs specifically for the women but they still provide medical help whenever there is a need for it like rushing a patient to the hospital, financial support, etc.

A plot of land is provided by the headman of the village to the women organization where they cultivate broom plants, pineapple, oranges, muga plant for seri-culture and with the money they get from selling the end products they invest the money on the betterment of the village. The last broom sale brought them a good amount of money with which they bought a number of dustbins for the village. Other than this the money is deposited in the bank to be used for the welfare of the women.

The women organization also have active role to play during the any cultural and religion festivals in the village, they concern with the preparing lunch, snacks for the program.

The unequal power status between men and women of this matrilineal village can be seen in the power distribution among the genders. On one hand the women are not allowed in the process of election of the headman. On the other hand the advisor of the women organization is always a male and appointed by the headman.

The changing scenario of the world has already started affecting the mind sets of the women of the community, many want that there be equal opportunities for both men and women in the village or the community at large. They feel that it is necessary for the women of the community to be allowed to take active participation in each and every aspect as the men.

Throughtheir endless efforts the women of Saiden have achieved a strong hold in the society they have not only limited themselves to the social works but have active indulgence in all spheres.By large women of India accepted modern sports and games rather late due to their conservative society. They usually had their own traditional games which they used to participate within themselves. During pre-independence era some selective participation was noticed in some selected states but in totality it was rather negligible. During initial period of independence the trend was more or less same. It was encouraged later in the north east states of India since in all respect awareness arrived late.

After independence both men and women were encouraged to participate in modern sports and games. Women of the north east arrived late in the scene but soon picked up very fast to establish their credentials. More are coming up in athletics too a few are attracting attention.

In Saiden the participation of women in sports can be seen to be in rise as a result of the efforts put in by the Women Organisation. One of the extraordinary women is Please Mee Rani, an active member of the Women Organisation and the Sports Club, she started running again and in 2nd October 2008 she won first prize in a 10 kilometre marathon in Shillong on the occasion of Rajiv Gandhi AkshyaUrjaDiwas. It was the first time she had gone out of the village she was supported by the Saiden Sports Club. After this there was no stop to her racing career.

She ran again in a 21 kilometre marathon in Shillong. On 2014 she stood second in the marathon Run for Democracy at Shillong in the women category above 50 years. Again in 25th January 2015 she took part in Run for Democracy marathon on the occasion of National Voters Day in which she again stood second and won the sum of 15,000 and a certificate.

She again participated in a marathon in 2015 on Meghalaya Day Run and received first prize a sum of 10,000 rupees and a certificate. According to her Run for Democracy was her biggest achievement in 2014 and 2015.She plans in pursuing her dreams further even at the age to 55 she says she would continue to run until she can no more.

Conclusion

Women though have a very high status culturally in the Matrilineal Khasi society they are still trying to gain a lot more socially. Women are regarded to be *kabalang Shi-bor* (having one power) in local term *kakyntheikabalang Shibor.* Meaning women having only one power, this is how a Khasi woman is perceived by the society. According to the people of Saiden the one power of the women refer to the physical strength of the women.This concept evolved during the early ages where the women could not hunt, efficiently as the men or smelting irons for making tools women could not complete with the men where there was the need for use of muscular and physical strength involved. The phrase "*kakyntheika long kum i kheiwkhyndew*" means a woman is like a small pot, depicting she has little power or strength.

Another explanation given by the people of Saiden in the as to why women have only the power also goes back to the role decision making. Women are not considered fit to be a member of any council especially in deciding matters concerning the welfare of the clan, the village, the Raid/Raij and the Hima- the four levels of local administration prevailing in the society. According to the people of Saiden a woman is not considered fit to take part in making laws nor is she allowed to take part in legal proceeding or to become a priest.

These restrictions have therefore deprived her of the chance to share the responsibility in the most of the matters like the political or the religious matters considered fit only for the men.

So in comparison to women, men are said to have twelve powers. Men are considered to be physically stronger. They are also considered to be mentally and intellectually stronger. And because they are physically stronger, therefore they are able to perform many arduous activities which women cannot do. Again men are also considered to possess were reasoning power and having higher rational ability in taking decisions that concern the welfare of the members of the clan, the village, the *Raid* or the *Hima.*

These have led to the moulding of the attitude of the society to consider men as being "*u rang khatar-bor*" (*rang*- male, *khatar*- twelve, *bor*-power), or in other words the one having twelve powers.

Though traditionally the women (especially the youngest one) are supposed to inherit ancestral property, today this system is fast changing due to factors like education of the young generations, modernization, and also religion, other daughters other than the youngest also get equal share in the family property, even men do inherit property today due to the changing society as the people of Saiden call it. Though earlier female used to more or less dominate in the field of various economic activities now-a-days men are involving rapidly in different activities mainly the modern economic sectors which is further more declining the status of women.

More females are uneducated than male. Data reveals that, now the high collar jobs are mostly occupied by the men in majority though there are women who occupy high jobs in saiden but the income of the female-headed households are relatively less, because men have the economic advantage of being the bread earner of the family in many cases. Yet the female better manage the family and give more emphasis on the human development indicators like education, health etc. "Women in the rural Khasi society are free from any limitation and can participate freely in any function of social and religious importance." this is the general idea about women of the North East but this prejudice is not very true the women do respect the men and so they are not entirely free, also referring to the religious freedom there are many limitations for the women, a women *Lyndogh*is rarely seen till date. There are many instances where the consent of men is very much required and the decision making is mutual between men and women in the family.

But psychological the women are not free and they feel much dependent on men. Still now, the rural Khasi women are not well aware of their political rights as women are kept aloof from the political sphere. To them political decision-making is not much important. Though local body like *Dorbar* is much powerful, their participation in such bodies also minimal. Even most of them do not believe in reservation in the local bodies or other constitutional areas that would help raising their status in the society. Rather they like to devote more on their social and economic activities for their welfare.

Though the Khasi society is known to be matrilineal and the women do exercise certain privileges still the main authority behind the mask of matrilinity is always a male, the *kni*. So we can well imagine the position of women in a society where they are perceived to hold high status but this is not the entirely picture. They only have privileges in certain spheres like inheritance of property and the decision making sphere also seem to be more or less equal with the men. But in the political and religious sector the women of the village have very less participation as well as low status.

Economy is one sector where the women can be seen doing much better in the society. There are many women who are earning and this provides an advantage in controlling of the family economy, in turn leading to a higher status of women in the family, especially for those who do not inherit the family property.

Inheritance in khasi society has always have been the domain of the women but here also there are disparities within women themselves. Only the youngest daughter is entitled to inherit the ancestral property and the other daughters do get their share yet the lion's share always goes to the youngest daughter.

The residence after marriage can also interpret the status of individuals in the society. The Khasi follow the matrilocal residence system but again this is only in the case of the youngest daughter or the one who inherits the family property (often the youngest daughter), only in cases of the death of the youngest daughter the other daughter gets the property instead. Also the youngest daughter cannot convert religions. If she does, she will lose her ancestral wealth and properties, but this is no more relevant since almost the whole population of Saiden follows Christianity.

It is however essential to adopt new measures for the improvement of education, income of the females to fill the gap between male and female. As female manage family better they would be able to further the welfare of the family members and thus the society.

References

Eckert, Penelope and Ginet, Sally Mcconell. 2013. *Language and Gender.* Cambridge: Cambridge University Press.

Kessler, Suzanne. J. and Mckenna, Wendy. 1978. *Gender: An Ethnomethodological Approach*. Chicago, University of Chicago Press.

West, Candace and Zimmerman, D.H. 1987. *Doing Gender*. Gender and Society 1:125-51.

37

Understanding Life in the Inter-State Borderlands of Assam and Arunachal Pradesh

Ratna Tayeng

Introduction

This paper is based on my ongoing research on Assam-Arunachal Pradesh borders. This border is an administrative interstate border dividing the two states of a single nation. Put differently, it is a boundary that divides hill and plain set up by the colonial rulers. The sole purpose of creating this border was to contain the movement of the people into the neighboring plain which were caused problems to the British administration. Their concern with the hillmen was that they should not come in the way of acquisition of land and forest areas required for establishing tea gardens (Reid, 1942).

However, with the passing of time the political influence of "dividing line" has grown stronger. It ultimately helps in developing a sense of distinctiveness among the people and a sense of imaginative communion – "Arunachali". Today, the people of the state argue that peace, development and prosperity of the state lie in this border. It gives them a sense of security and freedom. According to Berdalh Daphne (1999) "borders are artifacts of history and are subject to change over time. When borders shift, lands and peoples are subjected to changes".

The history of this borderland begins on June 30, 1947, when The North East Frontier (Assam) Tribal and Excluded Area Sub Committee (popularly known as Bordoloi Committee) was constituted under the leadership of Gopinath Bordoloi and Mr. Justice Bijan Kumar Medhi. The Committee was asked to prepare a report on the future pattern of the administration of North East Frontier Tracts and submit it to the President of India before August 25, 1950.

The Commission submitted its report on August 22, 1950 to the President of India. The committee recommended that govt. of Assam to take over the administration of NEFT. However this recommendation was overlooked and centre continued to administered North East Frontier Tracts as "excluded area" through the governor of Assam. Their recommendation for transfering of certain plain areas of the North East Frontier Tracts to Assam on the ground that "the people of these plain areas should not be denied the advantages of franchise and regular administration" was accepted. This report was accepted by the Minority Sub Committee of the Constituent Assembly presided over by Late Sardar Ballabh Bhai Patel in 1950. And once the presidential assent was obtained, Assam, having the authority, formally notified the report on 23.02.1951 that demarcated the 756 kms boundary between the then NEFT and Assam.

The notification excluding these areas from the North East Frontier Tracts was issued on 23-02-1951. As a result a new territory was produced which three years later became the North Eastern Frontier Agency popularly called NEFA (present Arunachal Pradesh). Presently, the boundary between Assam and Arunachal runs from the tri-junction of Assam, Arunachal and Bhutan at Bhairabkundo on the west bank of Dhansiri River to the tri-junction of Assam, Nagaland and Arunachal on the Tiok River on the east. It has a length of about 716 kilometers.

The Boundary

Located on the periphery of the Indian state, Arunachal Pradesh had a long cultural and economic isolation, as a consequence, the feeling of being isolated and being different is predominant among Arunachalee — a sense of separateness and otherness from the heartland and its population, economically, culturally, and historically. This boundary as object of cultural differences was planted when our first Prime Minister Pandit Jawaharlal Nehru proclaimed that "we should not allow NEFA people to be engulfed by the masses of Indian humanity. We should avoid-over- administering these areas and in particular, sending too many outsiders into tribal territory (quoted from Elwin, 1957). Ever since then, fear of being dominated by 'plains culture' through the influx of 'outsiders' remain a reality. Nevertheless, this is an understandable fear considering small tribal population, standing at around one 15 lakhs as per 2001 census.

The problem with this distinction is that it presumes that there is a unified 'plains' culture and similarly a unified 'hill' culture, or even unified Arunachali culture. According to Sanjib Baruah "The issue has become politically volatile because the present day Arunachal engulfed with many refugee migrants. The hegemony of the discourse is maintained through perceptions of influx". People had premonition that Arunachal is going to be the next Tripura, as the tribes in Tripura were politically and numerically outnumbered by the immigrants. As a consequence, recently railway connectivity was suspended for almost three month on the ground that railway authority and state government does not regularize Inner Line Pass.

The reason for maintaining such social boundary is because it gives them a sense of distinctiveness and freedom. Anto Rukbo, a well known Adi writer once noted that "We and Biharis are like north pole and south pole. We are generous, they are misers; we speak what we mean, they have a hidden intention in what they speak". Fredrik Barth noted that "Ethnic distinctions do not depend on an absence of social interaction and acceptance, but are quite to the contrary often the very foundations on which embracing social systems are built (Barth, 1969: 9-10).

The more interesting aspect of this boundary is the occasional tension that breaks within it. Police stations are there on either side of the border, though the one in Arunachal is more prominent. The calm exterior is sometimes disrupted by an occasional boundary dispute. People, who were there for more than a decade or two would tell the occasional listener how sometimes quarrels would break between persons on either side and take a hilarious turn.

The economicties

Socio-economic implications of border market have been the topic of sophisticated studies in economy, archeology, and to a lesser extent, in anthropology (Ramirez, 2014: 100). Here brief attempt is made to analyze the nature of the traditional relationship, particularly economic relationship, of plains and hills people and try to highlight how it has changed in present context.

Historically, this borderland is a product of colonial commercial interest, where colonial administration converted large tracts of land into tea plantations. Today, vast areas of the Arunachal-Assam foothills border are covered with tea plantations. So far trade relations is concerns, almost all the tribal groups of Arunachal Pradesh had trade relation with people of neighbouring areas. Monpas of Tawang has close ties with Tibet, Nah tribe of Upper Subansiri share close affinity with crossborder tribe, Bokar tribe of Adi has close ties Lobha of Tibet. Idu Mishmi of Upper Dibang valley share many affinities with people of China. Wachos, Tangsa and Nocte also share a common nomenclature with across the border.

According to B.K. Roy Barman, "Sometimes in the border, certain communities may play the role of bridge communities and certain others may play the role of buffer communities. For instance, the Mishmies in NEFA seem to have served as a sort of link for maintaining commercial and political contact between the tribes of the north, like the Abors on the one hand, and the tribes of the south and east on the other" (2004:96). Many communities sharing the borderlands continue to maintain social, cultural, and economic affinities with the people across the border.

Historically, this commercial relationship was more marked with the Abors (present day Adis) of the Sadiya Division. This was so because a considerable part of the Sadiya area remained within the boundaries of the Ahom kingdom for quite a long time. Passes (Duar) were therefore opened at Sadiya, Pasighat, Dhola for which they used to pay some kind of duty (Cosh, 1837: 144, Michell, 1883, Gait, 1906: 321).

Border markets are important economic aspects of people living in Arunachal Pradesh. Lila Gogoi write "The tribal people inhabiting the NEFA region always have to keep close touch with the neighboring people for the supply of their bare necessaries of life. It is not easy for the NEFA areas to be independent in matters of food and other things of daily requirement. In order to procure these things they always have to go to the plains" (Gogoi, 1958).

Assam-Arunachal border has its own distinctive character of market in the border. People across the border come and visit such market. It is distinctive because it is held once a week on Wednesday or on Friday or on Saturday. In fact, most of the Arunachal borderlanders survive on such border markets and equally all border markets is survives on the Arunachal people. But there also regular market exists in the region which people regularly attend. Arunachalee have been participating in such border markets for many years.

Likabali of West Siang is a small town along Assam Arunachal border. It is located just adjacent to the Silapathar town of Assam.

Bhalukpong of East Kameng is also a small administrative town located along Assam-Arunachal inter-state border.

The growth of border market centres like Bhalukpong, Banderdewa, Harmutty, Likabali, Jonai etc. along Assam-Arunachal borderlands have been the result of improvements of roads and development in the last two-three decades. Among the items, household utensils, vegetables, electric appliances and dress materials are the two most important items for Arunachal people whereas for Assam people mostly come to purchased local agricultural products.

Banderdewa is one of the most important hubs of trade and business center along Assam-Arunachal borders.

Harmutty is also an important border market along Assam-Arunachal borders.

In all the market, the vendors are mostly from Assam, coming from far flung area. For example in Paglam Bazar, big traders come from Dhola and Dibrugarh. Vendors coming from Arunachal mostly bring agricultural products that include vegetables, baby pig, fruits and wild products. Neighboring villagers sell whatever is in season. Wide varieties of goods are for sale in the market.

Other Economic Relations

Border villages of Assam and Arunachal maintain various forms of economic relations with the surrounding villagers on both sides of the state border. Firstly in many places Arunachal people do owned land in Assam which makes the ties stronger. Most of the owned lands are agricultural land (paddy cultivation), and often people from Assam are employed to look after the land in a share hold basis.

Interestingly, most of the share-croppers who are employed to look after the plot are mostly Napalese, Mishing, Assamese and Musalman. Generally in this system, the land holder is to provide land and monetary help to the share-cropper and the share cropper in return to give almost half of the production of land. Normally the landowner give seeds and animal for cultivation, sometimes rice also during the cultivation seasons. The owner only visits the land twice or thrice a year during agricultural seasons. On enquiry it was found that most of the Arunachalee who owned land in Assam used agricultural labor from the same locality where their lands are situated in a share hold basis.

Most of the agricultural labors working in the adjoining border areas of East Siang are Mishing and Musalman. They are mostly from bordering villages of Assam. Not only in agricultural field but they are also invited for fencing the bamboo garden, kitchen garden, cutting the field for ginger field, cutting of bamboos from bamboo garden, and cutting of wood etc. Many also involve themselves in construction work, agricultural labor and other patty business in every part of Arunachal. Kerosene selling is one of the profitable jobs that most of the Mishing youth of the area do. Apart from men, women folk especially small girls' age between 10-20 years are kept as housemaid by many Adis.

Borderland areas of East Siang and Dhemaji of Arunachal and Assam lie in between the foot hills of Himalayan range. There are two reserved forests located along this inter-state boundary namely Daying Ering wildlife sanctuary and the Poba Reserve Forest. During my stay at Jonai I visited a number of villages inside these reserved forest such as New Leku, Abor Leku and Jhelom.

This reserve forest and sanctuary are home to varieties of medicinal plant. As a consequence, there are many folk therapist and shamans in the locality who are specialist in the treatment of some common diseases like jaundices, malaria, women's menstrual problems and bone fracture etc. There are many of them who have special abilities to diagnose and treat health problems such as infertility, broken bones, jaundice, malaria, dysentery, typhoid etc. They often visit people across the border on an invitation. Some of them even earn living out of it.

Socio-cultural Network

Lila Gogoi (1958) writes that "The hills and the plains of Assam are not separate identities. Before the advent of the British, except its positional distinction there was no difference whatsoever in the social and cultural field between the hills and the plains people. There existed an unbreakable friendship with the tribes that surround the boundaries of Assam (Gogoi, 1958: 11, 12). Today, the socio-cultural network has become more integrated across political boundary.

It is said that there are around 10,000 Nyishis living in Assam, inhabited mainly in the Sonitpur and Lakhimpur border districts of Assam. Some of them were migrated back to mountain terrain of Arunachal when the boundary demarcation was made in 1951, but still many remain there. Some of the remaining Nyishi clan of Assam are Welly, Chuku, Techi, Tana, Taw, Sengdo, Wahge, Chiri, Yumlam, Rari, Tachang, Nabam, Taku etc., They inhabited in the areas of Phuloguri, Rangagarah, Boroli Basti, Dolong Basti, Hodubari, Gormara, Dubea, Soibari, Jorhat, Rangajan of North Lakhimpur district and Rangajan and Charduar of Sonitpur district.

Nyishi Elite Society (NES) has shown an interest to hold up their Assam Nyishi brethrens affair as they are being marginalized by the government of Assam. NES is a non profitable, non political and non-governmental apex organization of Nyishi tribe with the full initiatives of educated people for looking the welfare activities of the tribe. Dr. Joram Begi, a retired Director of Higher and Technical Education, Government of Arunachal Pradesh was the founder President of Nyishi Elite Society (NES) and also longest serving president of NES. Presently, Nyishi Elite Society (NES) is headed by Bengia Tulom as the President and Tarh Tabin as General Secretary. The emergence of educated social group among the Nyishis has been playing a very significant role in brining about a series of changes in the society. The socio-cultural awareness movements have been carried out by NES have been playing decisive role in forging a Nyishi identity.

In an interview with Vijay Sonam (former general secretary of Nyishi Elite Society) on April 25, 2013 noted:

> "The Nyishi of Assam are the real inhabitant of Sonitpur, they were already there prior to the British and Ahom arrival. In fact, these areas were part of the NEFA territory (Balipara Frontier Tract) which was transferred to Assam in 1951. Till today, Nyishis of Assam are not given ST (Scheduled Tribes Status) unlike the Garos, Singhpho, Khampti and Nagas, whom the Assam government notified as the Hills Tribe of Assam. It has caused a lot of hardship and difficulty in reservation of job and political representation. It is time that we think afresh for the Nyishi people of Assam who are being deprived of constitutional rights and benefits, such as ST status in their own land of origin and habitat".

As a matter of fact, the native of this borderland not only contend with their local issues, pan tribal issues but also with the trans-state political and economic dynamics and with the expression of indigeneity in the trans-state forums. In recent year, series of cultural exchange programme going along Assam-Arunachal borderland. For example, Nyishi-Bodo tribe of Arunachal and Assam had number of cultural exchange programme conducted in recent years. The first historic summit called 'Bodo-Nyishi Peace Summit' was conducted at Itanagar on 11th April 2002. So far both the communities have signed two accords on February 11, 2002 at Banquet Hall, Itanagar and February 16, 2012 at Seijosa of East Kameng district of Arunachal Pradesh.

Sarit Chaudhuri (2013) noted that "The ongoing process of identity formation of this state has a very interesting feature which can throw light on the evolving transformation process itself". Firstly, one can identify a trend of identity construction among the Tani tribes of the state, the identity construction among Nyishi, Adi, Apatani, Galo, Tagin, Hill Miris and Mishing of Assam etc or so called the sons of '*Abotani*'.

Abotani is the mythical ancestor Tani tribes. Literally, Abo-means father and Tani mean Man, so etymologically it means father of man or ancestor of Tani tribes. Among Tani tribes there are many legends that narrates how Abotani introduced the art of farming and cultivation, how he conquered "Uyu" evil spirit. The tales of Abotani and belief in Donyi-Poloism is what binds all the tani tribes of Arunachal today in various walks of their life since the ancient past.

This pan-Tani movement is based on the basis of commonalities in cultural traits and more importantly, on the basis of genealogy of origin, which illustrate their brotherhood (Ibid). This identity consciousness is stimulated by some educated youths to promote their language and identity. The key issue of their movement is to develop a common dialect for Tani groups. Taba Taku, one of the leading cultural activists and President of Arunachal Pradesh Abotani Community Confederation (APACC) is of the opinion that: "the aim of our group is to create a sense of nationalism inside the hearts and minds of every single Tanis....it is our duty to let the whole world know that Tani Clans is one of the existing strong rather than just a myth and stories". Arunachal Pradesh Abotani Community Confederation (APACCC) is a newly formed organization, active in Arunachal Pradesh headed by Taba Taku as the President and Subu Kechi as General Secretary.

There is also a forum called the Tani Federation Forum which claims to work to revive indigenous culture and language across Assam-Arunachal border. It is a Guwahati based forum. The organization was formed in 16 June 2007 at Lakhimpur, Assam. J.K. Riba is the president, Dheeraj Pao is the Secretary General and Tagam Nabam is the convener. According to Nabam Tagam,

> "Tani unification is only possible if we all really think for unification, for that we really need to think beyond our social and territorial boundary, at the same time we also need to respect other social and territorial integrity. And for that to happen, there should be an Annual Tani meet fest every year".

Since 2010, there is also a dialogue going on to form a Taniland. It is often told that there has been plan to form a Taniland province comprising of northern Mising tribe bordering Arunachal Pradesh of the Brahmaputra valley. Apart from Pan-Tani Movement, there is also a movement of Pan Nagas or Greater Nagalim active in bordering areas of Changlang, Longding and Tirap district of Arunachal Pradesh. Interestingly, it has been observed that recently, Arunachal Nagas like Nocte, Wancho, Ollo, Tangsa, Tutsa now did not want to identify themselves as Nagas. Recently, on February 20, 2014, thousand of Nocte, Wancho, Ollo, Tangsa, Tutsa, singphos took out a procession against the NSCN's demand to integrate Naga areas in its proposed 'Greater Nagalim'.

Emergence of inter-tribal political association is a new development, where some of the major tribes attempt to incorporate some of the comparatively smaller similar population within their fold. According to Sarit Chaudhuri (2013) "there are also attempts by some tribes and sub-tribes to come out of the larger generic umbrella in search of their distinctive identities. Further, a few smaller tribes are also found trying to unify themselves under a new umbrella in order to consolidate their position. For instance, the Nyishis, numerically largest tribe, were in favor of incorporating a few tribes, such as Sulung (Puroik), Miji (Bangro), Hill Miri, and the Tagin within their fold. Except Tagin, other groups in recent years started emitting their festival and lifestyle thus reducing the independent identity of themselves to almost nothingness.

Similarly, the Adis are also attempting to incorporate Mishing into their fold. Mishing on the other hand, also attempting to recognize themselves as part of Adis, so that they can get the benefits of constitutional incentives reserved for scheduled tribes in the state of Arunachal Pradesh. Thus, establishment of political authority and ascendency to position of power wields influence in acceleration the process of fusion of populations.

There is also a dialogue going on to reunite the Adi and Galong which is separated now constitutionally by amending their tribe from Galong to Galo in parliament in December 19, 2011. In an interview with Behon Jamoh, an Adi social activist say that "It's the right time for reunification of Adi and Galo as we witness that there is no good in being separate. It was solely due to some power hungry politicians who cannot stand our unity we got separated. If the West Germany and the East Germany could reunite then why cannot us".

The debate over granting of ST to Deories of Arunachal Pradesh is one interesting borderlanders problem. The Deories of Arunachal Pradesh are the ethnic group inhabiting in the border regions of Assam and Arunachal Pradesh. They inhabited in the Mahadevpur, Lekang, Namsai, Deopani and Sunpura areas of Arunachal Pradesh. They are originally from Joydam Hill and Manambhum area of Patkai Hills of present Myanmar. The history says that they migrated to present Arunachal Pradesh before 13th Century.

In the census report of 1901 as reported by B.C. Allen: '' Their original home was on the banks of the Kundil river east of Sadiya, but when the Ahom power began to decline, they were hurried by the hill tribes in the neighborhood, and at the beginning of the century they migrated to North Lukhimpur, and from there moved to the Majuli, the Dikrang river, Sissi Mukh, and the Baligao manza in Jorhat. The Mongolian type is much more strongly marked in them than in the ordinary Chutiya and they might easily be mistaken for Miris (Allen, 1906: 110-111).

On 10th November 2013, in the general convention of All Arunachal Pradesh Tribal Welfare Association (AATWA) at Mahadevpur, Arunachal Pradesh, the president of DTWA (Deori Tribal Welfare Association) Mr. Rajiv Deori noted that "No tribe is indigenous in Arunachal, all migrated one after another, some came early and some lately... If you can accept Tai Khamtis as

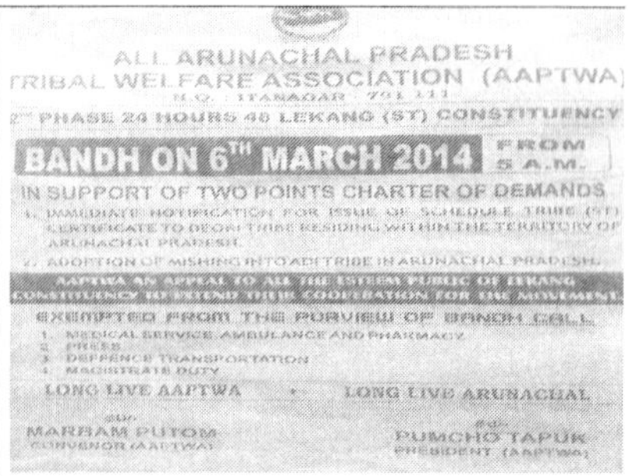

one of you, as one of the Indigenous tribes of the state then why can't you accept Deoris. Tai Khamptis along with their Tai Ahom brother came in the region much later in and around 16th Century. Even Historical Text of Hem Boruah Gohain's "The Prehistory of the Ahom" confirmed that Deories are here since 13 century, followed by Singhpho people from Burma. But then the area was captured by Tai Ahoms and then Tai Khamtis and again regained by the Tai Ahoms at last till British came. Now if khamtis and Singpho are given ST in Arunachal then why cannot the Deories?".

He further noted that "the present names of Dibang, Lohit, Namsai, Naamchum and Chowkam is said to be adopted from Deori words, who inhabited in the region long before Singphos and Khampti people came. There is no denying fact that they are non-indigenous then Singphos and Khamptis whom the dominant natives considered as native and indigenous. Unfortunately in 1991, the Government of Arunachal Pradesh stops giving them ST right in the state. As a consequence, Deori childrens were barred from issuing free books and schools dresses. They were not allowed to stay in government school hostel. And more importantly the government has stopped issuing PRC to them". At the same time, Lisus (Yobin), who were immigrated from Myanmar in recent history, are now considered more indigenous and being granted both Indian citizenship and APST status simultaneously recently at the behest of state government.

The Mishing Issue

The Mishing tribe living along the borderland areas of Arunachal Pradesh is one of the most marginalized borderland communities. They inhabited mainly in the districts of East Siang, Lohit, Lower Dibang Valley and Changlang. However, they are mostly concentrated in the Mebo circle of Pasighat sub-division and Sille oyan circle of the Ruksin sub-division of East Siang district. Although, the Mising of Arunachal consider themselves as natives of the soil, so far the dominant natives of state don't consider as native, as a result till today they are not given the Scheduled Tribes status of the state.

The root of the present problem of statelessness of the Mising in Arunachal Pradesh lies in the creation of Assam-Arunachal Border in 1951. According to Unkung Regon in a interview (12.09.2013) "The minority Mising people living in Arunachal Pradesh fell prey to the plan of Gopinath Bordoloni, who convinced the gathering at Sadiya to join Assam instead of remaining in the state of Arunachal Pradesh (then NEFA). As a result many areas of Arunachal Pradesh (the then NEFA), inhabited by them was relocated to Assam. Those who resisted and wanted to remain in Arunachal became today's Arunachal Mising and till today many of them were given Adi ST while few of them were denied the ST rights".

The recent submission of memorandum by Adi Bane Kebang (ABK) at Pasighat to Chief Minister of Arunachal Pradesh demanding Scheduled Tribe status for Mising people under the Adi ST, the issue has escalated into a major controversial issue among the socio-political circles of the border state. The move that has been strongly seconded by Adi Students' Union (AdiSU) is resented by the apex student body of the state All Arunachal Pradesh Students' Union (AAPSU) and Student Union Movement of Arunachal (SUMA). The AAPSU said that there was "no question of granting the status to Mishing people since they were already recognized in the state of neighboring Assam". On the similar line a noted academician of the lone university of state, Nani Bath (2010) argues that "....APST status cannot just be granted to the Mishing of Siang as Mr. Apang wanted."

The demands made by the Adis clearly manifested the desire for incorporating Mishing into their fold with conditional surrendering of Mishing identity into Adis. Some of the Mishing elders responded "for us it is only option, it is the only feasible option to end the prolonged alienation and social exclusion, since our Arunachalee brothers are not ready to accommodate us".

Even some of the Mising educated youth of Arunachal also raise voice against this development and advocated for retaining their ethnic identity at all cost. The President of Arunachal Misings Student's Union (AMSU), Mr. Suman Pao says:

> "To be born as Mising in Arunachal is a sin...I am an Arunachal Mising, not Adi, definitely our Mising have some cultural affinity with Adis, but our Mising also share certain similarities with all Tani tribes of Arunachal...I reject the idea of forceful conversion of Arunachal Mising into Adi. It is an insult to our Mising tribe; Our Mising tribe is not any sub-tribe of any tribe. Tiger and Lion both belong to cat family but we cannot say Tiger as Lion or Lion as Tiger. Similarly, Mising and Adi are both Tani tribes but Mising cannot be Adi and Adi cannot be Mising."

On 24th December 2013, a hunger strike was organized at Ruksin. The hunger strike was organized by Mishing Students of Arunachal Pradesh headed by Suman Pao. According to Suman Pao, the aim of organizing the Dharna was to wake up the government as well as the general public to the sufferings of our Mishing brethren in Arunachal who are at the edge of suffering.

However, it appears that majority are quite content with the Adi-Mising unity. As a result, two days cultural exchanges meet was organized between the Adi community of Arunachal and Misings of neighboring Assam and Arunachal at Jonai on 4th and 5th April 2013. The chief organizer of the 'Adi-Mising Cultural Exchange meets' and the President of Adi-Mising Lemo Kebang (AMLK), Raju Medok says:

> "The sole purpose of organizing such meet is to exchange our feeling to foster unity and brotherhood…We all are sons and daughters of Abotani…There is no denying fact that Adi-Mishing don't have a bio-socio-cultural bond….The Assam-Arunachal boundary was created for administrative convenience of the governments, but the demarcation can never distort the parental relation between Adi and Mising".

Adi-Mishing Lemo kabang (AMLK) is a newly formed organization of Adi and Mishing, formed on 6 February 2013 under the leadership of Okom Yousung and Raju Medok. The objective of forming this organization

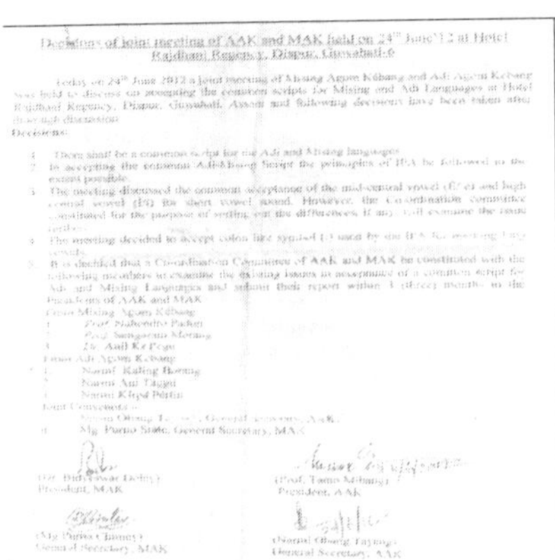
Decisions of joint meeting of AAK and MAK held on 24th June'12 at Hotel Rajdhani Regency, Dispur, Guwahati-6

Decisions:

(Dr. Bidyeswar Doley)
President, MAK

(Prof. Tamo Mibang)
President, AAK

according to them is to promote brotherhood feeling among Adi and Mising of Arunachal and Assam.

In another development, Adi Agom Kebang (AAK) and Mising Agom Kebang (MAK) are working together to develop a single language for Adi and Mising. In 17 November 2013, the third Joint Meeting of Adi Agom Kebang (AAK) and Mising Agom Kebang were held at Gogamukh, Assam. The joint meeting was attended by Mishing Agom Kébang President Dr Bidyeswar Doley, General Secretary Purna Kr. Chintey and Adi Agom Kebang President Nini Pertin, AAK General Secretary Obang Tayeng, AAK advisor member Prof Ani Taggu.

As a matter of fact, one of the Mishing subs-groups called Somuwa resides in the Namsai circle of the Lohit district of Arunachal has already switched the identity of Adi tribe. They are now known as Adi Somuwa. According to Omak Darin (2008) "They were actually the Moying subgroup of Mising tribes who are presently inhabited Buroi-Bharali Banks of Dibrugarh". He further pointed out that how the Somuwa Misings have switched their surnames from Pegu to Megu, Narah to Ratan, Pame to Pagduk, Taye, Payeng to Tayeng, which is an Adi clan, etc. and accommodated themselves to the new identity. Similarly, this kind of identity transformation has been also observed among the Oyan-Ruksin subgroup of Mising tribe of East Siang district of Arunachal Pradesh. Many among the Oyan-Ruksin sub group of Misings have already switched to Adi surnames from Mising surnames.

Another interesting development along Assam-Arunachal borderlands is the emergence of kinship unions (Opin Kebang) among the Mising and Adis. Such meetings are held every year in the month of January and February. In my last fieldwork in January 2014 "Pegu and Megu kin meet (Opin Kebang)" was held at Jonai, Assam. At the meeting, many solidarity speeches were given and many proposals were given to strengthen the brotherhood bonds. One interesting proposal also came to observed restrain marital relations among such kin members.

In fact, such meeting or kebang does take place every year among various Adi and Mising kin groups. For instance, between Jerang of Adi and Regon of Mising, between Pangam of Adi and Bori of Mising, between Mije and Taye, between Doso, Danggen and Dang, between Morang and Borang and between Lego and Mili etc. These kinship groups regard themselves as descendent of a same ancestor. They regard themselves offspring of the same father and mother. In such meeting, grand feast and cultural exchange program are organized to showcase their brotherhood and giving the younger generation a platform to know each other.

Despite some social problems, the Assam-Arunachal borderlanders had maintained strong social and marital relations across the state boundary. Marital ties have been established among Mising of Arunachal and Assam, between

Mising and Adi, between Galo and Mising, among others. My host where I stayed at Jonai two daughters married Adi from Arunachal.

Conclusion

Since this border is an interstate many borders villages of Assam and Arunachal maintain various forms of socioeconomic networks and relations with the surrounding villagers on both sides of the state borders. The narratives of the people resides at this border is clearly indicates boundary matter little for all practical reasons, people on both sides existing more or less, and it is not easy to differentiates, from one another. This is because the people have been living along the boundary engage in individual occasion, influences cultures, exchange among people.

The administrative boundary of the state does not stand in the way of the rational choice of markets for economic transaction. All market along Assam-Arunachal survived on the Arunachal people. Market don't differentiate customer on the basis of citizenship after all it is all about trade. In fact, it is the place where mixed people share memories together, and these memories can be identify in the form of festival like Bihu, Ali-Aye Ligang, Diwali, Durga Puja, where lots of cultural exchange take place by participating in the festivals.

NH-52 as a boundary line, it is a mutually agreed line between the two states and it is there for the ages, and the people alongside respected this demarcation and without questioning it reality. The daily experience of the people living there is not rigid, materiality boundary is presence but people don't look at it as subject of resistance, this boundary is became more like a acceptance, inner line permit is check in people who visiting from the outside, it is boundary is constructing and communicating identity of self and the collective life of the people living around.

Politics of Arunachal Pradesh has been increasingly designed by various ethnic movements after the independence of India. The demographic composition of the state is diverse with existence of various ethnic groups having distinct historical memories, cultural features, beliefs, languages or dialects. This multi-ethnic state since 1960s is facing the crisis of assertion by the various ethnic groups, which is basically to protect and preserve their identity. We see a chain of identity movements where many ethnic groups demanded assurance of their socio-cultural and political identity. A quick outcome was formation of Adi Bane Kebang, Nyishi Elite Society, Galo Welfare Society among others, as a common political platform of different tribes all across the state. Among all the welfare society, ABK and NES is the most popular organization running across the state.

During my visit to many border villages, I found out that many developmental activities are taking place especially in Assam side. Border Area Development Programme (BADP) though operating in the state, concentrating mostly in the international borders, leaving aside inter-state borders. It appears that in Arunachal Pradesh, BADP is only mean for international border areas not for inter-state border areas. Nowhere in Assam-Arunachal border areas you will find any developmental activities in the name of Border Area Development Programme whereas in Assam side you will find numbers of culverts, irrigation canals, river embankment raised clearly written in the name of Border Area Development Programme. Only exception is of Amarpur area of Dibrugarh district of Assam, which remain cut off from Assam during rainy season. Otherwise all place I visited road communication is established connecting every villages. At the every entry and exit point of roads was written "funded from BADP".

Foothill regions of Assam-Arunachal Border, traditionally which was supposed to be the place of economic exchange between the hills people and the plains, turned into a violence ground with the emerging ideas of 'territoriality'. The situation of this long foothills bordering Assam and Arunachal Pradesh became more complex when Assam's demand for inclusion of reserved forest and contiguous areas inhabited by Assamese emerged out. In order to solve the problem a series of meetings at different level also have taken place and a number of agreements have been signed between the two states but there has been no effective result till date- creating fear and crisis for security among the people residing in the region.

References

Allen, B. C. 1906, Assam District Gazetteers, Volume VIII: Lakhimpur. The Pioneer Press, Allahabad, page 110-111.

Acharya, S. K. Ethnic Processes in North-Eastern India, Economic and Political Weekly, Vol. 23, No. 21 (May 21, 1988), pp. 1068-1077, Published by: Economic and Political Weekly, Stable URL: http://www.jstor.org/stable/4378523S, page 1074.

Barman, B. K. Roy, Structure of Bridge and Buffer Communities in the Border Areas in Arabinda Basu, Biman, K. Das Gupta, and Jayanta Sarkar (Edt), 2004, *Anthropology for North-East India: A Reader*, Indian National Confederation and Academy of Anthropologists, Indian Anthropological Society and National Museum of Mankind, Calcutta, (Page-96-99).

Chaudhuri, Sarit K., 2013. Oral Narratives and Identity Construction among the Tani Tribes of Arunachal Pradesh, in A.K. Danda, Nadeem Hasnain and Dipali G. Danda edited volume "Contested Identities in the Globalized World" INCAA Occasional Paper, Jhargram, West Bengal.

Cosh, John M'. 1837, Topography of Assam, G.H.Huttmann, Bengal Military, Orphan Press, Calcutta

Darin, Omak, 2008. A Study on the Social Group 'Adi Somua' and their Identity Formation, An unpublished M. Phil Dissertation submitted to AITS, Rajiv Gandhi University, Itanagar.

of rural population....villagers' participation in the larger polity, whether by foot or vote, is formed at a level which is in many ways, different from and even alien to the different world of civil society, elected office and independent judiciary "(Ruud 2003).

The headman looks after all the important work in the villages of Meghalaya. Villagers also play an important role in the village; similarly in the Saiden village where it is ruled by the headman and its duty of headman to maintain peace in the village. Villagers elect their representatives as a headman through their traditional practice.

"Dominant castes, as kings, have right to rule, to deliberate, to take pre-eminence (in rituals, for instance). They also have an obligation to protect subjects, to nourish and sustain. Kings have an elevated position because they are protectors of society....The king as protector is also the king as benevolent provider, the distributor of boons, engaging in magnanimous acts of largesse. He generously gives paddy to the needy and land to his subjects..." (Ruud, 2003).

When it comes to generosity, all leaders do not possess this quality but the headman of Saiden is different. Apart from being hard worker, he is very generous. His role in the village is like a ruler who is looking after everyone in the village, as he occupies a curtail position in the village constitution and represents the interests of the villagers. He not only settles disputes in the village but is also involved in others matters in birth, death, illness etc. He is also symbolized as the prominent figure in the village and often states cooperative identity of the village.

"He had to see that his villagers keep the village clean, hoe paths, use latrines, follow agriculture and veterinary regulations, pay tax etc" (Srinivas, 1976).

Interestingly similar kind of responsibility is found out from the headman of Saiden. E.K Lapang initiated different plans and policies in his village for the betterment of the village, he clearly state the villagers to take part in cleaning their village on every Saturday. With the help of his executive members collect certain amount from villagers for the purpose of village development.

"Chieftainship in the Trobriands is the combination of two institutions: first, that of headmanship, or village authority; secondly, that of totemic clanship, that is the division of the community into classes or castes, each with a certain more or less definite rank" (Malinowski 2005).

It is true that every tribal state has their own traditional political rule; Saiden village is one of them. As Malinowski had already state in his book "Argonauts of western pacific" place is rule first by headman, same kind of tradition is followed in Saiden where village is governed by headman with the other sub headmen and executive members. This kind of practices is not new it has been practice by the Khasis since time immemorial.

In the case of monarchy in Nepal, it has been seen that King Mahendra dismissed the elected government in 1960 and promulgated a new constitution in 1962. Under this constitution, the King continued to rule, but was advised by an assembly or panchayat, which was part elected, part appointed. Political parties were forbidden, because, as sectional expressions of private interest, were alien to the distinctive moral ethos of the Nepali polity, in which the collective welfare of all was embodied in the singular person of the King."(Spencer 2007) This shows the power of the head of the state. Likewise, Richard Burghat in 1984 travelled to Nepal on a project to investigate attitudes to drinking water and hygiene. Along with this project he was also fascinated by events in the country like Nepal Polity. Though they got new constitution but they never give up their ethnic practices which is much more similar to Saiden. Though Meghalaya is now a democratic state, people participate in democratic functions and appoint their elected representatives, they still have their traditional one like *syiem, sirdar, myntries, rongashonong etc.* Same case in Saiden village where they still follow their customary rules and regulations like *rongashonong* or headman. Though there is a new scheme of state democratic government but the village is still rule by headman of village who is appointed by the people of village (male member).

So it can be concluded that the headman is an important figure in governing a village or even his role as an important leadership in the village. Whether the title is hereditary or not, or whether it has anything to do with the state government, their importance in the village administration is never fading away. People of Saiden needed their headman for the protection or to safeguard their customary laws not only today but for future generations. The present study aims to provide descriptive account of village administrative system. Attempt has been made to understand the role of *Dorbar*, headman, sub headman, executive members and gender equality in the village administrative system.

The study area was conducted at the Saiden village; to identify their traditional system of village administration and its relevance in today's modern society. A simple questionnaire was prepared to discuss with the local people to understand the concept of village administration in details. And the data for this study were collected by interacting with village headman, women, and youth's members through observation, participant observation, questionnaire, autobiographical, interviews and comparative methods through the period of 18th January to 8th February 2015.

Result and Discussion

Socio-economic Status

According to the survey conducted at Saiden Village of Meghalaya, overall descriptions of the 201 households from study area were studied, and

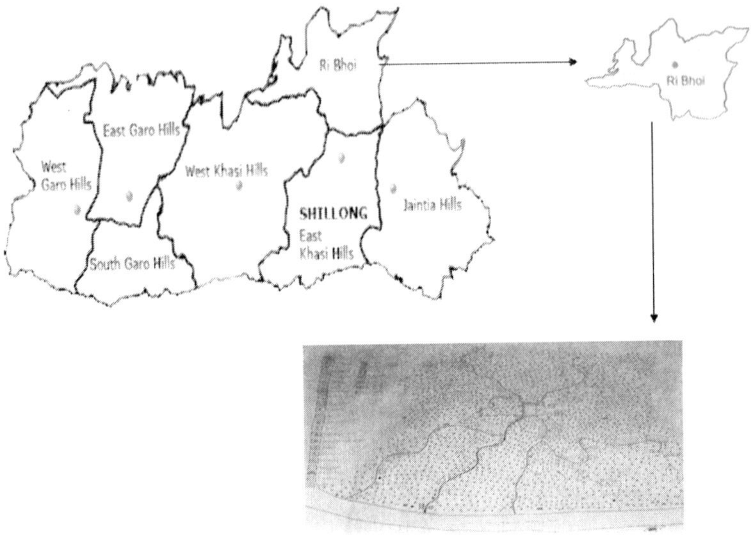

Figure 38.1: Map showing Study Area

it was found that 191 out of 201 household were pakka house. Total populations of village were 1141 and majority was Christian in religion. They live as Nuclear family followed by joint family as shown in Fig 38.2.

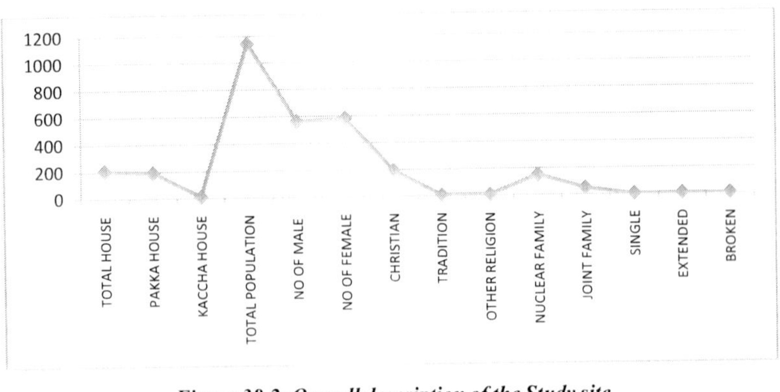

Figure 38.2: Overall description of the Study site

An attempt was also made to study the education status of Saiden village, where number of students was found higher in secondary level followed by primary, High secondary, Graduate, Post Graduate and few M. Phil as shown in Figure 38.3.

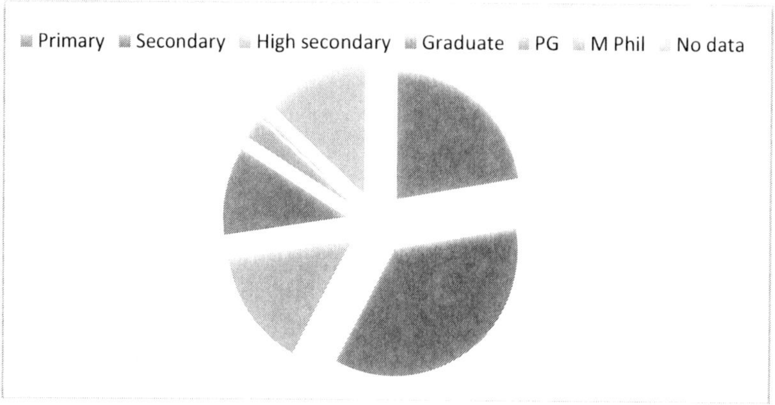

Figure 38.3: Educational Status

Study was also done about the occupation of the villagers. Agriculture was the main occupation for the people of Saiden, where most of them were engage in agricultural activities, like cultivation of cash crops like broom plants, pineapples etc. Some are also engaged in poultry farming, some people also work as wage laborers, school teachers, carpenter, shopkeeper, government jobs, business etc. Out of 1,141 of total population, 153 populations are farmers, 152 are working in private sector, 140 are government employees, 501 are students, 130 are housewives and 25 are retired from their respective work and 40 are jobless as shown in Figure 38.4.

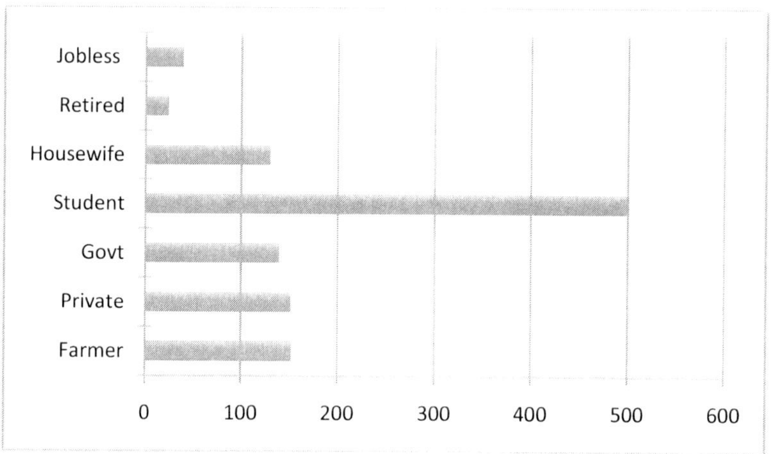

Figure 38.4: Occupational Status

Political Institution

The sixth schedule of the Indian constitution (1983) guarantees preservation of tradition customs, laws and institutions of the tribal societies of the north-eastern region of India. It has also provided autonomous district councils in the state of Meghalaya, which has been established to protect the customs, customary laws, traditional institutions and the interests of tribal societies. It also gives them the legislative, judiciary and executive powers. According to the Indian Constitution, the state of Meghalaya has a dual system of administration: The modern bureaucratic administration as found in other states of country; and the traditional (customary) system peculiar to tribal societies inhabiting the state. Under the bureaucratic administrative system the Khasi hills are divided to three districts i.e. The east Khasi hills, The West Khasi hills and The Ri-Bhoi district.

Traditionally, Khasi villages have enjoyed autonomy in the organization and management of their own affair focus and have exercised collective control over their natural and human resources. The village is exercised by a council of elders of the village called the village council or *'Dorbar Shnong'*. Saiden falls under the jurisdiction of *"Hima"*. The true name of this *Hima* from its existence is the *Hima* 12 *Lyngdoh Syiemship*. This *Hima* got its own special custom, culture and tradition since olden times before the coming of the British till date. Some of the important functions of *Hima* includes.

1: *The Dorbar Hima*- this is the apex most which holds and strengthensa the custom culture and tradition of the whole *Hima*. It's important members' are: the *syiem* who is the ruler, the three *myntris*, the twelve *Lyndoh* from the twelve separate raid.

2: *The Dorbar Raid*- it witness in all the important decision in its own respective Raid. Six Raid falls under this: *Raid Nongkharai, Raid Nonglyngdo, Raid Nongpoh, Raid Nongkyrha, Raid Sohkwai*. Saiden village falls under *Raid Nongpoh Sirdar Elaka as " Raid"* of distinct village. The *Nongpoh Sirdarship Elaka* have a *Sordar*, Three *Myntries, Lyngdohship* to look after the villages and how to regulate the inter –village relationship and sometime to solve the disputes and conflicts between the inter-village for controlling the land or water resources which are not owned by any particular village.

In Nongpoh Sirdarship Elaka, W.Syiem Nongshai, hold a post of *Sirdar*, which is hereditary system. He is the head of the *Raid* presided over the meetings of the *dorbar raid* and the executive committee of the *dorbar*. He has to maintain law and order in the *raid* and cases of the disputes in the *dorbar* and he also has to interact with the state government officials in pursuance of the interests of the *raid*.

Political system of Saiden village

The study area was Saiden which is located between the nation highway 40(NH40) of Guwahati and Shillong. Oral history states that before all the people of Saiden used to live in Nongrim Saiden 80 household were there. One day all the houses caught fire and they had to move out to another place, 40 households moved to *Mawthum*(rock chimney) and the remaining 40 household moved to present Saiden. The Saiden is derived from a water body *Umpyrli* which is running parallel to the Guwahati Shillong highway. Oral history says that the word Saiden came from the word sai and den which means a thread like rock, which is at *Thwei* Saiden near old

Picture: (A) Dorbar (B) Headman of the Village (C) Village Women (D) Village people (E) Sub-Headman (F) Traditional Food

Saiden *(Nongrim* Saiden*)* lies south of the present Saiden village. This threat like rock acts as a barrier to the flow of the *Umpyrli* and this is why there exists a pool of water in same place. The total area of this village 40sq kilometers and consists of seven localities. They are *Lumpdeng* (middle hills), *Lumsohram* (hills of jackfruits), *Mawdaron (maw* meaning rock and *daron* meaning a filter used to filter alcohol), *Nongkyndang (*it is a *Garo* name, oral history tells that the *Garo* people were migrated from a place called *Nongkyndang,* since then the place got the same name), *Mawpadang (Maw* meaning rock and *Pdang* meaning crack), *Ladiewsier* also called as *Dipu* presently (*ladiew* – junction and *sier*-deer meaning junction to the market of deer), and lastly the *Lewiser(*market of deer, where animals came to drink in river which contain salt water).

In Saiden village, headman is the prominent figure in the village who is responsible to look after the village and its people. Headman is called as" *Rongbashonong*" which is not hereditary, and the village has unique way of appointing the headman. *Rongbahshnong* means a Khasi male adult administrative head or village headman nominated unanimously by *u khun u hajar* (the citizens) of the village *dorbar*, under the administrative control of the khasi *Hima*(s). Again here the citizens include only the male members of the village who is above 18years. They don't have the system of ballet box, and they simply have to raise their hand, if they like the candidate. The elected headman has to work as voluntary service if he goes against the law and the rules of the village than the villagers have the power to dismiss him from his post as a headman. The post is for three years and before they elect another headman from the village. Headman in Saiden is voluntary service they don't get paid from the government like Panchayats in other states. Though they adapt the rules of state government they never neglect their own system. They give more importance and save their customary law, which is still prevalent in modern society today. Headman in Saiden is a voluntary service, as it is already mentioned in the previous chapter. Headman ship in Saiden village is very unique and is one of the interesting things about the village. We discovered in the field that the headman doesn't get salary from government like Panchayats form the village of other states. Headman in the village is not hereditary system like Srinivas' Rampura village which is hereditary which we thought it's going to be a same case.

The political system of the village is interesting and unique, where village still follow their traditional governing system (*Rongashonong).* The village is governed by a headman, though it is not a hereditary system but village still follows their customary rules and they elect an able headman in every three years. This system has been practiced since 1940 and it is still continued by the people of the village. The main purpose of electing the headman is to safeguard their customary laws, and also to continue and follow the traditional rules made by their ancestors. As a headman of the village he is respected by all the villagers who also obey his decisions regarding village matters. Another interesting fact about the headman is he can work in government or any institution and hold the post of headman at the same time. The *dorbarshnong* was mainly concerned with the law and order, the main function of the headman is to look after the village with the help of sub headmen of different localities and look after the village matter along with others executive members (Nongkynrih 2002).

Dorbar

Dorbar is another important part of village administration, traditionally known as "*dorbarshonong*" started around 1900; this is the only place in village where they conduct every meeting of village. Like general assembly where there is a different member with their own function, similarly village's *dorbar* also has different members who consist of headman who is the head of the *dorbar*, seven sub headman from all the localities of the village and the executives' members with their own duties who work along with headman in village's development.

The main aim of the *dorbar* is to protect and conserve all community and forests lands. The main function of the *dorbarshonong* is to ensure general discipline, social order, tranquility in village in case of intra and inter village affairs. Like general assembly where there is a different member with their own function, similarly village's *dorbar* also has different members who consist of headman who is the head of the *dorbar*, seven sub headman from all the localities of the village and the executives' members with their own duties who work along with headman in village's development.

Many meetings of the village are held at *dorbar* and the presence of headman is very essential if he can't manage to attend one then he has to give his responsibility to one of the sub- headman as in charge. The "grand meeting" which is held once in a year in the village, for such meetings headman's presence is necessary with certain rules and regulation should be followed like wearing silk turban which is important for them to wear during important occasions which is red and yellow in color. Wearing turban in such meeting signifies many thing like :it is the symbol of being wise, reasonable person and higher mental strength, symbol of being respectable, symbol that the wearer is a person of high authority, symbol that wearer is also a person with responsibilities and full of duties.

Rongbadong, who is the head of their own *dong* (locality). Along with the headman the appointment of *rongbadong* is important and it is also a tradition of the village. Villagers (male members) appoint sub headman to make the work of headman easier. There were seven sub headmen from seven blocks, their appointment is very necessary in village, as headman alone cannot look after all the matter in the village, if there is someone in the locality who looks after their own block then it will be easy to deal with situation. Sub headman usually looks after the development of their own localities without any salary from the government and they are also engaged in both the sectors.

Executive members are also important members or one may say they are the important organs of the village *dorbar*. Without them village *dorbar* is of no use is what I have understood personally, one may also says as a "palace without ministers". There are many executive members in the *dorbar* working under the village headman. The different members of the dorbar consist of Headman, Advisor, Secretary, Assistance Secretary, Chairman of village employment council, Finance Secretary, Treasurer, Farmer's club, Vigilance committee, and Village Defense Party.

Women and politics

Gender is a sociological construct as it is not something we are born with, and somethimg we have but something we do as explained by (West and Zimmerman, 1987). In more recent history, gender roles have changed rapidly and with growing modernisation women have been able to achieve an elevated status in the society but still the equality gaps have infact widened in many aspects. Women got employment but then again created new divisions and new inequalities between genders.

The role of the both the gendered are fixed from the beginning, where in all the cultures women have assumed particular cultural roles. During hunter gatherer society women were generally the gatherers, their main activities was to collect fruits, berries, yams, shoots, etc. while the men goes for hunting. During pastoral societies the men went to graze animals whereas women are associated with household and dairy products. While in agricultural societies women were more confined to their houses, even though they were involved with agricultural activities but they were not permitted for the leading roles in the field of agriculture.

India after its independence showed a remarkable change in the position of women's status in the society. Today the situation has changed; women started working along with the men in different sectors. The constitution of India framed and amended with the objective of ensuring equal status of women in the country but even after years of independence the position of the women is seemed to be not equal as men especially in the Indian society. Instead of having such constitutional guarantee they are not enjoying equal opportunity in economics, social and political fields. Whereas if we see the role of women in the tribal societies are different than the non tribal societies, in tribal communities there are some groups who follow matrilineality or matriarchy; in such cases the women plays an important role in the society and the different organizations like political, social and economic. They are not only involved in inheriting movable or immovable properties but they also share primary occupation with men. A different practice of tribal societies like Bride price, staying of groom at the bride's house is one of the reasons that place women in such advantages positions. Khasis are such tribe in India who are still known for such practice where the descent is traced through mother. The inheritance of property is from female line, i.e. daughter inherits property from her mother. As regards to the income of a khasi man, his mother is entitled to get his income before his marriage where he stays at his mother house, similarly after marriage his income will go to his wife after he starts living with his wife at her house. Instead of such tradition the Khasi women do not enjoy absolute supremacy. Man is neither dominated nor ill treated by women. He is respected by women folk and he maintains immense authority in their household in the post-marital period. Though the mother is the custodian of the family property, but the authority to manage property and maintain the tradition is in the hand of the *Kni* (maternal uncle).

In terms of political sphere women do not posses any significant role, they are not even allowed for the selection of the leader, they are still subordinate to the man. The main power lies in the hand of men which is clearly visible in the election of headman. Women participation is hardly seen in the political sphere, society doesn't allow women to take part in political decision making and selection of the leaders due to age old customary law practices which doesn't allow women to be a part of politics. Till now we hardly found any head women in such villages, they do not participate in politics nor attend such important meetings of *dorbar*. Moreover, most of the women don't seem any interested in politics due to their customary law and mostly because of their daily job which keeps them busy all day long. Women now feel that they are being neglected in the field of politics and they started questioning about the age old practices and a system of headmanship. This change may now bring the status of women as equal as men in the field politics.

Conclusion

To run the village administration smoothly the person is the village headman as the headman played an important role the social and political life of the villagers. He was also regarded as the chief, head, leader, protector and administrative head of the village. He maintained law and order in the village, had authority to settle disputes, make decisions over petty theft, mischief, public nuisance, littering, drunkenness assault and other wrong doings. People always counted on him to represent them in many matters in and around the village. The title of the headman was not a government recognized position. If there was anything coming from the government in matters dealing with the village, they had to consult him and he would look after the matter accordingly for the benefit of the village. He was also like an immigration officer for any outsiders or travelers passing through village. They needed his approval for their stay in the village. He is titled as the representation of customary roles in the village, which has challenged the traditional system, with the coming up of the new legislations like village administration bill today, where many people are raising their voice against the election of headman. Which is simply by raising hand or by "proposed panel" and demanding to conduct through a non political party electoral possess of secret ballot like the election of church elders in the some Christians denominations where the post of *rangbah shonong,* secretary shonong, finance secretary etc are given to those with highest votes from both men and women.

References

Bareh, H. 2001. *Meghalaya.* New Delhi: Mittal Publications.

Bareh, H. 1997. *The History and Culture of the Khasi People.* New Delhi: Mittal Publications.

Census 2001. Meghalaya profile. http://www. cencus 2011. co. in/census/state/ meghayala. html (accessed on 15 May 2015).

Dikshit R, Dikshit K, Jutta K 2014. North East India: Land, People and Economy. New York, Springer.

Gurdon.P.R.T. 2010 (1863) *The Khasis*. New Delhi: Akansha Publishing House.

Harris. M 1989 'Life without Chiefs, New Age Journal November/December.

Lapang, E.K 2010 Project Work on the Packages of the Integrated Child Development Schemes (ICDS) with Special Reference to Saiden Anganwadi Centre-1, Ri Bhoi District, Meghalaya.

Malinowski B. 2005(1922) Argonauts of The Western Pacific, London, Taylor and Francis e- Library.

Nongkynrih A.k (2002) Khasi Society of Meghalaya: A Sociological Understanding, New Delhi Publishing Company.

Rudd A.E (2003) Poetics of Village Politics: The Making of West Bengal's Rural Communism, New York Oxford University Press.

Srinivas M.N (1976) The Remembered Village, University of California Press Berkeley.

Shadap-Sen, N.C (1981) The Origin and Early History of the Khasi-Synteng People, Calcutta:Firma KLN Private Ltd.

Spencer J (2007) Anthropology, Politics, and The State: Democracy And Violence In South Asia, Cambridge University Press.

West, Candace and Zimmerman, D. H. (1987) Doing gender. Gender and Society 1:125-51.

39

Cervical Cancer and Cultural Vulnerabilities of Meitei Women

Arundhati Devi Maibam

Introduction

Cervical cancer is cancer of the cervix which is the narrow part of the lower uterus and an important part of the female reproductive system. It is the commonest cancer cause of death among women in developing countries (Denny, 2012). ICO Information Centre on HPV and cancer (as cited in Sreedevi et al., 2015) reported that 122,844 women in India are diagnosed with cervical cancer and 67,477 die from the disease annually. India has a population of 432.2 million women aged 15 years and older who are at risk of developing cancer (ibid). It is the second most common cancer in women aged 15–44 years (ibid). According to latest estimates by Indian Council of Medical Research (ICMR), it has emerged as a major killer among Indian women, overtaking breast cancer deaths as over 62,000 women died of cervical cancer in 2015, accounting for 24 percent of the total cancer-related deaths of women in India (Dey, 2016). In Manipur, cervical cancer is one of the leading causes of death among women. It is the second leading site of cancer among women (National Cancer Registry Programme, 2009).

HPV has been found to be a necessary but not sufficient cause for cervical cancer. The long interval between initial infection and disease indicates involvement of other factors such as sexual habits, reproductive factors, other sexually transmitted diseases, co-infection with HIV, smoking, nutritional deficiency, genetic susceptibility, use of hormonal contraceptives, and high parity . Socio-economic and cultural factors greatly influence the health seeking behavior of women. Women often ignore health problems, especially reproductive health problems. They avoid medical treatment and resort to traditional healing until the problem becomes serious. Cultural practices related marriage and cervical cancer, early age at first pregnancy also emerged as a risk factor. Among women with age at first marriage ≤18 years, 70.58 percent were pregnant within the first year of marriage. In their study, Dutta et al. (1990) also observed that the relative risk of acquiring the disease was 6 times more in case of women who had first parity before 18 years of age ($p<0.0001$) as compared to those who had the first parity after the age of 18 years. Lower age at first parity was found to be significantly associated with subsequent development of cancer cervix. This may be attributed to early sexual activities, hormonal changes during pregnancy or may be due to cervical trauma during delivery at a relatively younger age of mother.

Not only in rural settings, traditionally womanhood is directly related to motherhood, and being mothers is perceived as the main if not unique life project and meaning for women. Particularly in rural and indigenous settings, such expectations, implicit and explicit cultural norms are linked to feminine prestige (BID 2010:28), and also impact on the partner's male prestige. In many contexts the pressure is not only over the number but on the sex of the children; boys are socially, culturally and economically higher valued. This implies that women "must" have at least one boy. Even in urban cases this frequently implies that women are pressured to have more children until a boy is born. It must be noted, however, that cultural norms are not always or necessarily represented in negative terms; on the contrary, a large family with many children is frequently associated to plenitude, happiness, security, protection. Nevertheless, the implicit and/or explicit pressure, aggravated by educational, economic and social disadvantages of women, limit their real alternatives to make decisions regarding their reproductive life and health; furthermore, "oftentimes it is their spouses, uncles, mothers-in-law or even neighbours and health workers that make decisions for them" (Camacho et al. 2006:361).

Singer and Monaghan (2000) explained that the mechanism by which the early experience of first sexual intercourse and first pregnancy influence the risk of cervical carcinogenesis could be due to the steroid hormonal influence on HPV infection and on the host's immune response to HPV during pre-adolescence and adolescence. During adolescence and pregnancy, the cervix is exposed to augmented levels of hormonal changes. Oestrogen stimulation facilitates acidification of the vaginal cavity, a determinant of squamous metaplasia when the endocervical epithelial everts (Elson et al., 2000). When this oestrogen-stimulated metaplastic transformation occurs in the presence of HPV, the probability of cell transformation increases, resulting in neoplastic changes (Elson et al., 2000; Shai et al., 2007, 2008; Hwang et al., 2009). This phenomenon is dependent primarily on parity, and is more likely to occur during the first pregnancy rather than subsequent pregnancies (Singer and Monaghan, 2000). Although it has been postulated that these metaplastic changes are also influenced by the trauma and repair experienced during delivery, Münoz et al. (2002) observed no increased risk for cervical carcinoma when traumatic partition was evaluated.

The society expects newly married women to become pregnant soon after marriage. Women, therefore, never think of delaying pregnancy. Failure to bear a child immediately after or within one year of marriage puts a woman in an awkward position. In such situations, every available help is sought for to avoid social stigma attached to barrenness. A feeling of insecurity develops within the woman and fears abandonment by the husband. So the general concept is: the sooner, the better; not realizing the dangers and impediments to health due to early pregnancy and child birth.

Multiple pregnancies

The religious ideal of womanhood intrinsically linked to motherhood and the restricted vision of sexuality in terms of reproduction can paradoxically increase the exposure of women in general and young women in particular to unwanted pregnancies and to the risk of cervical cancer. Women in Manipur, despite being projected as important agents of social control, still remain subdued within the household. They do not enjoy the liberty to restrict pregnancies and avoid abortion. Decision on the number of children primarily rests with the husband and his mother (if any). Women have no choice but to abide by the decision of their husbands who do not understand the importance of checking the physical status of their wives in relation to pregnancy. Multiple pregnancies cause trauma to the cervix and leave it vulnerable to infections which can lead to dysplasia and ultimately cancer. But as the women do not have knowledge about it, they raise no objection for fear of being scorned by their husbands and family members. In most cases, the abortions were conducted without the knowledge of the husband. One major factor for abortion is non-adoption of effective modern birth control measures.

Personal hygiene

Personal hygiene of women in the present study is found to be bad as majority of the women did not take much care about their reproductive organs. Women in general use the inner clothing to dry their genitalia after urinating and seldom wash themselves after intercourse. There is also a practice of sharing clothes including inner garments amongst siblings and between mother and daughter. Though these areas were not investigated, the general information collected on hygiene reflects the existence of these practices among the patients. Infections may have spread from one to another which persisted and in due course of time caused dysplasia. Most of the women in this study made use of cloth during menstruation as they had no knowledge about any other alternative.

Conclusion

The study showed various cultural practices that make women vulnerable to cervical cancer. Cultural practices such as early marriage, early pregnancy, multiple pregnancies, sexual silence, childbearing decision and personal hygiene are habits which can be changed to prevent cervical cancer. There is, therefore, a great need to intensify behaviour change communication and curtail the social and cultural factors that predispose to cervical cancer. Primary and secondary prevention mechanisms such as awareness creation, vaccination and screening targeting particularly the women at high risk should be widely initiated and strengthened.

References

BID (2010): Salud de la mujer indígena: Intervenciones para reducir la muerte materna. Washington D.C.: BID.

Camacho, A., Castro, M., & Kaufman, R. (2006). Cultural aspects related to the health of Andean women in Latin America: A key issue for progress toward the attainment of the Millennium Development Goals. *International Journal of Gynecology and Obstetrics, 94*, 357-363.

Denny, L. (2012). Cervical cancer: prevention and treatment. *Discov Med., 14*, 125–131.

Dey, S. (2016, May 4). Cervical cancer back as top killer among women. *Times of India*, p. 1. Retrieved from http://timesofindia.indiatimes.com.

Dutta, P. K., Upadhyay, A., Dutta, N., Urmil, A. C., Thergoakar, M. P, & Ganguly, S. S. (1990). A case control study of cervix cancer patients attending Command Hospital, Pune. *Ind. J. Cancer, 27* (2),101-108.

Elson, D. A., Riley, R. R., Lacey, A.,…& Arbeit, J. M. (2000). Sensitivity of the cervical transformation zone to estrogen-induced squamous carcinogenesis. *Cancer Res., 60* (5), 1267–1275.

Francis, S. A., Battle-Fisher, M., Liverpool, J.,...& Mofammere, N. (2011). A qualitative analysis of South African women's knowledge, attitudes, and beliefs about HPV and cervical cancer prevention, vaccine awareness and acceptance, and maternal-childcommunication about sexual health. *Vaccine, 29* (47), 8760–8765.

Hwang, L. Y., Ma, Y., Benningfield, S. M., …& Moscicki, A. B. (2009). Factors that influence the rate of epithelial maturation in the cervix in healthy young women. *J Adolesc Health. 44*. 103–110.

Munoz, N., Franceshi, S., Bosetti, C., … & Bosch, F. (2002). Role of parity and Human papillomavirus in cervical cancer: the IARC multicentric case control study. *Lancet, 359*, 1093-1101.

National Cancer Registry Programme. (2009) *Annual report of Population based cancer registry, Imphal, Manipur State*. ICMR.

Shai, A., Brake, T., Somoza, C., & Lambert, P. F. (2007). The human papillomavirus E6 oncogene dysregulates the cell cycle and contributes to cervical carcinogenesis through two independent activities. *Cancer Res. 67*, 1626–1635.

Shai, A., Pitot, H.C., & Lambert, P.F. (2008). Loss synergizes with estrogen and papillomaviral oncogenes to induce cervical and breast cancers. *Cancer Res. 68*, 2622–2631.

Singer, A., & Monaghan, J. (2000). Colcoscopy of the normal cervix: a prerequisite to establish the diagnosis of cervical precancer. In A. Singer & J. Monaghan (Eds.), *Lower Genital Tract Precancer: Coloscopy, Pathology, and Treatment* (pp 43–70). Oxford, UK: Blackwell Sciences Ltd.

Sreedevi, A., Javed, R., & Dinesh, A. (2015). Epidemiology of cervical cancer with special focus on India. *Int J Women's Health*, *7*, 405-414.

40

Inter-tribal Marriage among the Thangal Tribe of Manipur-continuity and Change

Maibam Monoranjan Singh and
Arundhati Devi Maibam

Introduction

Marriage is a social institution determined by culture. It defines all the institutional demands, rights, duties, privileges and immunities of the pair as husband and wife (Hoebel & Frost, 1979). It is a method in which cultural tradition is passed on to the children by parents. All societies have prescriptions and proscriptions regarding who may or may not marry whom. In some societies these restrictions are subtle, while in some others, individuals who can or cannot be married are more explicitly and specifically defined.

Manipur is a state inhabited by different tribes, each with its own distinctive marriage system. The Thangal tribe is one of the Scheduled tribes of the state inhabiting in Senapati district. As in all societies, the Thangal society prescribes rules of marriage to establish a family. Monogamy is the prescribed rule though polygamy is permitted (Thangmi, 2006). Marrying a cousin from the maternal side through engagement is the usual type of marriage (Lisam, 2011, p. 386). Marriage through negotiation is the preferred type though elopement is on the rise (Thangmi, 2006). Selection of mate is done by the parents of the boy on attainment of marriageable age. Clan exogamy is strictly observed and penalty is imposed on the person who marries within the clan. Marriage within the clan is held equivalent to marrying his own sisters. Breach of this rule amounts to expulsion from the village if initial attempts to separate the boy and girl fail. Though intra-tribal marriage is the preferred type, which has been boosted recently by the Thanga Naga Union, the apex body of the tribe; intertribal marriage is a common practice since immemoriable times.

Relationships with neighbouring villages are established through marriage ties. Intertribal marriage fosters unity and is regarded as a good mechanism to minimise differences. However, it would be wrong to overlook the disadvantages which can lead to serious problems in the society, especially in loss of language. Though inter-tribal marriage is a good means to nurture/foster unity among the groups, it is also a contemporary index of language loss among youths (Ofodu, 2014, p.45).

The present study has been taken up to understand the status and extent of intertribal marriage among the Thangal, its impact on language and to identify the reasons for change in the age-old practice.

Methodology

The study is based on both secondary and primary data. The secondary data related to the Thangal tribe in particular and all scheduled tribes in general have been obtained from Census of India, 2011. Journals, books and Ph.D. dissertations related to the topic have been consulted for a broad theoretical framework. Primary data have been collected through interviews with elderly and knowledgeable residents of Thangal villages.

The Thangal

The Thangal, is a small indigenous Scheduled Tribe of Manipur, India. Formerly known and recognized as Koirao, they are found clustered in eleven villages in Senapati district, which is situated on the northern side of Manipur. The villages are Angkailongdi, Makeng Taphou, Katomei Makeng,Katomei MakengChajinba. MapaoThanga, Mayangkhang, Mayangkhang Ning-thoupham, Thangal Surung, Tumnoupokpi, TumuyonKhunou (Yaikongpao) and Tumuyon Khullen. Physically, they are indistinguishable from the neighbouring indigenous tribes who are of Mongoloid stock. The 2011 Census of India reports that the population of Koirao now identified as Thangal is 4475 individuals comprising of 2208 males and 2267 females and it made up 0.38 percent of the state tribal population.

The etymological meaning of the term 'Thangal' is still obscure and the views are varied. According to H. Khangba of Tumnoupokpi village (ex-President of Thangal Naga Union, Manipur), the Thangals represent one of the Naga tribes who are found on the southernmost part of Manipur. The name Thangal is believed to have been derived from the term "*Thangkaimi*" (meaning the southernmost people) by the other Naga tribes. Late K. Lengkham, former Chief of Thangal Surung village, opines that the name 'Thangal' has been derived from the name of a Thangal king named 'Thangkaba' meaning most superior. The people of the valley referred to him as "Thanggraba". Rev. Th. Thangmi, also from Thangal Surung and ex executive secretary of the Thangal Naga Baptist Association (TNBA), is of the opinion that "Thangal

Hill range is so long that it was commonly known as 'Thangkan' in the olden days. Under the jurisdiction of Thangal Surung village, there are two Kuki villages, namely, Thangkanphai and ThangkanThanglunpa. Having extracted some portion of the village names, the word 'Thangkan' has been coined in naming their village. The neighbouring Kuki villagers used to call the people of ThangalSurung village as 'Thangkan'. This could be one of the reasons of popularising the term 'Thangal' to mean their people" (Thangmi, 2012, p. 56).

The Thangals are patriarchal, patrilineal and patrilocal. The household head in a Thangal family is generally the senior most male member and follow ultimomogeniture system of inheritance with sixteen exogamous clans. Monogamy is the general rule in the society. In the olden times marriage among the Thangals were prohibited as all the Thangals are regarded as brothers and sisters. Nowadays marriage among the Thangals is allowed while strictly maintaining clan exogamy. However, the long tradition of Thangal male acquiring mates from the other tribe is still in vogue, on the other hand many non- Thangal men who took temporary refuge at various Thangal villages have in time married Thangal women. Some of them have become permanent residents while some are taking temporary shelter. Those who have become permanent residents have been inducted into the Thangal society with a proper clan name and recognised as full-fledged Thangal men.

Thangal is both the name of the tribe and language. It is known by alternate names like Khoirao, Khoirao Naga, Koirao, Kolya, Mayangkhang, Miyang-Khang, Ngari, Thangal, Thanggal, Tukaimi (Lewis et al., 2015). Dr. Grierson (1987) considered Thangal (Koirao)language as belonging to the Naga-Bodo sub-group having close affinity with Kabui and Kacha Naga languages. The language code of the Thangal language is ISO 639-3 and it has been classified under Sino-Tibetan (*ibid*) as shown below.

Sino-Tibetan
- Tibeto-Burman
  - Sal
  - Kuki-Chin-Naga
    - Zeme
    - Naga, Thangal

The Thangals are multilingual and communicate with non-Thangal people primarily in Manipuri and use Roman script in writing their language. There is no regular radio or doordarshan programme in the language except for some occasional cultural programmes. Though it is a recognized language, it is neither included in the curriculum of the formal education nor taught in the school as the number of speakers of the language is few. It has limited published works with only the holy bible and a few song books in Thangal as a result of revitalisation started by a section of dedicated social workers.

Marital relationship of Thangal with other tribes

i. Maram

Owing to close affinity in traditional attire, folklore and custom, large scale exchange of wives between Thangal and Maram has been in practice since time immemorial. As majority of the Thangal speak Maram dialect, wives from Maram never felt the need to learn the Thangal dialect. Children with a Thangal father and Maram mother grew up in a bilingual environment. They could understand both the dialects but failed to speak either with perfection.

ii. Kabui

As noted by Mc Culloch, Thangal and Kabui have close socio-cultural and linguistic affinities. Easy communication and regular contact between the two tribes brought them closer in physical proximity, particularly Thangal Surung and Yaikongpao. Consequently marriage between the two became inevitable as closeness nurtures fondness.

iii. Liangmei

Thangal and Liangmei share a common myth of origin. Both claim to have originated from Makhel with close linguistic affinity. Socio-cultural similarity and geographical proximity led to high rate of inter marriage between the two. Liangmei women are found in almost all the Thangal villages.

iv. Mao

As in the case of Liangmei, Mao and Thangal believe to have originated from Makhel. Socio-cultural similarities led to inter marriage of Mao and Thangal, particularly the northern settlers who were the first to convert to Christianity under the influence of the Mao.

v. Tangkhul

According to a legend, Thangal and Tangkhul of Hundung village are brothers. Like the Liangmei, the Tangkhul also claim to have originated from Makhel thus establishing a close relation with the Thangal. Similarity in culture is evident from the shawl called *Chongkhom Karong* used by the Tangkhul which is of Thangal origin. Large scale intermarriage took place between the Tangkhul and the southern Thangal.

Intermarriage between Thangal and other tribes, particular with those mentioned above, have been in practice for along time and is still continuing. The reason behind selection of wife from other tribes may be either due to large-scale migration to new habitats or due to living at close range with neighbouring villages of other tribes or because of the attraction they draw with their reputation as good warriors, men of valour and skill. Above all, few decades back the Thangals did not completely forbid marriage within the tribe, they did not encourage it as they had the notion or belief of considering the Thangal women as their own sisters, hence the Thangals have the tradition of taking wives from other tribes. The following charts (adapted from Thangmi 2006) gives a picture of tribal affiliation of marriage partners of Thangal men (76.71 percent) and tribal affiliations of the marriage partners of Thangal women and non-Thangal men staying at Thangal villages (23.28 percent).

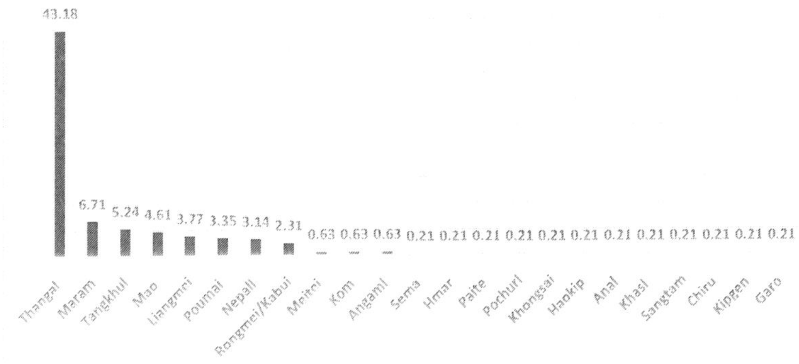

Chart 40.1 : Tribal affiliation of marriage partners of Thangal men

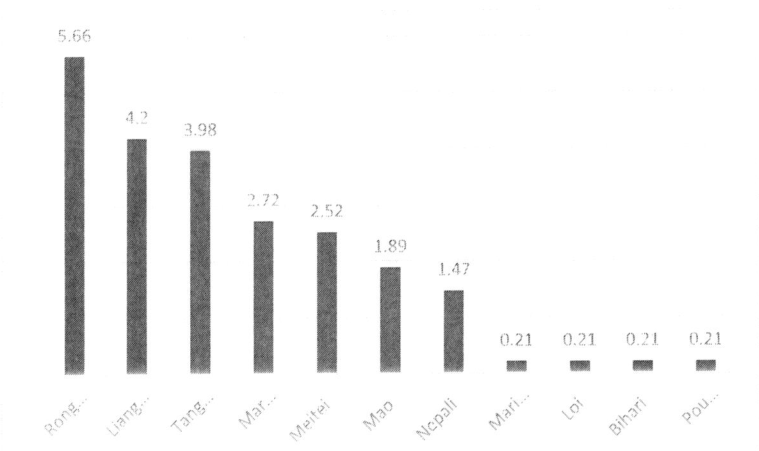

Chart 40.2 : Tribal affiliations of the marriage partners of Thangal women and non-Thangal men staying at Thangal villages

As the Thangal males were taking wives from other tribes, Thangal women were married to men from other tribes. As a result, there was a circulation of women among the Thangal and the neighbouring tribes. On the other hand, men from the other tribe marrying Thangal women who are taking refuge at Thangal villages is also common as indicated in table table 2. These circumstances has led to the high rate of miscegenation and population admixture among the Thangals.

Decline in intertribal marriage

After embracing Christianity under Baptist denomination which dates back to 1937, education among the people improved with establishment of private English medium schools. The educated undertook a venture to translate the Holy Bible into Thangal to facilitate easy understanding among the common mass. The venture became a great challenge as appropriate Thangal words could not be identified easily. The people became aware of an acute problem of language loss. On keen investigation, they realized that traditional recruitment of women from other tribes into the Thangal society through marriage led to reduced use of Thangal dialect at home and among children born to couple of different tribal affiliation. Such a situation motivated the Thangal Naga Union, the apex body of the tribe, to take a decision to encourage intra-tribal marriage. Though intertribal marriage has not been banned completely, intra-tribal marriage has been boosted by giving first preference to daughter-in-laws from within the tribe.

Impact of intertribal marriage on language

A number of research studies show that intertribal marriages are influential in shaping the linguistics environment at home. The Thangal being a group which regularly chooses marriage partners from outside the group arefaced with the problem of language loss. Such findings have been observed in studies conducted by Borberly (2000); David (2008); Martin (2005) and Martin and Yen (1992). In situations where spouses come from different linguistic background, there is a clear need to establish a common language for the home. In some situations, a linguistic compromise is made which often does not include the use of either spouse's mother tongue. In other situations, one of them will adopt the spouse's language if it is the dominant one in the society. Both situations involve a lack of mother tongue usage which discourages the maintenance of such language (Lasimbang, 1997). Singh (2016) observed high rate of miscegenation, rapid decline in the use of the mother tongue and sign of language shift among the Thangals.

Almost all the Thangals are bilingual suggesting co-existence of minor language with a major one which is an indication initiation or precursor of language shift. A large section of the population choose to speak *Lamjan / chinglon* (*lingua franca*) as the most convenient language in most social domains which pose a threat to the native language and identity of the people as well .

Use of Thangal language at home has declined remarkably and some of the younger generation cannot communicate in Thangal. It is also observed that in some Thangal villages large numbers of individuals in the younger generation no longer prefer to communicate in Thangal though they can understand and speak satisfactorily as observed by Crawford (2007).

Conclusion

Despite a growing trend of intramarriage among the Thangal, inter-tribal marriage is still practised. The traditional practice of exogamy and recruitment of wife from other groups has not only led to a high degree of miscegenation but also to a high degree of mixture in language. A shift from the native Thangal to a new *lingua franca* called *Lamjan* in some Thangal villages is a distinct sign of language shift. This needs to be checked with well formulated policies. A timely intervention to check the gradual shift is immediately needed. Unless a resolution to learn and promote Thangal language is adopted, chances of complete loss of the heritage within a few decades cannot be ruled out.

References

Borbely, A. (2000). *The process and the factors of language shift and maintenance: a sociolinguistic research in the Romanian minority in Hungary.* Retrieved May 7, 2009 from http://rss.archives.ceu.hu/ archive/00001138/01/146.pdf.

Thangmi, C.A. (2006). *The Thangal nana tribe of North East India.* New Delhi: Mittal Publications.

Crawford, J. (2007). Seven Hypotheses on Language Loss Causes and Cures. In Gina Cantoni (Ed.), *Stabilizing Indigenous Languages* (pp. 45-60). Flagstaff: Northern Arizona University.

David, M.K.(2008): Language choice of urban sino-Indians in Kuala Lumpur, Malaysia[Electronic version]. *Migracijskeietni ke teme*,3,217–233. Retrieved February 20 2015, from http://hrcak.srce.hr/index. php? show = clanak &id clanak jezik = 48622.

Grierson, G.A. (1987). *Linguistic Survey of India.* Vol.III, part II &III. Delhi : Motilal Banarsidas,

Hoebel, E.A. & Everett, L.F. (1979). *Cultural and Social Anthropology*, Tata McGraw-Hill Publishing Company Limited, New Delhi.

Lasimbang, R. (1997). SituatsibahasaKadazandusun masa kini[The Kadazandusun language situation]. Paper presented at the *Seminar Pendidik Kadazandusun* [Seminar for Kadazandusun Educators], Donggongon, Penampang, Sabah, Malaysia. July.

Lewis, M. P., Simons, G. F., & Fennig, C.D. (eds). (2015). *Ethnologue: Languages of the World*, Eighteenth edition. Dallas, Texas: SIL International.

Lisam, K.S. (2011). *Encyclopaedia of Manipur* Vol 2. (p. 386), Delhi: Kalpaz Publications.

Martin, P. W. & Yen, E. (1992). Language use among the Kelabit living in urban centers. In P. W. Martin (Ed.), Papers from the second bi-ennial international conference: *Shifting patterns of language use in Borneo* Vol. 3. (pp. 147-164). USA: The Borneo Research Council, Inc.

Martin, P. (2005). Language shift and code-mixing: a case study from Northern Borneo. *Australian journal of linguistics*, 25(1), (pp.109 – 125).

Ofodu, G.O. (2014). Governance and Language Loss among Youths in Nigeria. *IOSR Journal of Humanities and Social Science* ,19(5), ver.II:pp 42-49.

Singh, M.M. (2016). Language Loss among the Thangal tribe of Manipur. In Dhanaraju (Ed.),*Voice of the Other* (pp. 264-288).New Delhi: Gen Next Publication.

41

Impacts of Hinduism on the Meitei Society

S. Sumanta Singh and Thiyam Rabikanta Singh

Introduction

Whether desirable or not, cultural assimilation often brings a drastic change to a society. But, the cultural assimilation does not guarantee social homophily between cultures as the dominant culture was culturally different. Earlier ethnic identities can be preserved and reaffirmed even where extensive assimilation may have taken place (Yinger, 1997, p 42). There may produce integrative shift of culture, but rapid amalgamation in assimilation may also effect dissimilation. The present paper delineates the assimilation of the Meiteis in the historic period by compelling authoritative power of kings through the change of religion. It may relate to their geo-strategy insights but the assertion of religion-ethnicity connection was perpetuately criticized through the passage of time.

The Meiteis are the dominant inhabitants in the central valley of Manipur, a northeastern state of India along with several tribes of the surrounding hills. People of different colours, contrasting attitudes and varied aptitudes merged in the Meitei society and fused and interfused with various anthropoid species during the protohistorical and historical periods. The easterners (*Nongpok Haram*) and westerners (*Nongchup Haram*) were the main immigrations in the Meitei population. The immigrations of the agents and carriers of Hindu religious order have started since 1514 and 1516 A.D. as corroborated by the record (Ibungohal & Khelchandra, 2005). No deceptive information having the upper hand of bribery and corruption is kept in abeyance in matters relating to the migrations and settlements of the Brahmans in Manipur. Even though the Brahmans were in the lower class and not permitted to participate in the annual Meitei athletic sporting meets they were trained in the art of oration and oratory since their childhood by their household /family elders or by a reputed teacher, specially engaged by their parents. So they could speak in such a way as to draw the attention of the hearers, and listeners, etc. As they were habituated in their religious rites, rituals and ritualistic affairs, it was automatic on their part to speak or tell stories, myths, legends, etc. from the puranas, epics, etc. in which they were well-versed. Therefore it is observed that the influences of the Brahmanic religious order had prevailed during period prior to their entering into the socio- political sphere of Manipur (Ibungohal & Khelchandra, 2005, pp. 59, 66, 68) and much earlier than their first initiation to Brahmanic religious order. In the present study an attempt has been made to dissect the impacts of Hinduism in positive and negative ways in the Meitei society.

Methodology

The study was carried out by using interview method as well as secondary sources. In-depth interview after chalking out the key informants who belong to bamon group as well as Meitei scholars was adopted.

Acceptance of Impacts

The Meiteis, even though they loved and regarded their indigenous properties in their socio-cultural and religious realm, could understand the essentials, requirements, and necessitated materials brought about by the wheel of time against their nature cult and cultural riches, treasures, etc., because their motherland was more precious and valuable to them than their lives. They conceived that if they lost the motherland their everything was lost. So they are ready to give up anything, and to sacrifice everything to protect their mother country from the loss of her freedom and independence.

When the time of need came to retain prestige and honour as mentioned above by seeking aid and assistance to withstand a superior force of the Burma empire, Meitei –lord Tubee Charairongba embraced Hindu Sakta Sect and Kalika worship cult to secure help and support of the Hindu countries to the west of Manipur. Here lies the first Hindu impact of the Brahmanic religious order on the local Meitei society in the aspect of acceptance. As the Meitei monarch Tubee Charairongba had the intention and inspiration to adopt Hinduism and the initiation or conversion needed a Brahmin to carry out the Hindu consecration for becoming the preceptor in the best wish, the Brahmins were raised to a high status and standard.

With the help of their religious initiation and appreciation the Brahmins were given a room of honour in the Manipuri local society and foreign diplomatic politics and policies and were employed as envoys. The first statement of the royal chronicle in this regard goes as follows:

"…Nongthonbam Khommagee kum Shaka 1627…Thawan tha 27ni Langmaichingda Bamon Takhen changba Kamdevasung Chandrashekharsung 2ma thoklak-e!!" (Ibungohal & Khelchandra, 2005, p.69).

Translation

On Sunday the 27th day of Meitei lunisolar month of Thawan in 1627 Saka (corresponding to a date in the 2nd week of September, 1705 A.D.), the year of Nongthombam Khoma's sponsion, the Brahmins, namely Kamdeva and Chandrasekhar, (who had gone on duty to Takhen, the present Tripura State) have arrived.

The Brahmins' participation and sharing in the political, social, economic and allied fields, etc., were approved and accepted by the Meitei society. Even though these were the indirect results, effects and influences of Brahmanical religious propagation and popularization, the results paved the way for ascending the ladder of the social stratification of people in the Meitei society. Soon the Brahmins who converted the social units of Meitei society were accepted by the Meiteis not only as the recognized and acknowledged subjects of the Meitei king and the kingdom but also were admitted into the universal, national and communal brotherhood of the Meiteis. Besides, the Brahmins of present generation are the descendants Brahmin fathers and Meitei wives.

Reformation under Hinduism

When Meitei king Garibaniwaza reformed the Meitei society into a Hindu society the country was renamed under the name and style of Mekhali or Mekhalidesha (Ibochouba et al. 1995) and the Hindu culture of cremation in the disposal of the dead was introduced and linguistic designation of *Maharaj* which means emperor or king (appeared) in 1735 A.D. (Ibungohal & Khelchandra, 2005, p. 85) Sanskrit in the Manipuri vocabulary arrived to an extent and in cultural aspects and respects began to lay out a great deal of Brahmanic cultural and religions elements to the local Meitei society. The then Meiteis perceived and absorbed them in their socio-political and socio-economic lives as the acceptance of the Brahmanic religious order.

During the reign of Meitei-lord Garibaniwaza, the pilgrimage in Hindu thought and feeling to the foreign country beyond the territorial jurisdiction of Manipur started in 1725 A.D. (Ibungohal & Khelchandra, 2005, p. 85) but the direct visit to the holy places, rivers etc., outside Manipur began since 1735 A.D. and 1741 A.D. (Ibungohal & Khelchandra, 2005, pp. 95, 105)The pilgrimage to eye witness the Hindus' holy river Ganga was accepted by the Meiteis and the first and foremost Hindu ideological visit is recorded in the royal chronicle of Manipur as the following:

"Thangga Takhen gee Kum Shaka 16660...Hiyanggei tha...27 ni Leipakpokpada Mahapurus Bila Oikhi-e (Nongka-ye)...Poinu tha 11 ni Leipakpokpda Sheeja Guru Ongbina Gangga Eeruppa Chatkhiye. 12 ni Yumshakeishada Kriparam Mayang chenkhi–e!! ... Sanasam Maichougee Kum Shaka 1667...Thawantha ...13 ni Yumshakeishada Bamon Ramgopalna Sheeja Tampha, Sheeja Atom 2magee Loobu Gangga You-o haiduna peekhi–e!! ... Poinu tha...3 ni Eeraida sheeja guru ongbeega Kreparamga Kanjkadagee thunglei –e!" (Ibungohal & Khelchandra, 2005, p. 111).

Translation

On Tuesday the 27th day of the Meitei lunisolar month of Hiyanggei in 1666 saka (corresponding to a date in the 2nd week of December in 1744 AD), the year of Thanga Takhen's sponsion the great man (preceptor Shantidas Mahanta) breathed his last in the Burmese country...On Tuesday the 11th day of Poinu (corresponding to a date in the last week of December in the same year) the princess who had married with the royal preceptor went on pilgrimage to have a holy dip in the sacred river Ganges. On Wednesday the 12th instant Kriparam left for the Dimasa Kingdom ... on Wednesday, the 13th day of the Meitei lunisolar month of thawan 1667 saka (the year of Sanasam Maichou's sponsion), Brahmin Ramgopal was entrusted to drop the bone remains of the princesses namely, Tampha and Aton in the holy Ganga...on Friday, the 3rd day of the month of Poinu (a date in the 3rd week of December in the same year) the princess who wedded the royal preceptor and Kriparam arrived from their pilgrimage of the holy Ganges.

The above statement indicates Meitei pilgrimages to the holy places, rivers, etc., thereby respecting for the Brahmanic religious sacred shrines, rivers, places, monuments and others. The Brahmin cited in the above statement under the name of Kriparam who had rendered Gati (Sanskrit meaning help, assist etc.) to the princess who espoused the royal preceptor Shantidas in her pilgrimage by guiding and acting as caretaker during the course of pilgrimage was conferred the surname of Gatimayum to his household for his act and help offered to the princess (named Champakalata). His family under the said surname is still enduring in present Manipuri society.

The Brahmanic tradition of the cremating 'chaste woman' alive with the corpse of her dead husband in the same pyre under the style of *sati daha* was interestingly accepted by the Meitei society and it prevailed in Manipur since 1725 AD during the regime of Meitei-Lord Garibaniwaza till 1784 AD during the reign of Meitei-Lord Chingthangkhomba. The recorded information in this regard is summed up as under:-

Translation

(1) On Thursday, the 25th Eenga in 1647 saka (a date in the 2nd week of July 1725 AD), the year of Langmaithem Loija, prince Murari died, his corpse was cremated at Manglen (in the Kangla capital complex) and his two consorts had committed to die with their husbands by jumping in the burning pyre of their husband (Ibungohal & Khelchandra, 2005, p. 86).

(2) On Sunday, the 18th Mera in 1655 saka (a date in the first week of November in 1733 AD), A Shatpam man who held the position of Khwairakpam died at the village near the foothill of Chinga and one of his wife committed Sati with her husband in the same pyre (Ibungohal & Khelchandra, 2005, pp. 93-94).

(3) On Thursday the 7th Sajibu in 1657 saka (third week of April in 1735 AD), the year of Loukrakpam Moiramba's sponsion Brahman Lakhon expired and his two wives followed the Sati tradition (Ibungohal & Khelchandra, 2005, p. 96).

(4) On Thursday the 6th Kalen in 1657 saka (a date in the 3rd week of May in 1735 AD), the year of Loukrakpam Moirambam's sponsion. One Wayenbam Moirangthem man who held the portfolio of Nongthonba expired and his two consorts performed the Hindu rite of burning the chaste woman (Ibungohal & Khelchandra, 2005, p. 96).

(5) On Tuesday the 10th Thawan in 1706 saka (a date in the last week of August 1784 AD) two spouses consisting of the son and daughter-in-law of Petwa of Mayang Ningthounai (Ningthoukhong) committed suicide at a time in concept of chastisement of female spouse (Ibungohal & Khelchandra, 2005, p. 147).

From these findings, it is evident that the culture of Sati burning prevailed for a period of about half of a century in the 18th century AD but became obsolete by itself. But this Hindu rite continued till the abolition of "Sati" during the tenure of Lord William Bentinck (1828-35AD), the Governor General East India Company. The abolition of this rite in India is portrayed as under (Majumdar, 1979, p. 232).

Lord William Bentinck earned undying fame by notable reforms. The chief among those was the abolition of Sati. According to a long standing custom among the Hindus the wife of a man, who has just died used to burn herself along with her husband. Sometimes she was forced to do so by her relatives. Cases are on record where unwilling victims jump out of the fire, but her half burnt body was forcibly thrown back into it. The cruel and revolting practice was stopped by legislation.

Two peepal trees, symbolizing 'the burnt chaste woman' and 'fire afraid woman' under the names and style of 'Sati Khongnang' and 'Meikibi Khongnang' respectively, in the concept of **"Sati burning rite"** (*Sati Daha*) are still standing on the bank of river Imphal in vicinity of Bangoon village of Mayang Imphal, Imphal west-II, Manipur. Thus, though the culture flourished for a short period the acceptance of Sati rite by the local Meitei society has testimony till today.

Diffusing Hindu concept in local rites and festivals

The acceptance of the impact of the Brahmanic religious order in the local Meitei society is vividly seen in many aspects and respects of Meitei social and cultural heritages, festivals, rites, rituals, ritualistic ceremonies, celebrations, functions, etc. and religious and religiously festive performances, observances and commemorations such as funs and amusements, dramatic ballets, devotional choirs, folk and modernized songs etc. Ample examples may be set but only two are depicted as under:-

(i) *Ravana Kappa*: It is a festival of Meitei dress and ornamental competition and martial arts demonstration, named *Kwak Tanba* (driving the crows to fly away). Ravana Kappa (shooting of Ravana, the demon emperor) is the symbolic shooting of a rude image of Ravana with bow and arrow in the concept of the Hindu festival of killing Ravana by Rama performed in dramatized feature elsewhere in Uttar Pradesh, Rajasthan, and Maharashtra, Thailand, etc. This programme, as it bears the observation of ominous signs for the natural and artificial phenomenon to be ensued in the kingdom in the following year is still enduring. By observing the direction of crows when driven away is read and prediction is done. Crowning of Senapati and conferring of *pana* administration to Senapati at Ramji Prabhu (one of Hindu temple of Lord Ram) is also performed on this day. *Pana* is the administrative regional division of Meitei kingdom (Ibungohal & Khelchandra, 2005, pp. 110-111).

(ii) *Shajibu Cheiraoba*: It is the Meitei/Manipuri celebration of the New Year's Day in the lunisolar calendar. It is held in the month of *Sajibu* and date is fixed on 13th April. The festival was also diffused with the Hindu festival called *Charak puja*. On this day of *Chei* (*Chahi*) *lauba* (proclamation of the end of the past year and commencement of a new year), handing over and taking over of sponsors of the preceding and ensuing years is carried out before divine Govindajee. Because the king of Manipur in the spiritual and mythic context of the polytheistic sphere is divine Govindajee and his Yuvaraja (crown prince) and Senapati (Chief of Army) are divine Vrindavanachandra/ Vrinamchandra and Ramjee Prabhu respectively (Singh, 1976, pp. 25- 26). Prior to the sponsors of the preceding and following years, termed in Meitei dialect as *Chei/Chahi thaba* (enumerators of years) there is the ceremony of Yuvaraj *amasung* Senapati *Boriba* which is the crowning and conferring of powers, and functions, of the Crown prince and Chief of Army by the King of Manipur, who is conducting and witnessing oath taking of both the sponsors of the years. The crowning and conferring of powers etc., of the Senapati at divine Ramjee Prabhu Complex is also taking place in the morning programme of *Kwak Tanba*.

Emerging forms of festivals, art and rites-de-passage

The religious festivals observed in Manipur since the reign of saint king Bhagyachandra with omissions and additions during the time of succeeding Kings. Some of cultural additions are: (1) Maha Rasa on Mera Waphukpa, (2) Kunja Rasa on Mera Wayungba, (3) Basanta Rasa in Shajibu, (4) Jhullon Jatra, (5) Ratha Jatra, (6) Dol Jatra or Holi, (7) Vasanti Puja, (8) Sharadiya Devi Puja, (9) Govardhana Puja, (10) Ram Navami, (11) Shivaratri, (12) Vishwakarma Puja, (13) Kali Puja, (14) Lakshmi Puja or Deepanita, (15) Nitya Rasa, (16) Diva Rasa, Goshtha, (17) Goura Lila, (18) Vasaka, (19) Khubak Eeshei, (20) Heikru-Hidongba, etc.. Almost all the festivals appear to have been in the acceptance of the local populace.

The life's ceremonies celebrated in accordance with Hindu Brahmanic thought and philosophy under the acceptance of the Meitei society are enumerable as :- (1) Swasti Puja (the adoration of the Goddess presiding over the sixth day of the newborn child), (2) Anna Prasha/Prashang (the ceremony of giving a new born child food for the first time) otherwise termed in Manipuri as *chaumba*, (3) Vidyarambha (arrangement for learning/education), (4) Vivaha (marriage), (5) Shradha (the ritual ceremony after the final disposal of the dead), (6) Sambalsharik Shradha (the ritual ceremony on the first death anniversary), etc. Almost all these ceremonies appear to be in the life cycle of a Meitei who belongs to the twice born castes Irom (Amubi et al. 1994, pp. 86, 223).

The impact of the Brahmanic religious order, Hinduisation and Sanskritisation appear to retain in almost all the political, social, economic, judicial and their allied affairs, of Manipur and Meitei society. Even though some additions and modifications to remove cultural shortages and deficiencies were made during the reign of Sir Churachand Singh (1891-1941 AD) the completion of Hinduisation and sanskritisation of Meitei society are presumed to have occurred during the second reign of Maharaj Chandrakriti Singh (1850-86 AD). This period of Maharaj Chandrakriti Singh may be accounted "The Golden period "of Hinduised" and sanskritised culture. As the people accepted the impacts of these Brahmanic religious orders the common man managed to insert or put one or two Sanskrit words while speaking his mother tongue and such a man is considered to be a man of standard, dignity, high status. The fact of the preceding statement can be seen from the writing of scriptures and books written during the reign of Maharaj Chandrakriti Singh. Two examples are portraying hereunder:

1. "*Shree Radha Krishna bhyang Namah/Shree Govinda Prana Shree Ramachandra-na Thawaigee Lanbu Oinariba Shri Maumanipur Puuroudara Shree Pancha Yukta Garibaniwaza Mabudhou Ibungo Maharaja-na Linglamba Vangshabalee Adubu* ... "(Amubi et al. 1994, p. 222).

2. "*.... Ningthou Nangee Vangshabalee Purana-dasung Tangja Linna Mee Pok-e Haiba Asidi Ut-Pat-ne, Desha Nareibaksung Manipur Kou-e, Vabrubahonagee Santan-ne Hairakpa...* " (Amubi, 1979, p. 63P).

The underlying words in the above two versions are names with Sanskrit lexicon or words or derivatives of Sanskrit. Thus the acceptance of impacts of Brahmanic religious order was vigorous enough to ensure speedy spread of the impacts even when there were minor collisions and strife in the course of the current as unanimous scholars/writers had imagined in the former time.

Resistance of Impacts

The most important authentic and realizable source of history of Manipur in almost all aspects and respects is generally and conventionally considered to be the records and information transacted in *Cheitharol Kumbaba*, the royal chronicle of Manipur. There is little information with regard to the resistance of the impacts of the Brahmanic religious order. But some books/ manuscripts written by some anonymous and nicknamed writers were out of the framework of formal writing rules, and norms. They were written during the period ranging from 1850 to 1960 AD. For the purpose to repay their grudge in inferiority or superiority complex, these writers and authors reproduced some past events with the additions of manufactured and forged accounts of history.

The Meitei scriptures like *Sanamahee Laihooy (Achouba)*, or *Khagemba Langjei*, *Sanamahee Laikon*, *Miyat*, *Larei-Lathup*, etc. appear to be in favour of the resistance of the impacts of the Brahmanic religious order but those anonymous writers/authors have followers, patrons, and sympathizers, who do not change even their own Sanskritised names. Meitei scripture *Sanamahee Laihooy (Achouba)* or *Khagemba Langjei* and its modified stylistic book *Sanamahee Laikon* or *Laikanlon* appear to be the books of advocates pleading the resistance of the impacts of the Brahmanic religious order or elements. The anonymous writers are acting as the barrister of darkness as they are depending upon the Sanskritised culture and dialects as they have no alternatives. The anonymous barristers of darkness and the recent advocates of resistance of impacts of Brahmanic religious order are working studying the historical, cultic, cultural sequences of Manipur. An instance is the personalization of Moirang Lanhaba, the Kotwal (Kotwal, the chief of city town police or police officer in-charge of a police station) and follower of Meitei lord Garibaniwaza in following the Ramandi/Ramat Vainshnavite sect and who accompanied him till his murder by the patricidal son Aton or Shatrughana Shai or Tolentomba in January 1752 AD (Ibungohal & Khelchandra, 2005, pp. 120). The identity hiding writers and copyists identified Moirang Lanhaba as the royal physician and a priestly man, a scholar in Meitei theology adoring blessings of lord Sanamahee (*Lai-wa- heiba, Phalou khomba* or *Taibang khaiba*) and a person who was always in contact or occasional contact with divine Sanamahee with or without trance or ecstatic state (Bhogeswhwar, 1974, pp. 67-82, 84-89). He is attributed to have established the authority of divine Sanamahee in the spiritual and religious realm of Meitei thought and theistic school (Bhogeswhwar, 1974, pp. 67-89). The writers of *Sanamahee Laihooy* and *Sanamahee Laikan* plead the similarity and equality of the qualities, virtues, powers, functions etc., of divine Sanamahee with those of the Lord Vishnu who always associates with the Lord Shiva (Bhogeswhwar, 1974, pp. 92-99).

From the above facts and circumstances, it is brought to light that there were someone who had the strong desire to resist; the currents of the impacts of the Brahmanic religious order but they could not fight openly with speeches and actions due to insecure state of their lives. During this period, those who organized for uprising against the Meitei monarch were given the sentences of capital punishment or banishment. Those aspirants who dreamt of raising the barriers against the non-stop flows of Sanskritization of the Brahmanic religions were remaining and living silently keeping the then occurrences in their minds. But some of them dared enough to put something in black and white so that the future generations can imagine the pitiful, condition of the Meitei society. During the last decade of the kingship of Maharaja Churachand Singh, the knight Commander of Star of India and Commander of British empire, some men in the personalization of revivalist rose to save and reform the Meitei society from the Brahmanic religious impact and continuous and gradual Sanskritization of the local Meitei cultural and cultic elements. The progress of revivalism of the said Meitei cultic and ethnical cultural revivalists is still running by following the descriptions of once black listed manuscripts. The social structure has been somewhat changed from the former Hindu social system. For instance, even during British period there was sharp distinction of the people of valley in the Hindu caste line. The census report surveyed by R. Brown, the Political Agent speaks about the then population of the Brahmins and some other sections of Manipuri as follows.

The numbers of houses in section Khoai (Khwai) are 2,267, Khurai 649, Oangkhai (Wangkhei) 703, and Jaskul (Yaiskul) 2118, in all 5737. Allowing on the average of the persons to each house, the population will be 28,685.

Caste	*House*	*Population*
Brahmins	308	1,540
Ganaks	31	155
Raja's Family	101	505
Kshatrias	4,256	21,280
Baisyas	42	210
Kayastha or Kyasts	99	495
Sudras	498	2,490
Hari or Chamars	97	485
Musalmans	305	1525
Total	5,737	28,685

The above given numbers of house and population are only for the Imphal urban area of 1867 to 1875 A.D. Even though Imphal was most thickly populated area of the then Manipur there were Brahmins in the thinly populated rural areas of Manipur. Again, the percentage of the population of the Brahmins to the general population of the then Imphal stood on 5.73. The census also shows the social stratification due to Hinduisation. Caste was the gift of the transformation in religion. It was also an attempt to assimilate in a totally Hindu society.

At present, such a division of the Meitei population is truly not found. The ethics of the Meitei axial cult (Sanamahee cult) in the Polytheistic aspiration seems to be the object of the stated revivalism. But their scope and sphere of views become broader and extended to approach towards the universal modernity of religious context. It is because of the fact that to maintain and retain the ethnic or national identity is given top priority to this day.

Conclusion

Before the Brahmans were first elevated up to the rung of common people in the social stratification of Meitei people, they were unrecognized people. They were not allowed to participate in the states functions. In the historic period the Meteis were not always in good terms of diplomatic relations with Burma. Frequent expansive wars to dominate Meiteis in those days left Meiteis in the notorious seven-year devastations. The Meiteis had no alternative other than western states for seeking helps in totality to cope with that peril. To establish a long lasting relationship to get military aids and refuge, matrimonial relationship was only the solution. As western neighbours who were in good relation were Hindu Kingdoms so also Meitei Kingdom was ought to adopt Hinduism as a means of political economy is a philosophical version of adopting Hinduism. At that very juncture role of Brahmins were a much with their initiation and employing them as convoy, matrimonial relations were established, and Meitei Kingdom was able to protect from Burmese incursion forever as such. Hinduisation of Meitei in the past might be in compulsion as demanded by time and place only to save the kingdom. There may be other versions regarding the conversion of the Meiteis under the advisor-ship of Hindu Brahmin. But, it is the fact that it was with the intention of cultural assimilation with the change in religion. Along with the dissimilation traits linger underneath. So, one section of the present Meitei society moved for the revivalism into their traditionalism. Besides, during the strict Hindu period, the people followed the Hindu faith in fusion with elements of traditionalism. Sanamahi, the household deity was worshipped and the belief system around Sanamahi was used for the revivalist movements.

References

Amubi, I., Kulachandra, N., Bhogeshwor, O.,& Ibochouba, N. (1994). *Sagei Solairol,* Imphal: State Kala Academy

Brown, R. (1981). *Stastical account of Manipur.* New Delhi: Motilal Publication,

Ibochouba, N., Chitreshwor, A., & Kulachandra, B. (1995). *Meitei Bamon Hourakpham.* Imphal: Aribam Sanahanbi Devi.

Ibungohal, L., & Khelchandra, N. (2005). *Cheitharol Kumbaba.* Imphal: Manipur Sahitya Parishad.

Irom, A. (1979). *Awangamba.* Imphal.

Majumdar, R.C. (1979).*A brief History of India.* Calcutta

Oinam, B. (1947). *Sanamahi Laikan.* Imphal: Laishram Lalit Singh,

Singh, L. M. (1976). *Manipuri Devalaya Grantha.*Imphal

Yinger J. M. (1997). *Ethnicity.* Delhi: Rawat Publications.

Section - IV

Ethno-Archaeology

42

Subsistence Pattern of the Poumais, Towards Understanding of the Application of Ethnographic Postulates of the study of Ethno Archaeology

N. Sanatombi Devi and
Kh. Manglembi Devi

Introduction

Ethno-archaeology is "the direct observation field study of the form, manufacture, distribution, meaning and uses of artifacts and their institutional setting and social unit correlates among living, non-industrial people for the purpose of constructing better explanatory model to aid archaeological analogy and inference", Stanislawski (1974). Lewis R. Binford (1968) has utilized the knowledge of the present day societies to successfully interpret the past human society and its culture to a large extent. He (1977, 1978, and 1983) has also studied Nunamiut Caribou hunters of Alaska and the Navajo developed cybernetic theory that explains the parallelism between Prehistoric and Contemporary pre-literate societies. Ethno-archaeology studies the modern simple societies and attempts at reconstructing the life ways of early man on the ground of spiritual and tangible cultural information, Medhi (2002). Ethno-archaeology is now basically based on the premise that the study of the traditional socio-cultural and behavioural patterns of a group of people along with traditional tools can lead us to the knowledge of the past cultural life of human groups. The reasoning in the case of this kind of research is based on analogy derived from the comparison of the artifacts explored in archaeological studies with the traditional artifacts used by the people under observation Devi (2007).

The main aim of the study is to formulate the ethnographic postulates about the subsistence pattern of the Oinam people by making ethnographic observations from a close range so that an empirical insight into how their economic activities, such as, gathering, hunting fishing, agriculture, weaving, pottery, etc. that are interrelated with the techno-material basis of their life ways continued from their past to the present. Such postulates resulted from the ethnographic observation lead to the formulation of hypothesis. However the present study mainly deals with the ethnographic study of a hill people in Manipur from which the ethnographic postulates are derived on the presumption that these can havea correlation with archaeological past. Both primary and secondary data have been used. Various techniques of data collection like observation, key informant interviewing, case history method and scheduled method are used as the situation and nature of the data demanded. Secondary data are based on data such as written records, books, journal and internet searching.

Subsistence Pattern

For the present study the Oinam Hill Village which is located at a distance of about 125km to the north of the Imphal town has been selected in order to know the total way of life of the Poumais. The village is under the jurisdiction of purul sub-division of Senapati district with a total population of 1032 individuals .It consists of five localities *khels* namely *Rinita, Dainita, Thoulaomi, Singnemi and Lanemi*. A representative from each *khel* is nominated as a member of the village authority to assist the village head man in administration. The Poumais following their tradition, believe that they had come out from a cave. Though the origin of the Poumais is lost in mystery, their tradition points to Makhel a placein the Mao area,to the north of the Oinam village as a place of earliest settlement during the course of their migration from south west china, through Burma and islands of South east Asia to Manipur before their settlement to the present habitate. They named the village as *Ngimai* (Oinam in Manipur), which means a village discovered through smelling of soil. Therefore, naming of Oinam is quite related and significant with the making of earthen pot. Linguistically, they belong to Tibeto-Burman Family. Rice is their staple food. They are patrilineal society following patrilocal type of residence. Monogamy is the preferential form of marriage, However, polygamy is also permissible. Clan exogamy is strictly followed. Besides marriage within the same locality (*khel)* is also prohibited. They practice agriculture as a way of life but not as a profession. Moreover, it is also a fact that gathering, hunting, fishing are still a part of their livelihood though they live a food producing economy. Both men and women are engaged in agriculture. Besides, in the lean season males are engaged in making basketry and household utensils whereas females are closeted in weaving and pot making. The pots prepared by the Poumai are known as *Pouli*.

Gathering

It is a part and partial of their economy. Besides they are expert in collecting honey comb frog, snake, and a type of edible insect locally known as *Lung*. They collect six types of bees such as *Khaoda, Nou, Khapou, Khabou, Khaolukhao and Raokhane.* Menstruating women are not allowed in the honey collection. It is because of the common belief that if such women are present in the honey collection, the bees would bite all the persons who have come to collect it. Three kinds of edible frogs are also known to them – such as *Nana', Sola* and *Kaopu*. The *Nana type* of frog cannot be consumed during its egg laying period. Both men and women can gather such frogs.

They have the knowledge of differentiating the poisonous snakes from the non-poisonous one. The non–poisonous snakes have rounded heads whereas the poisonous ones have pointed heads. They consume both poisonous and non-poisonous snakes however poisonous snakes are consumed after cutting the heads of about three inches in length. Some of the snakes which are found in the village are locally termed as *No Khoji, No Thamavah, No Leno, No Da* and *Du La No*. Another food items, collected from the wet agricultural field and nearby streams includes molluscs, specially the snails. Both men and women use to collect these faunas. Besides they also collect three kinds of crabs namely – *Vao sing, Vaopo* and *vao Bungne.* These are mainly found in the small streams flows down the hills. During the rainyseason, thesecrabs usually comes out of their holes and the villager stake this opportunity to catch them. They consumed it after frying and roasting. Crabs have medicinal value also and it is belief that consumption of the crabs can cure cough. They also collect wild vegetables and fruits (Plate No2, 3 & 4).

Hunting

Hunting is still a continuing practice, though not frequent; by the people of the Oinam Hill Village and some underlying factors that make them continue in the system include geographical isolation, environmental conditions, cultural system etc. Such factors make it possible for hunting activities. In this village the mode of transportation is poorly developed. It is a hilly and forested area where various kinds of wild animals are abounded. Its climatic condition and rainfall are also quite favourable for the luxuriant growth of wild vegetation and animals. Many a time's villagers follow their traditional patterns of hunting. They practise both individual as well as group hunting. There is no particular culturally determined season or timing for hunting, but they can hunt at their spare time. However they mainly hunt animals in the dry season, during the months of January to April. Women are not allowed in hunting activities. It is believed that if women are participated in a hunting trip, it would be unfruitful. So, hunting is done by men only. Hunting techniques practised by the Oinam males can be grouped under three main categories i.e. hunting by weapons, trap, and tame animals. The hunting implements used by the people are wooden club, bamboo spear, spear with iron blade, catapult, pallet bow, dao and axe. For capturing big games like bear, boar and tiger they used such traps as pit-fall trap (*Rao-trap*) and automatic spear trap (*Peih-trap*).The other traps used for capturing small land and arboreal fauna are neck trap for porcupine, monkey trap, squirrel trap and guinea pig trap. All these traps except pit- fall trap others are based on principle of leverage.

Dogs also play an important role in hunting and every hunting expedition is accompanied with dogs. Meats of the hunted animals are shared among the individuals who took part in the hunting expedition. It is reported that head of a hunted animal is shared to the person who is the owner of the dog that accompanied with the hunting expedition. The portion of the lung, kidneys and some part of hunted animal are shared to the dog, though other remaining parts of the animal are distributed equally among the hunters.

Fishing

Fishing is another means of getting food though it is not a regular practice among them. It is done in the nearby rivers, ponds and ditches. Both individual as well as collective fishing are practiced using weirs, poisons, nets, traps, baited hooks, spear and bar hand. Except the baited hook and fishing spear, others are made of bamboo strips, cane and plant fibre. Sometimes, they prepare a pond or a ditch in their paddy field in order to collect the naturally available fishes in the rainy season. Long bamboo poles are used to gather the scattered fishes in the paddy field into the ditch. Receptacle, locally known as *Kha-Bung* for the females and *Bung* for the males are used for keeping and carrying the fishes while fishing.

Domestication of Animals

Animals which are reared by the people are dog, pig, cattle, buffaloes, cat and fowl. Pig and fowl are used for religious offering. Dog is mainly used for hunting whereas buffaloes are engaged in ploughing and drawing carts. They seldom keep the buffaloes at home as the animals are allowed to stay in the nearby jungles all day long. When the owners need their services, they will collect them from the jungles. As they face constrain for individual cowshed, they reared the cattle collectively in a common cow shed comprising a few families and these are mainly for their meat requirements. Cow dung is shared among the families for using as manure.

Agriculture

Agriculture is the main economic pursuit of the Oinam Hill People. They practice both wet and dry cultivation on the hill slopes within their village boundary. Both men and women are engaged in agricultural activities. They use simple technologies in agricultural operation using hoe and plough for tilling the soil. Two types of ploughs are found namely *Mipho* and *Loupho. Mipho* is mainly used in the wet cultivation whereas *Loupho* is used in both wet and dry field. Four persons are required in the operation of *Mipho* and drawn by man only where as one buffalo and two individual persons are required in the operation of *Loupho*. Both are similar in structure .However, *Loupho* is larger in size than the *Mipho*. Besides, narrow working edge type of hoe is also used in the tilling of fields. It comprises iron blade and wooden or bamboo handle. It is reported that in the earlier days they used scapula of the cattle or buffaloes as digging hoe. A Wooden implement known as *Lang* is used for levelling of already tilled fields. It also comprises, some pointed wooden tips and a long wooden handle. For terrace cultivation, ploughing starts during the month of March to April. In the month of May-June transplantation of young paddy saplings are carried out particularly in the wet fields. Before this transplantation, mud walls of these terrace fields are made. In the month of June- August weeding is carried out in the both wet and dry fields. It is done with the help of a long bamboo knife, broad working edge type of hoe and naked hand. Weeding is continued upto the month of August. Harvesting is started from the first week of October upto the first week of November in the wet field with the help of sickle, wooden beater, wooden base and mat. From the month of November to February, they planted seasonal vegetables such as mustard, cabbage, cauliflower, pea, tomato, potato, brinjal, onion, ginger, garlic, coriander leaf, etc. They can do it with the help of a broad working edge type of hoe and Knife. Above all, different kinds of agricultural and kitchen gardening activities are done by both men and women. They can produce only their sufficient food for their own consumption. They do not use any chemical fertilizer in their fields. They use only cow dung and organic manure of vegetables in their fields as manure (Plate No.1, 5 & 6).

Weaving

Women weave cloths for their family members. They weave clothes on their simple looms. They spin the thread for weaving purpose from the locally grown some plants. *(Utricaparviflorus),(cannabis sativa), (corchoruscapsularis), vah-Lurka and Khailoro* are the locally harvested during the months of September and October. Yet they used simple technologies in the process of spinning and weaving. Fiber can be extracted from the bark of these fibre extracting plants by the naked hand. Then, it should be spinned by the naked hand keeping it on the thigh of the spinner. Such spinned fiber should be boiled in the water with ash for about one hour. After this it should be pounded by a bamboo or wooden beater. Then it should be thoroughly dried by exposing to the sun light for about one day. But in the case of bad weather it takes about two or five days. While drying, powdered rice should be spread to it. After this step it can be used for making cloths. They used simple wooden implements namely *Dae, Lamothing, Pao, Pa and chongthing.* These are dorso-ventrally flattened small wooden implements. *Mu* is a wooden spinning implement. Weaving is engage by women only in order to supply cloths for their family members.

Ethnographic postulates on Oinam Subsistence Economy

Ethno archaeology is studied by different scholars and researchers using different methods and techniques on the basis of the different perspectives such as social and cultural perspective, ecological perspective, etc. of the contemporary societies. Subsistence economy is one of these perspectives. So, ethno archaeology can be studied on the basis of this subsistence economy. Here ethno archaeological perspectives of the Oinam are reconstructed on the basis of their subsistence economy.

On the basis of the present study on the Oinam subsistence pattern, the following ethnographic postulates can be made which may have somepre-historic archaeological significances in reconstructing the subsistence pattern of the past having similar ecological and topographical characters.

1. The subsistence economy of Oinam People that centres around gathering, hunting, fishing, domestication, agriculture, shifting cultivation, weaving and pottery have been made effective by way of organising labour on the basis of age and sex within the economic unit of family on one hand and collective economic effort at the level of the community on the other.
2. The resource mobilisation has been successfully made by organising economic activities in line with an annual economic cycle based on the exhaustive indigenous knowledge about the life cycle of the different varieties of plants and animals available in their surroundings.
3. Domesticated animals occupy an important position in the economic life of the people, for some economic activities such as hunting of some wild games and tilling of soil are carried out with the help of dog and buffaloes respectively. Such animals also served as the important source of protein for the people. Most of the households rear pigs as to keep some reserved food for them. A closer analysis has, however, established beyond doubt that is nothing but an economic strategy, for pigs are the walking food reserved. Moreover, it is also a socifact that what ever reserved for the pigs are the leftovers of their daily food thereby making a provision for storage of their waste food in the form of living pigs in order to make them enable to use the same whenever necessity arises. There lies the economic rationality of the indigenous knowledge of the people by

means of which they can maximise their life chance by adapting to the prevailing situation demanded by their habitat.

4. Oinam women weave cloths to supply their family members. They weave cloths on their simple looms. They spin the thread for weaving purpose from the locally grown some plants.

Conclusion

The present study that vigorously attempts to make a bridge between the life way of two different groups of people, one living at the ethnographic present and the other at the prehistoric past by making specific ethnographic postulates formulated from the ethnography of the Oinam subsistence pattern will be able to throw light on the reconstruction of the probable behaviour related to the subsistence pattern of prehistoric man. The fact that the Oinam people are still practicing gathering, hunting, fishing, agriculture and weaving as a part of their way of life and that the prehistoric man also lead a life of gathering and hunting. The theoretical understanding of the ethnographic postulates employed in the attempt to reconstruct the fossilised behaviour and cultural pattern related to the subsistence economy of the prehistoric man once lived in the prehistoric past in Manipur against the backdrop of the culture of the Oinam people living in the ethnographic present has led to the formation of the following generalizations about the subsistence life ways of the prehistoric man of Manipur.

The prehistoric people, who share similar life ways of gathering, hunting and fishing with the Oinam people, as done by their living counterpart, might have organised their labour along the age and sex lines within the economic unit of family in particular and at the level of the community in general to make their economic pursuit more effective.

The Oinam People have mobilised the resources available in their surrounding by following strictly an annual economic cycle made operative in line with the seasonal availability of the different varieties of plants and animals. Moreover, they are also fully informed about the life cycle and habitat of those plants and animals. The prehistoric people, like their ethnographic counterpart, might have successfully exploited their available plant and animal resources by scheduling their economic activities in accordance with their exhaustive knowledge about the availability of different varieties of plants and animals at different places of their habitat and in different seasons of the year.

Weaving as revealed by the ethnography of the Oinam people is in the domain of household chores and consequently it is the monopoly of that Women folk. The same may hold true in case of the prehistoric forerunners.

References

Binford, R.L. 1968 'Methodological Considerations of the archaeological use of ethnographic data'. In, R.B. Lee and I. De Vore (eds), *Man the hunter.* Pp.268-273. Aldine: Chicago.

Binford, R.L. 1977 General Introduction. In *Theory building in Archaeology,* Binford, L.R. (ed). Pp. 1-10. New York: Academic Press.

Binford, R.L. 1978 *Nunamiut Ethnoarchaeology,* New York: Jovanoviah, Academic Press.

Binford, R.L. 1983 *In Pursuit of the Past,* London and New York.

Devi, Kh.Manglembi, 2007, A Study of the traditional Subsistence Pattern of the Kabuis and its relationship with the Prehistoric Cultures of Manipur, *Unpublished Ph.D Thesis* Manipur; Manipur University.

Medhi, D.K. 1993*Man and Environment* in *North East India,* Vol.1. New Delhi: Omsons Publication.

Roy, IndraniBasu, 2003- *Anthropology: The Study of Man, S. Chand,* New Delhi.

Stanislawski, 1974 – *The Relationship of Ethno-archaeology, Traditional and Systems Archaeology,* California.

43

Change and Continuity of Monuments among the Chothes of Purum Tampak Village, Manipur

Kh. Manglembi Devi and
Kamlenthang Khongsai

Introduction

The Chothes are one of the indigenous tribes of Manipur. The general concentration is in the hills and foothills near the valley in Chandel district of Manipur with a population of 2675 individuals (Census of India 2001). Purum Tampak village is situated at a distance of about 60 km to the south east of Imphal, the capital city of Manipur with a population of 462 individuals. They have close similarity in their traditional culture with that of the Meiteis. Khiyang (1985) reported that the genesis of the Meitei and Chothe had great similarity. The worship of Pu Pakhangba and Pu Soraren is found in practice among Chothes of non-Christian villages. The entire life of the Chothes is rich in legends and folktales that explain either their origin or a pattern of social behavior, the people have had a story to fall back on. The Chothes follow their tradition belief that they had come out from a cave known as Huipithoranga (Khiyang, 1985).

The first progenitor of Chothe tribes were Kachokte and Thanidam of which the name of the tribe "Chothe" was derived. They are patrilineal society following patrilineal type of descent and patrilocal type of residence. Monogamy is the preferential form of marriage; however, polygamy is also permissible. Both cross-cousin marriage (MBD) and parallel cousin marriage are strictly prohibited. They have seven clans. As the custom goes, some clans are bride givers where as some clans are bride takers, (Chothe, 2016).

The idea of erecting monuments either for the self-glorification or for the welfare of the people and for commemoration is still in vogue. People in individual capacity or in group organized to dig ponds (*Pukhrihongba)* and plant trees (*Khongnanghongba)* for the village or for the habitat. From the viewpoint of modern world, it may be interpreted in many ways as preservation of biodiversity or maintaining of environment to go green. They may also erect stone pillars and place flat stones at the village boundaries including its gate to mark its village map and geographical possession as well as to perform as a resting place. They erect large stones at the centre of its habitation area and worship with rites and rituals as village gods and goddess. They may build community hall and churches and or any other structures to mark a particular event or occasion or period. Sometimes, people may also perform it in one's individual capacity purely for his or her own interest and with feast of merit. With the passage of time, deep into the modern society, these structures and symbols of human action and thought were better known as monuments and it retold many stories of the past to the generations to come.

Therefore, a monument may be defined as anything enduring that serves to commemorate, especially structure, building or memorial stones. With the dawn of civilization, men began to diversify their activities in many allied fields – some for their wellbeing, and other for aesthetic values and self-glorification. All their enduring norms become unwritten history that retold in volumes to generations after generations down the memory land of human kind. In other words, monuments are not only a tangible items of culture but also embodiment of knowledge relating to the different aspects of the life ways of the people. Like any other items of culture they are subject to change and continuity. Moreover, their change and continuity have theoretical bearing on ethnographical and ethno-archaeological study of total ways of the life of the people. The present study made an attempt to highlight the change and continuity of monuments erected within the Purum Tampak village and its boundary.

Methodology

Both primary and secondary data have been used. Primary data relating to monuments in the pre and post-Christian period have been collected from the village through interview and observation technique. Elderly persons were interviewed regarding the monuments erected in the village, their change and continuity in the course of time. Secondary data are based on books, journals and the internet searching.

Monuments found in the Village

The types of monuments found in the village are broadly classified chronologically into two types-Traditional (Pre- Christian) Monuments and Modern (Post- Christian) Monuments.

Traditional (Pre-Christian) Monuments

Lungchungpa

Lungchungpa, the traditional god of the Chothe people, is derived from the term, '*Lung'* means stone,' *Chung*' means up or above and '*Pa*' means father or one. It is believed to be the stone that blocked the entrance of the cave in course of their migration. The people also believed that it has protected them from wild beasts and evil spirits that dwelled in their surroundings. They worshiped *Lungchungpa* in every villages in the pre-Christian period.

According to P.B. Vincent Chothe, Asst. headmaster of Purum Tampak High School, *Lungchungpa* was represented/symbolized by two huge stones-one large stone of about 4ft height erected vertically and another flat stone measuring 2 square feet placed in front of it. It was placed in habitation area 300 metres away from the village. Banana, milk, and bursted rice are offered to *Lungchungpa*. The rituals are done by the *Thiempu*, who belong to the Thao and the Lungkung (Khyang) clan on the day of Sajibu nongma panba/ Cheiraoba (a New Year day of the Meitei's) and during festivals.It was their belief that god *Lungchungpa* was the protector of the people from the evil spirits. However, if they neglect him, they will get the curse of the god *Lung-chungpa*. In this regard, there were two incidents- one at Pallel and the other at Ahu-Kansui in the course of their migration.During the settlement at Pallel, people suffered, untold miseries because of curse of god *Lungchungpa.*People became more materialistic and did not like to worship with rites and rituals. Therefore, they threw away the god *Lungchungpa* in the Sekmai River. They believed that God was not pleased with them and so he cursed them. Because of the curse, children died suddenly every day. All children of one generation died at this instant. So, they again picked the thrown god Lungchungpa from the river and started worshipping, due to the order of the then chief of the Tribe. Then only the curse was calm (Plate 1).

Thelhongba

It is also an age-old practice prevalent and common in the past among the people living in the hilly area, which is closely associated with the making of resting place and boundary of the village. A person generally from a well to do family with a social mindset dragged stone and prepared *Thel* for the people of the locality. The *Thel* are usually prepared at the outskirt of the village on the side of the village road. After due completion of making of the Thel, a ceremonial function known as *Thel* Hongba is performed with traditional rites. It is rather a function to dedicate the *Thel* to the people of his locality. In such functions, a grand feast is always offered to the invites for social recognition for his work. When a person is ready to perform the ceremony, then he would inform the head of the village, then they would fixed a day for the ceremony. The host would bear all the expenses involved in the ritual. There is one *Thel* in the village, which is located on the outskirt of the village near the Litan border by the side of Litan- Purum Tampak inter village road. This*Thel* is known as Leikhamjao *Thel*.At present, only some remaining part of the *Thel* is present. The vertical stone measures 120cm. in height, 47cm. in breadth and 27cm. in thickness, whereas, the flat rounded stone measures 117cm. in length, 74cm. in breadth and 20cm. in thickness (Plate 2).

Khongnanghongba- Abunghung

Khongnanghongba is an age-old practice in vogue in Meetei society, which is still practice in the village. It commemorates a person, his works for the society, his contributions, and devotion for the society by observing the banyan tree. From the views of modern society, it is helping in mitigating climate change, in sustaining and preserving biodiversity. A banyan tree locally known as *Abung* is a sacred plant for the Chothes. It is their tradition and custom to plant a banyan tree at a new settlement area or village. Since it is considered as a sacred plant, the one who plant a banyan tree usually dedicate for the village and perform a ceremony with feast of merit when the banyan tree attains a certain height. This practice is known as *Abung Hung* in the local dialect.*Abung-Hung* involves many procedures in which the one who plant a banyan tree has to seek permission from the village chief and after the formal procedures, the chief give his assent to the person to perform the ceremony. Then the day for the ceremony is fixed.

On the day of the ceremony, the host was carried by *Tolai* from his house to the place where the ceremonial function is to be performed. He was dressed in full Chothe traditional attire and carried by four men. A large crowd followed the person who sit on the *Tolai* and sang a song of dedication to the host, which was composed by one elder of the village. Then, the ritual was performed by the *Thiempu*. After the completion of the ceremony, they all returned to the house of the host and there was merrymaking and feast. Then the *Maksa (*Son in laws of the host) presented him a shawl and in return, the host presented a portion of meat to his *Maksa*. The significance of this practice is not only giving shade to the people of the village but also to retold the achievement of the person who perform it to the generations to come by observing the symbolic tree without any written record (Plate 3).

Pukhrihong

It is also an age-old practice very prevalent and common in the past, which is closely associated with the storing and supplying of potable water in the locality and its people. A person with a social mindset digs pond both for himself and for the people in the locality. After due completion of the pond, a ceremonial function known as Pukhri Hongba is perform with the traditional rites. It is rather a function to dedicate the pond to the people of his locality. In such functions, a grand feast is always offered to the invites for social

to the Lord on the 10th December, 2013 by Rev. Dr. W. Konghar, General Secretary, Manipur Baptist Convention in the presence of Rev. Kh. Hranun Executive Secretary, Ch.BCA to mark the inaugural function the newly constructed Purum Tampak Baptist Church. It consist of two parts- a plinth or a flat slab measuring 81 cm. in height which serves as a foundation of a column and a three faceted elongated column stone measuring 168 cm. in height and 48.5 cm. at the bottom of the column, respectively. The first face of the monuments has the name of the person who unveiled the stone, the dignitary present at the event and the name of donor of the memorial stone. The second face has the name of the Church Board Members, Auditors, executives of the Women and the Youth Department. In addition, the third face has the name of the Building Construction Committee and the Donors of the Memorial Stone (Plate 10).

St. Thomas church Golden Jubilee Monument

The three faceted memorial stone is situated on the eastern part of the village between the village pond and St. Thomas Church. It was erected on 9th February, 2003 commemorating the 50 years of the Church's establishment in the village. The monuments consists of two parts-a plinth or a flat slab measuring 103 cm. in height having 4 steps which serves as the foundation of a column and a three faceted elongated column stone measuring 178 cm., 50 cm. and 25 cm. in height, broad at the bottom and top of the column respectively. Name of the pioneers and the persons who unveiled the monuments along with the date of inauguration are inscribed on the first face of the monument. The chronology of the local catechists with their year of service is written on the second face of the monument. On the third face, an encouraging verse from the Bible, the first priest who visited the Purum Tampak village and the donor of the memorial stone is written on it (Plate 11).

Groto

The Groto is a statue of Mary erected at St. Thomas Church campus. The Monument was donated to the Church by Mr. Kh. Tomchou Anthony and his family in memory of his beloved wife (L) Mrs. Lochini Rose Mary Chothe. The Groto measures 141cm. wide and 193.5cm. in height. The Catholics used to pray before the Groto honouring Mary (Plate 12).

Memorial Stones in the Homestead Area

There are 10 memorials stones in the homestead area of the village. The dead bodies were buried in their common burial ground but memorial stones were erected on their homestead area for their remembrance. Most of the memorial stones for the dead have a two faceted elongated stone placed above a plinth or a flat slab, which serves as a foundation of a column while some are made with a cross above the plinth. Name and date expiry of the person, the year in which the person was born and the pastor or the father who unveiled the memorial are inscribed on the face. The cost of memorial stone are borne by the family of the deceased and a Pastor in the case of the Baptists and the Father for the Catholics are invited to unveil the stone (Plate 13).

Plate - 8

Plate - 9

Plate - 10

Plate - 11

Plate - 12

Plate - 13

Modern (Post Christian) Monuments: Plate 8: CLAM Golden Jubilee Monument; Plate 9: Purum Tampak Baptist Church Golden Jubilee Monument; Plate 10: Baptist Church Inaugural Monument; Plate 11: St. Thomas Church Golden Jubilee Monument; Plate 12: Groto; Plate 13: Memorials at the homestead area; Plate 14: Memorials at burial ground; Plate 15: Family Chronology of M. Noren Chothe.

Memorials at the Burial Ground

There are altogether 59 memorials found in the village. The memorials in the burial ground are made either with stone or cement as well as with wood resembling the shape of a cross (Plate 14).

Family Chronology

This is the only family chronology monument erected on the eastern part of the village in the homestead area of M. Noren Chothe in his life time. The stone was donated by his son named M. Dhiren Chothe. It consist of two parts- a plinth or a flat slab measuring 84.0 cm. in height which serves as a foundation of a column and a two faceted elongated stone (column) measuring 91 cm. in height. It has a maximum of 71cm. and 13cm. in breadth and thickness respectively. On the first face of the monument, the genealogy of Shri M. Noren Chothe from his grandparents to his down line is written in chronological order. The significance of the monuments is that it clearly show the family chronology of Shri M. Noren Chothe from his grandparents to his down line are clearly written on it (Plate 15).

Conclusion

The idea of keeping monuments or memorials either for the self-glorification or for the welfare of the people is still alive in the mind of the Chothes. Consequently, their age old tradition of observing *Pukhrihongba* and *Khongnanghongba* is still in vogue. However, there are visible changes in the mode of observation as the observance of some traditional rites and rituals of the Pre-Christian period is now being replaced by Christian prayers. While the core trait of the tradition - the performance of the feast of merit - is still practice in the post-Christian period too. The practice of *Pukhrihongba* and *Khongnanghongba* is also a part of the tradition of the Meiteis. The fact of sharing this same tradition both by the Meiteis and the Chothes may be explained in the light of the theoretical understanding of diffusion that might have taken place in the historical past.

The worship of their traditional god *Lungchungpa* represented by a Megalith, who is believed to be the protector of the people is no more performed in the village. Instead they built churches, erect memorial stones, and worship Jesus Christ and Mother Mary. Erection of memorial stone in the form of either simple, unworked megalith or worked and decorated megalith for the commemoration of a dead person is still in vogue but in a modified form. The Pre-Christian monuments are found associated with symbolic expressions connected with activities of the deceased. For instance, the memorial stone is decorated with mithuns or buffaloes at the shade of banyan tree. However, all these are, at present, replaced by Christian symbol, i.e. Cross mark. The history relating to origin, settlement, spread of Christianity, formation of Students' Union are all documented on the memorial stones erected on the eastern side of the village near the village playground. The activities of a person or persons which were once transmitted from generation to generation through the symbolic inscriptions made on the monuments are now replaced by monuments inscribed with historical facts.

References

Census of India, 2001, Manipur: Directorate of Census Operations, Manipur.

Chothe, P.B. Vincent 2016. The History of Phaihu (Purum Tampak) *in Souvenir 2016 Foundation Day Celebration,* Purum Tampak (Phaihu), Chandel District, Manipur.

Khiyang, Thambaljao, 1985. The Original history of Chothe (Chote) tribes in *Proceedings of the Symposium on Purum (Chothe) Revisited (eds)* Biman K. Das Gupta, Ababinda Basu, Bikash Raychaudhuri and Pabitra Gupta, Anthropological Survey of India, Calcutta.

Index

I

J

K

L

M

T

Y

Z